Drawn by J.W.Barber.

EASTERN VIEW OF PLYMOUTH FROM THE HARBOR.

The first church, on the left, is the Orthodox; the next south, the Robinson church; between these is seen Watson's Hill; the Universalist, and the Unitarian churches, Gothic structures, appear in the central part, back of which is seen Burying Hill; the Pilgrim Hall is on the right; the Court House with a spire is seen westward of the Iona Wharf.

EPITAPHS

FROM

BURIAL HILL,

PLYMOUTH, MASSACHUSETTS,

FROM 1657 TO 1892.

With Biographical and Historical Notes.

ILLUSTRATED.

BY BRADFORD KINGMAN,

MEMBER OF NEW ENGLAND HISTORIC GENEALOGICAL SOCIETY; CORRESPONDING MEMBER OF WISCONSIN
STATE HISTORICAL SOCIETY; PILGRIM SOCIETY, PLYMOUTH; WEBSTER HISTORICAL SOCIETY,
BOSTON; WEYMOUTH HISTORICAL SOCIETY, WEYMOUTH; BOSTONIAN SOCIETY,
BOSTON; ESSEX INSTITUTE, SALEM; AUTHOR OF HISTORY OF NORTH
BRIDGEWATER, MASS., AND KINGMAN MEMORIAL.

CLEARFIELD

Originally published
Brookline, Massachusetts
1892

Reprinted by
Genealogical Publishing Co., Inc.
Baltimore, Maryland
1977

Library of Congress Catalog Card Number 77-82297

Reprinted for Clearfield Company by
Genealogical Publishing Company
Baltimore, Maryland
1994, 2014

ISBN 978-0-8063-0780-0

Reprinted from a volume in the collection of
The Rhode Island Historical Society

Made in the United States of America

TO

THE MEMORY OF

The Pilgrim Fathers

AND

Their Descendants,

WHEREVER LIVING,

THIS WORK

IS

RESPECTFULLY DEDICATED

BY THE AUTHOR.

Memory of the Dead.

Many ages ago the eloquent Pericles, in an oration in honor of the hero-dead who fell fighting for the liberties of Greece, declared in true and burning words the good of doing honor to the memory of the noble dead. It was not that they — immortal in their deeds — needed temple or column to perpetuate their fame or reward their virtues, but because the living, by thus spurring emulation of the good and heroic dead, inspired and ennobled themselves. Their homage was proof that they were not ungrateful, nor insensible to the deeds that constitute glory and renown. No wreath is given, and no monument reared by a nation to the memory of its illustrious dead, but it blossoms with good for the living through all future time. Virtue is encouraged, patriotism kindled, and all that is noble in our nature inspired to action, by this homage to the greatness and goodness of our race.

PREFACE.

"Time corrodes our epitaphs and buries our very tombstones."

The practice of erecting memorials of some kind is almost coeval with the existence of the human race, but at what precise date epitaphs were first introduced, and by what nation, is involved in obscurity. The first we have been able to find is that about 876 B.C., when Sardanapalus, the last King of the Assyrians, ordered the following inscription to be engraved on his tomb, which was found at Anchiale in the time of Alexander, 543 years later: —

" Sardanapalus built Anchiale and Tarsus in one day. Go, Passenger, eat, drink, and rejoice. for the rest is nothing."

Epitaphs have long been declared as a means of communication between the living and the dead; a means of instruction as well as a reminder of our mortality. It is that we may make acquaintance with those who have lived before us, to inquire into their habits, their peculiarities, to investigate their history, which is not the least interesting object of the student and the antiquary, and to the biographer they are legitimate sources of inquiry.

The importance of monuments and inscriptions cannot be too strongly stated. But for these, many persons, as well as events worthy of remembrance, would have been forgotten. In the early days of epitaphial writings, inscriptions were prohibited except upon the monuments of illustrious persons; but now it is the universal custom among all classes of people to adopt them.

An epitaph to the honor of the dead has ever been regarded as of all praise the most noble and the most pure, especially when it expresses the character and actions of the good. Private virtues are as much entitled to this homage as public ones, and the title of a good parent, a good friend, and a good citizen is worthy of being engraved on brass or marble. Thus the tomb of a good man may in some degree be made to supply the want of his presence, and attach a veneration to his memory, and prove a benefit by his example. " Records on tombstones," says Leigh Hunt, " are introducers of the living to the dead, makers of mortal acquaintances; and ' one touch of nature,' in making the whole world kin, gives them the right of speaking like kindred to and of one another."

An eminent writer says, " When I properly look upon the tombs of the great, every emotion of envy dies within me, — when I read the epitaphs of the beautiful, every inordinate desire goes out, — when I see the grief of parents for children, my heart melts with compassion, — and yet, when afterwards I have beheld the tombs of parents themselves, I see the vanity of grieving for those that we must follow, — when I see kings lying, perhaps, by those who deposed them, —

when I consider rivals who are placed side by side, or the great men who divided
the world with their contests and disputes, in the same situation, I reflect with
sorrow and astonishment on the little competitions, factions, and debates of man-
kind, — and finally, when I read the several dates on the tombs of some who died
recently and some who died many years ago, I consider that great day when we
shall be all cotemporaries and make our appearance together."

The author of this work has for a long time been exceedingly interested in col-
lecting memorials of persons who have been distinguished as citizens as well as
in the annals of fame, and whose memory should be cherished with a reverence
due to their position.

Among the many places that the writer has visited, none has exceeded in
interesting associations that of Plymouth and of "*Burial Hill*," and as the interest
attached to this beautiful spot, once trodden by the steps of our early fathers,
has become so universal, the long-cherished purpose of preserving the memorials
of this locality has at last been realized, and the results are now offered to the
public in this volume, with the hope that all may find as much personal gratification in its perusal as has the writer in its compilation.

Epitaphs descriptive of the personal character and social lives of those who
lie beneath them are interesting and instructive, especially when drawn with
truth and discrimination, and the advice given to the living in many of them are
worthy of more than a passing thought. It would seem but natural that in a
burial ground found in the oldest town of New England, the grave-stones should
be the earliest to be found anywhere; but such is not the case. There are found
elsewhere many whose records antedate those on Burial Hill, but none more
interesting. Those buried here are mostly descendants of the early Pilgrims, as
will appear by a careful perusal of the index at the end of this volume.

Here there are not only single graves representing a family, but whole house-
holds, — parents, brothers, sisters, children, and grandchildren, — all grouped
together in immediate proximity; these, united in life, are not separated in death.
Among these occupants of the soil may be found persons of prominence as well as
those from the ordinary walks of life. Here rest the remains of many of the earliest
settlers of the colony and children of the next generation, none of whom are now
living. Here, too, may be found ministers who led the devotions of the sanctuary near by, which, for many years, was the only church in the town, and those
who, by their lengthy terms * of faithful pastoral duties, manifested an interest in
their fellow-worshippers, and desired to remain in their midst after death.

Here moulders the dust of several prominent physicians who completed their
terms of usefulness to their fellow-townsmen, and lie within this sacred enclosure
beside those whom even their skill could not save.

Here also may be found the names of those who were called to take an active
part in the councils of the nation when the country was in peril during the revolution, and a long list of those who died in their country's service in the late
rebellion.

Many also who have lost their lives on the perilous sea have found their final
resting-place beneath the turf in these grounds.

At the time of commencement in copying these epitaphs, nearly forty years
since, there were a large number of badly broken and defaced grave-stones lying
about the ground. Since the work was begun a still larger number of slates

---

* Rev. Dr. Kendall was pastor of the First Church for nearly sixty years.

have given way to the ruthless storms of years, or have been removed and others of a more imposing kind have taken their places, in the form of marble monuments and tablets or enduring granite. This will account for some of the inscriptions being found in different places in the volume, as the earlier ones are printed as found on the slate stones which afterward were removed, and on the new monuments the same names and dates were placed.

There are also a large number of inscriptions herein for which no stone can be found. The list of such will render this work the more valuable, as it will preserve the names of many which otherwise would have been forgotten.

It was originally intended to print these epitaphs to the year 1858, but time has wrought so many changes, and so many additions have been made since that date, it was deemed advisable to bring them to the present time. Great pains have been bestowed in the copying, and it is believed the results will be of great value to the antiquary, the genealogist, and the historian, as well as to the public at large.

It will be noticed that much labor and expense have been bestowed on this work in illustrating many of the monuments which it is thought would add much to the interest as well as value to the volume.

The author would respectfully acknowledge the kind assistance and encouragement he has received from many friends in Plymouth as well as elsewhere, during the progress of this work, and would especially mention Hon. William T. Davis, late president of the Pilgrim Society, as well as historian of Plymouth; Dr. Thomas B. Drew, curator of the Pilgrim Society at Pilgrim Hall; also to the family of the late William S. Russell, Esq., who did much in preserving the historical records of Plymouth, and publisher of " Recollections of the Pilgrims; " also to David Pulsifer, Esq., the well-known antiquary of Boston.

To Captain Charles C. Doten, editor of the " Old Colony Memorial," he is indebted for the free use of files of that paper; and to his son, Charles M. Doten, Esq., correspondent of the Boston Herald, for the kindly assistance rendered, he tenders his hearty thanks.

Bradford Kingman.

BROOKLINE, MASSACHUSETTS,
August 1, 1892.

LIST OF ILLUSTRATIONS.

VIEW OF BURIAL HILL, PLYMOUTH, MASS., U.S.A.

INTRODUCTION.

BURIAL HILL.

NEXT to the famous rock on which the Pilgrim Fathers landed there is nothing of more interest to the many thousands of visitors to the old town of Plymouth than the above named locality. The stranger upon his arrival in town, whether by steamboat or rail, cannot fail to notice, directly in the rear of the main street, a beautiful elevated spot of ground appropriated to the purposes of burials. There rest the remains of many of the early settlers of the old colony and their descendants for several generations.

This commanding and elevated ground was early selected by the pilgrims, while reconnoitering for a place on which to locate, as appears by their records, viz. : —

"On the other side of the river also much Corne-ground cleared; in one field is a great hill, on which wee poynt to make a platform and plant our ordnance, which will command all round about. From thence we may see into the Bay, and farre into the Sea, and we may see thence Cape Cod."

This hill is one hundred and sixty-five feet above the level of the sea, and contains about eight acres.

This was their first measure of precaution against any sudden attack of the Indians, and served as a protection for the two rows of dwellings they had designed to construct.

At a little later date, in 1622, in consequence of threatened hostility from Canonicus, the distinguished and powerful sachem of the Narragansett Indians, it appears they erected a larger fort, and so built it in the interests of economy as to answer for protection from the natives as well as for a place of worship.

"This somer they builte a fort with good timber, both strong and Comly, which was of good defence, made with a flate rofe and battlments, on which their ordnance were mounted, and wher they kepte constante watch, espetially in time of danger. It served them allso for a meeting house, and was fitted accordingly for that use."—*Bradford.*

OLD PILGRIM FORT AND MEETING HOUSE.

For a full account of this hill as it appeared a few years later, we find the following in a letter written by Isaac De Rasieres, a French Protestant, to Gov. Bradford in 1627:—

"New Plymouth lies on the slope of a hill stretching east towards the sea-coast, with a broad street about a cannon shot of e'ght hundred [yards] long, leading down the hill, with a [street] crossing in the middle, northwards towards the rivulet, and southwards to the land. The houses are constructed of hewn planks, so that their houses and court-yards are arranged in very good order, with a stockade against a sudden attack; and at the ends of the streets there are three wooden gates. In the centre, on the cross street, stands the Governor's house, before which is a square enclosure, upon which four patereros [steen-stucken] are mounted, so as to flank along the streets. Upon the hill they have a large square house, with a flat roof, made of thick sawn planks, stayed with oak beams, upon the top of which they have six cannons, which shoot iron balls of four and five pounds, and command the surrour'ing country. The lower part they use for their church, where they preach on

Sundays and the usual holidays. They assemble by beat of drum, each with his musket or firelock, in front of the captain's door; they have their cloaks on, and place themselves in order, three abreast, and are led by a sergeant without beat of drum. Behind comes the Governor, in a long robe; beside him, on the right hand, comes the preacher with his cloak on, and on the left hand the captain with his side-arms and cloak on, and with a small cane in his hand; and so they march in good order, and each sets his arms down near him. Thus they are constantly on their guard night and day."

Thus did our forefathers worship God—with a Bible in one hand and a sword or a musket in the other.

Again in September, 1642, according to the records of the town, repairs were made to the fort:—

"It is agreed that every man shall bring two peeces more of viii. foote long to finish the fortyfycacon on the fort hill, and that Richard Church shall speedyly make the carriage for another piece of ordnance."

And on the 23d of September, 1643, a watch was established at Plymouth, and "it was agreed upon that there shall be a watch house forthwith built of brick, and that Mr. Grome shall sell us the bricks for xi. s. p. thousand." This is the first instance where bricks are mentioned in the colony.

Again in February, 1676, there were fears of an invasion of the natives under King Philip and his tribe, afterwards known as King Philip's war, which caused the citizens of the town to make more extensive preparations for defence, as appears by the following vote:—

February 19th, 1676. "It was ordered by the Towne that there shal be forthwith a fortification built upon the fort hill att Plymouth; to be an hundred foot square, the pallasadoes to be ten foot and a halfe longe; to be sett two foot and a halfe in the Ground; and to be sett against a post and a Raile; every man is to doe three foot of the said ffence of the fortification; the pallasadoes are to be battened on the backsyde one against every two, and sharpened on the topps, to be accomplished by every male in each family from sixteen yeares old and upwards, and that there shal be a watch house erected within the said ffence or fortification, and that the three peece of ordnance shal be planted within the said ffence or fortification.

"Agreed with Nathaniell Southworth to build the said watch house, which is to be sixteen foot in length and twelve foot in breadth and eight foot studd, to be walled with board, and to have two flores, the uper flore to be six foot above the lower flore; and hee is to batten the walls and to make a smal paire of staires in it and to frame two smal windowes below, to make two gebles to the Roofe on each syde one, to Cover the Roofe with shingle; onely the frame to be brought to the place att the Townes Charge; and for the said work hee is to have eight pounds to be paid either in money or other pay equivolent."

In the year 1679 this watch house was granted to Samuel Jenney "to dwell in, or remove when he pleaseth." The remains of the old fort were sold to William Harlow, and formed part of his dwelling-house. The cannon were used in Revolutionary times for the defence of Coles' hill, and afterwards, as we learn, sold, to be wrought into more harmless forms of human use.— *Town Records, Vol. 1. p. 83.*

It seems that this hill was used not only as a central point for protection from any sudden attack upon the town, but as a place of burial from 1676, the date whence it ceased to be used as a fort.

BURIAL HILL, PLYMOUTH.

The first mention of it as a burial place was in 1698, when Chief Justice Sewall, holding court in Plymouth, says in his diary, "I walk out in the morn to see the mill, then turn up to the graves, come down to the meeting-house, and seeing the door partly open went in and found a very convenient opportunity to pray."

And again in the deed of the lot of land, where "Davis Building" now stands, from Nathaniel Howland to Francis Le Baron, of the same year the seat of the Le Baron family.—*Davis Ancient Landmarks.*

The following is a description of the Hill as it appears to-day, and of those who visit the same for the first time, as well as the impressions of a stranger from foreign lands.

"The 'Burying' Hill is the most remarkable spot in Plymouth. From whatever side we approach the town, it rises conspicuously above all its buildings; a lofty green mound, covered with dark gray tombstones, the first place to receive the rays of the sun, and the last upon which they linger.

"Let us ascend to it by the narrow foot-path from the head of Leyden-street, worn deeply to the thick and mossy turf, and, seated on one of the tombstones, look out upon the surrounding scene. What a Sabbath stillness reigns buried among its leafy groves; though the curling smoke tells of many a cheerful home concealed amidst the foliage. It is morning, the tide is in, the wide expanse of the bay glitters with light, and a fresh and bracing sea-breeze pleasantly salutes us. The robin red-breast, a much larger bird than his elder brother in England, hopping from stone to stone, seems to haunt this fresh and breezy eminence. The view that it commands is pleasing from its wide expanse of sea and shore. But the spot whereon we stand, the cemetery, is itself the most striking feature of the scene.

"In wandering about this venerable place of sepulture, I was particularly struck with the longevity attained by a large proportion of its tenants. It is remarkable that many of those who survived the first winter, fatal to half their companions, and became accustomed to the climate, which, if keen and cutting, is remarkably pure and salubrious, should, with their immediate descendants, have lived to eighty, ninety, and, in some few instances, above even a hundred years of age.

"Such, in its main features, is the Burying Hill, the most venerable, if not the most beautiful, necropolis to be met with on the soil of America."—*Bartlett's Pilgrim Fathers.*

"When the modern pilgrim finds his way to Plymouth, and, with filial veneration, directs his steps to the sacred spot where rest the fathers of New England, he is peculiarly struck with the remarkable objects which are presented to his view. When he has ascended the high hill, and looks around upon the innumerable gravestones which affection has placed as the last tributes to the memory of departed parents, relatives and friends, he seeks in vain for any ancient memorial to mark the graves of the Mayflower pilgrims of 1620. In vain he inquires for the graves of those who came in the Fortune in 1621, in vain for those of the Ann and Little James, in 1623. In vain he asks, in vain he seeks. Of all these, Thomas Cushman alone of the Fortune, and Thomas Clark alone of the Ann, are remembered by tablets. Their graves alone were surely designated by gravestones on Burying Hill. One of the old comers, Phineas Pratt, was similarly remembered in the old burial-ground in Charlestown. Uncertain tradition, however, has attempted to point out the burial places of a few others, and modern memorials have been erected to their memory.

"In an elevated position in one part of this field of the dead may be seen the shaft erected in memory of William Bradford, not only emphatically the Governor of the Plymouth Colony, but the faithful chronicler of the Pilgrims, his associates in the great enterprise. In another direction is the large slab commemorating the life and services of the venerable John Howland; and still, in another portion of the field, the monument which the filial regard of the Cushman family has raised over the graves of their pious ancestor, the excellent Elder.   These, indeed, are modern erections, but not the less honorable.

"The site upon Burying Hill on which the Cushman monument stands has hallowed family associations, and is not in itself entirely devoid of interesting recollections of a more general character.   It is the identical spot selected for the burial place of Elder Cushman by his bereaved friends and religious associates; and beneath the turf which has grown for ages, and whose verdure has only now and then been disturbed, as a new tenant has been admitted to the community of the dead, to mingle ashes with those of the venerated sire, rest the remains of the earliest of this Pilgrim family, — the Cushmans.   Around the Elder's humble grave were buried many of the Church, who, from their feelings of attachment, desired to be near him in death, as they had been with him in life; among these were the officers of the church, with whom he had for so many years ministered; but his pastor was not permitted to be with him in his long sleep, but is quietly reposing in the distant regions of the sunny South. From this spot the turf has now been removed, but the sacred remains are still there.   The turf has given place to more enduring granite.

"While standing within this ancient cemetery, the stranger is forcibly struck with the appearance of the large number of monumental tablets and burial mounds which he notices on all sides, compared with the smaller number of buildings in the village at its base,—that the dwellings of the dead far outnumber the dwellings of the living.   The immediate scene presents a vast assemblage of the past and a more limited population of the present—the quiet remains of other days above, and busy and bustling life of to-day below.   Here is where the forefathers lie with their children of more than two centuries, gathered together in family clusters, awaiting the call of the last great day.   And where could they lie more appropriately than in the chosen land of their American pilgrimage?

"Extending the eye beyond the hill at his feet, and beyond the village and a few sparsely scattered houses adjacent, the stranger will witness the placid and hospitable waters, formed into a safe and quiet harbor, by the almost surrounding headlands and projecting beaches.   His attention will be drawn to the Gurnet, at the eastward, with its twin beacons, and to Saquish, noted for affording food for the almost famished voyagers; to Clark's Island, on the north, where the Pilgrims, after their arrival in their new home, first passed the Christian Sabbath in prayer; to the fields of Duxbury and the green elevation there, which bears the name of the redoubtable Captain Standish; to the

lands of Kingston, where piously dwelt good Elder Cushman
and his devoted Mary, beside their never-failing spring* of living water, and where they terminated their earthly pilgrimage;
and to the meanderings of Jones's River, and Rocky Nook,
and Plain Dealing; and more westerly, to the chain of undula-
ting hills, upon the chief of which is the national monument to
the Pilgrim Fathers, and to the fresh waters of Billington Sea,
and the numerous crystal lakes of the townships. More southerly
will be seen the Town Brook and Pilgrims' Spring, where the
Pilgrims first quenched their burning thirst, and Watson's Hill,
where first appeared human friendship, in the person of the
almost civilized Massasoit. Further to the east, following the
circuit, the villages of Wellingly and Eel River, and the far-
famed beach, and the warning and inviting Manumet are seen
rising nearly 400 feet above the ocean. Extending his vision
across the bay, a distance of twenty-five miles, the white cliffs
of Cape Cod appear as if suspended in mid-air by some secret
enchantment of nature.

"All these the stranger sees; and he may also see, almost at
his feet, the famous Leyden street, where were the first dwellings of the Pilgrims, and the Middle street, and the North
street, lying parallel to each other, and at right-angles with and
between the Main street and the Water street at the Water
side, where were the first allotments of land; and he may see
Forefathers' Rock, the place of landing, and Cole's Hill, where
were laid to rest, during the first winter, half of the precious
freight of the Mayflower. Well may we say to him, as he stands
beside the graves of the Fathers;

" 'Stranger!—As from this sacred spot, hallowed by the remembrance of the true-hearted, who sleep beneath its turf, you
cast your eyes around and view scenes unsurpassed in interest and
beauty,—while you behold flourishing towns and villages abound-
ing in industry, prosperity, and happiness, where once all was
dreary, inhospitable, and desolate; think of the self-sacrificing
forefathers, learn to emulate their virtues, and firmly resolve to
transmit unimpaired, to the latest posterity, the glorious lessons
of their noble examples.' "—*Pilgrim Almanac.*

---

* This spring on the premises of Samuel P. Cole, at Kingston, is well worth a
visit; as near by the visitor can see where one of the old Pilgrims had a home. The
electric cars take one quite near to the same.

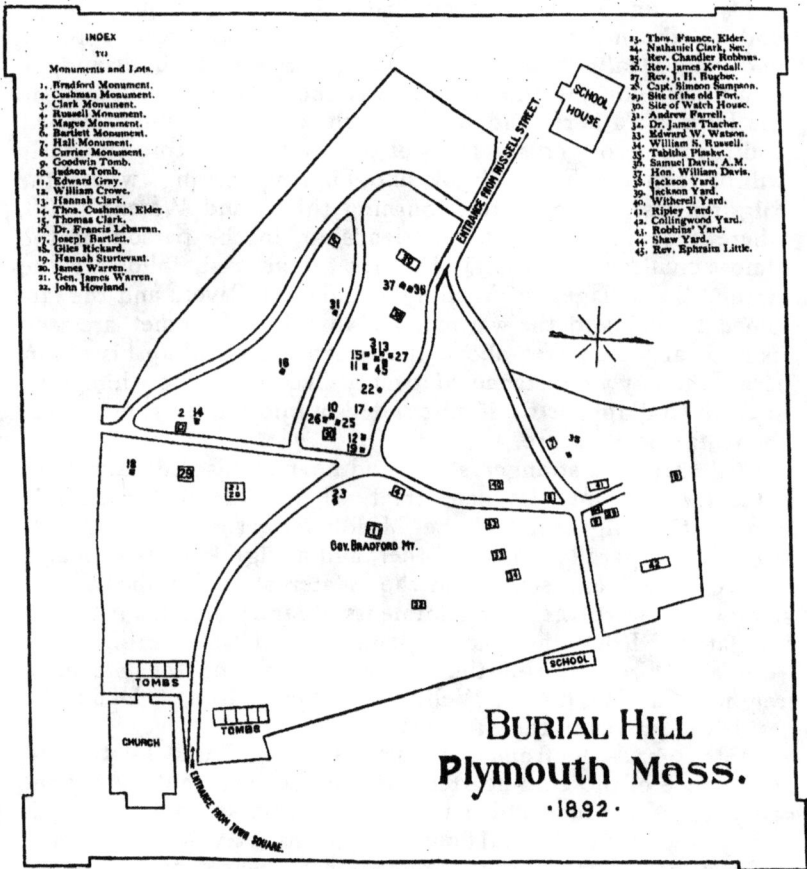

SCHOOL HOUSE

ENTRANCE FROM RUSSELL STREET.

Gov. BRADFORD MT.

TOMBS

TOMBS

CHURCH

ENTRANCE FROM TOWN SQUARE.

SCHOOL

BURIAL HILL
Plymouth Mass.
·1892·

EPITAPHS

BURIAL HILL,

PLYMOUTH.

A neat monument was erected on the site where, it has long since been ascertained, the remains of Governor Bradford were deposited. The monument consists of a solid block of granite, thirty inches square and eighteen inches thick, on a stone foundation. On the granite is a block of white marble twenty inches square and ten inches thick, on which is a white marble shaft, six feet high, in the form of a pyramid, fifteen inches square at the base, and eight inches square at the top, making the total height eight and one-half feet, erected in 1835 under the direction of Alden Bradford of Boston, late Secretary of State, a descendant of the Governor.

The following persons contributed to the same: Mrs. James De Wolf, of Bristol, R. I., Mrs. Collins, of Newport, wife of the late Lieutenant Governor of Rhode Island, Hon John Davis, of Boston, LeBaron Bradford, of Plymouth, Capt. Gershom Bradford, of Duxbury, William J. A. Bradford, Duncan Bradford, George P. Bradford and Ezra Weston, Jr., Esq., of Boston.

(NORTH SIDE.)

יְהוָה עֵזֶר חַיָּי *

1. Under this stone | rest the ashes of | WILL^M BRADFORD, | a zealous puritan & | sincere christian: Gov. of Ply. Col. from | April 1621 to 1657, | (the year he died | aged 69) except 5 years | which he declined.

† *Qua patres difficillime*
adepti sunt nolite turpiter
relinquere.

(SOUTH SIDE.)

H. J. | WILLIAM | BRADFORD | of Austerfield | York-shire | England was the | son of WILLIAM | and ALICE BRAD-FORD | He was Governor of | Plymouth Colony | from | 1621 to 1633 | 1635 | 1637 | 1639 to 1643 | 1645 to 1657.

Governor WILLIAM BRADFORD was born in Austerfield, a small and rather obscure village in the southerly border of Yorkshire, England, in March, 1588. His father

---

* Jehovah is the help of my life.

† What our fathers with so much difficulty secured, do not basely relinquish.

died in 1591, leaving him to the care of his grandfather, who died in 1596. He was then placed in care of his uncle Robert of Scrooby, a small village five miles only from Austerfield in Nottinghamshire, and near to the manor house of Brewster. His father was an husbandman, and William was brought up as an agriculturalist. He inherited considerable property from his father. At an early age he became an attendant upon the preaching of Richard Clifton, and became a member of his church, over which he and Robinson presided. Brought up to labor he received only a scanty education, although he was much inclined to literary pursuits. He became quite proficient in Dutch, Latin, French and Greek, and was a very devoted student of Hebrew, as "he wished to see with his own eyes the ancient oracles of God in their native beauty." He was fond of history and philosophy but theology was his favorite study. He early adopted the views of the separatist divines, with an enthusiasm peculiar to his nature, and having become at an early age a leading man in the community where he resided, at the age of eighteen he joined with those who emigrated to Holland, where the commercial spirit had tolerated free religious opinions. In this attempt the company was betrayed by the captain of the vessel in which they had embarked and they were thrown into prison in Boston, Lincolnshire, but he was soon liberated on account of his youth. In the spring of the following year he made another unsuccessful attempt, but finally succeeded and joined his brethren at Amsterdam. Here he learned the art of silk-dyeing. Upon arriving at the age of twenty-one years he came into possession of his estate in England, and engaged in commercial pursuits in which he was not successful.

After a residence of about ten years in Leyden, the church which had been formed by Mr. Robinson prepared to remove to America. In this movement Bradford engaged with that zeal with which he entered into everything. He embarked for England July 22, 1620, and on the sixth of September set sail from Plymouth with the first company of about 100 persons, in the *Mayflower*, arriving in sight of Cape Cod on the ninth day of November. While the vessel lay in Cape Cod Harbor, he became one of the foremost in the selection of a site for a settlement; and while he was on an exploring expedition, his wife fell overboard from the ship, December 7, 1620, and was drowned.

Soon after the death of Governor Carver, April 5, 1621, Bradford was elected to fill the vacancy as Governor of the Colony. He was annually elected to that office till 1657, excepting the years, 1633, '34, '36, '38, '44. He had then become conspicuous among the people for wisdom, piety, fortitude and benevolence.

He lived almost through the whole period of the English Commonwealth, and saw other flourishing colonies, the offspring of that at Plymouth, rising around him and forming the germ of an immense nation, by all of whom he was regarded with the love and veneration due to a patriarch, and in the words of an ancient writer he "was the very prop and glory of Plymouth Colony during the whole series of changes that passed over it." In the office of chief magistrate he was prudent, temperate and firm, and would suffer no person to trample on the laws, or to disturb the peace of the colony.

He wrote a history of "Plymouth plantation," beginning with the first formation of the church (in 1602, and ending with 1647) which was published by the Massachusetts Historical Society in 1856. After an infirm and declining state of health for a number of months, he was suddenly seized by an acute disease in May, 1657. In the night his mind was so enraptured by contemplating upon religious truth and the hopes of futurity, that he said to his friends in the morning, "The good Spirit of God has given me a pledge of my happiness in another world and the first fruits of eternal glory." The next day, May 9, 1657, he was removed from the present state of existence, greatly lamented by the people not only of Plymouth, but in the neighboring colonies.

> "The ninth of May, about nine of the clock,
> A precious one God out of Plymouth took:
> Governor Bradford then expired his breath."—*Morton.*

Governor Bradford's first wife was Dorothy May; his second wife was Alice Southworth, widow of Edward Southworth, 1623. He had one son by his first wife, William; Mercy and Joseph, by his second wife, from whom has sprung a large and honorable list of descendants, many of whom have lived and died in the Old Colony, and led active, useful lives, and have been highly respectable, as well as prominent in public life in New England and without her limits.

Alice, the wife of Governor Bradford, was no doubt buried near this monument.

The Old Colony records have the following:

"On the 26th day of March, 1670, Mistress Alice Bradford, Seni'r, changed this life for a better, having attained to four score years of age or thereabouts. Shee was a godly matron, and much loued while shee lived, and lamented tho' aged when she died, and was honorably interred on the 29th day of the month aforesaid: at New Plimouth."

A few years since Hon. John Howland, who died November 5th, 1854, at the age of ninety-seven years and five days, President of the Rhode Island Historical Society, Providence, R. I., and a descendant in the fifth generation from John Howland, the Pilgrim, caused a grave-stone to be erected over the remains of his ancestor, consisting of a large slate-stone, upon which is the following inscription:—

2. *Here ended the Pilgrimage of* | JOHN HOWLAND *and* ELIZABETH *his* | *wife. She was the dau'tr of Gov. Carver* | *They arrived in the Mayflower Dec. 1620;* | *they had 4 Sons & 6 dau'trs from whom* | *are descended a numerous posterity* |

"1672 Feb'y 23ᵈ JOHN HOWLAND of | *Plymouth deceased, he lived to the age of 80* | *yr's. He was the last man that was left of those* | *that came over in the Ship called the Mayflo-* | *wer that lived in Plymouth."* — [Plymouth Records.]

There is a painted sign board at the side of this gravestone containing the following inscription:—

The grave of | JOHN HOWLAND | died | Feb. 25, 1672.

It has been frequently published that Mr. Howland married a daughter of Governor Carver. This we think is a mistake. In Bradford's History we find that John Howland married Elizabeth, the daughter of John Tillie. Mr. Howland was a distinguished man, and devoted to the interests of the Colony, both in relation to its civil and religious institutions. He was Deputy and Assistant for several years. His early residence was on Summer street, but afterwards removed to Rocky Nook, where he died. The remains of his cellar are visible a short distance north of the residence of the late Hezekiah Ripley.

The colonial records say, "He was a godly man and an ancient professor in the ways of Christ, and proved a useful instrument of good in his place." His descendants are quite numerous. The late Reverend John Howland of Carver, Mass., was grandson of Mr. Howland. He was the last man of them that came over in the Mayflower, who settled in Plymouth. On the passage to this country in the Mayflower the weather was tempestuous, and in a severe storm Mr. Howland fell overboard and came near losing his life. The following is a record of the accident in Bradford's own words. : —

"And in one of them as they thus lay at hull, in a mighty storme, a lustie yonge man (called John Howland) coming upon some occasion above ye grattings, was, with a seele of ye shipe throwne into [ye] sea; but it pleased God yᵗ he caught hould of ye tope-saile halliards, which hunge over board, & rane out at length; yet he held his hould (though he was sundrie fadomes under water) till he was hald up by ye same rope to yᵉ brine of ye water, and then with a boat hooke & other means got into ye shipe againe, & his life saved; and though he was something ill with it, yet he liyed many years after, and became a profitable member both in church and comone wealthe."

3. Here Lyeth yᵉ Body | of EDWARD GRAY | Gent Aged Abovt | 52 years & Departᵈ | this life yᵉ Last of | June 1681.

Mr. GRAY came to this conntry with his brother Thomas about 1643. Thomas removed to Tiverton, R. I., and Edward settled in Plymouth. His name frequently appears in the records of that town, and he became a large owner of real estate. By his habits of industry and good management, he acquired a large property, his estate having been estimated the highest in the colony, at one time amounting to £1250 sterling. He was a large owner of land at Rocky Nook, Kingston, where the old family mansion still stands on the old road leading from Plymouth to Kingston, and is now owned and occupied by his descendants.

Beside his gravestone is a painted sign erected by the town of Plymouth, as follows:—

The grave of | EDWARD GRAY, | Died | June 1681.

4.   Here lyes buried | yᵉ body of Mr. | WILLIAM CROWE | Aged Abovt 55 years | who decᵈ· January | 168¾.

He married Hannah, daughter of Josiah and Margaret (Bourne) Winslow, a brother of Governor Edward Winslow, in 1665. She afterward became the wife of John Sturtevant, and died March, 1708-9.

Beside this gravestone is the following inscription on a painted signboard:—

The grave of | WILLIAM CROWE | Died | Jan. 1683.

5.   Here Lyes yᵉ Body of | Mʳˢ HANNAH CLARK wife | To Mʳ·WILLIAM CLARK | Decᵈ Febʳʸ yᵉ 20ᵗʰ | 1687 in the 29ᵗʰ | year of her age.

6.   Here Lyes yᵉ Body of | Mʳ THOMAS CLARK Aged | 98 Years departed | this life March | yᵉ 24ᵗʰ 1697.

"It is a well received tradition that this ancient man was the mate of the Mayflower, and the one who first landed on the island in Plymouth Harbor which bears his name.   Little is known of the life and circumstances of the mate of the Mayflower; his name is not among the signers of the original compact, nor mentioned among the first settlers.   It may therefore be conjectured, that he was considered merely as an officer of the ship, and that he returued to England in her with Captain Jones, and subsequently came over and settled in this town.   We find his name among those who received allotments of land in 1624; and he also shared in the division of cattle in 1627.   He resided at Eel River, and it is supposed that his family were among the sufferers in the house of William Clark, when attacked by a party of savages, March 12, 1676.   He being himself absent at meeting escaped, while eleven others were massacred and his son tomahawked, who ever after wore a silver plate on his head from which he was called Silver-Head Tom.   Numerous lineal descendants from Thomas Clark now reside at Eel river in this town, and in other parts of the Old Colony.   There is a handsome China mug whose pedigree is traced through the Clark family back to Thomas Clark, which had been presented to the cabinet of the Pilgrim Society by Betsey B. Morton, a descendant, and also a leathern pocket-book with the initials T. C. impressed on its cover, presented by Amasa Clark.   These relics afford additional evidence that the mate of the Mayflower died in this town, and that his ashes rest in the grave in our burial place designated by a stone with the above inscription."

There is a sign board at the side of this gravestone on which is the following inscription:—

The grave of THOMAS CLARK | Died | March 24, 1697.

7. Here lyeth buried ye body | of that precious servant of | God, Mr THOMAS CUSHMAN, who, | after he had served his | generation according to | the will of God and | particularly the Church of | Plymouth for many years in | the office of a ruling Elder, | fell asleep in Jesus Decm^r | ye 10th 1691, and in y^e | 84th year of his age.

Elder CUSHMAN came to Plymouth in the "Fortune," in 1621. He was brought up and educated in the family of Governor Bradford, and was always his intimate and confidential friend. He served the church of Plymouth as Ruling Elder nearly 43 years, having been chosen April 6, 1649. His gravestone is on the southerly brow of the Hill in a beautiful locality commanding a full view of the harbor of Plymouth as well as the town, the green hills in the distance, and of the "Meeting House," where, for over seventy years he had prayed and worshipped. This gravestone was erected by the church in 1715, twenty-five years after his death, and is a plain slab of mica slate, probably imported from England. It is in a good state of preservation, and the inscription is still distinct and legible.

His wife was Mary, daughter of Isaac Allerton, who came over in the "Mayflower" the previous year.

Soon after his marriage he removed to "Rocky Nook" in Kingston, (then Plymouth). The locality of his house has often been visited by antiquarians and others interested in early Colonial matters. There is a famous spring of excellent water near his residence, that has received the title of "Elder Spring," near the railroad on land now owned by Mr. Samuel P. Cole in Kingston.

At the grave of Elder Cushman is a signboard of recent date, directing the visitors to the grounds to the grave of one of the most noted of the old Pilgrims.

The grave of | Eld. THOMAS CUSHMAN | Died | Dec. 10, 1691.

CUSHMAN MONUMENT.

On the 15th of August, 1855, the descendants of the Cushman ancestors and their relatives, met together to Plymouth, in honor of their venerated ancestors, Robert Cushman, the right hand of the Plymouth forefathers, and Elder Thomas Cushman, his son, who for about forty-three years acceptably served the church of the Pilgrims as Ruling Elder. On the following day the persons assembled from almost every State in the Union, visited the grave of their ancestor, the Elder, and before parting resolved to erect an enduring monument over the remains of this venerable man. This object was subsequently consummated; and on the 16th of September, 1858, in commemoration of the sailing of the Mayflower from Plymouth, in England, for the new home in New England, the monument was consecrated with becoming exercises and ceremonies.

The Cushman monument stands in a conspicuous position within the ancient cemetery of the Plymouth fathers, upon Burying Hill, within sight of the hospitable harbor where the Mayflower lay safely moored in the inclement winter of 1620; and also, of the far-famed solitary rock of that sandy shore whereon the forefathers first set foot on the memorable twenty-first of December, and almost beneath the drippings of the first Christian sanctuary in New England.

The monument is a massive and tasteful structure, built of smoothly hewn Quincy granite, of the finest and most durable quality, and is highly creditable to the skill and faithfulness of Messrs. C. R. & C. Mitchell, the contractors. Its form is that of an obelisk with plainly chamfered edges, having a Grecian base standing upon a ornamented pedestal, also chamfered to its base, and containing sunken panels; the pedestal rests upon two square plinths, and the whole structure upon blocks of hewn granite occupying the whole space enclosed by a quadrangular fence, constructed with large stone posts and substantial iron rails. The whole height of the monument, including the stone blocks on which it stands, is about twenty-seven and one-half feet; the base of the pedestal is about five feet square, and of the lowest plinth about eight feet. The space within the railing is about twelve feet square. The tablets, which contain the inscriptions in raised letters, occupy the four panels of the pedestal, and measure about thirty-six by twenty-two inches.   They are of metallic bronze, and were cast at the foundry of Messrs. Henry N. Hooper & Co., in Boston.

The following are the inscriptions on the tablets:—

(Front or East Side.)

ERECTED | BY | THE DESCENDANTS OF | ROBERT CUSH-MAN | IN MEMORY OF THEIR PILGRIM ANCESTORS | XVI SEPTEMBER, MDCCCLVIII.

(North Side.)

FELLOW EXILE WITH THE PILGRIMS IN HOLLAND, | AFTER-WARDS THEIR CHIEF AGENT IN ENGLAND, | ARRIVED HERE IX NOVEMBER, MDCXXI, | WITH THOMAS CUSHMAN HIS SON: | PREACHED IX DECEMBER, | HIS MEMORABLE SERMON ON "THE DANGER OF SELF–LOVE | AND THE SWEETNESS OF TRUE FRIENDSHIP." | RETURNED TO ENGLAND XIII DECEMBER, | TO VINDICATE THE ENTERPRISE OF CHRISTIAN EMIGRATION; | AND THERE REMAINED IN THE SERVICE OF THE COLONY | TILL MDCXXV, | WHEN, HAVING PREPARED TO MAKE PLYMOUTH | HIS PERMANENT HOME,

(West Side.)

HE DIED LAMENTED BY THE FOREFATHERS | AS "THEIR ANCIENT FRIEND, — WHO WAS | AS THEIR RIGHT HAND WITH THEIR FRIENDS | THE ADVENTURERS, AND FOR DIVERS YEARS | HAD DONE AND AGITATED ALL THEIR BUSINESS | WITH THEM TO THEIR GREAT ADVANTAGE."

"AND YOU, MY LOVING FRIENDS, THE ADVENTURERS | TO THIS PLANTATION, AS YOUR CARE HAS BEEN FIRST | TO SETTLE RELIGION HERE BEFORE EITHER PROFIT | OR POPULARITY, SO, I PRAY YOU, GO ON.—

I REJOICE——THAT YOU THUS HONOR GOD | WITH YOUR RICHES, AND I TRUST YOU SHALL BE REPAID | AGAIN DOUBLE AND TREBLE IN THIS WORLD, YEA; | AND THE MEMORY OF THIS ACTION SHALL NEVER DIE."— [*Dedication of the Sermon.*]

(South Side.)

THOMAS CUSHMAN, | SON OF ROBERT, DIED X DECEM-BER, MDCXCI, | AGED NEARLY LXXXIV YEARS. | FOR MORE THAN XVII YEARS HE WAS | RULING ELDER | OF THE FIRST

CHURCH IN PLYMOUTH, | BY WHOM A TABLET WAS PLACED, TO MARK HIS GRAVE | ON THIS SPOT, | NOW CONSECRATED ANEW BY A MORE ENDURING MEMORIAL.

MARY | WIDOW OF ELDER CUSHMAN AND DAUGHTER OF ISAAC ALLERTON | DIED XXVIII NOVEMBER, M.D.CXCIX, AGED ABOUT XC. | THE LAST SURVIVOR OF THE FIRST COMERS IN THE MAYFOWER.

8. NATHANIEL yᵉ Son | of NATHANIEL | THOMAS ESQ & | MARY his Wife | Died yᵉ 5th of | April 1697 | in yᵉ 23ᵈ Month | of his age.

9. Here Lyes Interred three | children—three | sons of Revᵈ Mr | JOHN COTTON who | died in the work | of the Gospel | Ministry Charles | town in South | Carolina Septʳ yᵉ 18th | 1 6 9 9, | Where he had great | success And 7 | Sons of JOSIAH COTTON | Esqʳ who Deceased | in their infancy.

Rev. JOHN COTTON was born in Boston, March 13, 1640. Graduated at Harvard College, 1657. Settled pastor of the First Church in Plymouth, June 30, 1669. Dismissed, October, 5, 1697. Sailed for Charleston, S. C., Nov. 15, 1698. Preached in Connecticut and Martha's Vineyard, 1664 to 1667. He was eminent for his knowledge of the Indian language, and frequently preached to the aborigines at Plymouth in their native tongue. He revised and corrected Eliot's Indian Bible, printed at Cambridge in 1685. His residence was on the north side of Leyden street. His sons, John, Roland and Theophilus, were clergymen.

Hon. JOSIAH COTTON, son of the above Rev. John, was born in Plymouth, Jan. 8, 1680. Studied theology, but was not ordained over any church; taught school in Plymouth seven years; acquired a knowledge of the Indian language, and preached to the Indians of Plymouth and vicinity for a long time. He was author of an Indian grammar; became Clerk of the Inferior Court of Common Pleas, and afterward Judge of the same; was also Register of Deeds for the County of Plymouth. He died Aug. 19, 1756.

10. Here Lyeth | Buried yᵉ Body | of JOSEPH | BARTLETT who | Departed this | Life Aprill yᵉ 9th | 1703 | In yᵉ 38th year | of His Age.

On the footstone are the following lines:

J.   B.

Thousands of years after blest Abell's fall,
Twas said of him being dead he speakᵗʰ yet;
From silent grave methinks I hear a call,
Pray fellow mortal, don't your death forget
You that your eyes cast on this grave,
Know you a dying time must have.

It is said by some elderly persons that the gravestone of Mr. BARTLETT was the first placed on Burial Hill, although by the records he died subsequent to Edward Gray. He was son of Joseph and Hannah (Fallowell) Bartlett, who was son of Robert Bartlett, a passenger in the Ann, in 1663, by Mary, a daughter of Richard Warren.

HERE LYES Ȳ BODY OF
Ȳ HONOURABLE MAJOR
WILLIAM BRADFORD
WHO EXPIRED FEBY 20
170¾ AGED 70 YEARS

HE LIVED LONG BUT STIL WAS DOING GOOD
IN HIS COUNTRES SERVICE LOST MUCH BLOOD
AFTER A LIFE WELL SPENT HES NOW AT REST
HIS VERY NAME AND MEMORY IS BLEST

11. Here lyes yᵉ body | of Honourable Major | WILLIAM BRADFORD | who expired Febʳ yᵉ 20th | 170¾ Aged 71 years.

He lived long but still was doing good,
& in his country's service lost much blood.
After a life well spent he's now at rest,
His very name and memory is blest.

Major WILLIAM BRADFORD, son of the Governor, early obtained high distinction in the Colony, having been elected an Assistant and chief military commander soon after the decease of his father. He was a Major in the army, and was an active officer in King Philip's war. When the colonial government terminated, in 1692, he became Deputy Governor, and afterward a Counsellor of Massachusetts.

He had fifteen children, nine sons and six daughters. The late Ebenezer Cobb of Kingston, who lived to the remarkable age of 108 years, well remembered the funeral of Deputy Governor Bradford. The public road between Kingston and Plymouth was obstructed by deep snow, and the corpse was carried from his family residence near Jones' River, along the seashore, it being the expressed desire of the deceased to be buried near the body of his father. His tombstone indicates the spot where the Governor was probably buried, the father lying on the east side of the son, while Joseph lies in another row, northerly.

12. MARY GRAY dau to | JOHN & JOANNA | GRAY his wife | March 17th | 170¾ | yᵉ 16 year | of her age.

13. Here lyes yᵉ body | of Mr FRANCIS LE BARRAN | Phytician who | Departed this life | Augˢᵗ yᵉ 8th 1704 | In yᵉ 36 year | of his Age.

Dr. FRANCIS LeBARON was a surgeon on a French privateer, fitted out at Bordeaux, and cruising on the American coast, was wrecked in Buzzard's Bay. The crew were carried to Boston as prisoners of war. Dr. LeBaron came to Plymouth, and having performed a surgical operation, the selectmen petitioned the executive, Lt. Governor Stoughton, for his liberation, that he might settle in that town. This was granted; and he married Mary Wilder, and practised medicine in Plymouth, where he died at the age of 36 years.

His religion was Roman Catholic. He made a donation of ninety acres of wood land to the town. He had a son, Lazarus, who was a physician in Plymouth for a long time.

It is probable that nearly all of this name in this country descended from Dr. LeBaron, and have become quite numerous and highly respected.

14. Here Lyes y^e | body of | JOSEPH CHURCH | aged 25 year^s | died Octo^r y^e | 13th 17 0 7.

15. Here lyeth | y^e body of | WARREN Gent. | who dece– Oct | y^e 29, 1707 in y^e 48th | year of his age.

16. Here lyes | y^e body of | GILES | RICKARD | Aged 30 | years died | January y^e — | 1709.

17. Here lyes y^e body | of Mrs HANNAH | STURTEVANT aged | Above 64 years | dec^d in March | 1 7 0 $\frac{8}{9}$

18. Here lyes y^e body | of REBECKAH y^e | wife of JOHN | CHURCHELL aged | 52 years died | April the 7th | 1709.

19. Here Lyes | Buried y^e Body of M^{rs} | HANNAH BART- LETT wife | to Mr JOSEPH BARTLETT | Deces^d March y^e 12th | 1710, In y^e 72^d year | of her age.

20. Here Lyes y^e | body of Mr JOSEPH | BARTLETT De- ceased | Febru^{ry} ye 18th 1711, In y^e | 73^d year of his age |
Lo here their bodys near togather lay
Till ye bright morn of ye Resurection day.

21. Here lyes buried | ye body of | JOHN RICKARD | Aged about 55 years | Deces^d March y^e | 25th 1712.

22. Here lyes buried | ye body of | MARY RICKARD | Aged 35 years | deces^d August y^e | 28th 1712.

23. Here lyes buried | ye body of M^r | THOMAS LITTLE | Practioner in | Physick & Chyrurgery | Aged 38 years dec^d | Decem^r ye 22, 1712.

Mr. LITTLE was born in Marshfield, Mass., 1674, graduated at Harvard College, 1695, married Mary Mayhew, 1698. He was a lawyer and physician, and at one time was a large owner of real estate in the central portion of Plymouth.

24. SARAH LITTLE daugh^r | to CHARLES & SARAH | LITTLE aged 17 | M^o Dec^d January | ye 3^d 1714.

25. NATHANIEL | CHURCHELL | aged 21 years | died March y^e | 24th 1714.

26. WILLIAM son of | NATHANIEL THOMA^s | Esqr & MA- RY | his wife Dyed | ye 23^d of June | 1714 in y^e | 11th day of his | age.

27. REBECCA | COLE, aged | 18 years | died July | ye 2^d 1714.

She was the daughter of Ephraim and Rebecca (Gray) Cole.

28.   Here lyes ye body | of Mr JONATHAN | BURNES Aged | about 73 years | died Aug^st ye 20th | 1714.

29.   Here lyes y^e | body of ELKNEY | CUSHMEN aged | about 37 years | died Jan^ry ye 9th | 1714-15.

Mr. CUSHMAN married Hester, daughter of Jonathan and Elizabeth Barnes, February 23, 1702.   She married for her second husband, Benjamin Warren, October 25, 1716, a grandson of Richard, who came over in the Mayflower, by whom she had four children.   His gravestone is about five feet from the grave of Elder Thomas Cushman.·

30.   Here lyes y^e | body of MARCY | COOK who decd | Feb^ry ye 8th | 1 7 1 4-5 in | ye 36th | year of | her age.

31.   Here lyeth ye body | of the Honourable | JAMES WARREN Esqr | who deceased June | ye 29th 1715 | in ye 50th year | of his age.

Mr. WARREN was son of Nathaniel and Sarah (Walker) Warren, and grandson of Richard of the Mayflower.   He was a sheriff of Plymouth County and held other public offices of great integrity and capacity.   The records of the first church say he was "an exceeding loss to the Church, Town and County." He was taken suddenly ill while on his way to the assembly.

32.   Here lyes interred ye body of | Mr JOSEPH BRADFORD son to the | late Honourable WILLIAM BRADFORD | Esqr Governor of Plymouth | Colony who departed | this life July the 10th 1715 | in the 85 year of his age.

Mr. BRADFORD was born 1630, married Jaël, daughter of Rev. Peter Hobart, the first minister of Hingham, May 25, 1664.   She died 1730.   His residence was about one mile from the mouth of Jones' River, at a place called "Flat House Dock" in Kingston, Mass., so called from the fact that his house had a flat top.

33.   Here lyes y^e | body of Mr SAMUEL | RYDER who dec^d | July ye 18th | 1715 about | ye 85th year | of his age.

34.   Here ye lyes ye body of | HANNAH WARRE^n | wife of BENJAMEN | WARREN, aged 37 | Died | November ye 3^d | 1715.

35.   Here lyes ye body of | Mrs MARY CHURCHELL | wife to Mr ELEAZAR | CHURCHELL aged 60 | years deces^d Dec^r | ye 11th 1715.

36.   Here lyes ye body of | Mr ELEAZAR CHURCHELL | died March ye 25th 1716 | in ye 64th year of | his age.

37.   Here lies ye body of | NATHANIEL CLARK Esqr | dec^d Jan^ry 31st 1717 | In the 74th year | of his age.

38.   Here lyes y^e | body of MARYE | CURTIS wife to | Eb^eNEZER CURTIS | died March y^e | 17th 1717 | in ye 31st year | of her age.

39. Here lyes ye body of | Mrs JANE FAUNCE | wife to Eld^r THOMAS FAUNCE | Augst ye 6th 1717 | in the 67th year | of her age.

The husband of Mrs. Faunce was the last ruling elder of the First Church in Plymouth.

40. Here lyes ye body of M^r | ROBERT BARTLETT died | January the 3^d | 1718 | In ye 55th year | of his age.

41. Here lyes the | body of EB^{e}NEZER | SPOONER who died | Febry the 5th | 1717-8 | About ye 52^d | year of | his age.

42. Here lycs ye body of | Mrs SARAH BARNES | Aged about | 32 years Dec^d | April ye 11th | 1718.

43. Here lyes ye body | of MARTHA HOWLAND | aged about 46 | years dec^d | Augt ye 11th | 1718.

44. Here lyes ye body | of Mrs HANNAH | COOPER wife to M^r | RICHARD COOPER dec^d | Decr y^e 16th | 1718 in | y^e 57th year | of her age.

45. 1718 | 40th year | his age.

The above is a loose fragment on the ground.

46. SAMUEL A— | JOSIAH y^e sons of | JOHN COTTON | JOSIAH, ANONYMOUS, | EDWARD, JOSIAH, EDWARD | ROLAND, ROLAND, 7 son$f$ | of JOSIAH COTTON | who died between | y^e year 1719 | & 1734.

47. Here lyes y^e body | of Mr JOHN WARD | dec^d March y^e | 15th 1719-20 | In y^e 53^d year | of his age.

48. Here lyes y^e body of | EPHRAIM KEMPTON, | who | dec^d dec^r | —th 1720 | In y^e 18th | year of his age.

49. Here lyes y^e body of | JOHN DREW aged 79 | years died July | The 27th 1721.

50. Here lyes y^e body | of Mr CALEB COOK | who dec^d Feb^{ry} | y^e 5th 172$\frac{1}{2}$ | in the 72^d | year of | his age.

CALEB COOK, son of Jacob and Damaris (Hopkins) Cook, born March 29, 1651, and resided at Rocky Nook, Kingston. He will be remembered as the person connected with the death of King Philip. He was a soldier under the lead of Col. Benjamin Church, and while closely pressing the Indians, Cook, and an Indian named Alderman, of the Seaconet tribe were placed on duty to watch Philip, lest he should get out of a swamp, where he had hidden, and if possible to kill Philip. He soon had a chance, and fired at him, but his gun missed. He then bid Alderman to fire, and he soon became their victim, having been shot through the heart. Mr. COOK exchanged guns with the Indian, and the gun which did the fatal work has been kept in the COOK family till quite recently. The old flint lock was taken off and presented to the Massachusetts Historical Society. Part of the gun is in the Cabinet of Curiosities in Pilgrim Hall, Plymouth.

51. Children of Mr JOSIAH | CARVER (the 1st born) | JO-
SIAH dec^d July | 6th 1722 Ag^d 7 D^a | A daugh^r dec^d April |
29th 1723 Ag^d | 1 D^a. | DOROTHY dec^d Jan^r | 2^d 1730 Ag^d |
3 y^r 7 m^o 13D^a | JAMES dec^d Jan^r | 15 1730 Ag^d | 1 y^r 8 m^o |
A dau^r dec^d Jan^r | 17 1730 Ag^d | —

52. JAMES BARTLET | aged 22 years | died Jan^{ry} | y^e
13th | 1723.

53. Here lyes ye body | of JEHOSEBETH ROBB | ENS
died March y^e | 28 in ye year | 1723 in ye 83 | year of her age.

54. Here lyes y^e | body of Mr JOHN | FOSTER J^{ur} who |
dyed April y^e | 26th, 1723 and | aged 22 years.

55. Here lyes ye body | of Mrs HANNAH | CHURCHELL
wife to | Mr JOHN CHURCHELL | dec^d April ye 29th | 1723 in y^e
61st | year of her age.

56. Here lyes ye body of | Mr JOHN CHURCHELL | de-
ceased June y^e | 13th 1723 | in ye 66th year | of his age.

57. HANNAH dau^t to | Deacon JOHN | ATWOOD & | SARAH
his wife | dec^d July ye 14th | 1723 aged | About 4 mon^{ts}.

58. Here lyes ye body | of LOTHROP BARTLETT | ſon to
SAMEUEL | & ELIZth BARTLETT | Aged 16 weeks | dec^d Sep^t y^e
27 | 1723.

59. Here lyes buried the body of | the Reverend M^r EPH-
RAIM LITTLE | Pastor of the Church of Christ at | Plymouth
aged 47 years 2 m^o & 6 D^s | Deceased Novr ye 24th 1723.

Rev. EPHRAIM LITTLE was the son of Ephraim and Mary (Sturtevant) Little ; born
1673. Graduated at Harvard College 1695; ordained as pastor of the Plymouth Church
1699, married Sarah, daughter of William and Hannah (Griswold) Clark 1698, and
died leaving no children. The town supported his widow by annual grants to her
during her life. He was the first minister buried on the hill. "He was a gentleman
more inclined to the active, than the studious life; but should be remembered for his
useful services as a minister, and for his exemplary life and conversation, being one
of good memory, of quick invention, having excellent gift in prayer, and in occasional
performances also excelling. But what can never be sufficiently commended, was the
generosity of his spirit, and his readiness to help all that were in distress."

60. Here lyes y^e | body of MARY | STEPHENS wife to |
EDWARD STEPHENS | dec^d Janry ye 25th | 1723-4 in | ye 35th
year | of her age.

61. HOLM^{e}S CRYMBLE | son to QUINTIN | and ELIZA-
BETH | CRYMBLE his wife | dec^d March ye 20th | 1724 In | ye 4th
year | of his age.

62. Here lyes y^e | body of ^{Mr} RICHARD | COOPER who dec^d | March ye 29th | 1724 in | ye 85th year | of his age.

63. —CRYMBLE | Dau to QUINTIN | & ELIZABETH CRYM | BLE his wife | dec^d April ye 14th | 1724 In | ye 5th Month | of her age.

64. ELIZABETH— | y^t was still | Borne Oct^{br} y^e | 10th 1724.

65. Here Lyes Buried | The Body of | Mr ISAAC DOTEN | died April ye 15th | 1725 In ye 46th | year of his Age.

66. Here lyes buried | y body of M^{rs} | SARAH WATSON wife | to JOHN WATSON | of Plymouth Esqr | Deceased July ye 2^d | 1725 Aetatis 31.

67. JOHN son to | Mr JOHN & M^{rs} | BETHIAH CHURCHILL | his wife: dyed | Sepr ye 28th | 1725 | Aged 1year | 11Months.

68. Here lyes y^e | body of ABIGAIL | RIDER who Dec^d | Novm^r ye 8th | 1725 | In ye 26th | year of | her age.

69. Here lyes the | body of ^{Mrs}SARAH | ATWOOD wife to | Deacon JOHN ATWOOD | Dec^d Jan^{ry} y^e | 22^d 1725-6 | in ye 37th | year of | her age.

70. Here lyes interred | ye body of ANNA | Dau^{tr} to ye Rev^d | Mr NATHANIEL LEO | NARD Born Nov^{br} | ye 23d 1725 | dec^d Feb^{ry} ye 12th | 1725-6.

Rev. NATHANIEL LEONARD was the son of Major George and Anna (Tisdale) Leonard of Norton, Mass., born March 9, 1700. Graduated at Harvard College 1719, the first from that town. He was called to settle as pastor of the First Church in Plymouth, February 13, 1724, and was ordained on the twenty-ninth of July following. On account of failing health he was obliged to resign in the early part of 1756; and in June, 1757, he removed to Norton, and resided in Barrowsville till his death, June 11, 1761. He married Priscilla Rogers of Ipswich, Mass., by whom he had sixteen children. Rev. Abiel Leonard, D D. of Woodstock, Conn., and Dr. Thomas Leonard of Norton were his sons. He was buried in Norton.

71. Here lyes ye body | of MARCY COB wife to | EBENEZER COB dec^d | March ye 2^d | 1725-6 in ye | 53^d year | of her age.

72. Here lyes y^e | body of ELISHA | MORTEN Dec^d | Oct^{rb} ye 23^d | 1726 | in ye 15th year | of his age.

73. Here Lyes y^e | body of JAMES | COLE who dec^d | Nov^{br} ye 24th | 1726 In | ye 22^d year | of his age.

74. PELEG son to | Mr PELEG & | Mrs MARY DURFY | his wife dec^d | Dec^{br} ye 3^d | 1726 in | ye 3^d year | of his age.

75. NATHAN son | to JOHN & | MARCY HOLMES | his wife: decd | Decbr ye 23d | 1726 in | ye 8th year | of his age.

76. Here lyes buried 2 | sons to Mr NATHANIEL | & Mrs HOPE THOMAS | his wife; ye 1st decd | Janry 26th 1729-7 | Aged 23 mons 21 Days | ye 2d son decd Febry | ye 27th 1726-7 | Aged 31 days.

77. Here lyes buried | ye body of Mrs MARY | BARNES wife to Mr | JOHN BARNES: decd | Febry ye 20th | 1726-7 in | ye 55th year | of her age.

78. Here lyes ye | Body of Mr NATHANIEL | HOLMES, who decd | July ye 25th | 1727 in | ye 84th year | of his age.

Mr. HOLMES was the son of John, who was in Plymouth as early as 1632, and in 1634 was a messenger of the general court &c, from whom most of the name in Plymouth and vicinity are descendants. He married Mercy, sister of Elder Thomas Faunce, and daughter of John Faunce, who came in the Ann in 1623, and Patience Morton.

79. Here lyes ye body | of Deacon GEORGE | MORTON who decd | Augst ye 2d | 1727 in | ye 82d year | of his age.

Deacon GEORGE MORTON was the son of Ephraim and Ann (Cooper) Morton, born 1645, and grandson of George Morton who came in the Ann in 1623, whose wife was Julian Carpenter of Wrentham, England, and married in Leyden in 1612. Ephraim, the father, was born on the passage to this country and died in 1663. No stone is said to mark the place of his burial, or that of his brother Nathaniel Morton, who was Secretary of the Colony, and died in 1685, although he was probably buried near to Deacon Morton's grave.

The above is the oldest grave-stone on the hill bearing the name of Morton.

80. ABIGAIL dautr of Mr NICHOLAS & Mrs | REBECKAH DREW | his wife, died | Augst ye 22d | 1727 aged | 3 years 11 Mo | & 8 days.

81. Here lyes ye | body of JOSHUA | WETHREIL, died | Septr In ye | year 1727 | aged about | 45 years.

82. Here lyes ye body | of Mrs HOPE THOMAS | wife to Mr NATHANIEL | THOMAS decd May | ye 3d 1728 | in ye 26 year | of her age.

83. Here lyes ye Body | of Mrs JOANNA | wife to Deacon | MORTON who decd | June ye— | 1728 in | ye 83d year | of her age.

84. JOSEPH ye son | to JOSEPH & | ABIGAIL RIDER | his wife decd | July ye 5th | 1728 | Aged 8 weeks | & 3 days.

85. Here lyes ye | body of WILLIAM | RING who decd | Decbr ye 25th | 1728 in | ye 31st year | of his age.

86.　Here lyes y^e | body of Mr WILLIAM | RING who dec^d |
Sum time in April | 1729 in | ye 77th year | of his age.

87.　Here lyes buried | ye body of MA | RGARET dau^r to |
Mr SAMUEL & M^rs | ELEZABEH BARTLET | dec^d April ye 25th |
Anno 1729 | Aged one year | & 3 Days.

88.　Here lye 2 child^rn | to Mr JOHN & M^rs | HANNAH
SPARHAWK.
HANNAH| Dec^d June | ye 15th| | JOHN | Dec^d June | ye 20th |
1729| Aged| A Bout| 2 Mon^ts. | 1730 | Aged| A Bout |6 Weeks.

89.　Here lyes y^e | body of Mrs MARY | OSMENT who
dec^d | Aug^st ye 17th | 1730 in | ye 72^d year | of her age.

90.　Here lyes ye body | of MARY dau^r to | ye Rev^d M^r |
NATHANIEL LEONARD | & PRISCILLA his | wife dec^d Sept | 26
1729 | Aged 2 Month | & 18 days.

91.　Here lyes y^e | body of JOB | CUSHMAN who dec^d |
Nov^br the 12th | 1729 in | ye 19th year | of his age.
Mr. CUSHMAN was the son of Job and Lydia (Arnold) Cushman, who was an inn-
holder of Plymouth: born 1710.　His grave is ten feet south of the grave of Elder
Thomas Cushman.

92.　Here | lyes ye body of | CALEB CURTTIS who | dec^d
Nov^br ye 19th | 1729 in ye 18th | year of his Age.

93.　Here lyes y^e | body of M^rs | REBEKAH DREW | wife
to M^r | NICHOLAS DREW | who dec^d Nov^br | 1729 in | ye 45th
year | of her age.

94.　FREEMAN LOTHROP | son to Mr ISAAC & | M^rs HAN-
NAH LOTHROP | Aged 4 weeks & 5 D^s | dec^d Jan^ry ye 9th | 1730.

95.　Here lyes ye body | of Cap^tn WILLIAM | SHURTLIFF
who Dec^d | Feb^ry the 4th | 1729-30 In | the 72^d year | of his age.
Captain WILLIAM SHURTLEFF was the son of William and Elizabeth (Lettice)
Shurtleff; born in Plymouth 1657.　Married Susanna, daughter of Barnabas and
Elizabeth (Hedge) Lothrop.　He was a Selectman of Plymouth several years, and
a delegate to the Provincial Assembly in 1694, and held other positions of honor and
importance.

96.　Here lyes buried | the body of | Mrs MARY WESTRON
wife | to Mr THOMAS WESTRON | aged about 28 years | dec^d
Feb^ry ye 13th | 1730.

97. Here lyes buried | the body of M^rs | HANNAH THOMAS wife | to Mr NATHANIEL THOMAS | dec^d Feb^ry ye 19th 1730 | in the 23^d year | of her age.

98. Here lyes ye body | of Mr JOHN | CHURCHILL who dec^d | Feb^ry ye 25th day | 1729-30 | in ye 39th year | of his age.

99. EXPERIENCE, dau^tr | to Deacon JOHN | & Mrs SARAH | ATWOOD his | wife dec^d | July ye 7th | 1730 in | ye 6th year | of her age.

100. ELIZABETH dau^tr | to RICHARD & | MARY WAITE | Aged 13 M^o & 20 | D^s dec^d Sepr ye 16: 1730.

101. Here lyes ye body of | SARAH COLE wife to | EPHRAIM COLE, dyed Octr y^e | 26th 1730 Aged | about 32 years. their son EPHRAIM aged 12 years | dec^d 1730 SARAH, | their dau^tr aged 7 | years dec^d 1730.

102. Here lyes ye body | of M^rs REbECKAH MORTON | wife to Mr ELEAZAR | MORTON who dec^d | Nov^br ye 6th | 1730 in | ye 66th year | of her age.

103. Here lyes ye bodys of PELEG | & MAREY DURPHEY his wife.
He dec^d | Nov^b 16th | 1730 | She dec^d | Octr ye 23^d | 1730 in | ye 34th year | of his age. | in | ye 33^d year | of her age.
PELEG their son dyed Nov^br y^e | 19th 1730 aged 4 years.
The mother was daughter of Ephraim and Rebecca (Gray) Cole.

104. ELISHA son to | THOMAS & LOIS | FOSTER his wife | dec^d Nov^br y^e | 19th 1730 | aged 6 Mont^s | & 7 days.

105. Here lyes buried | the body of M^rs | HANNAH LOTHROP wife | to Mr ISAAC LOTHROP Junr: | dec^d Decr ye 11th 1730 | in the 22^d year | of her age.

106. Here lyes ye body | of Mrs DOROTHY CARVER | wife to Mr JOSIAH | CARVER dec^d Jan^ry | ye 20th 1730-1, aged | 28 year^s 11 Month^s | 17 days, & Near | her 5 of their Chil^n | as may be seen | on ye foot ston.

107. Here lyes ye body | of Mr EPHRAIM | COLE who dec^d ⌈ May ye 15th | 1731 in | ye 71st year | of his age.

108. Here lyes buried | the body of | Mr THOMAS MOR-
TON | Son to M^r | THOMAS MORTON | & Mrs MARTHA | his
wife who | dec^d July ye 10th | 1731 in | ye 31st year of | his age.

109. Here lyes buried | the body of | Mrs JEMIMA SAM-
SON wife to | Mr LAZARUS SAMSON | Dec^d July ye 20th 1731 |
in ye 27th year | of her age.

110. Here lyes y^e | body of FRANCIS | LEBARON who
dec^d | August ye 6th | 1731 in | ye 31st year | of his age.

FRANCIS LEBARON son of Dr. Francis and Mary (Wilder) LeBaron, married Sarah,
daughter of Joseph and Lydia (Griswold) Bartlett.

111. Here lyes the body of | Mr SAMUEL COLE | dec^d
Augt ye 18th | 1731 | in ye 23^d year | of his age.

112. Here lyes y^e | body of SAMUEL | WEST who dec^d |
Aug ye 22^d | 1731 in | ye 20th year | of his age.

113. Here lyes y^e | body of JOHN | COB who dec^d | Augst
ye 22^d | 1731 in | ye 23^d year | of his age.

114. Here lyes the | remains of | JOHN WATSON Esqr |
who deceased Sep^{tr} | the 9th 1731 | in the 53^d year | of his age.

JOHN WATSON, ESQ., son of Elkanah and Mercy (Hedge) Watson; born 1678.
He was a useful and respectable inhabitant, and afforded employment to a large number of people.   At one time he was supposed to have been the largest owner of real
estate in the country, and was charitable to the poor and destitute.   He married, 1st,
Sarah, daughter of Daniel Rogers of Ipswich; 2d, Priscilla, daughter of Caleb
Thomas, of Marshfield.   His son John was the second President of the Pilgrim Society, Plymouth.

115. Here lyes ye body | of SARAH BARTLET | wife to
JOHN | BARTLET dec^d | Sepr ye 28th | 1731 In | ye 30th year | of
her age.

116. Here lyes ye body | of HANNAH DREW | wife to
LEMUEL | DREW who dec^d | Oct^{br} ye 25th | 1731 in | ye 36th
year | of her age.

117. Here lyes ye body | of Mrs HANNAH DYRE | who
dec^d Octr ye 27th | 1731 aged about | 22½. She was late | wife to
Captⁿ WILL^m | DYRE formerly wife | to Captⁿ TOMSON | PHILLIPS
who was | drowned at sea Dec^{br} | ye 6th 1729.

118. ELIZABETH Dau | to Deacon HAVI | LAND & M^{rs} |
ELIZABETH TORREY | his wife dec^d | Nov^{br} ye 2^d | 1731 | aged
7 Monts.

119.   Here lyes yᵉ body | of Mʳ NATHANIEL | MORTON who decᵈ | Novᵇʳ yᵉ 7ᵗʰ | 1731 in | yᵉ 25ᵗʰ year | of his age.

120.   Here lyes yᵉ body | of Mrs ELIZABETH | DOGGETT wife To | Mʳ—EBENEZAR | DOGGETT who decᵈ | Decᵇʳ yᵉ 7ᵗʰ | 1731 in | yᵉ 38ᵗʰ year | of her age.

121.   Here lyes yᵉ | body   of Mrs ELIZAbETʰ | BARNS wife to | Mʳ JONATHAN BARNS | who decᵈ Decᵇʳ yᵉ | 15ᵗʰ 1731.

122.   Here lyes yᵉ body | of Mrs ELIZAbᵉTH BARNS | wife to Mʳ | JONATHAN BARNS | who decᵈ | Decᵇʳ yᵉ 15ᵗʰ | 1731 in yᵉ 86ᵗʰ year | of her age.

Number 122 is the same person as number 121.

123.   Here lyes yᵉ body | of MARCY HOLMES | wife to Mʳ NATHⁱˡ | HOLMES who decᵈ | Febʳʸ yᵉ 11ᵗʰ | 1731-2 in | yᵉ 81ˢᵗ year | of her age.

124.   Here lyes yᵉ | body of Mʳ EPHRAIM | MORTON who decᵈ | Febʳʸ yᵉ 18ᵗʰ | 1731-2 in | yᵉ 84ᵗʰ year | of his age.

125.   Here   lyes   buried | the   Body   of | THOMAS LEWIS | son of Capᵗ | PHILIP & Mrs | MARTHA LEWIS | who died April | 6ᵗʰ Anno Domini | 1732 in yᵉ 22ᵈ | year of his age.

Here lyes buried | yᵉ body of Capᵗ | PHILIP LEWIS | of Boston who | died April 6ᵗʰ | Anno Domini | 1732 in   yᵉ 56ᵗʰ | year of his age.

126.   HANNAH dauᵗʳ to | Mʳ SAMUEIL & Mrs | ELIZABETH BARTLETT | his wife decᵈ | April yᵉ 21ˢᵗ | 1732 | aged 8 Monˢ | & 6 days.

127.   ROBERT son to | ROBERT BROWN | E—& PRISCILLA | his wife died | June yᵉ 18ᵗʰ | 1732 | Aged 10 years.

128.   EXPERIENCE dauᵗʳ | to Deacon JOHN | ATWOOD & | Mrs EXPERIENCE ATWOOD his | wife: Decᵈ | June yᵉ 19ᵗʰ | 1732 | Age 15 Monᵗʰ.

129.   JERUSHA BARTLET | Dauᵗʳ to JOHN | & SARAH BARTLET | his wife Decᵈ | July yᵉ 9ᵗʰ | 1732 In | yᵉ 9ᵗʰ year | of her age.

130. HEAVILAND son to | deacon HEAVILAND & | Mrs ELIZABETH TORREY | his wife dec^d | July ye 13th | 1732 in | ye 17th year | of his age.

131. Here lyes y^e | body of NATH^l. | FAUNCE who dec^d | Aug^st ye 29th | 1732 | Aged 26 years | & 2 days.

132. HANNAH dau^tr to | LEMUEIL and | HANN^aH DREW | his wife: dec^d | June ye 18th | 1733 in | ye 11th year | of her age.

133. Here lyes y^e | body of GERSHEM | FOSTER who dec^d | July ye 11th | 1733 in | ye 25th year | of his age.

134. In Memory of | MATHEW Son to | Mr MATHEW | LEMOTE & Mrs | MARY his | Wife Born Aug^s | ye 18th 1730 | Dec^d July ye 15th: | 1733.

135. In Memory of | JOSEPH Son to | —MATHEW LE | MOTE & Mr^s | MARY his Wife | Born Nov: ye 30th | 1732 Dec^d | July ye 22^d | 1733.

136. ZACCHEUS son to | Mr STEPHEN & | Mrs EXP^eRIENCE CHURCHILL | his wife. Dec^d | Sepr ye 19th | 1733 aged | 13 year 10 Mo | & 19 days.

137. Here lyes | ye Body of | RICHARD HOLMES | Who Dec^d | Nov^br ye 12th | 1733 | in ye 15th | year of | His age.

Here Lyes | ye Body of | NATH^il HOLMES | Who Dec^d | Nov^br ye 14th | 1733 | in ye 32^d | year of | his age.

138. Here lyes | Body of | ELENER HOLMES | Who Dec^d | Decr ye 12th | 1733 | In ye 24th | year of | Her age.

Here Lyes | ye Body of | JOSHUA HOLMES | Who dec^d | Dec^br ye 13th | 1733 | In ye 29th | Year of | His age.

139. Here lyes ye body | of Mrs HANNAH DYER | wife to Cap^tn JOHN | DYER who dec^d | Dec^br ye 23^d | 1733 in | ye 68th year | of her age.

140. JOSEPH Son to | Mr ABIEIL & Mr^s | BETHIA PULSI-FOR | His wife depart | ed this life | Dec^br ye 28th | 1733 | Aged 3 Weeks.

141. Here lyes ye body | of DANIEL son to | ye Rev^d M^r | NATHANIEL LEONARD | & PRISCILLA his | wife dec^d Jan^ry | 18th 1733-4 Aged | 9 days.

142. Here lyes y^e | Body of Mrs PHEBE | HOLMES Wife to M^r | EBENEZER HOLMES | Who Dec^d April y^e | 16th 1734 In | ye 62^d year | of her age.

143. ELIZ^th daut^r to | Mr TIMOTHY & M^rs | MARY MORTON | his wife dec^d | May ye 3^d | 1734 aged | 1 year 4 M^s | & 14 days.

144. In Memory of | ABIGAIL Daugh^r | to Mr MATHEW | LEMOTE & M^rs | MAREY his | Wife. Born June | ye 6th 1733 | Dec^d Octr ye 25th | 1734.

145. Here lyes y^e | Body of JOHN | FAUNCE who dec^d | Nov^br ye 28th | 1734 in | ye 26 year | of his age.

146. Here Lyes y^e | Body of ELEAZAR | RING who dec^d | Feb^ry ye 3^d | 1734-5 in | ye 31st year | of his age.

147. Here lyes y^e | Body of NATH^il | KING who dec^d | Feb^ry ye 7th | 1734-5 in | ye 28th year | of his age.

148. Here lyes y^e | Body of Mrs MARY | MORTON wife to M^r | TIMOTHY MORTON who | died Ma^rch ye 22^d | 1735 in | ye 47th year | of her age.

149. Here lyes y^e | Body of HANNAH | HOLMES who died May ye 10th | 1735 in | ye 23^d year | of her age.

150. Here Lyes y^e | body of | PRISCILLA HOLMES | who deceased | August ye 8th | 1735 In | ye 21st year | of her age.

151. Here Lyes Inter^d | ye Body of M^rs | BETHIAH PULSIFER wife | to Mr ABIEL | PULSIFER who died | Septr ye 25th | 1735 aged | 21 years 3 mon^ts | & 17 Days.

152. Here lyes ye body | of Mr NICHOLAS | DREW who departed | this life Oct^br y^e | — 1735 | Aged about | 51 year.

153. Here Lyes Inter^d y^e | Body of Mrs MARTHA | WAITE who Departed | this Life Nov^br y^e | 28th 1735 In·| ye 79th year | of her age.

154. Here lyes y^e | Body of M^rs | RELIANCE MORTON | Wife to Mr JOHN | MORTON who died | Dec^br ye 4th | 1735 in | ye 55th year | of his age.

155. To | Mr ABIEL & Mrs | BETHIAH PULSIFER | His wife Dec^d | Jau^{ry} y^e—th | 1735-6 | Aged—

156. HANNAH Dau^r To | Mr THOMAS & Mrs | ReBECKAH WITH | ERLY his wife | Dec^d June y^e | 10th 1736 | Aged 3 years | & 10 Mon^{ts}.

157. Here lyes buried | ye body of | PRISCILLA FAUNCE | Daug^r to Elder | THOMAS FAUNCE | who dec^d Sepr y^e | 8th 1736 in ye 53^d | year of her age.

158. LOIS Dau^{tr} To | JOHN & LOIS | HOLMEs his wife | Died Spt^{er} y^e | 11th 1736 | aged 20 Mon^{ts}.

159. Here lyes y^e | Body of ELIsAbETH | PHILLIPS who dec^d Jan^{ry} ye 5th | 1736-7 in | ye 50th year | of her age.

160. Here lyes the body | of Mrs PENELOPE | WARREN the wife of | JAMES WARRBN Esqr | who departed this | life May the 25th | 1737 in the 33^d | year of her age.

161. TILDEN son to | M^r Jo^sEPH & Mrs | AbIGAIL RIDER | his wife aged | 1 year 4 M^o | 25 days died | June ye 30th | 1737.

162. Here Lyes Buried | ye Body of M^r | JOƒEPH RIDER who | Departed this life | July ye 18th | 1737 | Aged 46 yearƒ | Job 7 : 8, 9, 10.*

163. Here lyes inter'd | the Body of | JOHN THOMAS Esqr | who died Augt ye 7th | 1737 | in ye 41st year | of his age.

164. Here Lyes ye Body | of Mrs MARY WAIT^e | wife to Mr RETURN WAITE she Dec^d | Sep^{br} ye 29th | 1737 in | ye 69th year | of her age.

165. Here lyes interr'd the | Body of the Honourable | NATHANIEL THOMAS | Esqr who Departed this Life | February the 24th 1738 | in the 75th year of his age.

166. Here lyes y^e | body of Mr THOMAS | MORTON who dec^d | March ye 8th | 1738 in | ye 48th year | of his age.

---

*8. The eye of him that hath seen me shall see me no *more*: thine eyes *are* upon me, and I *am* not.

9. *As* the cloud is consumed and vanisheth away; so he that goeth down to the grave shall come up no *more*.

10. He shall return no more to his house, neither shall his place know him any more.

167. LEMUEL Son To | Mr Thomas & Mrs | Rebekah
Wethreil | His Wife Dec^d | Octr ye 13th | 1738 In | ye 9th
year | of his age.

168. Here lyes y^e | Body of Mr JOHN MORTON who dec^d |
Feb^{ry} ye 4th | 1738-9 in | ye 59th year | of his age.

169. GERsHEM ƒon to | Garƒhem & Lydia | Holmes his
Wife | Died Augst ye 22^d | 1739 | Aged 10 M^o | & 2 Days.

170. MATHEWƒon to | Mr Mathew Le | mote & Mrs |
Marcy his Wife | Born June ye 25th | 1738 Dec^d | Sep 1739.

171. Here lyes y^e | Body of Mrs LYDIA | BARTLETT
Wife To M^r | Benjn Bartlett She | Dec^d October ye 21st |
1739 In | ye 37th year | of her age.

172. Cap^{tn} | Thomas | Howland | Dec^d 1739.
This inscription appeared on a foot-stone.

173. Nathl son to | Mr Nathl Forster | & Mercy his |
wife died Dec^{br} | ye 11th 1739 | Aged 4 Month^s | & 2 days.

174. Here Lyes y^e | Body of MARG^{tt} | Dau^{tr} of Sam^{il} |
Bartlett Esqr & | Elizath His wife | Born April y^e | 15th
1737 | Dec^d Dec^{br} y^e | 31st 1739.

175. Here lyes y^e | Body of Mrs | LYDIA DREW | wife to
M^r | Nicholas Drew | Dec — | 1736.

176. In Memory of | ISAAC TOTMAN | who died March |
ye 20th 1740 Aged | 13 Months & 9 days | son of Mr Simo^n | &
Mrs Sarah Totman.

177. Here lyes y^e | body of JOHN | MORTON he died |
March ye 21st | 1740 in | ye 24th year | of his age.

178. Here lyes ye body of | HOLMES | dau to Nathl |
Holmes who dec^d| July ye 6th | 1740 in |ye 32^d year| of her age.

179. HANNAH Dau^r To | Mr Thom^s Wethreil | Ju^r &
Elizabeth | his wife died | July ye 26th | 1740 | Aged 14 Mo^n |
& one day.

180. ELIsABth dau^{tr} to | Frain^{cis} Courties | ju^r & Elisa-
beth | his wife died | Jan^{ry} ye 26th | 1740-1 | Aged 17 Mo^n | &
26 days.

181. SAMUEL BURN y^e | son of Mitchell | & Elizth
Burn | Died May 8th | 1741 | Aged 7 months.

182. In Memory of M^{rs} | DEBORAH CROADE | ye Consort of | Mr JOHN CROADE | And Daught^r of | ye late Honble | NATH^l THOMAS Esqr | who died in y^e | 73^d year of her | age June ye 14th | 1741.

183. Here Lies Buried | Capt JOHN DYAR | who Died | October 18th | 1741 | In ye 70 year | of his Age.

184. Here lyes buried the | Body of | Deacon JOHN FOSTER | who Departed this Life | December ye 24th 1741 | in ye 76 year of his age.

185. Here Lyes ye Body | of Mrs RUTH JACKSON | Wife To Mr NATH^{il} | JACKSON who Dec^d | March ye 29th | 1742 In | ye 79th year | of Her age.

186. JOSEPH son of | M^r CON^sIDER & M^{rs} | RUTH HOWLAND | He Died May | ye 11th 1742 | Aged 3 Mo | & 3 Days.

187. Here lyes buried | ye body of M^{rs} | LIDIA LEBARON wife | to Doc^{tr} LAZARUS | LeBARON who Dec^d | May ye 29th | 1742 aged | 44 years 4 M^o | & 29 Days.

188. MARY Dau^{tr} To | Mr JAMES & Mrs FAITH | SHURTLEFF His | Wife Died May | 1742 In y^e | 13th Month of | Her age.

189. Here Lyes y^e | Body of MARY | KEMPTON wife To | THO^m KEMPTON she | Died Sep^{tr} ye 13th | 1742 In | ye 30th year | of Her age.

190. CONSIDER Son to | Mr CONSIDER & M^{rs} | RUTH HOWLAND | Died Feb^{ry} y^e | 16th 1742-3 | Aged 7 years | & 16 Days.

191. Here lyes ye body | of DANIEL JOHNSON | jun^r son to DAN^l | JOHNSON Esqr & | BETTY his wife | who died March ye 27th | 1743 | in ye 17th year of | his age & in | ye 5th month of his | Apprentisship with | ROB^t BROWN Esqr.

192. Here Lyes y^e | Body of M^{rs} | FAITH SHURTLIFF | wife to Mr JAMES | SHURTLIFF She Dec^d | March ye 28th | 1743 In | ye 27th year | of Her age.

193. Here Lyes Interr^d | ye Body of M^r | THOMAS WETHREIL | who Dec^d April y^e | 21st 1743 in | ye 63^d year | of His age.

194.   Here lyes Interr'd y^e | Bodyes of NATHANIEL & LUCE | THOMAS, children to NATHANIEL | THOMAS ESQ^r & ELIZABETH his wife. | NATHANIEL Born Octr 17th 1742 | Dyed June 16th 1743. LUCE Born | Decem^r 5th 1743 Dyed 18th Instant.

195.   Here Lyes Buried | The Body of | Mr NATH. JACK-SON | who died July y^e 14th | 1743 In the 79th | year of his age.

196.   Here lyes Inter'd the Body | of the Honble | ISAAC LOTHROP Esqr | Who Departed this Life | Sep_t 7th 1743 in the 71st year of his age.

197.   Here lyes Buried | the Body of | Mrs LOIS FOSTER the wife of Mr THOMAS FOSTER | who died September y^e 21st | 1743 with one child buried | in her arms and five more | by her side. Viz. ELISHA, JOHN | GERSHOM, GERSHOM & HAN-NAH.

198.   Here Lyes Buried | The Body of | Mr LEMUEL COBB | Died Octr 22^d 1743 | In The 38th year | of his age.

199.   MARY ye Daughter | of NATHANIEL | THOMAS Esq & | MARY his Wife | Died ye 3 of | April 1744 | in ye 5th year | of Her age.

200.   Here lyes buried | the Body of | Mr JOHN BARNES | Dec^d May the 15 1744 | in the 76th year | of his age.

201.   Here lyes Buried the | Body of Madam | PRISCILLA BROWN | the wife of ROBERT BROWN | Esqr who Died September | the 7th 1744 In the 44th | year of her Age with three | Children Buried by her Side viz | ROBERT, MARTHA & MARGRET.

202.   In memory of JOſIAH ſon to | Mr JOHN COBB & SARAH his | wife who died Sep^t ye 10th | A. D. 1744 in ye 6th year of his Age | Like^{wise} A daughter not | named Aged 11 Days.

203.   Here Lyes the Body | of SAMUEL FOSTER | son of Mr SAMUEL FOSTER | & MARGARET his wife | aged 18 years 1 | M^o & 7 D^s who died | Sep ye 27th 1744.

204. In Memory of | ZACHEUS CURTIS | son to Mr |
ZACHEUS CURTIS | aud LYDIA his wife | who died Sep yᵉ 12ᵗʰ |
1744 Aged 11 | months & 9 days.

205. Here lyes Buried | the Body of Mʳˢ | ELIZABETH
WARREN | Daughter of JAMES | WARREN Esqʳ & SARAH | His
Wife Decᵈ Novʳ | yᵉ 5ᵗʰ 1744 Aetatis 33.

206. Here Lyes Buried | The Body of | Mʳˢ SARAH BART-
LETT | wife To Mʳ ROBERT | BARTLETT who Died | Febʳʸ yᵉ
8ᵗʰ 1744-5 | In y² 74ᵗʰ year | of Her age.

207. Here lyes Buried | The Body of | Mʳˢ MARTHA
DOTEN wife | To Mᵗ ISAAC DOTEN | Died Septʳ 9ᵗʰ 1745 | In
yᵉ 65ᵗʰ year | of Her Age.

208. Here lyes buried the Body | of Mʳˢ ELIZABETH
BARTLETT | the virtuous wife of SAMUEL | BARTLETT Esqʳ
and daughter | to the Honᵇˡᵉ ISAAC LOTHROP Esqʳ | (Decᵈ)&
ELIZABETH his wife | departed this life Novʳ yᵉ 1ˢᵗ | 1745 in the
41ˢᵗ year of | Her age and lies inter'd by | 5 of Her Children |
only one child surviving.

209. Here Lyes Buried | the Body of Mʳ | SAMUEL JACK-
SON He | Departed This Life | Novᵇʳ yᵉ 2ᵈ | 1745 In | yᵉ 55ᵗʰ
year | of his age.

210. Here lies buried | Mr JOHN BARNES | who decᵈ
decemʳ | yᵉ 11ᵗʰ 1745 | in yᵉ 52ᵈ year | of his age.

211. Here lyes buried | the body of Mʳˢ | MERCY WAR-
REN | who died Janʳʸ | the 17ᵗʰ 1745-6 | in yᵉ 42ᵈ year | of her
age.

212. Here lyes buried | the Body of | Mʳ THOMAS
FAUNCE | ruling Elder of the first | Church of CHRIST in |
Plymouth deceaſed Febʳʸ | 27ᵗʰ An: Dom 1745-6 in | the 99ᵗʰ
Year of his age. | The Fathers, where are they. | Bleſsed are the
dead who | die in the *Lord*.

Elder THOMAS FAUNCE was the son of John and Patience (Morton) Faunce.
Born 1647; married Jane daughter of William and Martha (Ford) Nelson 1672; ordained Deacon of the First Church of Plymouth, December 26, 1686, also Town Clerk
of Plymouth from 1685 to 1723 His father having died when he was a child, Captain Thomas Southworth took him by the hand at the grave, led him to his own home,
and from that time bestowed on him paternal affection. In the family of Mr. Southworth he was educated and instructed, and here his mind received the rudiments of
those principles of humility and piety, by which he was so remarkably distinguished

in after life. It has been related, that the Elder has often been heard to say that for
this education he should have reason to bless God to all eternity. He was first chosen
Deacon and afterwards Elder, and was the last who held that office. In those
days the office of Elder was one of great consideration. An Elder was regarded as
the virtual representative of the church, and on an equality with the Pastor. He
was bound to keep a watchful eye over the doctrines preached as well as the principles and practices of the brethren.

The Elder's house stood on the west side of the road near Eel River bridge. His
descendants are numerous, and are represented in the names of Kempton, Doten,
Paddock and Finney, as well as by his own family name.

213. Here lyes buried | the Body of | Capt BENJAMIN
WARREN | died May ye 30th | 1746 in ye 76th | Year of His
age.

214. Here lyes buried | the Body of M^{rs} | ELIZABETH
BARTLETT | the daughter of | SAMUEL BARTLETT Esqr | &
ELIZABETH his wife | born Augt 25th 1725 : | died Sep^{tr} 30th
1746.

215. The Remains of Mrs MERCY FOSTER | wife to M^r
NATH^l FOSTER who | died Decem^r ye 24th 1746 | in ye 33^d year
of Her Age | daugh^{tr} to the Revd Mr PETER | THATCHER late of
Midleh dec^d | April the 22^d 1744 | The Remains of SUSANAH
daug^r | to Mr NATH & Mrs MERCY FOSTER | died Jan^{ry} ye 20th
1746.

216. Here Lyes buried | the Body of | Mr NATH^l HOW-
LAND | Died Decr ye 29th 1746 | In the 76th year | of His age.

217. Here lyes buried | the Body of Mrs HANNAH | FOS-
TER the wife of | Deacon JOHN FOSTER | died April ye 30th
1747 | in the 77th year | of her age.

218. ABIGAIL DELENO | dau^r to Mr NATHAN | & M^{rs}
BATHSHEBA | DELENO aged 1 year | 6 m^o & 4 D^s died | May y^e
10th 1747.

219. In memory of | HANNAH FOSTER | Daughter to
Mr | THOMAS FOSTER | Jun & MERCY his | wife who Decs |
April 25 1748 | aged 7 Months | & 6 Days.

220. Here Lyes The Body | of MARY BARTLETT Dau^r |
To Mr JOHN and M^{rs} | SARAH BARTLETT who | Died Augt 16th
1748 | In ye 18th year of Her age.

221. Here lyes Buried | the Body of | Mrs SARAH SAM-
SON wife | to Mr JONATHAN SAMSON | died Augt ye 21st 1748 |
in the 22^d year | of Her age.

222. Here lies buried | the Body of | Mrs EXPERIENCE LOTHROP | the wife of | Capt BENJAMIN LOTHROP | died Sept 5th 1738 in the | 47th Year of her Age.

223. In Memory of | MARY BOWEN Who | decd Sept ye 21st | 1748 in ye 27th | year of Her | age.

224. Here lies the | body of Mr | JONATHAN BARNES | Who decd | Octbr ye 2d | 1748 aged | 45 years.

225. Here lyes ye Body | of PETER MORTON | Son of Mr JoſEPH | MORTON Junr & Mrs | ANNA his Wife Who | died Novbr 16th 1748 in | ye 9th year of his age.

226. Here lies buried | the body of Mrs | MARY THOMAS | the wife of Doctr | WILLIAM THOMAS | Aged 26 years | Died April ye 23d | 1749.

227. Here lies Buried Mrs | ELIZABETH Wife of | Mr DOUGHTY RANDALL | & daughter of Capt | EDMOND TILLSON & ELIZABETH his Wife | who died July 22d | 1749 in ye 28th | year of her Age.

228. JENNY Dau To | Mr JOHN & Mrs SARAH | BARTLETT Died | Sept 16th 1749 | In ye 10th year | of her age.

229. GEORGE WATSON | son to Mr GEORGE | & Mrs ABIGAIL WATSON | who departed | this life | Septr ye 26th 1749 | Aged 27 Days.

230. In Memory of Mr EPHRAIM | CHURCHELL Who Decd Decmr ye | 14th 1749 in ye 41st Year of his age : | In Memory of Mrs PRISCILLA | ye Wife of Mr EPHRAIM CHURCll | Who Decd Decmr ye 17th 1749 | Aged 41 Years.

231. Here lies ye Body | of Mr JOHN GODDARD | who decd Feby | the 3d 174— | aged 33 years.

232. Here lies buried | the Body of | Lieut SAMUEL BARTLETT | who died March the 9th | 1750 in the 59th | year of his Age.

233. Here lies Interr'd the Body of | Mrs ABIGAIL WATSON wife of | GEORGE WATSON Esqr | and Daughter to the Honble | RICHARD SALTONSTALL Esqr | who departed this Life |

March ye 15th 1750 Æ 22 | al/o | their son stillborn March 11th .1750.

234. This Stone is | erected to the memory of | that unbias'd Judge | faithful officer sincer^e Friend | and honest Man | C^{oll} ISAAC LOTHROP | who resigned this Life | on the 26th day of April 1750 | in the 43 year of his age.

> *Had Virtues Charms the power to save*
> *Its faithful Votaries from the Grave*
> *This Stone had ne'er possess'd the Fame*
> *Of being mark'd with LOTHROP'S name.*

ISAAC LOTHROP Esq., was the son of Isaac and Elizabeth (Barnes) Lothrop; born 1707; married 1st, Hannah, daughter of Edmund Freeman, 1729; married 2nd, Priscilla (Thomas) widow of John Watson, 1733. He was a Justice of the Court of Common Pleas, and his death was lamented throughout the county. At the opening of the Court, at the next term of the Court after his death, the Chief Justice, Nicholas Sever, and Peter Oliver, an Associate Justice of the Court, both expressed their great grief and sorrow with which the Court and bar were affected by the melancholy event, and observed that Col. Lothrop was held in profound regard as a Judge, and was greatly respected for his moral and Christian virtues. He possessed a large estate, and transacted extensive business in the mercantile line, in which he sustained an honorable and upright character. Few men have been more beloved, nor any whose death could diffuse more heartfelt sorrow among the poor, and in every social circle. He had five children, four sons and one daughter.

235. To the memory of | Mr WILLIAM RIDER | who | was born June 17 1750 | and | died May 5 1815.

> *Our life is ever on the wing,*
> *And death is ever nigh;*
> *The moment when our lives begin,*
> *We all begin to die.*

236. Here lies Interr'd | the Body of M^r | JOHN COBB | who departed | this life July y^e | 16th A. D. 1750 | in the 41 year | of his Age.

237. Here lies Interr'd | the Body of | Mrs ELIZABETH WATSON | the wife of | JOHN WATSON Esqr | who departed this Life | September ye 14th 1750 | Æ 28.

238. In Memory of | MERCY HARLOW | Dau^r of Mr SAMUEL & | Mrs MERCY HARLOW | who died Sepr 22^d | 1750 aged 13 | months & 12 days.

239. Here Lies Buried | The Body of M^{rs} | HANNAH CHANDLER | wife of Capt REUBEN | CHANDLER died Feb^{ry} | 25th 1750-1 | In the 28th year | of her Age.

240. Here lies buried | the body of M^r | NATHANIEL BRADFORD | died March 27th | 1751 | in the 36 year | of his age.

241. Here Lyes Buried | the Body of | Mr WILLIAM BARNES | who died March ye 31st | 1751 in the 81st | year of his age.

242. Here lies | Buried Mr | WILLIAM | HARLOW Who | Dec^d April | ye 11th | 1751 | in ye 59th | year of | his Age.

243. Here lyes Buried | the Body of | Mr STEPHEN CHURCHELL | died Septr 5th 1751 | in the 36 Year | of his Age.

244. Here Lyes inter'd the Body of | Mr THOMAS MUR-DOCH Son | of JOHN MURDOCH Esqr | who Departed this Life on | the 30th Day of September | 1751 And in the 50th | year of His Age.

245. In memory of | LYDIA HOLMES wife | of M^r JO-SEPH | HOLMES, Formerly | wife of Mr JOSEPH | BARTLETT (Dec^d) | who dec^d Jan^{ry} | 6th 1752 in ye 81st | year of her age.

246. Here Lies Buried | Mr JOHN STURTEVANT | Who Died | February 4th | 1752 | Aged About 92 | years & 5 months.

247. Here lies Buried | Mrs RUTH DOTEN | ye Wife of Mr JAMES | DOTEN who dec^d March | ye 22^d 1752 in ye 24th | year of her Age.

248. Here lies buried | the body of | Mrs SARAH CHURCHILL | the Wife of | Mr JOHN CHURCHILL | who died March 31st 1752 | in the 22^d Year of her Age.

249. Here lies ye Body of | Mr EBENEZER COBB | who Died | July 29th | 1752 | In ye 71st year | of his age.

250. REBECCA HARLOW | Dau^r to Mr AMAZIAH | and Mrs LOIS HARLOW | aged 11 Months | died Septr 30th | 1752.

251. In Memory of | SARAH Daught^{er}; | To Mr THOMAS | JACKSON J^{ur} & | Mrs SARAH His | Wife ye Child | Born April y^e | 22nd 1752 | Dec^d Octr ye 3^d | 1752.

252. Here lies | buried the Body of | JOHN WATSON Esqr | who departed this Life | Jany 3^d 1753 | in the 37th year | of his age.

253. Here lies the | Body of M^{rs} PHE | BE BARNES widow | of Mr JONATHAN | BARNES who | dec^d May y^e 23^d | 1753 aged | 49 years.

254. In Memory of | BATHSHEBA MAY | who died Ju^ly y^e 31 | 1753 in | y^e 5th year of | Her Age A DAUght^r | of Mr JOHN MAY | & BATHSHEBA | his wife.

255. THOMAS Son of | The Rev^d M_r | JACOB BACON & | MARY his Wife | Born Feb^{ry} y^e 15th | 1753 Died | Auguſt 6th| 1753, N. S.

Rev. JACOB BACON was born in Wrentham, Mass., 1706; graduated at Harvard College 1731. Settled over a church in Keene, N. H. about ten years. Installed pastor of the First church in Plymouth in 1749, where he continued his labors of love, till 1776, when he was dismissed by mutual consent. After preaching about eighteen months in Plympton, Second Parish, now Carver, he retired to Rowley, where he died, 1787, in the eighty-first year of his age.

256. Here lyes the | body of JOHN | MAY who died | August ye 7th | 1753 | in ye 2^d year | of his age.

257. In memory of | BETHIER CHURCHEL | who died December | ye 28th 1753 | Aged 2 Months | & 28 days A | Daughter of | Mr EBENEZER | CHURCHEL & MERCY | his wife.

258. Here Lies Buried | Mrs SARAH BRAMHALL | who Died January 26th | 1754 In y^e 25th year | of her Age Relict to | Capt JOSEPH BRAMHALL | who Died at Jamaica | Jan^{ry} 26th 1753.

259. Here lyes buried | y^e body of M^r | JOSEPH MOR-TON | Who Departed this life | Feb^{ry} y^e 24th 1754 in y^e | 71st Year of His Age.

260. In Memory of | M_r JOHN MAY | who died June | y^e 3^d 1754 | in y^e 67th year | of his age.

261. The memory of y^e Juſt is Bleſſed | Here lyes the Body of | Mr JOHN ATWOOD, Who Died | on the 6th of Auguſt A. D. | 1754 Ætatis 70 years.

"He was a Man of Piety & Religion | Adorned with every Christian grace | & Virtue & therefore well qualified | for ye office of a Deacon, which he | diſcharged in ye first Church of |

Christ in this Town for about 40 | Years with Honesty & upright-
nefs | and in the Courfe of his Life | adorned ye Doctrine of his
Saviour | by a well ordered Converfation:"

262. Here lies Buried the | Body of Mr ELEAZER
HOLMES | who died Aug^st 21st | 1754 | Aged 65 Years 10
Months | & 5 Days.

263. In Memory of | Mr ELEZAR | CHURCHILL | Who
Dec^d | Septr ye 21st | 1754 In y^e | 72nd Year of | His Age.

264. Here Lies Buried the | Body of that Virtious | Woman
Mrs RUTH | TURNER Wife To M^r | DAVID TURNER &
Daugh^tr | To Mr NATHANIEL JACK^son | She was A Member of |
The 1st Church of | Christ in Plymouth | She Dec^d March y^e
28th | 1755 Aged 55 | years & 5 Months.

265. In Memory of Mrs | BATHSHEBA DELE | NO the
Wife of | Capt NATHAN | DELLENO Who dec^d | April 21st 1755|
Aged 51 years & | 5 Months.

266. Here Lies the | Body of MORIAH | HOWES Daught |
er of Mr JEREMI | AH HOWES & Mrs | MORIAH his wife | who
dec^d May y^e | 31st 1755 in her 13th | year of her age.

267. In Memory | of | *Mrs REBECAH | WETHRELL* wife
of | *Mr THOMAS | WETHRELL* | Dec^d died Nov^r | 1755
Aged—.

268. In Memory | of Mrs MARY | BRIMHALL Who | Dec^d
Decem^br | ye 21st 1755 | In ye 49th year | of Her Age | Wife of
M^r | SILVANAS BRIMHALL.

269. In Memory of M^r | JOHN RIDER Who | Dec^d March
ye 11th | 1756 Aged 47 | years Wanting | 4 Days.

270. Here Lyes Entred | The Body of JOHN | MURDOCK
Esq who | Departed this Life | March y^e — 1756 | In y^e — year
of | His Age.

271. In memory of | EXPERIENCE Da | ter To M^r GID-
EON | WHITE & JOANNA | His wife who | Dec^d May ye 5th |
1756 aged 9 | Days.

272. Here lyes ye Body of | Mrs HANNAH COTTON | Wife
of | JOSIAH COTTON Esq | who Died | May 27th 1756 | Aged 69
years | and 1 Month.

273. In Memory of | LOTHROP BARTLETT | son of SAM-
UEL | BARTLETT Esq & | Mrs ELIZABETH his | Wife Born Aug-
ust | ye 7th 1755 Decd | June ye 13th 1756.

274. Here lies the Body of | DANIEL WATSON son | of
JOHN WATSON Esqr | & ELIZABETH his wife | Died June 29th
1756 | Aged 6 Years 9 months | & 13 Days.

275. In Memory of Mr | EDWARD STEPHENS | who Decd
July ye 30th | 1756 in ye 77th year | of his Age.

276. Here lyes the Body | of the Honble | JOSIAH COTTON
Esq | who Died | Auguſt 19th 1756 | Aged 76 years | and 7
months.   (See page 7.)

277. In Memory of Mr | JOHN MURDOCK | Who Decd
Sept ye 17th | 1756 | In ye 65th year | of His Age.

278. In Memory of hANNah | Daughtr of Mr | BENJAMIN
MORTON | born Augst | ye 15th 1755 decd | Octr ye 16th 1756.

279. Here lyes ye Body of | Mrs MARCY MORTON Wife |
to Mr JOSEPH MORTON | Who Departed this Life | Octr ye
18th 1756 in ye | 72d Year of Her Age.

280. In Memory of SETH FOSTER | Who died Octr ye 18
1756 In | ye 4th year of his age) | & of EUNICE FOSTER died
March | ye 16th 1757 aged one Week | Both children of | THOMAS
FOSTER Esqr | & MARY his Wife.

281. In Memory of Mrs | LYDIA LEBARON | Wife to
Doctr | LAZARUS LEBARON | Who decd Octbr ye 28th | 1756 in
ye 37th | year of her Age.

282. Here lyes Buried | Mrs ELIZABETH TILLSON | ye
wife of | Mr PERES TILLSON | the only daughter of | Coll.
THOMAS DOTY | who died November 8th | 1756 In ye 32d | year
of her age.

283. In Memory of MAR | GARET Daughter to | Doctr
LAZARUS & Mrs | LYDIA LE BARON Born | July ye 5th 1755 |
Died Novbr ye 20th | 1756.

284. In Memory of | ELIZABETH Daugh | ter to Mr
GIDEON | WHITE & Mrs JOANNA | His Wife Born April | ye 1st
1751 died | Decmr ye 26 1756.

285. Here Lies The Body | of SARAH HOWES | Daughter of Mr | JEREMIAH HOWES & | Mrs MORIAH His | Wife who Dec^d Dece^r | y^e —th 1756 in her | 6th year of her age.

286. Here Lies ye Body | of Mrs MERIAH | HOWES ye Wife of Mr | JEREMIAH HOWES | Who Departed | This Life Feb^{ry} ye 14th | 1757 In Her 43^d | year of Her Age.

287. In memory of JOSEPH | son to Mr WILLIAM | TORREY & MARY his | Wife who died April | ye 25th 1757 aged | 18 months & 4 | days.

288. Here lies buried the Body of | Coll^o *JAMES WARREN* Esqr | who departed this Life | *July* the 2^d 1757 | In the 58th year | of his Age.

Col. JAMES WARREN was the son of James and Sarah (Doty) Warren; born 1700. Married Penelope, daughter of Isaac and Sarah (Wensley) Winslow, of Marshfield, 1724, and had five children, one of whom, General *James*, became famous as an officer in the Revolutionary war.

289. Here lies the Body of | *GEORGE WATSON* son of | *GEORGE WATSON* Esqr | & *ELIZABETH* his wife | Died August 10th | 1757 | Aged 16 Days.

290. In Memory | of Mrs HANNAH | CHURCHILE | (wife of Mr | ELEAZER CHU | RCHILE) who | died Sept ye 19th | 1757 in y^e | 66th year of | her age.

291. In Memory of | WILLIAM son to | Mr JAMES DREW | & Mrs MARY his | Wife born Dec^{mr} | ye 29th 1755 | Dec^d Sept ye 25th | 1757.

292. In memory of Mrs | PRISCILLA DREW y^e | wife of Mr LEMUEL | DREW who dec^d | Oct ye 2^d 1757 | Aged 25 years | 5 months & 2 days.

293. Here lies Buried | Mrs RUTH DOTY | (the Wife of | Coll^o THOMAS DOTY) | Who Departed this Life | October 11th 1757 | In y^e — year | of her Age.

294. Here lies Interr'd | the Body of | Mrs ELIZABETH LOTHROP | Relict to the | Honble ISAAC LOTHROP Esqr | She departed this Life | Octr the 19th 1757 in the | 81st Year of her age.

295. Here Lies The | Body of EBENEZER | HOWES son of Mr | JEREMIAH HOWES | & Mrs MORIAH His | Wife who Dec^d No | vem^r ye 7th 1757 | In ye 16th year of | His Age.

296. In Memory of | JAMES HARLOW | son of M^r
SAMUEL & M^rs | MERCY HARLOW who | died Decr ye 26
1757 | Aged 7 weeks & 6 days.

297. In Memory of | Mrs HANNAH | HOLMES y^e
Widdow | of Mr ELEZER | HOLMES Born | March ye 15th |
1692 dec^d | April ye 7th | 1758 | Aged 66 years.

298. In Memory of | LYDIA Daughter | to Mr CORNELIUS |
HOLMES & M^rs | LYDIA his Wife | Who dec^d July | ye 19th
1758 | Aged 1 year 6 | Months & 13 | days.

299. In Memory of | Mrs MERCY LEMOTE | Wife to M^r
MATTHE^w | LEMOTE She Dec^d | Aug^st ye 8th | 1758 in ye 54th |
year of her Age.

300. In memory of | BRADFORD son to M^r | CALEB
STITSON & | Mrs ABIGAIL his | Wife Who Dec^d | Sep^t ye 5th
1758 | Aged 1 year 3 | months & 13 | Days.

301. ELIZABETH Daughter | to Mr PEREZ TILLSON | &
ELIZABETH his Wife | And grand daughter of | Capt THOMAS
DOTY | Died Octr 26th N. S. | 1758 In ye 7th | year of her Age.

302. Here Lies Buried | Mr LOTHROP RICKARD | Who
Died March | ye 6th 1759 | Aged 27 years.

303. THOMAS | (son of Capt | GIDEON & | Mrs JOHANNA |
WHITE) Died | April ye 10th | 1759 Aged | 10 Months | & 10
Days.

304. In Memory of DEBORAH | ye Daughter of M^r |
THOMAS & Mrs SARAH | DAVEE Who Dec^d | May ye 4th 1759 |
Aged 9 years 11 Month^s | & 26 Days.

305. In Memory of | BENJAMIN ſon to Mr | EBENEZER
SAMSON | & Mrs HANNAH | His Wife Who Dec^d | June ye 21st
1759 | in ye 19th Month | of his Age.

306. In | Memory | of | M^r CONſIDER HOWLAND |
who | departed this life | Augt 8th 1759 | aged | 60 years.

307. In Memory of | Mrs ESTHER HOLMES wife | of M^r
ELEAZER HOLMES | who died Augt 26 1759 in y^e | 39 year
of her age.

308. In Memory of M^r | BENJAMIN BARNES | son of Mr WILLIAM | BARNES He Dec^d April | ye 12th 1760 in ye 43^d | year of his age.

309. In Memory of M^r | *ZEPHENIAH* | *MORTON* who | dec^d Oct^o ye 19th | 1760 in y^e | 46th year of | his age.

310. In Memory of M^{rs} | LYDIA HOLMES Wife | Of Mr GERSHUM | HOLMES Who Dec^d | Novr ye 20th 1760 | In ye 47th year | of Her Age.

311. Here lyeſthe body of | Mr *JOHN COOPE*^r | who decd Decemb^r | the 6th 1760 aged | 62 yearſ 11 monthſ—& 14 dayſ.

312. In Memory of | Capt JABEZ SHURTLEFF | Who Dec^d Janu^{ry} ye 22^d | 1761 In y^e | 77 year of His | age.

313. Here lies buried | Doc^{tr} JOſEPH LEBARON | Who dec^d May ye 11 | 1761 In ye 39th | year of his age.

Dr. JOSEPH LEBARON was the son of Dr. Lazarus and Lydia (Bartlett) LeBaron; born 1722; was a physician in the West Indies for a time, and returned to his native town where, he died, as above.

314. In Memory of | Capt JOSIAH | MORTON Who | Dec^d May ye 19th | 1761 in y^e | 74th year of | his Age.

315. In Memory of | M^r JOB COBB | who died | June ye 8th | 1761 | in ye 45th year | of his age.

316. In Memory of | BENJAMIN SAMSON | son to Mr EBENE | ZER SAMSON & M^{rs} | HANNAH His | Wife Who Dec^d | Sept ye 5th 1761 | in ye 16th Month | of his Age.

317. In Memory of | SARAH MAY Dau^{tr} of | Mr JOHN MAY & M^{rs} | BERſHEB^a his wife who | Dec^d Sept ye 13th 1761 | Aged 2 years & 4 days.

318. In Memory of | — DAVEE | —Sept^t y^e | —1761 | aged 41 Years | 7 Months & 6 | Days.

316. In | Memory of | EPHRAIM Son | to Mr ZACHEUS | CHURCHILL & | Mrs MARY his | wife Who Dec^d | Nov ye 7th 1761 | Aged 1 year & | 2 Months.

320. Here Lyes | Buried ROBY Son | of Mr NATHANI^{el} | GOODWIN & M^{rs} | LYDIA his Wife | Who Dec^d Decemb^r | ye 5th 1761 | Aged 4 Month^s | & 14 Days.

321. Mr JOB | MORTON | 1761.
The above inscription is found on a foot-stone.

322. In Memory of | Capt BARNABAS HEDGE | who
Departed this Life | January the 18th | 1762 | Aged 56 Years &
22 Ds.

323. Here lies buried | Mr SEATH BARNES | Who decd
March | ye 21st 1762 | In ye 63d year | of his Age.

324. In Memory of | Mrs EXPERIENCE | ATWOOD
Widow to | Deacon JOHN | ATWOOD She Decd | April y: 14th
1762 | in ye 58th Year | of Her Age.

325. In Memory of | Mrs MERCY HARLOW | the wife of
Mr SAMUEL | HARLOW who departed | this Life July the
4th | 1762 In the 34th year | of her Age.

326. Here lies Interrd | ye Body of Mr | JOHN COBB | who
departed | this Life August | the 7th A. D. 1762 | in the 27th |
Year of his | Age.

327. In Memory of | WILLIAM son of | Mr JOHN MAY | &
Mrs BERSHEBA | his wife who Decd | Augst ye 14th 1762 | Aged
13 days.

328. In Memory of | 3 children of JOHN & MARY GODDARD |
Viz. MERCY died Augt 10 1762 aged | 6 years. LYDIA died
Augt 14 1762 | aged 2 years & 3 months. POLLY | died June
15 1767 aged 2 years & 6 | months.

329. In Memory of | ABIGAIL daughter | to Mr BENJAMn |
MORTON born | Febry 18th 1761 | decd Augst | ye 20th 1762.

330. In Memory of Mr | MATHEW LEMOTE | Who Decd
Oct | ye 27th 1762 | Aged 57 Years | & 20 Days.

331. Here lyes the Boody | of Mrs JOANNA ATWOOD| ye
wife to Mr JOHN | ATWOOD who decd Octo ye | 29th 1762 in ye
46th | year of her age.

332. In Memory of | Mrs REBEKAH | BARNS ye Wife |
To Mr CORBAN | BARNS She Decd Novbr | ye 3d 1762 In ye
26th | year of Her Age.

333. Here Lies | Buried ye Body of | Mr THOMAS SPOONER | who Departed this | Life Decem^{br} 19th | Anno Domini 1762 | in ye 68th year | of his | Age.

334. In Memory of M^r | JOSHUA BRAMHALL | Who decd Janu^{ry} y^e | 21st 1763 In | ye 80th year of his | age.

335. Here lye∫ the body of | Mrs HANNAH COOPER y^e | wife to Mr JOHN COOPER | who dec^d March ye 14th | 1763 aged 52 year∫ | 4 Months & 18 days.

336. In Memory of M^{rs} | ELEZEBETH MORTON Widow | of Capt JOSIAH MORTON | Who dec^d March y^e | 21st 1763 | In ye 71st year of | her age.

337. Here lies buried | Mr SAMUEL CLARK | who died April | ye 2^d 1763 | aged 76 years.

338. Here Lies Buri | ed ye Body of M^{rs} | HANNAH JACKSON | widdow of Mr JEREMIAH JACK | ∫ON who Decea∫^d | June 29th 1763 | in ye 84th year | of her | Age.

339. In Memory of ELIZABET^h | Daughter to M^r | SAMUEL & Mrs EXPERIN^{ce} | JACK∫ON his Wife who | dec^d July ye 31st 1763 | Aged 11 days.

340. In Memory of | ABNER Son to M^r | EBENEZER RIDER Jun & | Mrs SARAH His | Wife Boren June | ye 29th 1760 | Dec^d Augst | ye 19th 1763.

341. In Memory of M^{rs} | SARAH STEPHENS ye wife | of Mr ELEAZER STEPHE^{ns} | who dec^d Oct^o ye 28th | 1763 In ye 43^d year | of her age.

342. Here lies ye body | of Mrs ABIGAIL HEDG^e | Daughter of M^r | BARNABAS HEDGE | & Mrs MERCY his | Wife who dec^d | Decm^{br} ye 9th 1763 | Aged 26 years.

343. Here lyes buried | 4 children of Mr EPHRAIM | SPOONER & Mrs ELIZABETH his wife | Viz 1∫^t A Son born April 1∫^t 1764 | lived 20 hours, 2^d ELIZABETH dec^d | April 17th 1767 Aged 1 year 7 | Months & 12 Days, 3^d EPHRAIM | dec^d Decr 2^d 1769 Aged 2 years | & 7 Months, 4th EPHRAIM dec^d | Aug 4th 1775 Aged 4 years | & 4 Months.

344. Here lies buried | ELIZªBETH Daughter | to Mr
Bᵉɴᴊᴀᴍɪɴ | Bᴀʀɴs & Mrs Eʟɪᴢªʙᴇᴛʜ | his Wife who | Died
April yᵉ 21st | 1764 aged one | year & 8 months.

345. Memento Mori | In Memory | of | Capt JOSEPH
FULGHUM | who | Departed this Life June 14th | 1764 Aged
about 44 Years.

346. In Memory of | ELIZABETH WATSON | Daur of
GEORGE | WATTSON Esqr & | *ELIZᵗʰ* his wife | Died Septbr
14th | 1764 | Aged 15 Days.

347. Here Lies buried | the Body of Mr | THOMAS
BARTLETT | who Departed this | Life Sept yᵉ 28th 1764 | In
yᵉ 71st year | of His Age.

348. Here Lies buried | the Body of Mrs | ABIGAIL
BARTLETT yᵉ | wife of Mr Tʜᴏᴍᴀs | Bᴀʀᴛʟᴇᴛᴛ who Depar-
ted | this Life March yᵉ 13th | 1765 in yᵉ 68th | year of her age.

349. In Memory of | BARNABY son to | Mr Bᴇɴᴊᴀᴍⁿ |
Mᴏʀᴛᴏɴ born | Janaʸ yᵉ 28th | 1759 decd Augst | yᵉ 28th 1765.

350. Here Lyes Buried | Mrs MARY CLARK | yᵉ Widow
of Mr Sᴀᴍᴜᴇʟ | Cʟᴀʀᴋ who Decd | Octᵒ yᵉ 1st 1765 | in yᵉ 73d
year of | Her age.

351. Here lies buried | Mrs PRUDENCE Widow to | Mr
Tʜᴏᴍᴀs Wᴇ*f*ᴛᴏɴ | who decd Janry yᵉ 4th | 1766 In yᵉ 59th |
year of her age.

352. Here lies Buri | ed yᵉ Body of | That Virtuous | Woman
Mrs REBE | CCA TURNER | (wife of Mr | Dᴀᴠɪᴅ Tᴜʀɴᴇʀ) |
Who died Janr | yᵉ 21 1766 Aged | 54 Years 10 Mont | hs & A
11 Days.

353. Here lyes buried | 5 Children of Capt *SIMEON* |
SAMSON & Mrs *DEBORAH* his wife | Viz 1st SIMEON born
May 6th 1765 | decd March 22d 1766 | 2d SIMEON born Decr
8th 1766 | decd Decr 10th 1766 | 3d A Son *f*till born Sepr 15th
1770 | 4th MARY born June 3d 1775 | decd Octr 1st 1777 | 5th
MARTHA WASHINGTON born Sepr | 4th 1779 dec'd Sept 25th
1780.

354. Here Lies buried | ANNA Daſtr to Mr | NATHANIEL GOODWIN | & Mrs LYDIA his wife | who Decd July ye 14th | 1766 Aged 11 Months | & 3 days.

355. Here lies ye Body | of *HANNAH ROBBINS* | Daur of the Revd | Mr *CHANDLER* & | Mrs *JANE ROBBINS* | Died July 17th 1766 | Aged 10 Months.

356. Here lies buried ye Body of | Mr WILLIAM RICK-ARD | who departed this Life | Auguſt 20th 1766 | Aged 32 Years.

357. In Memory of | ABIGAIL RUSSELL | Daughter of Mr *JOHN* | *RUSSELL* & *MERCY* his wife | Aged 18 Months | Died Octr 23d 1766.

358. Here lies buried | Mrs ABIGAIL RIDER | ye Widdow of Mr | JoſEPH RIDER Daughtr | to Capt BENJAMIN | WARREN Decd who | Departed this life Decemr | ye 5th 1766 in ye 67th | year of her Age.

359. Here lyes buried | JOSEPH RIDER | —Decd | Decr 29th | 1766 In | ye 95th year | of his Age.

360. Here Lies buried | Mrs SUſANNA | STEPHENS Wife to Mr | ELEAZER STEPHENS who | Decd Decemr ye 30th | 1766 in ye 37th year | of her Age.

361. Here lies Interr'd | the Body of Mr | JAMES CURTIS | who departed | this Life January | ye 15th A. D. 1767 in | ye 32d year of his | Age.

362. Here lies Interrd | the Body of Mrs | *SARAH SPOON* | ER who dece | aſed January | ye 25th A. D. 1767 | in ye 72d Year of | her Age She was widow | to THOMAS SPOONer.

363. Here Lies buried | Mrs PATIENCE | JOHNſON | ye wife | of Mr JoſIAH | JOHNſON who | Decd Febry ye 1st | 1767 | aged 38 years.

364. Here Lies buried | REBEKAH Daſtr | to Mr ANDREW | CROſWELL & Mrs | MARY his wife | who Decd feb | ye 2d 1767 | Aged 5 days.

365. Here lies buried | Mrs ELIſABETH HILL wife | To Mr ANDREW HILL who | Decd Febry ye 3d 1767 | In ye 22nd year of | her Age.

366. Here Lies Interr'd the Body of | Mrs. ELIZABETH WATSON | the wife of | GEORGE WATSON Esqr | & Daughter to the | Honble *PETER OLIVER Esqr* | who Departed this Life | February ye 19th 1767 | Aged 32 years.

367. Here lies Interr'd | the Body of | Mrs *PATIENCE WATSON* | the wife of | Mr *ELKANAH WATSON* | She Departed this Life | April 20th 1767 | In the Thirty fourth Year of her Age.

368. In Memory of Mrs | HANNAH WATERMAN ye wife | of Mr JOHN WATERMAN Who | Died May ye 4th 1767 In ye | 54th yr of her age | & of 6 of their Sons & 2 | Daughters buried by her | who all Died In their | Infancy; their Son ELKa died | In Jamaica Augst ye 31st 1759 | In ye 27th year of his Age.

369. Here lies buried LIDEAY | Daughter of Mr THOMAS | JACKſON Junr & Mrs SARAH | his Wife was Born | Janry ye 16th 1767 | Decd June ye | 12th 1767.

370. Here Lies Interred | the Body of | Capt SAMUEL | HARLOW who | Departed this Life | June ye 17th 1767 | In ye 41st year of | his Age.

371. Here lies the Body of Mrs | BATHſHEBA DREW Wife | to Mr NICHOLAS DREW | who departed this | Life June ye 18th | A. D. 1767 Aged 55 | years & 3 Months.

On this foot-stone is the following inscription.

372. BATHſHEBa | DREW | 1767.

373. Here Lies Interrd | the Body of Capt. | JAMES NICOLSON | who departed this | Life August ye 4 1767 | Aged 58 Years 1 Month | & 17 Days.

374. Here Lies buried | NOAH Son to Mr | SILVANUS HARLOW & | Mrs DEſIRE his wife | who Decd Augustt | ye 23d 1767 | Aged 3 Weeks.

375. In Memory of | Mr PEREZ TILſON | Who Decd Sep ye 3 | 1767 in ye 42nd Year | of his age.

376. Here lies buried | DEBORAH Daſtr to | Mr SAMUEL JACKſON | & Mrs EXPERIENCE | his wife Born octo | ye 17th 1766 Decd | octo ye 9th 1767.

377. Here lies buried | ye Body of I∫AAC | SYMMS Son to M^r | I∫AAC & Mrs HANA^h | SYMMES who depar | ted this life Nov^br ye 1st | 1767 aged 5 Months.

378. Here lies buried | Capt HEZEKIAH | JACKSON who | dec^d Feb^ry y^e | 6th 1768 | In ye 30th year | of his Age.

379. In Memory of JOSEPH | Son of Capt JOSEPH | & Mrs LURAINA FULGHUM | who | Departed this Life | Feb^ry 6th 1768 Aged | 11 Year^s & 8 months.

380. —M^r— | & Mrs ELIZABETH his | wife Born march y^e | 17th 1768 Dee^d | march ye 26th 1768.

381. In Memory of | THOMAS SPOONER ∫on of | Mr THOMAS SPOONER & | Mrs DEBORAH his wife | who was Drown'd near | Clarks Island June 21^∫^t | 1768 aged 12 years.

382. Here Lies buried | M^rs ELI∫ABETH DIMAN | ye wife of M^r | DANIEL DIMAN | who Dec^d July ye 11th | 1768 In ye 38th | year of her age.

383. Here lies Buried BENj^aMAN | son of Mr CORNELIUS | HOLMES Ju^r & Mrs LYDIA | his wife who died | Aug^st ye 7th 1768 | aged one year 7 | months & 14 days.

384. Here lyes the body | of ye Revd Mr WARD | COTTON late Minister of | ye Go∫pel at Hamp^ton | who dyed at Plymouth | Novr ye 27 1768 | Aged 57 years 2 | Months & 8 days.

385. In Memory of | Mr DAVID TURNER | who Dec^d | Jan^ry ye 18th 1769 | In ye 76th year | of his Age.

386. Here lies Enterd | ye Body of | SAMUELL BAR- TLETT E∫q^r | who departed this | life March ye 25th | 1769 Aged 72 year^s.

387. Here lyes Inter'd the | Body of SALOME | Daughter of | WILLIAM HALL | JACK∫ON & DEBORAH | his wife who de | parted this life y^e | 27 of July A. D. 1769 | Aged 10 Mounths | & 2 days.

388. Here lies Interrd ye body | of Mrs *MERCY THOMAS* | ye wife of Doctor | WILLIAM THOMAS | who departed this life | Augu∫t ye 3^d A. D. 1769 | in ye 44th year of her | Age.

389. Here Lyies Inter'd | the Body of M^r | SAMUEL
MARSON | who departed this | Life Augt 28 A. D. 1769 | aged
67 years | 4 Months & 25 Days.

390. In Memory of | Mr JOHN MAY | who Dec^d Sep^t y^e |
4th 1769 Aged | 46 years & 8 months.

391. Here lies buried | EXPERIENCE Daugh^tr | of Capt
JABEZ HARLOW | & Mr^s EXPERIENCE | his wife who | dec^d Sep^r
ye 17th 1769 | aged 13 years 4 | Months & 18 days.

392. In Memory of | Mr^s BETHIAH | WATERMAN | Who
Dec^d | Sep^t ye 19th | 1769 | Aged 18 | years & 1 | Day.

On a foot-stone is the following inscription.   Also the letters B. J.

393. 1769 | 18th year of his age.

394. Here lies buried | Mr^s SARAH BARN^s | ye Wife of
M^r | SETH BA^rNS | who dec^d March | ye 19th 1770 | In ye 67th
year | of his Age.

395. In Memory of | Mr^s BETH∫HEBA MAY | ye widow
of Mr JOHN | MAY, who Dec^d May ye 20th | 1770 Aged: 45:
years | & 3: months.

396. Here lies buri^ed Mr^s | E∫THER WARREN | widow of
Capt | Be^nJAMIN WARREN who | dec^d Novb^r ye 1st | 1770 aged
88 years.

397. Here lies buried | Mr JOHN HARLOW | who Dec^d
Jan^ry | ye 30th 1771 Aged 87 | years 1 Month & 28 day^s.

398. Here lies Buried y^e | Body of Mr^s LYDIA HOV | EY
late wife of JAMES | HOVEY Esqr & Daughter | of ye late Dec^n
JOHN | ATWOOD dec^d she died | Feb^ry ye 23^d 1771 In y^e | 56th
year of her age.

399. In memory of | Mr THOMAS DAVIE | who died at
Sea | March 5 1771 aged 27 years | Also in memory of | Mrs
JANE DAVIE | who died Jan^ry 25 1824 | aged 75 years |
widow of the above | Blessed are the dead that die in the *LORD.*

400. Here lies Interrd | the Body of M^r | NATHANIEL
GOODWIN | who departed this Life | ye Twenty third Day of |
May one Thou∫and | ∫even hundred and | ∫eventy one | in y^e
forty eight year | of his Age.

401. Here lies Interr'd | the Body of | Mr MELATIAH LOTHROP | who Departed this Life | July 6th 1771 | Aged 70 years.

402. Here lies buried | DANIEL Son to M^r | DANIEL HO*f*EA & M^{rs} | HANNA^h his Wife | Born Jan^{ry} y^e | 29th 1769 dec^d | Sep^{tr} ye 27th 1771.

403. To | The Memory | of | Mrs ELISABETH CLARKE | who died | September 27th 1771 | ÆT. 26.

> *Tho' the pale corpfe is in the Grave Confine'd*
> *She leaves a Pattern for her Sex behind.*
> *The Sun of Virtue never can decay,*
> *It shines in Time, & gives eternal Day.*

404. Here lies Interrd | ye body of LEWIS | ye Son of JOHN BAR | TLETT & DOROTHY | his Wife who de | parted this Life | January ye 9th 1772 | Aged 1 year 9 mo | nths & 20 Days.

405. Here lies burie^d | Mrs MARCY HARLO^w | Widow to Mr | WILLIAM HARLOW | Who dec^d Janu^{ry} | ye 21st 1772 in y^e | 77th year of her Age.

406. To the memory of | HANNAH Daughter | of NATH^l GOODWIN | and MOLLY his Wife | Who died May ye 5 | 177² Ætatis 8 Days.

407. Here lies Interr'd the body | of Mr WILLIAM RIDER | Who departed this Life | June the 29th | A. D. 1772 | In the 49th year of his Age.

408. In Memory of | ELIZABETH Daughter of M^r | JAMES DREW & Mrs MARY | his wife who died July 24th | 1772 aged 2 years 10 months | & 12 days.

409. Here Lyes Inter'd y^e | Body of SOUTHWORTH | son to ICHABOD | SHAW & PRISCILLA | his wife he died | Septr ye 9th Day | A. D. 1772 | Aged 7 Month^s and | 6 Days.

410. Here lies Buried | 4 children of Capt JOHN BI*f*HOP | & Mrs ABIGAIL his wife | Viz 1*ft* MARY died Sepr 24th 1772 | aged 1 year & 11 months | 2^d ABIGAIL died Jany 17th 1774 | aged 7 days | 3^d MARY died Jany 15th 1774 | aged 15 days | 4th JOHN died Sepr 25th 1778 | aged 11 months.

411.   To perpetuate yᵉ memory | of *Mrˢ MARY BACON* |
Consort of yᵉ Revᵈ Mʳ | *JACOB BACON* who | departed this
Life much | Lamented, Nov. 17 1772 | in yᵉ 55 Year of her Age |
is this Stone here ſet | up & thus marked | with her name.

412.   Here lyes buried 4 children of Mʳ | JEſSE CHURCHELL
& Mrs ABIGAL his wife | Viz 1ᶠᵗ JEſSE born Novʳ 10ᵗʰ 1772 |
Aged 12 Days 2ᵈ ABIGAL WORCESTER | born June 25ᵗʰ
1778 Aged 2 Months | & 12 Days 3ᵈ ABIGAL born March |
23ᵈ 1782 dec'd July 24ᵗʰ 1783 | 4ᵗʰ DAVID born July 30 1784
dec'd | Janʸ 11 1788.

413.   REBECCA FULLER | Deceased Decemᵇʳ | 25ᵗʰ 1772
Aged 1 | year 4 months and | 13 Days Daughtᵉʳ of | Mʳ JOHN
FULLER and | REBECCA his Wife.

414.   Here lies Interrd the | Body of Mʳ | JOHN BAR-
TLETT | who departed this | life February the 6th | A. D.
1773 Æ 77 years.

415.   Here lies yᵉ body | of Capᵗ *JABEZ HAR* | *LOW* who
died | March yᵉ 8ᵗʰ A. D. 1773 | in yᵉ 40ᵗʰ Year of his | Age.

416.   In Memory of Mrs | HANNAH HOſEA | Wife of Mʳ
DANIEL | HOſEA who decᵈ Marᶜʰ | yᵉ 17ᵗʰ 1773 in yᵉ 24ᵗʰ | year
of her age : Daughᵗʳ | to Decⁿ JOSEPH BARTLETT.

417.   Here lies buried | JOſEPH Son to Mʳ | JOſEPH BAR-
TLETT & Mrs | MARY his Wife who | decᵈ March yᵉ 26ᵗʰ 1773 |
Aged 1 Month & 11 days.

418.   Here lies buried | the Body of | Mrs MARY CROS-
WELL | wife of Mʳ ANDREW CROSWELL | who departed this
Life Auguſt | 30ᵗʰ 1773 in yᵉ 29ᵗʰ year | of her Age.

419.   In Memory of | Doctor LAZARUS LE BARON | who
departed this Life | Sepʳ 2ᵈ 1773 Ætatis Sual 75.

> *My flesh ſhall slumber in the ground*
> *Till the last trumpet's joyful sound*
> *Then burst the chains with sweet surprise*
> *And in my Saviour's image rise.*

DR. LAZARUS LE BARON was the son of Dr. Francis and Mary (Wilder) Le Baron;
born 1698; married Lydia, daughter of Joseph and Lydia (Griswold) Bartlett, 1720.
Studied medicine and became an eminent physician, and had extensive practice from
1720 to the day of his death as above.

420. To the memory of | Mrs HANNAH SYMMES | the wife of | Mr ISAAC SYMMES | who died Oct^{br} 1^{ft} | 1773 Æt. 31.

421. Here lies | buried PATIENCE | Daugh^{tr} to M^r | DAVID TURNER | & Mrs DEBORAH | his Wife who | dec^d Decm^b y^e | 9th 1773 Aged | 4 Months | & 27 days.

422. In Memory | of | Mrs JOANAH HOLMES | who departed this | Life Decr 17th 1773 in | ye 76th year of her | Age.

423. In Memory | of | Mrs SARAH SPINKS | who departed this Life | April ye 3^d 1774 Aged | 38 years wife | of Mr NICHOLAS SPINK.

424. Here lyes Buried ye body | of Mrs MARY HOVEY late | wife of JAMES HOVEY Efq | fhe dyed on ye 2^d day of | June A 1774 in ye 44th Year | of her Age.

425. This Stone | is erected to the Memory | of | Capt ABRAHAM HAMMATT | who | departed this Life June 23^d | and in the year of our Lord 1774 | Ætatis 55.

426. This Stone is erected | to the memory of | Mrs PATIENCE HOWLAND | who departed this Life | July ye 23^d 1774 in ye 52^d year | of her Age she was Widow | of Capt *JOHN HOWLAND* | who died on ye Florida shoar | A. D. 1750 in ye 59th year of his Age.

427. In Memory of | SARAH Daughter of M^r | JOfEPH TRIBELL Ju^r & M^{rs} | SARAH his wife who died | Octr 28 1774 aged 1 year.

428. In Memory of | Mrs MARCY FOBES | widow of | Mr JOSHUA FOBES | who died Novr 19th 1774 | in ye 78th year of her Age.

429. In Memory | of | Mrs MARY TORREY wife to | De^acon JOHN TORREY | who departed this Life | Decr ye 31^{ft} 1774 in ye 43^d | year of her Age.

430. In | memory | of | Mrs RUTH HOWLAND | Relict of | M^r CONfIDER HOWLAND | who | departed this life | Jan 11th 1775 | aged 61 years.

431. In Memory | of | ROBERT BROWN | who | Departed this Life | January ye 21st A. D. 1775 | in ye 93^d year of his Age.

432. This stone is Erected | to the memory of ROBERT |
ROBERTS who died at the | Island of St. Domingo Apr. 12 |
1775 in the 32 year of his age | Also in memory of SARAH |
ROBERTS Widow of the Above | who died March 1 1826 |
aged 78 years | Also their Daughter SARAH | who died March
4 1775 | aged 2 years & 6 months.

Till Christ shall come to rouse the slumbering dead
Farewell pale lifeless clay a long farewell.

433. In Memory of | Mr NEHEMIAH RIPLEY | who
departed this Life | April ye 28th 1775 in y^e | 75th year of his
Age.

434. To | the memory | of | Capt JOHN HARLOW | who
died June 20th 1775 | aged 44 years.

435. In Memory of | REMEMBER Daugh^{tr} of | Capt
SAMUEL HARLOW | & Mrs REMEMBER his | Wife Born Nov^{br} y^e |
12th 1770 Died | June ye 23^d 1775.

436. In Memory | of | Capt THOMAS JACKSON | who
departed this Life | July ye 10th 1775 Aged | 75 years.

437. In memory of | SILVANUS ſon of Capt | SILVANUS
HARLOW and | Mrs DESIAH his wife | who died Sep^{tr} ye 5th |
1775 Aged 11 years.

438. In Memory | of | Mr EPHRAIM COBB | who departed
this Life | Sepr ye 6th 1775 Aged | 67 years.

439. In Memory of | Mr DAVID TURNER | who died
Octo^{br} | ye 4th 1775 in | ye 45th ye^{a}r of | his Age.

440. In Memory of | BENJAMIN ſon of | SETH HARLOW
and | SARAH his wife who | died Octr ye 17th | 1775 aged 11
years.

441. In Memory of | PACIENCE COLEMAN | TURNER
Daugh^{tr} to | Mr DAVID TURNER & | Mrs DEBORAH his | wife
dec^d Octo^{br} | ye 19th 1775 | Aged 10 Months | & 4 days.

442. In Memory of | Mrs ELIZABETH JACKSON | wife
of | Mr NATHANIEL JACKSON | who departed this Life Oct^r |
27th 1775 Aged 28 years.

443. In Memory of | the dec'd Children of M^r | WILLIAM & Mrs SARAH | LE BARON Viz WILLIAM | dec'd Nov^{br} 18 1775 aged | 7 days WILLIAM dec'd Oct^r | 21 1788 aged 17 months.

444. In Mem°ry of | REMEMBER Daugh^r | of Capt SAMUEL | HARLOW & M^{rs} | REMEMBER his wife | Born Aug^{ſt} ye 4th 1773 | Died Nov^{br} ye 20th 1775.

445. To the Memory of | JOSEPH Son of | Mr JOSEPH CROSWELL J^r | & LUCY his wife who | died Decr 8th 1775 | Aged 5 years 1 | Month & 11 Days.

446. To the Memory of | *DEBORAH* Daughter | of Mr *WILLIAM* | *HARLOW* & Mrs *SARAH* | his wife who died | Dec 23^d A. D. 1775 | Aged 7 Year & 6 months.

447. In memory of | JOHN LEWIS Son | of Mr JOHN BARTLETT | and Mrs DOROTHY | his wife who died | April ye 1st 1776 Aged | 2 years & 27 | Days.

448. In Memory | of | Mr NATHANIEL | *MORTON* ye 3^d who | departed this Life Nov^{br} | ye 20th 1776 in ye 23^d | year of his Age.

449. In Memory of | M^{iss} MERIAH Dau^{tr} of | Mr JEREMIAH & M^{rs} | HANNAH HOWES who | Died Decr 2^d 1776 | In ye 15th Year of | her Age.

450. In Memory of | Mrs HANNAH DIER Widow of | Mr JOHN DIER who died Decr 2 | 1776 in ye 79 year of her age.

451. In Memory | of | *JOHN TORREY* Esqr | who departed this Life | Decem^r ye 16th 1776 in ye 60th | year of his Age.

> *In Faith he dy'd, in Dust he lies:*
> *But Faith foresees that Dust shall rise*
> *When Jesus with almighty word,*
> *Calls his dead Saints to meet the Lord.*

452. To the memory of | Mrs ABIGAIL SAMPSON | wife of M^r | STEPHEN SAMPSON | who died of the | Small pox Jan^{ry} ye 9 A. D. 1777 | in the 45 year of her age.

453. In Memory | of | M^r *JOB FOSTER* | who departed this Life | Jany ye 22^d 1777 in ye 22^d | year of his Age.

454. In Memory | of | THOMAS FOSTER Esqr | who departed this Life | Jany ye 24th 1777 in ye 74th | year of his Age.

455. Here lies Buried the Body of | Mrs *HANNAH GOODWIN* the wife of | Mr *JOHN GOODWIN* and Daughter of | Mr *THOMAS* and Mrs *SARAH JACKSON* | who departed this Life March 8th A. D. 1777 | in the 22^d Year of her Age.

> *A Soul prepar'd Needs no delays*
> *The Summons comes, the Saint obeys*
> *Swift was Her flight & short the Road*
> *She clofed her Eyes & saw Her God*
> *The Flefh refts here till Jefus comes*
> *And claims the Treafure from the Tomb.*

456. In Memory | of | Mrs JERU*f*HA DOTEN | wife of Capt | THOMAS DOTEN | who departed this | Life Apriel ye 24th 1777 | in ye 31*ft* year of her Age.

457. In Memory | of | Mrs REBECCA MORTON | wife of Mr *NATHANIEL* | *MORTON* who departed | this Life May ye 15th 1777 | in ye 41st year of her age.

458. In memory of | CORBAN Son of Capt | CORBAN BARNES & M^{rs} | MARY his wife who | died July ye 21st 1777 | Aged 1 year 2 Months | & 15 Days.

459. Here lies buried | ANDREW *f*on of M^r | ANDREW & Mrs SARAH | CROSWELL who dec^d | Sepr 23^d 1777 Æt. 13 | months & 17 days.

460. In Memory of | 4 Children of Mr SAMUEL & M^r— | Viz SAMUEL died Sepr 28 1777 | If AAC died Sepr 14 1703 aged 5— | died Sepr 25 1786 aged 1 year— | 1791 aged 9 months & 19 days.

461. In Memory of | —HOS *f*on of Capt AMOS RIDER & | Mrs MEHITABLE his wife who died | Oct. 14 1777 | Aged 1 year 5 mont | & 25 days Al*f*o In Memory of | AMOS their 2^d *f*on who died Feby 14 | 1788 Aged 3 months & 11 days.

462. In Memory | of | Mrs HANNAH JACKSON | widow of Capt *THOMAS* | *JACKSON* dec'd who | departed this Life Jany y^e | 21^{ft} 1778 Aged 70 years.

463. In Memory | of | Mr NATHANIEL CURTIS who | was Drowned att Marfh | field March ye 8th 1778 Aged | 21 years 11 mon^{ths} & 12 Days.

464. In Memory of | JOS^h WARREN ALBER^{son} | son of Mr JACOB | ALBERSON & LYDIA | his wife who was | born June 25th 1778 | dec^d the same day.

465. In Memory | of | Mrs HANNAH DIMAN | wife of Deacon JON^a DIMAN | who departed this Life July ye 6th | 1778 in ye 65th year of her age.

466. In memory of | LAZARUS fon of | NATH^l GOODWIN Esqr | and Mrs MOLLY his | wife who decd July | ye 29th 1778 Ætatis | 6 Days.

467. ANNA WETHRELL | wife of | THOMAS WETHRELL | Born Feb 20th 1747 | Died Sept 12th 1778 | *WILLIAM* their son | Deceased Sep 6th 1770 | aged 1 year.

468. Memento Mori | In Memory of | Mrs LURAINA wife of | Capt JOSEPH FULGHUM | who Departed this Life | Novr ye 28th 1778 In the | 53^d year of her Age.

469. In Memory | of | Mrs SARAH BRAMHALL | Widow of JOSHUA BRAMHALL—who departed this Life | Decr ye 15th 1778 in ye 97th | year of her Age.

470. In Memory of | Capt | In Memory | of M^r DAN-JOHN | RUffEL Died | | IEL | HALL Died | Decm^{br} Decm^{br} | ye 26th 1778 | Aged | ye 26th | 1778 in | ye 25th 31 years. | year | of his Age.

Capt. JOHN RUSSELL, of Barnstable, Mass., was a commander of the marines, and DANIEL HALL was a Lieutenant on board of the brig "General Arnold," which was ship-wrecked in December 1778, at Plymouth, in which so many lives were lost. The stone to their memory is on the brow of the hill, south east side.

471. In memory of | Mrs MARTHA DARLING—wife of JONATHAN DARLING & | Daughter of JOSHUA BRAMHALL | who Departed this life | January the 7th 1779 | in the 63 year | of her age.

Why flow my tears why should I
Not rejoice—
At their deliv'rance from this combrows
Clay;
I soon shall meet them! hear their
Gentle voice—
Welcome my soul to everlasting day.

472.

IN MEMORY OF
SEVENTY TWO SEAMEN, WHO
PERISHED IN PLYMOUTH HAR
BOR ON THE 26th & 27th
OF DECEMBER 1778, ON BOARD
THE PRIVATE ARMED BRIG
GENERAL ARNOLD OF TWEN-
TY GUNS NUMBERING IN
OFFICERS AND CREW ONE
HUNDRED AND SIX PERSONS
IN ALL, JAMES MAGEE OF
BOSTON COMMANDER, SIXTY
OF WHOM WERE BURIED ON
THIS SPOT, AND TWELVE IN
OTHER PARTS OF THE HILL.

The inhabitants of Plymouth were called to witness a most distressing catastrophe in the month of December, 1778, of which the following is a reliable account as published in the Boston Gazette, June 4, 1779:

"On Friday, the 25th ult , at six a. m., the wind to the westward, sailed from this port the brig *General Arnold*, James Magee, commander; and about meridian the wind chopped round to north-east, and looking likely for a gale, they thought best to put into Plymouth, and came to anchor in a place called the Cow-yard. On Saturday, the gale increasing, she started from her anchor and struck on the White Flat. They then cut both cable and masts away, in hopes to drive over; but she immediately bilged; it being low water, left her quarter-deck dry, where all hands got for relief. A schooner lying within hail heard their cries, but could not assist them. On Sunday the inhabitants were cutting ice most of the day before they got on board, when they saw seventy-five of the men had perished, and thirty-four very much frozen, which they got on shore and on Monday they got on shore and buried the dead. Great part of her stores, etc., will be saved. Some evil-minded persons have raised a report that she was plundered by the inhabitants, which is entirely false, as they behaved with the greatest humanity. The following are the persons taken off the wreck of the General Arnold, that *survived* the ship-wreck : Capt. James Magee, John Steel, Jotham Haughton, George Pilsbury, Peter Moorfield, Robert Hinman, Dennis Flin, Thomas Farmer,—Stevens, John Bubbey, James Hutchinson, Andrew Kelley, Francis Fires, Daniel English, Robert Mitson, James Kent, —Robertson, James Rughley, of Boston: James Williams, David Williams, Chelsea; George Chockley, Bedford; Eleazer Thayer, — Potter, Providence; Wm. Russell, Vineyard; Abel Willis, Edward Burgess, Jethro Naughton, — Coffin, — Merchant, William Gardner, — Chapman, Martha's Vineyard; — Dunham, Falmouth; Barnabas Lathrop, Barnabas Downs, Jun'r, Barnstable."

The inhabitants of Plymouth provided for the comfort of the survivors in the best possible manner and ministered everything necessary to their restoration, with a tenderness and social sympathy characteristic of our best people.

On Monday the inhabitants passed over the ice to the wreck. Here was presented a scene unutterably awful and distressing. It is scarcely possible for the human mind to conceive of a more appalling spectacle. The ship was sunk ten feet in the sand: the waves had been for about thirty-six hours sweeping the main deck; the men had crowded to the quarter deck, and even here they were obliged to pile together dead bodies to make room for the living. Seventy dead bodies, frozen into all imaginable postures, were strewed over the deck, or attached to the shrouds and spars; about thirty exhibited signs of life, but were unconscious whether in life or death. The bodies remained in the posture in which they died; the features dreadfully distorted. Some were erect, some bending forward, some sitting with the head resting on the knees, and some with both arms extended, clinging to the spars or some parts of the vessel The dead were piled on the floor cf the Court House, and it is said that Dr. Robbins fainted when called to perform the religious services.

Among those who perished were Dr. Mann, of Attleborough, and Dr. Sears. Sixty persons were buried in one pit, on the south west side of the burial hill, at which is the above tablet.

473. In Memory of | Mr LEMUEL MORTON | who departed this Life | Jany ye 26th 1779 in ye 75th | year of His Age.

474. In Memory of | JOSHUA son of Mr | JOSEPH BRAM-HALL | & Mrs REMEMBER | his wife who died | Febry ye 5th 1779 aged | 3 months & 8 Days.

475. In Memory | of | Mrs ELIZABETH THOMSON | for-merly wife to THOMAS | MURDOCH decd she departed | this Life Feb ye 24th 1779 | in ye 75th year of her Age.

476. This Monument | is erected to | the memory of | Mr SILVANUS DUNHAM | who died in Martinico Febry | 1779 aged 29 years.

477. In memory of | Mr GIDEON WHITE | who departed this life March | ye 6th 1779 Aged 62 years | Alƒo In Memory of | Capt CORNELIUS WHITE | his son who Founder'd at Sea Sepr | ye 22d 1779 aged 35 years.

478. In Memory | of | Mr SILVANUS— | who departed this life | March ye 14th 1779 in ye— | year of his age.

479. In Memory of | JOHN HARLOW | who Dec'd March 10th 17— | in ye 73d year of his age | Alƒo In Memory of | Mrs MARY HARLOW | his wife who Dec'd April 2d | 1779 in ye 64th year of her Age.

480. In Memory of | Mr JOSEPH RIDER Jur | who departed this Life | May ye 13th 1779 in ye 65th | year of his Age.

481. In Memory | of | Mrs MERCY DAVIS | wife of | Capt THOMAS DAVIS | who departed this Life | Sepr ye 20th 1779 in ye 45th | year of her Age alƒo | their son Still born 18th.

482. In memory of | Mrs ELISABETH BARTLETT | wife of THOMAS BARTLETT | who departed this life | Sep 20 1779 | in the 32 year | of her age.

483. In Memory of | JOHN son of Mr JOHN | TORREY & Mrs MERIAH | his wife who died | Octr ye 7th 1779 | Aged | 1 year 4 Months & 19 | Days.

484. In | memory of | THOMAS SOUTHWORTH |
HOWLAND who | departed this life | Octr 15th 1779 | aged 45 |
years | In memory of | Capt CONSIDER HOWLAND who
was | lo*ft* at *f*ea Octr 1780 aged 35 years.

485. To the memory of | Mrs MOLLY GOODWIN | wife
of | NATHANIEL GOODWIN Esqr | who departed this life | Oct_r
y^e 22_d A. D. 1779 | Ætatis 30 years.

486. In Memory of 2 Children of | M^r CRO*f*BE LUCE &
M^{rs} | ELIZABETH his wife Viz. ELKANAH | died Novr 5 1779
aged 1 year | 3 months & 11 days CRO*f*BE | born June 25 1780
& died the | *f*ame day.

487. In Memory of | Mr EZRA ALLEN | who | departed
this Life Nov^r | ye 22^d, 1779 aged 61 | Years.

488. To the memory of | Mr JOHN CHURCHILL | Who
whas lo*ft* at Sea | In the year 1779 aged 34 years | Al*fo* | To
the memory of | Mrs OLIVE CHURCHILL | Died June 28th
1780 aged 29 years | Relict of | Mr JOHN CHURCHILL, | Here
lies interred | The body of | Mr JOHN CHURCHILL | Died
October 28th 1800 | In the 21st year of his age | only son to the
above Parents.

Hark! the Arch angel's trumpet rends the skies,
From Earth and Ocean, see the Dead arise,
The Parents — Son — and Daughter, meet again
*Where perfect love shall bani*fh *fear and pain.*

489. In Memory of | NANCY Daughter of M^r | JOHN
GOODWIN and | Mrs FEAR his wife who | dec'd Jan 17th 1780 |
Aged 1 Month & 25 Days.

490. *Sic Transit Gloria Mundi* | To | the memory | of |
M*i/s* HANNAH HOWLAND | who died | of a Languishment |
January ye 25th 1780 | Ætatis 26.

For us they languish & for us they die,
And shall they languish shall they die in vain.

491. In Memory of | REBECCA Daughter of | Mr JOSEPH
CROSWELL & | Mrs LUCY his wife | who died Feby ye 3^d | 1780
Aged 8 Months | & 5 Days.

492. In Memory of | Mr SAMUEL BARTLETT | who departed this Life | April 7th 1780 in ye 54th | year of his Age.

493. Mrs *ELLEN LOTHROP* | Con*f*ort to *NATH^l LOTHROP* | and only Daughter of the late Rev^d | Mr *NOAH HOBART* of Fair field | was born October 56th 1741 | and Died June 1st 1780 | This Stone | An unavailing Tribute of affliction | is Erected by her Hu*f*band | To her Memory.

To name her Virtues ill befits my grief,
What once was blifs can now give no relief,
A Hufoand mo^urns—The reft let friendship tell,
Friends knew her worth: a Hufoand knew it well.

494. In Memory of | Mrs HANNAH NICOLSON | wife of | Capt JAMES NICOLSON | who died Sep^t 24 1780 | aged 75 years.

495. In Memory of | JAMES HOVEY Esq | who dec'd Jan'y ye 7th 1781 | in ye 72^d year of his Age.

496. A. D. | 1781 | March 4 died | WILLIAM WATSON Jun | Aged 24 years | June 24 died | BENJAMIN WATSON | In the 21st Year of his Age | Only *sons* of WILL^m WAT*f*ON Esqr | And ELIZABETH his Wife. | And | Here lie | Interred | B. W. | W. W.

497. In Memory of | Mrs MARY MORTON | wife of | Mr NATHANIEL MORTON | who dec'd March 7th 1781 | in ye 63^d year of her Age.

498. In Memory of | Mrs MARGARET KEEN | widow of | Mr WILLIAM KEEN | who departed this Life April | 26th 1781 in ye 66th year | of his Age.

499. Memento Mori | In Memory of Mrs EUNICE | wife of Mr EBENEZER ROBINS | who Died June ye 4th 2781 | In ye 46th year of her Age | In Memory of EBENEZER their | son who died in Captivity In | the 21st year of his Age | Af*f*o | In Memory of 4 infant children | viz CO^nSIDER, LEVI, JOANNA & LEVI | who Lie buried by her.

500. In Memory of | MARY BENNET Daughter | of Mr JOSEPH BRAMHALL | & Mrs REMEMBER his | wife who dec^d July | ye 20th 1781 Aged 1 | year & 4 Days.

501. In Memory of | Mr NATHANIEL MORTON | who departed this Life | Augu*ſt* 13th 1781 in | ye 50th year of his Age.

502. In Memory of | STEPHEN *ſon* of | Mr WILLIAM BARTLETT | & Mrs MERCY his | wife who died Sep^r | ye 10th 1781 in ye 2^d | year of his age.

503. In memory of | JONATHAN *ſon* of | Capt ELKANAH BART | LETT & Mrs SARAH | his wife who died | Sept ye 17th 1781 | Aged 15 months.

504. To the memory | of | Mrs SARAH DELENO | wife of | Capt NATHAN DELENO | who died Sep^t 21*ſt* 1781 | in the 69th year of her age.

505. To | the memory of | Col. THEOPHILUS COTTON | who departed this Life | Feby ye 18th 1782—Ætatis 66 years.

> *" The firm Patriot there*
> *Who made the welfare of mankind his care*
> *Shall know he conquered."*

Col. THEOPHILUS COTTON was the son of Josiah and Hannah (Sturtevant) Cotton; born 1716, married Martha Saunders 1742. He was a zealous and active whig and patriot, and served sometime in the provincial army. He left several children.

506. In Memory of | Mrs LYDIA WASHBURN | wife of Mr *JOHN* | *WASHBURN* who dec'd | May ye 12th 1782 in y^e | 47th year of her Age.

507. To the Memory of | Mrs *MERIAH TORREY* wife of | Mr *JOHN TORREY* who dec'd | July ye 20th 1782 in ye 25th | year of her age.
Her | Life agreeable | Her | Death Triumphant | Through | Her Saviour.

508. In Memory of | FREDERICK *ſon* of M^r | JO*ſ*EPH & Mrs MARY | BARTLETT his wife, who | died July 27 1782 aged | 1 year 2 months & 27 days.

509. In Memory of | MARY BROWN Daughter | to ROBERT BROWN & | MARY his wife who | Expired on Sepr 27th | A. D. 1782 Aged 5 years | 1 Month & 14 Days.

> *Sleep ſilent Dust, till Christ our Lord*
> *The Omnipotent will speak the word*
> *Then Soul & Body both will arise*
> *To endless joys above the Skies.*

510. Here lies buried | SARAH daughter of | Mr ANDREW & Mrs SARAH | CROSSWELL who dec^d | Sepr 28th 1782 Æt^s | 1 year & 4 days.

511. In memory of | 2 Children of Mr LAZARUS | HARLOW & Mrs SARAH his | wife Viz. LAZARUS died Oct | 3 1782 aged 14 months | GRACY died April 21 1790 | aged 6 years.

512. In Memory of | Mr SILAS MORTON | who died Octo ye 30th | 1782 In the 55th year | of his Age.

513. Novr y— | Aged 11 years &— |

Not youth, nor parts, nor friends could save,
The unsuspecting victim from the grave
Like a fair flower that fades in early bloom,
In life's bright morn he met his early tomb
Tho' harsh the stroke and most severe the rod
Cease mourner cease—It was a stroke from God.

This stone is broken. On the foot-stone is inscribed:
ISAAC SAMSON | 1782.

514. In Memory of | Mrs MARTHA wife of | Mr SILAS MORTON who | died Decr ye 12th 1782 | Aged 52 Years | & 8 Months.

515. Here lies buried ye body | of Mrs *LOIS COLLINGS* | wife of Mr *JAMES COL* | *LINGS* with an Infant | in her armes who died | March 1st 1783 in ye 28th | year of her age.

516. In Memory of | Mrs JEMIMA TAYLOR | wife of Capt *JACOB TAYLOR* | who dec'd March 14th 1783 | in ye 52^d year of her Age | Alſo In Memory of Mr *JACOB* | *TAYLOR* their Son who was Drown'd | Novr 26th 1783 in ye 21^{ſt} year of his Age.

517. In Memory of | Deaⁿ JOSEPH BARTLETT | who died May 30 1783 | in ye 80 year of his age.

518. In Memory of | Mrs ABIGAIL DOTEN | Wife of Mr *WILLIAM* | *DOTEN* who dec'd | July 5 1783 Aged | 25 years.

519. In memory of | WILLIAM ſon of | DAVID & Mrs ELIZABETH | DREW who died July | 21^{ſt} 1783 Aged 1 year | 6 Months & 21 days.

520. In memory of | HENRY Son of M^r | BARNABAS & M^rs | POLLY his wife who | died July ye 22^d 1783 | Aged 10 months & 8 | Days.

521. In Memory of 2 Children | Sons of Mr RICHARD HOLMES | & Mrs ABIGAIL his wife | 1st REUBEN born June 8th 1782 died Aug. 2 1783 | 2^d REUB born Sepr 17th | died 26th 1785.

522. In Memory of | 2 Children Daughters of M^r | JUDAH DELANO & Mrs PENELOPE | his wife, Viz 1st SALOME died | Sepr 6th 1783 Aged 1 year 5 | months—Days, 2^d PENELOPE | died April 9 1784 Aged 2 Days.

523. In Memory of | Mrs ELIZABETH BARTLETT | widow of | Mr SAMUEL BARTLETT | who departed this Life | Sepr 12th 1783 in ye 48th | year of her Age.

524. In Memory of | THOMAS FORSTER PRINCE | Son of Mr JAMES | PRINCE & Mrs EUNICE | his wife who died Sep^r | 13th 1783 Aged 1 year | & 4 Months.

525. In Memory of | DAVID ſon of M^r | JOSEPH CROSWELL & | Mrs LUCY his wife | who died Sepr 29th | 1783 aged 1 year 2 | months & 8 days.

526. In Memory of | EZRA THAYER JACKSON ſon of | Mr THOMAS JACKSON 2^d & | Mrs LUCY his wife who | died Novr 23^d 1783 Aged | 25 Days.

What did the Little hasty sojourn^r
find So forbidding & disgustful in
our upper World to occation its
precipitant exit.

527. To the Memory of | Mrs HANNAH SYMMES | wife of | M^r IſAAC SYMMES | who died Decr 13th | 1783 Æt 35th.

528. To the memory of | 3 Children of ICHABOD HOLMES J^r | & REBEKAH his wife 1st a ſon | ICHABOD Died Auguſt 26 1784 | aged 11 days 2^d a daughter REBEKAH | Died Novr 13th

1786 aged 2 | months & 14 days 3ᵈ a ſon | ICHABOD Died Janʳʸ 13 1799 aged | 17 months.

> *Fresh in the morn the ſummer rose*
> *Hangs withered ere its noon*
> *We scarce enjoy the balmy gift,*
> *But mourn the pleaſures gone.*

529. In memory of | Mʳˢ DEBORAH HOWLAND | wife of | Mʳ CALEB HOWLAND | who departed this Life | Sepʳ 8ᵗʰ 1784 in yᵉ 48ᵗʰ | year of her Age.

530. In Memory of | Miſs BATHſHEBA HOLMES | Daughter of Mʳ ELNATHAN | HOLMES & Mʳˢ BATHSHEBA | his wife who died Sepʳ 11ᵗʰ | 1784 aged 16 years 11 monthˢ | & 4 days.

531. In Memory of | DANIEL ſon of Mʳ | DAVID DIMAN & Mʳˢ | LOIS his wife who died | Octʳ 9ᵗʰ 1784 Aged | 2 years & 5 Days.

532. In Memory of | JOHN ſon of Mʳ JOHN | TORREY & Mʳˢ ELIZABETH | his wife who died Octʳ 19 | 1784 aged 3 days.

533. In Memory of | Mʳˢ MARY ALLEN | Relict of | Mʳ EZRA ALLEN | why dec'd Janʸ 20ᵗʰ | 1785 Æ. 63.

534. Here lies Inter'd | Mʳˢ SUſANNA ATTWOOD | (& her Infant in her armes) | wife to | Mʳ WAIT ATTWOOD | died Feb 5 1785 in | the 35 year of her | Age.

535. To | the memory | of | Capt THOMAS DAVIS | who departed this life | March 7ᵗʰ A. D. 1785 | in the 63ᵈ year of his age | and here lies interred.

536. In Memory of | the deceased Children of | WILLIAM & LYDIA C. GOODWIN | to wit IſAAC born April firſt | 1785 & died the ſame day | CHARLES died Augᵗ 10 1791 | aged 14 months.

537. In Memory of | SARAH Daughter of Mʳ | LEMUEL MORTON & Mʳˢ | SARAH his wife who | was born April 3ᵈ 1785 | & dec'd yᵉ ſame day.

538. Here lies buried | the Body of | Mrs SARAH MORTON | wife of | Mr LEMUEL MORTON | who departed this Life | April 17th 1785 in ye 23^d | year of her Age.

In Her united all that^s Fair & good,
Short was her Race yct Virtues Path she trod.

539. In Memory of | EBENEZER ſon of M^r | SAMUEL DOTEN & M^{rs} | EUNICE his wife who | died April 28th 1785 | Aged 4 months & 3 | Days.

540. In Memory of | Mrs MARY BARTLETT | wife of Mr WILLIAM BARTLETT who died July | 16 1785 in ye 56 year | of her age.

541. In Memory of | Mrs MARY RIDER | widow of | Mr JOHN RIDER | who dec'd Augſt 24th | 1785 aged 69 years | 10 months & 25 days.

542. In Memory of | Mr ELEAZER STEPHENS | who departed this Life | Sepr 5th 1785 in ye 63^d | year of his Age.

543. In Memory of | 2 Children of Mr BARNABAS | CHURCHILL & Mrs SARAH his | wife Viz: BARNABAS died Sep^r | 14 1785 aged 10 months & 14 | days BARNABAS died Decr 8 | 1789 aged 10 months & 3 days.

544. In Memory of | Mrs SARAH BARTLETT | wife of | Deaⁿ JOSEPH BARTLETT | who died Decr 23 1785 | in ye 80 year of her age.

545. In Memory of | SAMUEL WEſT ſon of M^r | RICHARD BAGNELL & M^{rs} | BETHIAH his wife who died | Jany 12 1786 aged 4 months | & 24 days.

546. Here lies buried | the body of | Mrs ELIZABETH TUFTS | wife of | Mr JONATHAN TUFTS | who departed this Life | Jany 12th 1786 aged 39 years.

547. In Memory of | Capt. EZRA FINNEY | who was Lost at Sea | in the winter of 1786 | aged 37 yrs | Also *Mrs. HAN-NAH* his wife | who died | June 17 1814 | aged 64 yrs.

548. In Memory of | JOſEPH Son of M^r | LEMUEL DREW & M^{rs} | ELIZABETH his wife | who died March 4th | 1786 Aged 2 years | 3 Months & 17 Days.

549. Cap CHARLES DYER | died at Sea March | 1786 aged 47 y.rs | *BETHIAH* his wife | died June 8 1837 | aged 87 yrs | Their son *CHARLES*—died May 7 1822 | aged 46 yrs.

550. In Memory of | LEMUEL STEPHENS ROBBINS | Son of Mr Jofeph Robbins | & Mrs Elizabeth his wife | who died April 1ft 1786 | aged 3 years 2 months | & 7 days.

551. In Memory of | Capt GAMALIEL COLLINGS | The firft adventurer in the | whale fifhery to the Falkland Iflands | who died April 1 1786 in ye 44 | year of his age.

552. In Memory of | Mrs SUSANNA DIMAN | wife of | Mr Daniel Diman | who departed this Life | April 4th 1786 in ye 60th | year of her Age.

553. In memory of | Capt NATHAN BACON | who died at Sea | April 10 1786 aged 50 years | Also Mrs MARY BACON his wife | who departed this life | January 17 1825 | aged 84 years.
Blessed are the dead that die in the *Lord.*

554. In Memory of | Capt JAMES DOTEN | who departed this life | July 25th 1786 in ye 58th | year of his Age.

555. In Memory of | Mr SAMUEL COLE | who dec'd July 30th 1786 | Aged 30 years.

556. In Memory of | Mrs *MARY MORTON* wife of | Mr *THOMAS MORTON* who | died Augt 28 1786 in ye 52 | year of her age.

557. In Memory of | HENRY SAMPSON Son of | Mr David Bacon & Mrs | Abigail his wife who died | Jany 21 1787 Aged 14 Days.

558. In Memory of | Mr RICHARD HOLMES | who Dec'd June 5th 1787 | in ye 44th year of his Age | Alfo In Memory of | Mrs MERCY HOLMES | his wife who Dec'd May 20th 1779 | in ye 45th year of her Age.

559. In Memory of | ELIZABETH Daughter of Mr | Crosbe Luce & Mrs Elizabeth | his wife who died Auguft 5th 1787 | in ye 7th year of her age.

560. In Memory of | 2 Children of Mr IƒAAC | BARNES & Mrs
LUCY his | wife, Viz. SALLY died Octr 11 | 1787 aged 11 months
& 9 days | POLLY died Sepr 5 1789 aged | 2 years 1 month & 20
days.

561. In Memory of | THOMAS SMITH ƒon of | JOSIAH
COTTON Esqr & Mrs | LYDIA his wife who died | Octr 11th 1787
aged 4 | months & 18 days.

562. To | the Memory | of | the amiable *Mrs LYDIA COT-
TON* | Conƒort of *JOSIAH COTTON* Esqr | who died Nov
1ƒt 1787 in ye 35th year | of her Age.

> *'Tis God who lifts our comforts high,*
> *Or ƒinks them in the grave;*
> *He gives and (bleƒsed be his name!)*
> *He takes but what he gave.*

563. In Memory of | 2 Children of Mr WILLIAM & | Mrs
RUTH BRADFORD Viz | ELIZABETH died Novr 17 | 1787 aged
7 weeks JAMES | died Decr 28 1788 aged 7 | weeks & 6 days.

564. In Memory of | HANNAH Daughter of Mr | LEWIS
WEƒTON & Mrs LUCY | his wife who died Feby 9 | 1788 aged 1
year 4 months.

565. In Memory of | FREDERIC ƒon of Mr THOMAS |
JACKSON & Mrs LUCY his wife | who died March 15th 1788 aged |
1 year & 5 days.

> *O! Happy Probationer! accepted without*
> *being exerciƒed! It was thy peculiar Privi-*
> *lege not to feel the ƒlightest of thoƒe Evils,*
> *which oppreƒs thy ƒurviving kindred.*

566. In Memory of | GRACE Daughter of Mr | JoƒEPH
BRAMHALL & Mrs | REMEMBER his wife who | died March 17
1788 aged | 6 months & 12 days.

567. In Memory of | Mr EDWARD STEPHENS | who died
April 9 1788 in ye | 66th year of his age.

568. To | the memory | of | Capt JACOB TAYLOR | who |
died May 2 1788 | aged 59 years.

> *Through life he brav'd her foe if great or ƒmall*
> *And march'd out foremost at his Country's call.*

569. In Memory of | Mr JAMES DREW | who died May 5ᵗʰ 1788 in yᵉ 60ᵗʰ | year of his age.

570. In Memory of | Mʳˢ BATHſHEBA WAſHBURN ⟩ wife of Mʳ BENJAMIN | WAſHBURN who died July | 13 1788 aged 26 years.

571. In Memory of | JESſE ſon of Mʳ JESſE HARLOW ! —Mʳˢ HANNAH his wife | — died July 16 1788 | — 4 months & 19 days.

572. In Memory of | DAVID Son of Mʳ DAVID | DIMAN & Mʳˢ LOIS his wife | who died Augᵗ 4 1788 | aged 3 years 1 month & 26 | days.

573. Died Augſᵗ 22 1788 | DEſIRE JACKſON | Daughter of | Mʳ THOMAS JACKſON | & Mʳˢ LUCY his wife | Aged 2 months & 13 | days.

574. In Memory of | Mʳˢ ABIGAIL BARTLETT | wife of Mʳ SOLOMON | BARTLETT who died Sepʳ 11 | 1788 aged 40 years.

575. In Memory of | Mʳˢ SARAH NICOLSON | Conſort of | Capᵗ THOMAS NICOLSON | who died Octʳ 24ᵗʰ 1788 | in yᵉ 36ᵗʰ year of her age.

576. In Memory of | SARAH Daughter of Mʳ | EDWARD MORTON & Mʳˢ | SARAH his wife who died | Novʳ 12 1788 aged 7 years | 9 months & 9 days.

577. In Memory of | THOMAS ſon of Mʳ THOMAS | JACK-SON 3ᵈ & Mʳˢ SARAH his | wife who died Decʳ 24 1788 | aged 31 days.

Can the human heart remain untouch'd
With tender feelings when an Infant dies.

578. In Memory of | Mʳˢ NANCY DUNHAM | wife of | Capᵗ GEORGE DUNHAM | who died April 5 1789 in yᵉ | 41ˢᵗ year of her age | Alſo in Memory of George their ſon who | died Sepᵗ 3ᵈ 1773 aged 1 year & 3 months.

579. In Memory of | Mʳˢ REBECAH SEARS | who died April 14 1789 | in yᵉ 52ᵈ year of her age.

580. In Memory of | Mʳ SETH MORTON | who died April 17 1789 | in yᵉ 54 year of his age.

581. Died | Captain | SIMEON SAMSON | June 22 A. D.
1789 | Aged | fifty three | years.

> *O ye whofe cheek the tear of pity ftains,*
> *Draw near with pious reverence & attend*
> *Here lie the loving Hufband's dear remains*
> *The tender Father & the generous Friend*
> *The dauntless heart yet touch'd at human woe*
> *A Friend to man to vice alone a foe.*

Capt. SIMEON SAMPSON was the son of Peleg and Mary (Ring) Sampson; born in
Kingston, Mass., August, 1736. In early life he became a mariner, and was employed
in the merchant service from Plymouth. In the year 1762, Mr. Sampson was taken
prisoner by the French, in a vessel belonging to Goodwin & Warren, which was
redeemed by the captain for a large sum of money, and Mr. Sampson was left as a
hostage for the payment of the ransom. From this imprisonment he escaped by
assuming the dress of a female, and was soon restored to his family in Plymouth.

At the commencement of the revolutionary war, when a marine force was deemed
necessary to protect our commerce from the depredations of the British cruisers, he
was honored by the Provincial Congress of Massachusetts with the appointment of
the first naval captain in the service of the country. He immediately took command
of the brig Independence, belonging to the colony, and which was built at Kingston,
under his direction. In this vessel he was eminently successful, and in one cruise
captured and sent in five prizes, among which was the Roebuck, Captain White, in the
autumn of the year 1776. Immediately after this, he himself was captured by Capt.
Dawson, of distinguished memory in these seas. Capt. Sampson did not surrender,
until an engagement of a character as severe and bloody as perhaps is recorded in the
annals of naval warfare. The skill and intrepidity manifested by him was applauded
even by his enemies. Had he been sustained by all his men, he would undoubtedly
have been the conqueror, rather than the vanquished. It is said in the gazette of
that period, that he was driven to the awful necessity of running through the body of
two or three of his men, who abandoned their guns in the most trying moment of the
conflict. One of these victims was his third lieutenant. Soon after his return from
captivity, which was at Fort Cumberland, near Halifax, he was appointed commander
of the brig Hazard, a public vessel belonging to the state. In this vessel he likewise
took several prizes, among which was the ship Live Oak. In 1779 he was selected
to the command of the packet ship Mercury, built at Plymouth, by Mr. John Peck, for
Congress. She was employed to carry despatches to our ministers in France. In
this ship he returned from Nantz during the severe winter of 1780. Soon after
which, he was promoted to the command of the Mars, a large ship, likewise belonging to the state, and in this vessel he was employed in the most responsible trust, in
carrying despatches, and in one cruise carried out one of our ministers to Europe.
The British flag ship Trial was captured by him while in the Warren. At the close
of the war, he retired, like most of the faithful servants of our country, with a very
scanty estate, and a numerous family dependent upon him for support.

In 1788, Capt. Sampson disposed of his mansion in Middle street, Plymouth, and
purchased a farm in Plympton, where he terminated his earthly career by an apoplexy,
June 22d, 1789, at the age of 53 years. He was buried upon his own farm, and afterwards his body was removed to the burying hill in Plymouth, where his grave is
marked as above.

Few naval officers stood higher in public estimation, and few citizens were more
respected for domestic virtues, hospitality, and generous friendship. He married
Deborah, daughter of Seth Cushing of Hingham, Mass., who survived him, and died
in Homer, N. Y., in 1830, at the age of 90 years. He had twelve children, seven of
whom died young, and five of whom married.

582. In Memory of | Mrs ELIZABETH TURNER | wife of |
Mr LOTHROP TURNER | who died Auguft 16 1789 | in ye 24
year of her age.

583. To | the Memory | of | *JOHN COTTON* Esqr formerly a | Miniſter of the Gospel at Hallifax | (which Employ was ever his greateſt | Delight) who died Novr 4 A. D. 1789: | in ye 78 year of his Age.

> *'Tis Heaven's irrevocable Decree,*
> *That the great, the good, the pious ſhall fall,*
> *In the dark Grave undiſtinguiſh^d to lie,*
> *Till the laft Trumpet rends the azure ſky!*
> *When the Virtuous immortal will rife*
> *To Glory and joys 'bove the ftarry ſkies!*
> *The Vicious to pain, diſhonour, contempt;*
> *In realms below the fplendid Firmament!*

Rev. JOHN COTTON, son of Rev. Josiah and Hannah (Sturtevant) Cotton, born April 5, 1712; graduated at Harvard College 1730; ordained minister at Halifax, Mass., October 1736. In 1756, owing to a failing voice he requested a dismission which was granted. He succeeded his father as Register of Deeds, which office he held till his death, November 4, 1789,. He was considered an able theologian, and much beloved as a pastor and preacher. He was the author of the valuable Account of Plymouth Church, appended to Rev. Chandler Robbins' ordination sermon in 1760, which was afterward republished by the Massachusetts Historical Society in volume 4 of their collections. He also published several occasional sermons, including among them seasonable warnings to the churches of New England, and tracts on "Infant Baptism." He was chosen delegate to the Convention for revising a Constitution for the Commonwealth in 1780, and was one of the committee for Plymouth county to draft the constitution. He left several children, among whom was Rev. Josiah Cotton, minister at Wareham, Mass., who became a magistrate, and clerk of the Court for Plymouth county, and died April 19, 1819, leaving a son who became a physician in Ohio, and a daughter who married Isaac Lothrop Hedge Esq. of Plymouth. His other sons were Rosseter, who for several years was Register of Deeds in Plymouth. Rev. Ward Cotton, of Boylston, Mass., was his son. Another son, John, was lost at sea in 1800.

584. In Memory of | Mrs *DEBORAH* wife of | Mr KIMBAL CROMBIE | who died Novr 17 1789 | aged 21 years.

585. In Memory of | Miſs PATIENCE WARREN | Daughter of Capt BENJAMIN | WARREN who died Novr 27 | 1789 aged 74 years.

> *Hark from the tombs a doleful found*
> *My ears attend the cry*
> *Ye living men come view the ground*
> *Where you muft shortly lie.*

586. In Memory of | JOANNA Daughter of M^r IſAAC & Mrs JOANNA SYMMES | who died Decr 27 1789 | aged 5 years 2 months & 13 | days.

587. In Memory of | Mrs KETURAH HOVEY | wife of Capt *SAMUEL* | *HOVEY* who died Feby 14 | 1790 in ye 37 year of her age | Al/o in Memory of RACHEL their Daughte^r | who died Octr 14 1790 aged 18 months & 5 days.

588. Died March 14th | 1790 | STEPHEN Son of | Capt NATHANIEL | CARVER & JOANNA | His wife | Aged 49 days | And their daughter | NANCY died /ep^t 24 | 1798 | Aged 1 year & 8 months.

589. In Memory of | EDWIN Son of Mr THOMAS | JACKSON 3^d & Mrs SARAH his | wife who died April 20 | 1790 aged 22 days.

590. In Memory of | Mr JOHN BARTLETT | who died April 26 1790 in y^e | 53 year of his age.

>*Here lies the man who nev'r his friends denied*
>*Nor never gave them grief but when he died.*

591. To | the Memory | of | Mi/s ELIZABETH MORTON | who departed this Life | May ye 21/t A. D. 1790 in y^e | 20th year of her age.

592. In Memory of | Mrs HANNAH LEWIS | wife of | Mr NATHANIEL LEWIS | who died May 29 1790 | in ye 38 year of her age.

593. In Memory of | O/BORN /on | of M^r O/BORN | MORTON & Mrs PATIENCE his | wife who died Sepr 18 1790 | aged 4 years & 10 months.

594. In Memory of | JO/EPH Son of Dr STEPHEN | MARCY & Mrs LUCY his wife | who died Octr 16 1790 aged | 1 year & 9 months.

595. In Memory of | SUKEY THACHER who died Dec^r | 8 1790 aged 2 years & 8 months | & of JAMES THACHER who died | Decr 12 1790 aged 2 days | Children of Dr JAMES THACHER | & M^rs Su/ANNAH his wife Both of | who/e remains are depo/ited.

>*Sleep on my babes & take your quiet rest,*
>*'Twas God who called you when he thought it best.*

596. In Memory of | MARCY WARREN Daughter of | Mr BENJAMIN BRAMHALL & M^rs | PRI*f*CILLA his wife who died | Novr 11 1790 aged 1 year 7 | months & 7 days.

597. In Memory of | 2 Children of Mr JUDAH & M^rs | PENELOPE DELANO Viz HENREY | died Novr 14 1790 aged 2 years & 4 | months & 8 days died a Daughter | Feby 4 1785 aged 1 day.

598. In Memory of | Mrs MARY BRADFORD | wife of | Mr LEMUEL BRADFORD | who died Decr 21 1790 in y^e | 36 year of her age.

599. To | the memory | of | Mr THOMAS FINNEY | who died Jan^ry 5th | A. D. 1791 in the 53^d | year of his age.

600. In Memory of | Mrs HANNAH OTIS | wife of Mr *JOHN OTIS* | who died March 28 1791 | in ye 47 year of her age.

601. To the memory of 5 children of | Mr Wm BARNES & Mrs MERCY his wife | viz ELENOR died March 28th 1791 | aged 8 days | 2^d MERCY died Augu*f*t 12th 1801 | aged 3 months & 14 days | 3^d NATHANIEL died Septr 15th 1802 | aged 3 months & 9 days | 4th CALVIN CARVER died Octr 19th 1802 | aged 4 years & 2 months | 5th CALVIN CARVER died April 22^d 1805 | aged 1 year & 7 months | and 7 days.

> *In early days, away from us they fly,*
> *No more their plea*f*ing actions charmes our eyes.*
> *A happy change from earth to* f*ure above,*
> *Now take their dwelling in the realmes of love.*

602. ANCEL *f*on of Mr SAMUEL DOTEY | & Mrs EUNICE his wife who | died June 17 1791 aged 1 year | & 7 months.

603. In Memory of | Mrs *PATIENCE RIDER* | wife of | Major *BENJAMIN RIDER* | who died June 18 1791 in y^e | 42^d year of her age.

> *Why do we mourn departing friends,*
> *Or* f*hake at deaths alarms,*
> *'Tis but the voice that Jesus sends,*
> *To call them to his arms.*

604. In Memory of | Mrs SARAH CHURCHILL | wife of
Mr SAMUEL | CHURCHILL who died | June 26 1791 in y^e | 40.
year of his Age | Alſo in memory of their ſon | who was born
June 15 1786 | & died the ſame day.

605. In Memory of | EUNICE Daughter of M^r | EBENEZER
HOWARD & M^rs | BETHIAH his wife who died | July 10 1791
aged 3 years | 1 month & 7 days.

606. In Memory of | Mr KIMBALL CROMBIE | who died
July 13 1791 aged | 24 years.

607. In Memory of | Mrs RUTH MARſHALL | wife of M^r
BARTLETT | MARſHALL who died | July 24 1791 Aged | 37
years.

608. In memory of | *Mrs SARAH LUCE* wife of | *Mr SETH
LUCE* who died | July 26 1791 in the 53 year | of her age.

609. In Memory of | MARY Daughter of Dr | ROſſETER &
M^rs PRIſCILLA | COTTON who died Aug^t | 26 1791 aged 15
months | & 6 days.

610. Died | Mr ISAAC SYMMES | Auguſt 27 1791 | in
the 48 year | of his age.

> *Here lies a man who never was unjuſt,*
> *His body ſlowly mouldering into duſt*
> *But when Time ceaſes, joyfully he'll riſe*
> *And meet his Saviour's face in ſweet ſurpriſe.*

611. In Memory of 2 Children of M^r | SETH & Mrs ELIZABETH
CHURCHILL | Viz LUCY died Sepr 2 1791 aged | 2 years & 2
months, DAVID died | Sepr 30 1791 aged 9 months & | 3 days
alſo a 3^d SETH | died Sepr 24, 1795 aged | 1 year 4 months
& 5 days.

612. In memory of | POLLY Daughter of Mr JOHN | & M^rs
LYDIA EDWARDS who | died Sepr 11 1791 aged 5 | years & 3
months.

613. To the memory of | Mr JOSEPH MITCHELL | who
died December ye 30 | 1791 Ætatis 54 Mrs MARY | his wife
died May 22^d 1790 | Ætatis 51.

614. To the Memory | of | Mrs MERCY HEDGE | Relict of | Capt BARNABAS HEDGE | who died | December 25 A. D. 1791 | aged 83 years.

615. In Memory of | Mrs MARY DIMAN | wife of | Mr DANIEL DIMAN | who died Feby 15 1792 | in ye 55 year of her age.

616. Beneath this Sod | lies buried all that was mortal, | of Mifs LUCIA WATfON | (the youngeft Daughter of Mr ELKA-NAH | & Mrs PATIENCE WATfON) | who, at the age of 26 years | without one reluctant Sigh | Calmly refigned her Spirit | to the Creator who gave it | firmly perfuaded that in his | Infinite Benevolence | She fhould injoy an endless & | a happy Immortality | She was born November 11 1765 | Died March 20 1792.

617. In Memory of | Mrs HANNAH SAMfON | wife of Mr EBENEZER | SAMfON who died May | 13 1792 in ye 72 year | of her age.

No Pain, nor Grief, no anxious Care nor Fear
Invade fhese facred Bounds No mortal Woes
Can reach or vex the pious Sleeper here
May Angels gently watch her foft Repose.

618. To the memory of | Mr LEMUEL BARTLETT | who departed this life | May 20th 1792 Ætatis 77.

With filent fteps he meekly trac'd the way
To the bright relms of love his wish'd abode
Nor did he ask a moments longer stay
When the last fummons call'd his foul to God.

619. In Memory of | Mrs PATIENCE COBB | widow of *M^r* *JOB COBB* | who died July 26 1792 | aged 70 years.

620. In Memory of | NANCY Daughter of M^r | JOfIAH & Mrs REBECCA FINNEY | who died Augt 13 1792 aged 1 | month.

621. In Memory of | Capt JAMES RUffELL who died | Sepr 28 1792 aged 32 years | And alfo Mr THOMAS RUffELL | fuppofed to be loft at Sea in a fevere | snow ftorm Decr 4 & 5, 1786, | aged 24 years both Sons of the late | Mr JOHN & Mrs MERCY RUffELL.

622.   To the memory of | —LENOR CHURCHILL | Daughter of | Capt STEPHEN CHURCHILL | And LUCY his Wife | Who died Oct 3 1792 | in the 10th year | of her age.

623.   In memory of | MARTHA TORREY Daughter of | Mr JAMES & Mrs MARTHA | DOTEN who died Novr 26 | 1792 aged 11 months & 6 days.

624.   In Memory of | JOHN BARTLETT Son of M^r | JOHN & Mrs DOROTHY BARTLETT | who died Jany 25 1793 | aged 17 years.

Thofe eyes which once fo fparkled with delight
Are e'en now clofed in Death's eternal night.

625.   In Memory of | ZENAS *f*on of Mr ZENAS & | Mrs ELIZABETH STURTEVAN^t | who died March 24 1793 | aged 1 year 2 months & 15 | days.

626.   In Memory of | Mrs ELIZABETH BARTLETT | Relict of | SAMUEL BARTLETT Esqr | who died March 29 1793 in y^e | 77 year of her age.

627.   In memory of | DAVID BARNES | Son of JOSIAH & | RACHEL COTTON | who died April 27 1793 | aged Seven months.

Dear Babe sleep their in the dust
Till thy Saviour say arise with the Juft.

628.   This Stone is | Erected to the | Memory of JAMES | HERSEY THACHER who | Died 27th April 1793 | Aged 1 year And 4 months | And CATHERINE THACHER | Who Died 10 Febry 1800 | Aged 3 years Children of D^r | JAMES And Mrs SUSANNA THACHER.

Early Bright Transcint Sweet
As Morning Dew They Sparkled
Were Exhaled And went to Heaven.

629.   To the memory of | Mrs HANNAH HOWES | wife of | Mr JEREMIAH HOWES | Relict widow of M^r | STEPHEN CHURCHILL | who died June ye 12th | A. D. 1793 in ye 75th | year of her age.

630. In | memory of | two Sons of | Mr JOHN DOTEN & | Mrs SALLY his wife | JOHN Died July 18 1793 | aged 3 months | and nine days | WILLIAM Died Augt 24th 1794 | aged two years one | month & 16 days.

> *Our days were few on earth*
> *We could no longer stay*
> *The blefsed JESUS doth appear*
> *To bear our souls away.*

631. In Memory of | Mrs MARY JENNINGS | wife of | Mr JOSEPH JENNINGS | who died Augt 5 1793 in ye 43 | year of her age. Also In Memory of their | Children Viz 3 Sons & 1 Daughter who died in Infancy.

632. To the memory of | POLLY ROGERS | Daughter of | Mr WILLIAM ROGERS | & M^{rs} ELIſABETH his wife | who died Sepr 5th 1793 | aged 1 year & 10 months.

633. In memory of | HARRIET Daughter of M^r | SAMUEL & Mrs HANNAH | JACKſON who died Sepr 15 | 1793 aged 10 months & 15 days.

> *Babes thither caught from Womb & Breaft.*
> *Claim'd Right to fing above the reft*
> *Becaufe they found the happy fhore,*
> *They never faw nor fought before.*

634. In Memory of | MARY Daughter of—D^r | RoſſETER & Mrs PRISCILLA | COTTON who died Sepr 24 | 1793 aged 12 months.

> *Sleep on fweet Babes & take thy reft*
> *'Twas God that call'd when he thought beft.*

635. In Memory of | Mrs *LYDIA REED* wife of | Mr *NATHAN REED* who | died Octr 12 1793 in ye 32 | year of her age.

636. Mr TIMOTHY BURBANK | died Oct^{br} 13th 1793 Ætatis 90 | Mrs *MERCY* his wife | died Jan^{ry} 27th 1771 Ætatis 63 | and here lie interred.

637. In Memory of | SOUTHWORTH Son of M^r JOB & Mrs REBECCA RIDER | who died Octr 15 1793 | aged 6 years & 3 months.

638. To the memory of | two Children of Mr JOHN | PATY & DEBORAH his wife | viz SILVIA died Oct y^e 22 | aged 3 years 6 months & | 26 Days MERIAH Died Aug^t | y^e 11 A. D. 1793 aged 1 year —st | & 26 Days.

639. To the memory of | M^{rs} ELIfABETH NELfON | wife of | Capt SAM^l NICOLS NELSON | who died Oct 26th 1793 | aged 67 years.

640. In Memory of | Mrs PRISCILLA THOMAS | Con$f$ort of | Mr NATHANIEL THOMAS | who died Decr 6 1793 aged 36 years.

641. SAMUEL H— | SAMUEL HARMO— | LYDIA his wife— | 9 1793 aged 7 years | & 9 days.
This was probably the family of Samuel Harmon.

642. In memory of | Mr WILLIAM BRADFORD | who died in Roxbury Jany 14 1794 | aged 44 years | Also of Mrs RUTH BRADFORD his wife | who died May 22 1813 | aged 60 years | Also of two of their children | viz AMOS who died in Martinico | Augt 3 1794 | aged 17 years | And ISAAC who died March 16 | 1806 aged 21 years.

643. In Memory of | Mr SAMUEL LANMAN | who died Jany 19 1794 | in y^e 73 year of his age.

In thy fair book of life divine,
My God in$f$cribe my name,
There let it fill $f$ome humble place,
Beneath the $f$laughter'd Lamb.

644. , Here | lies   inter'd | the   Body   of | C^{oll} THOMAS LOTHROP | who   departed | this   Life | January 23 1794 | aged 54.

645. To | the   memory | of | Capt. *THOMAS DOTEN* | who | died Feb^{ry} 28th 1794 | in the 49th year of his age.

646. To | the   memory | of | M^r JOfEPH   RIDER | who died | March 19th 1794 | aged 65 | years.

647. In Memory of | BETfY Daughter of Mr | SAMUEL & M^{rs} BETfY BROOKS | who died April 19 1794 | aged 5 years & 6 months.

648. Here lies | inter'd the body | of Mi/s HANNAH | SYMMES elde/t Daughter | of Mʳ I/AAC & Mʳˢ HANNAH | SYMMES who at the early | period of 28 years after being | long exerci/d with bodily pain | with christian fortitude | yielded her Spirit to its | benevolent Author | Born Janʸ 30 1766 | Died May 27 1794.

649. To the | memory | of the amiable | Mʳˢ JANE DOGGET | who died May 31/ᵗ 1794 | in the 26ᵗʰ year of her age | also an infant Daughter by her /ide.

> *Come view the seen 'twill fill you with furprise*
> *Behold the lovelieft form in nature died*
> *At noon she flourifh'd blooming fair and gay*
> *At evening an extended corpfe fhe lay.*

650. In Memory of | Mʳ *JAMES DOTEN* Junʳ | who Died June 6 1794 | in yᵉ 32 year of his age.

> *Death is a debt too nature due,*
> *Which I have paid & fo muft you.*

651. In | memory of | WILLIAM W | Son of | WILLIAM & SARAH | STURTEVANT | who died | June 13 1794 | aged 2 years | and 4 mons.

652. In Memory of | Mʳˢ POLLY HOLMES | wife of JOSEPH HOLMES | who died July 3 1794 | aged 26 years.

> *Death is a debt to nature due*
> *Which I have paid & fo muft you.*

653. ET EGO IN COLUMBIA VIXI | To | The memory | of | Mʳˢ ANNA JACKSON | Wife of | WILLᵐ JACK/ON | Obiit | July 20 | 1794 | Aged | 28 years.

> *Death is the privilege of human nature*
> *And life without it were not worth our taking*
> *Thither the poor, the unfortunate, and Mourner*
> *Fly for relief, & lay their burdens down.*

654. In Memory of | PETER HOLMES | who died at Port Au Prince | September 15 1794 | aged 38 years | Also | MARY HOLMES | Consort of Peter | Who died Sept 2 1829 | aged 73 years.

655. In Memory of | Mʳ JOSEPH PLASKET | who died
August 1 | A. D. 1794 in the 48 | year of his age.

> *All you that doth behold my stone*
> *Consider how soon I was gone*
> *Death does not always warning give*
> *Therefore be careful how you live*
> *Repent in time no time delay*
> *I in my prime was called away.*

656. To | The Memory | of | THOMAS JACKSON Esqʳ |
This | Monument | Is erected | Obiit | September 19 | 1794 |
Aged | 67 years.

> *The ſpiders moſt attenuated thread*
> *Is cord is cable to mans tender tie.*

657. To the memory | of MARY BREWſTER HOLMES |
Daughter to ELNATHAN | HOLMES & DEBORAH his | wife who
died Sep 21 1794 | aged 2 months alſo | thare ſon who died
Sep 17 1795 aged 5 hours.

> *The Babe thats caught from womb & breaſt*
> *Claim right to ſing above the reſt*
> *Because they found the happy shore*
> *They never ſaw nor ſought before.*

658. To the memory of | Mʳˢ OLIVE WAſHBURN | wife
of | Mʳ ABIEL WAſHBURN | with an infant in her arms | who
died Oct. 14 1794 in | the 30 year of her age.

659. SARAH WETHRELL | wife of | THOMAS WETH-
RELL | Born Aug 6ᵗʰ 1753 | Died Oct 30ᵗʰ 1794 | *LUCIA* their
Daugh. | Deceased Oct 27ᵗʰ 1790 | Aged 1 year.

660. To the memory of | Mʳˢ MARY POPE | wife of | Mʳ
THOMAS POPE | who died Janʳy yᵉ | 9ᵗʰ 1795 in the 27ᵗʰ | year
of her age.

661. In Memory of | LYDIA PRINCE Daughter of | Mʳ
DAVID & Mʳˢ LYDIA | TURNER who died Janʸ 19 | 1795 aged 9
months & 12 days.

> *Of ſuch is the kingdom of heaven.*

662. Erected August 22 1824 | In memory of | JOSEPH BARNES who died | in Cape Francois January | 25 1795 aged 58 years | HANNAH BARNES Widow | of the above died November | 12 1815 Aged 76 years | HANNAH HARLOW wife of | ZACHEUS HARLOW & Daughter | of the above died December | 26 1807 Aged 47 years | Also NATHANIEL BARNES | who died in Martinico | July 9 1794 Aged 23 years.

663. To | the memory of | Mrs ELIZABETH FINNEY | wife of | Mr THOMAS FINNEY | who died | March 3^d 1795 in the | 53^d year of her age.

664. In memory | of | LAZARUS GOODWIN E∫q^r | who died | June 27th 1795 | aged 42 | years.

665. To the memory | of | Mr ROBART DAVEE | who died July 4th 1695 | in the 54th year of | his age.

666. Died Aug 18 1795 | PATIENCE CHURCHILL | Daughter to the late | Capt EBENEZER CHURCHILL | & Mrs JEAN his wife | in the 18th year of her age.

667. To the memory of | Mrs POLLY HOLMES | wife of | Capt ELEAZAR HOLMES | and Daughter of | Capt CORBAN BARNES | and *MARY* his wife | who died Sep 16 1795 Ætatis | 28 and her Infant Daughter Jenny | by her ∫ide who died Dec 5 Ætatis 1 year | and 8 months.

> *No age exempt the tender Mother fir∫t*
> *Bows to Deaths Empire & returns to Du∫t*
> *Scarce had th' afflicted Confort wip'd his tearful eyes*
> *When lo Heaven calls the lovely Infant dies.*

668. To the memory of | GEORGE COOPER ∫on of | Mr JOSEPH COOPER & LUCY | his wife who died Nov^r | 7 1795 aged 2 years | & 22 days.

669. To | the memory | of | JO∫IAH HARLOW | ∫on of | Capt ZEPHANIAH HARLOW | & Mrs PATIENCE his wife | who died Novr 10th 1795 | in the 16th year of his age.

670. Died Novr 13th 1795 | JENNE ELLIS | Daughter of | Mr NATHANIEL ELLIS | & Mrs JENNE his wife | in the 10th year of | her age.

671. To the memory of | Mrs MARY HILL | wife of | Mr JONATHAN HILL | who died Novr 14th 1795 | in the 42^d year of her age.

672. In | memory of | THOMAS TRIBBEL | son of | M^r JOƒEPH TRIBBEL | & Mrs MARY his wife | who died Novr 18th 1795 | aged 11 months | Alƒo | In memory of | MARY TRIB-BEL | daughter of | Mr JOSEPH TRIBBEL and | Mrs MARY his wife | who died Octr 18th 1799 | aged 1 year & 14 days.

673. In memory of | HENRY HOLMES | Son of | Mr NATHANIEL HOLMES | and MARY his wife | who died Decr 8th 1795 | aged 2 years | 8 months & 8 days.

674. To the | memory of | SUƒANNA NICHOLS | daughter of M^r MOƒES | & M^rs SUƒANNA NICHOLS | who died Decr 17th 1795 | in the 6 year of her age.

675. ABIGAIL LEACH | Died Decr 24 1795 aged 10 years | EBENEZER LEACH | Died Jany 31 1796 aged 13 years | Children of | Mr CALEB & Mrs ABIGAIL LEACH | And here lie interred.

676. To the memory of | Mrs *BETSEY SHAW* | wife of | Mr *ICHABOD SHAW* Junr | who died Decr 26 1795 | aged 20 years | alƒo her infant daughter | BETƒEY HOLMES by her ƒide | aged 7 months & 15 days.

677. To the memory of | Capt WILLIAM SHERMAN | who died at ƒea Jan^ry 9th | 1799 and was interred at Martha's Vineyard | in the 32^d year of his age.

> *On life's rough ocean toft a dark abode!*
> *By nature's optics he deƒcried a GOD:*
> *Reaƒon his pole ftar, by whoƒe friendly ray*
> *He fteered his courƒe to fhores of endless day.*

678. Capt. WILLIAM SHERMAN | died at sea | Jan 9 1796 | aged 32 years | ELIZABETH SHERMAN | his wife | died Oct 9 1849 : | aged 83 years | 10 months.

> *God calls our loved ones, but we lose not wholly,*
> *What he hath given;*
> *They live on earth, in thought and deed, as truly*
> *As in His Heaven.*

679. To the memory of | Capt COOMER WESTON | who died at Martha's Vineyard | (and is there interred) | January 10th A. D. 1796 | In the 34th year of his age.

That manly virtue which adorn'd thy bloom
Friendfhip recalls and weeps upon thy tomb
There fad remembrance drops a filent tear
And chafte affection ftands a mourner there.

680. To the memory of | ELIZABETH BARNES | daughter of | Mr JofEPH BARNES | & Mrs ELIZABETH his wife | who died Jan^{ry} 12 1796 | aged 3 years 5 months | & 22 days.

681. In memory of | ROfSETER fon of | RofSETER COTTON Efq | & M^{rs} PRIfCILLA his | Wife who died | January 30 | 1796 | aged two years.

682. To the memory | of SETH LUCE | fon of | Mr EBENEZER LUCE | & Mrs SARAH his wife | who died Feb^{ry} 14 1796 | in the 16 year of his age.

683. To the memory of | Mrs MARGARET COBB | widow of the late | Mr EPHRAIM COBB | who died Feb^{ry} 26 1796 | aged 85 years | Alfo to the memory of their fon | Capt LAZARUS COBB who died in Jamaica | 1771 aged 27 years.

684. In memory | of | Mrs LUCY HARLOW | wife of | Mr AMAZIAH HARLOW | who died March 6 1796 | in the 42 year of | her age.

685. To the memory of 3 Children | of RICHARD HOLMES jun^r & | SARAH his wife 1^{ft} a Daughter | EUNICE Died March 8th 1796 | aged 1 year 6 months & 18 Days | 2^d a Daughter MARCY Died Oct | 13th 1796 aged 7 months & 13 | Days 3^d a fon RICHARD Died Aug^{ft} | 6th 1798 aged 5 years & 10 months.

May their parents confolation find
May they never think that Heaven's unkind
nerring wifdom faw twas fit and beft
To call thefe Children early to their rest.

686. To the memory of | WILLARD SEARS | fon of | Mr WILLARD SEARS | & Mrs SARY his wife | who died May 22 1796 | aged 20 years.

687. In memory of | MARTHA COTTON | Relict of | Capt
THEOPHILUS COTTON Esqr | who | died April 10th | A. D. 1796
aged 79 years.

> *Many years I liv'd*
> *Many painfull scenes I pass'd*
> *Till God at last*
> *Call'd me home.*

688. Departed this Life | June 23^d 1796 | in the 90th year of
her Age | Madam PRISCILLA HOBART | Relict | of the Rev^d
NOAH HOBART | late of Fairfield in Connecticut | her third Hus-
band | her first and Second | were | JOHN WATSON Esq | and |
Honb^le ISAAC LOTHROP.

689. FREDERICK | Wm JACKSON | born July 21 1796 |
died Aug 16 1796.

690. Died Sept 10th 1796 | ANDREW CROSWELL | Eſq:
Aged 59 years & | 11 days | The ſweet remembrance of the
Juſt.

691. Died Sepr 10th 1796 | LUCY JACKſON | Daughter
of | Mr THOMAS JACKſON | & Mrs LUCY his wife | aged 1 year
3 months | & 9 days.

692. In memory of Miſs DOLLY | BARTLETT Daug. of
Mr JOHN & | Mrs DOROTHY BARTLETT who died | Sep^t 11 1796
in her 25 year.

> *The virtuous youth whoſe duſt is laid*
> *In the drear manſions of the dead*
> *Shall rise and leave its native ground*
> *At the last Trumpet's ſolemn ſound.*

693. To the memory | of | Mrs DEſIRE HARLOW | wife
of | Mr SILVANUS HARLOW | who died Octr 8th 1795 | aged 58
years.

> *Thrice happy thoſe thats gone to reſt*
> *For they ſhall be forever bleſt.*

694. In memory | of | Mrs SARAH LE BARON | wife of |
WILLIAM LE BARON Esq | died Oct 29th 1796 | aged 46 years.

695. To the memory | of Mrs SARAH DAVEE | Daughter
of Mr | ROBART DAVEE & Mrs | ELIZABETH his wife | who died
Novr 13th | 1796 in the 30th year | of her age.

696. In | memory of | WILLIAM HENRY VIRGIN | ſon
of | Capt JOHN VIRGIN and | Mrs PRIſCILLA his wife | who dieJ
Decr 9th 1792 | aged 5 days | Alſo | In memory of | WILLIAM
HENRY VIRGIN | ſon of | Capt JOHN VIRGIN and | Mrs PRIſ-
CILLA his wife who | died Sepr 13th 1798 aged 9 | months and 4
days.

> *Unblemiſhed innocence what beauty*
> *Huſht to reſt, ſhrouded from ills*
> *Which riper years infest.*

697. To the memory of | Mrs ELIZABETH DAVEE | wife
of | Mr ROBART DAVEE | who died Febry 11th | 1797 | aged 52
years.

698. Here reſt the   Remains | of | Dean JONATHAN
DIMAN | who reſigned his mortal | Life in hope of Glory |
Feby 25th 1797 in the 85th | year of his age.

> *Where ſhould the dying members reſt*
> *But with the dying Head.*

699. In memory | of | Mrs JANE WARREN | Conſort of |
Maj. BENJAn WARREN | who died | Febry 28th 1797 in | the 59th
year of her age.

> *See me behold me mouldering into duſt,*
> *As you ſee me ſo certainly you muſt.*

700. To | the memory | of | Mr THOMAS DAVEE | who
died April 6th 1797 | aged 26 years.

701. To the memory of | HENRY BIſHOP | ſon of | Dean
JOHN BIſHOP | & Mrs ABIGAL his wife | who died April 14
1797 | in the 8th year of his age.

> *'Tis God who lifts our comforts high*
> *Or ſinks them in the grave*
> *He gives and blessed be his name*
> *He takes but what he gave.*

702. To | the memory | of | Mrs REBEKAH BARTLETT |
wife of | Mr ELKANAH BARTLETT | who died July 17th 1797 | in
the 28th year of her | age | alſo REBEKAH their Daughter |
who in her 11th month died | June 9th 1797.

703. To | The memory | of | SARAH MAY JACKSON |
This Monument | is erected | by | Her afflicted Parents | M^r
Thómas Jackson Jun | and Mrs Sarah his Wife | died | Sept.
26th 1797 | aged 3 years 11 months.

704. To the memory of | M^r ELIſHA NELſON ſon of |
Mr Ebenezer NELſON & | Mrs Ruth his Wife | he died Oc^t the
6 | 1797 | In the 22^d year | of his age.

705. In | This ſacred ſpot | Are depoſited the remains | of
Capt ABRAHAM HAMMATT | Who died of a malignant |
Fever October 13th 1797 Ætatis 47 | And of his daughter
SOPHIA who | on the Fſt December following | Fell a victim to
the ſame | Diſeaſe Ætatis 13.

> Hers was the mildneſs of the riſing Morn
> And his the radiance of the riſen day.

706. In memory of | Mr. ISAAC CHURCHILL & Son | was
lost at Sea Octr 1797 | Mr ISAAC CHURCHILL aged 40
years | ISAAC CHURCHILL Ju^r aged 16 years | Also In
memory of | WILLIAM CHURCHILL | who died Augu^t 10
1817 | aged 21 years.

707. To | the memory | of | MARY W. HAYWARD |
Daughter | of | Dr Nathan Hayward | and | Joanna his wife |
who was born the 16th | and | died the 29th October | 1797.

708. To | the memory | of | Mr DANIEL DIMAN | who
died Decr 16th | 1797 aged 69 years | and 10 months.

> But the ſalvation of the Righteous is of the
> Lord he is their ſtrength in time of trouble.

709. WILLIAM RICHMOND | died 1797 | aged 56 yrs |
also | SALOME wife of the above | died June 8 1836 | in her
90th yr.

710. To the memory | of | Mr SETH CHURCHILL | who
died Jan^ry 15th | A. D. 1798 in the 44th | year of his age.

711. In memory of | Capt. THOMAS NICOLSON | who
died in the | Island of Guadaloupe | February 9 1798 | in the
fiftieth year | of his age.

712. To | the memory | of | Mr ELEZER HOLMES | who died Feb^{ry} 21 1798 | Ætatis 84.

Thro' a long life in devious paths I trod
And liv'd alas! forgetful of my God:
But oh! the triumph of redeeming Power
A Sinner ranfomed at the Eleventh hour
Repairs to Chrift the Lord his Righteoufnefs
And dies proclaiming free and fovereign Grace.

713. To the memory | of | Mrs MERCY BRAMHALL | relict of | Mr SILVANUS BRAMHALL | who died | March 21 A. D. 1798 | aged 77 years.

714. In | Memory of | Mr GEORGE D. THOMSON | Attorney at Law | who died April 2^d 1798 | aged 24 years.

Till the great Rifing Day this Duft muft lie,
Which loudly fpeaks, Reader, prepare to die.

715. Died July 27 1798 | M^{rs} BETfY HOLMES wife | of Capt LEWIS HOLMES | Aged 27 Year | alfo 3 children by her fide | REBEKAH DIMAN died 1796 | Aged 1 Year & 1 month | EfTHER 1798 Aged 5 Month^s | PHEBE LEWIS 1799 Aged | 11 Months.

716. To | the memory | of | Mrs RUTH CHURCHILL | wife of | Capt BENJAMIN CHURCHILL | who died Aug^{ft} 22^d 1798 | aged 73 years.

717. To the memory of | MOLLY I. GOODWIN | daughter of | Mr THOMAS & M^{rs} | ABIGAL GOODWIN of | Portland who | died Aug^{ft} 24th 1798 | aged 15 months.

718. Here lies intered | the remains of | Mrs ELIZABETH WATSON | wife of | WILLIAM WATSON Efq^r | who departed this life | Sep^{tr} 2^d A. D. 1798 in the | 66th year of her age.

719. To | the memory of | Mr LEWIS WEfTON who | Departed this life | Sept the 28th 1798 | In the 45th year of | his age.

720. To the memory of | DAVID TURNER | fon of | Mr DAVID TURNER | & Mrs LYDIA his wife | who died Sept 30th 1798 | aged 1 year 9 months & 20 | days.

And muft thy children die fo foon.

721. Died October 1 | 1798 | JOHN ROGERS ſon | of Mr
Wm ROGERS | & Mrs ELIZEBETH his | Wife Aged 2 year | & 1
week.

722. To the memory of | ANNA RIDER Daughter of |
Capt SAMUEL RIDER and | Mrs ANNA his wife who | died Octr
1ſt 1798 aged | 1 year 9 months & 14 | Days.

> *Why do we mourn departing friends*
> *Or ſhake at death's alarms*
> *'Tis but the voice which Jeſus ſends*
> *To call them to his arms.*

723. To the memory of MARY | SIMMONS GODDARD
Daughter | of Mr DANIEL & Mrs BEULAH | GODDARD who died
Octr | 19th 1798 aged 3 years 10 | months & 19 Days.

> *Memento Mori.*
> *Here lies the flower of our youth*
> *Great God forgive our morning ſin.*

724. To the memory of | Mrs SUſANNA DIMAN | wife of |
Mr JOſIAH DIMAN | who died Octr 24th | 1798 in the 33d year |
of her age | alſo in memory of their ſon JOſIAH who died |
Sepr 16th 1798 aged 7 days.

725. To the memory of | THOMAS MAY | ſon of | Mr
JOHN MAY and Mrs | MERCY his wife | who died Octr 1798 |
aged 18 years.

726. To the memory | of | Capt EDWARD TAYLOR | who
was drowned in | attempting to go ashore | from his veſsel Novr
25th 1798 | & whose remains were found | July 10th 1799 & here
interred | aged 33 years | alſo in memory of EDWARD ſon of
Capt EDWARD & Mrs MARY | TAYLOR who died Sept 15th 1798
aged 1 year & 4 months.

> *The wide Atlantic paſt his raptur'd ſight*
> *Beholds his wiſhed for home his best delight,*
> *Adverſe the tide—in boat the ſurge he braves*
> *And meets his fate beneath o'erwhelming waves,*
> *Thus fell the huſband kind the parent dear,*
> *The loving brother and the friend ſincere.*

727. To the memory of | Mrs ELIZABETH DREW | wife
of | Mr BENJAMIN DREW | who died Decr 6th 1798 | aged 60
years.

728. To the memory of | M{ıs} BATHSHEBA RICKARD |
widow of | Capt JOHN RICKARD | who died Decr 9th 1798 | in
the 72d year of | her age.

> *Far from our fight fhe's borne away*
> *To trace the realms of untried day*
> *There to difplay celeftial Love*
> *And fpeak Siraphically of God.*

729. To the memory of | Mrs HANNAH NELƒON |
Daughter | Of Mr EBENEZER NELƒON | & Mrs RUTH hiƒ wife |
Died December 20 | 1798 | In 29 year of her age.

730. Died | at Demerara | December 31{ſt} 1798 | Capt
LEWIS HOLMES Aged | 32 Years.

> *Their Cold remains though distant*
> *lands divide,*
> *To burft the bars of death the SAV-*
> *IOUR died,*
> *The eye of faith their union, fees*
> *again,*
> *Where fcenes of love and bliss im-*
> *mortal reign.*

731. In | memory of | Capt SAMUEL HARLOW | who
died at Charlestown | South Carolina in 1798 | aged 51 years |
Also | Mrs. REMEMBER HARLOW | wife of the above | who
died December 26 1829 | aged 79 years.

732. In | memory of | JOANNAH HOWLAND | who
departed this life | Feb{ry} 29th 1799 | aged 62 | years.

733. F W JACKƒON | obiit | March 23 1799 | Aged | one
year & 7 dayƒ.

> *Heav'n knows What man*
> *He might have made. But we,*
> *He died a most rare boy.*

734. This Stone | Con*f*ecrated to the memory | of the Rev*d*
CHANDLER ROBBINS D. D. | was erected | By the inhabi-
tants of the fir*ſt* | Religious Society in Plymouth | As their la*ſt*
grateful tribute of re*ſ*pect | For his eminent labors | In the min-
i*ſ*try | of *JESUS CHRIST* | Which commenced January 30*th*
1760 | and continued till his death June 30, 1799 | Ætatis 61 |
When he entered into the everla*ſ*ting re*ſt* | Prepared for the
faithful emba*ſ*adors | Of the most high God.

> *Ah! come heavn's radiant Offſpring hither throng*
> *Behold your prophet your Elijah fled*
> *Let faered ſymphony attune each tongue*
> *To chant hoſannas with the virtuous dead.*

Rev. CHANDLER ROBBINS, D. D. was the son of Rev. Philemon Robbins, of
Branford, Conn., who was a native of Cambridge, Mass. Born August 24, 1738,
graduated at Yale College in 1756, and was a distinguished classical scholar. He
was ordained to the work of the ministry January 30, 1760, the same day on which
Rev. Mr. Leonard was dismissed. He became early impressed with the truth and
importance of the christian system, and qualified, by divine grace, for the gospel
ministry. He commenced preaching this holy religion before he reached twenty
years of age. In him was an example of religion, united with taste and accomplish-
ments, of courteous manners, with an amiable cheerfulness of disposition. He always
manifested a deep interest in, and a solicitude for the cause of religion in general,
never forgetting the welfare and propriety of his church and society. In the discharge
of his parochial duties he was ever faithful and kind; and the sick and afflicted could
rely with confidence on his cordial sympathy and condolence. He had a peculiar
suavity of manners, and christian humility combined with such a felicity of expression
that rendered his religious sentiments acceptable to many who would not have
received them from another source. His voice was melodious, and his taste for
music, both vocal and instrumental was very refined. He preached chiefly without
notes, having only a skeleton of his sermon before him. In prayer he was peculiarly
devotional and fervent. Dr. Robbins lived during a remarkable period of the nation's
history. In the revolutionary struggle he was a most zealous advocate for liberty and
independence, and rendered essential service in his sphere of action. He was among
the foremost of our patriotic clergymen, and subsequently, when our political hemis-
phere was darkened by party spirit, he pursued a consistent course in the support of
order and good government. Mr. Robbins' wife was a niece of Rev. Thomas Prince
of Boston. He had five sons and two daughters who lived to an old age.
    A doctorate of divinity was conferred on him by Dartmouth College in 1792, and
by the University of Edinburgh in 1793. He was buried in old Burial Hill ground,
the Reverends Mr. Sawyer and Shaw officiating in the services in the First Church.
    The following is a list of published works by Dr. Robbins:
    Replies to Essays of Rev. John Cotton, on the practice of the half-way covenant.—
Sermon on the death of Madam Watson, consort of George Watson, Esq. of Plymouth.—Sermon on the death of Mrs. Hovey, wife of James Hovey, Esq.—At the
ordination of Rev. Lemuel Le Baron, at Rochester, 1772.—At the annual election,
Boston, 1791.—Address commemorative of the French Revolution, 1793.—Sermon
on the anniversary of the landing of the Fathers at Plymouth, December 22, 1793.—
Century sermon at Kingston, April 2, 1794, at the request of its subject, Ebenezer
Cobb.—Sermon before the Massachusetts Convention of Ministers, 1794.—Sermon at
the Ordination of Rev. Eliphalet Gillet, at Hallowell, August 12, 1795.—Address
before the Massachusetts Humane Society, June 14, 1796.—Sermon at the ordination
of Rev. Ward Cotton, at Boylston, Mass., 1797.

735. To the memory of | Mr WILLIAM GODDARD | who died at ſea & was buried | at Martha'ſ Vineyard July 10th | 1799 aged 26 years.

& Here lies buried WILLIAM ſon | of the above WILLIAM GODDARD | & SARAH his wife who died | Sept 22 1798 aged 1 year & 9 | months.

> *Why do we mourn departing friends*
> *Or ſhake at death's alarms*
> *Tis but the voice that Jeſus ſends*
> *To call them to his arms.*

736. To | the memory | of | Mrs MARY COBB | who died Augſt 6th 1799 | in the 58th year of her | age.

737. To | the memory of | Mr SILVANUS HARLOW | who died Augst 14 | 1799 | In the 62 | year of his age.

738. In | memory of | ELIZABETH HUEſTEN | COVENTON daughter of Mr | THOMAS COVᵉNTON & | Mrs ELIZABETH his wife | who died Sepr | 12th 1799 aged 1 year & 3 | months & 14 days.

> *The infant ſmiles in lisping ſpeech*
> *And in the grave in ſilence ſleeps.*

739. ENOCH RANDALL | Died Septᵉ 25th 1799 in | the 33 Year of his | Age | & is here Inter'd.

> *No more to foreign climes the bark he ſteers*
> *No more his ſafe return his kindred cheers*
> *Snatch'd in his prime; of life's best joys*
> *poſſeſt;*
> *Tis God's command, whose name be ever*
> *blest.*

740. In memory of | Mr BARTLETT MARSHAL | aged 45 | Also of | SAMUEL MARSHAL aged 16 | both lost at Sea in 1799 | Also of | BARTLETT MARSHAL Jᵘⁿ aged 19 | who died in Charleston S. C. | of a Malignant Fever 1799 | Also of | HANNAH MARSHAL who died | Septr 26th 1806 Aged 21 years | She only is here Interred.

> *Their ſudden change & ſhorten'd date*
> *Bid Youth & Age prepare:*
> *Their lifeleſs clay deſcribes our fate*
> *And shows how frail we are.*

741. In | memory of | Capt ABNER SYLVESTER | who died | October 9th 1799 | aged | 74 years.

742. In Memory of | MERCY JACKSON | died Octr 13th 1799 | Aged 29 years.

> *At thy command fhe meekly yields*
> *Her body to the duft*
> *Jefus, fhe trufts alone in thee*
> *And knows in whom fhe trufts.*

743. To the memory of | Mr JEREMIAH HOLMES Junr | who died | October 17th 1799 | in the 43^d year of his age | Also In memory of | Mrs NANCY his wife | who died at Orrington | in the County of Hancock | April 3^d 1797 | Aged 37 years.

744. Here lies buried | BARNABE Son to | Mr BENJAMIN | MORTON & M^{rs} | HANNAH his Wife | Who dec^d Nov^{br} | ye 7th 17-4 aged 10 day^s.

745. To | the memory | of | Mrs ELIZABETH WARREN | Relict of | Mr WILLIAM WARREN | & daughter of Capt ANfEL | LOTHROP Dec^d | who died Novr 26th 1799 | aged 58 years.

746. Here lyes y^e | body of M^{rs} AbIGAIL | DREW wife to M^r | NICHOLAf DREW | who dec^d—17—.

747. To the memory | of | Mrs DEBORAH CROMBIE | Con$f$ort of | Capt WILLIAM CROMBIE | who died Jan^{ry} 3^d | 1800 in the 32 | year of her age.

748. Mrs. IRENE THOMSON | died January A. D. 1800 | aged 53 years.

> *Weeping may endurè for a night,*
> *But joy cometh in the morning.*

749. To | the memory | of | Mr EZRA BURBANK | who died | Feby 25th 1800 | aged 62 years.

750. This Monument | is erected | To the memory of | Mrs HANNAH COTTON | who died May 25th 1800 | in the Seventy third year | of her age | Relict of JOHN COTTON Efq.

> " *Blefsed are the dead which die in the LORD*
> " *From henceforth, yea faith the Sperit*
> " *That they may reft from their labours,*
> " *And their Works do follow them.*"

751. To the | Memory of | SALLY DREW | Daughter of | Mr LEMUEL DREW | & Mrs SALLY his wife | Who died July 27 | 1800 | Aged 2 years | & 9 months.

752. To the memory | of | Mr EPHRAIM BARTLETT | who was drowned on the | Grand-bank Sepbr 9th 1800 in the | 34th year of his age.

> *The voice of this alarming fcene*
> *May every heart obay*
> *Nor be the heavenly warning vain*
> *Which calls to watch and pray.*

753. This ftone | confecrated to the memory | of Madam JANE ROBBINS | confort of the late | Revd Dr ROBBINS | who languifhed from his death | 30th June 1799 till 12th September 1800 | when in the 60th year of her age | fhe commenced her | infeparable union with her | much beloved Hufband and her God | is erected by the Piety | of her afflicted Children.

> *Unfading Hope when Life's laft Embers burn,*
> *When foul to foul and duft to duft return,*
> *Heav'n to thy charge refigns the awful hour;*
> *Oh then thy Kingdom comes Immortal Power!*

Mrs. JANE ROBBINS was the accomplished daughter of Mr. Prince, and niece of Rev. Thomas Prince of the Old South Church, Boston, the famous annalist of New England.

754. To the memory | of 2 children of | Mr LEWIS & Mrs | ELIZABETH WEfTON | 1ft a fon LEWIS died | Sept 21ft 1800 aged | 1 year 7 months and | 20 days 2d a fon LEWIS | died May 3d 1802 aged | 1 month and 23 days.

755. Hear Lies the Boddy | of Mrs ELIZABETH BATTLES | The wife of Mr JOHN | BATTLES who died Sept the | 29th 1800 Aged 23 years | And 5 Months.

> *Fragrant the rose but it will fade in*
> *Time. Such and so withering are our*
> *Early Joys which time or sicknefs*
> *Spiedly distroys.*

756. To | the memory | of | LILLIS GILL MARSH | Daughter of | Mr THOMAS MARSH | And Mrs MARCY | his wife | who died Octr 1st 1800 | Aged 15 months.

757. JOHN RUSSELL | died Oct 11 1800 | Æt. 42 |
CHARLES son of | JOHN & MARY RUSSELL | died Nov 2 1791
Æt 1 | *NANCY* daughter of | JOHN & MARY RUSSELL | died
Aug 10 1797 Æt. 2 | *MARY* | relict of JOHN RUSSELL | died
Oct. 18 1826 Æt. 65.

758. JOHN MAY WETHRELL | Son of | Mr THOMAS
WETHRELL Jur | & Mrs NANCY his wife | died Octbr 28th 1800 |
aged 8 months & 23 days.

759. THOMAS Born July 18th 1799 | died Novr 9th 1800 |
WILLIAM THOs Born April 14th | 1801 died Sepr 24th 1801
Children | of Capt THOMAS & Mrs | MARGARET Js BARTLETT
his wife | and here lie Enterred.

> *Surely life is, as a vapour that appeareth*
> *For a little time and vanifheth away.*

760. To the memory of | ELEAZER S. TURNER | fon of |
Capt LOTHROP & Mrs | SUfANNA TURNER who | died Novr 9th
1800 aged | 1 year & 39 days.

761. To the memory of | Two Children of | Mr HENRY
JACKSON & | Mrs HULDAH his wife | 1st a Son FOSTER | who
Died Novr 21st 1800 | aged 1 year & 8 months | 2d a Daughter
BETSY | who Died Sepr 7th 1807 | aged one year & 5 months.

> *Sleep on sweet babes and take thy rest*
> *While angels guard thy graves*
> *The almighty God the Sovereign king*
> *He takes but what he gave.*

762. To the memory of | JANE CRANDON | Daughter of |
Mr BENJAMIN CRANDON | & Mrs SUKEY his wife | Died | Novm
21 1800 | Aged 8 months.

763. In memory of | Capt ROBERT DAVIE | who Deceased
Decm the 17th 1800 | In the 32 year of his age | alfo | In mem-
ory of ELIZABTH DAVIE | Daughter to Capt ROBErT & Mrs
JERUfHA DAVIE | who Died Aug the 30th 1800 | Aged 11 months
and 4 Days.

> *Defstrefsing fcene to fee in life fair prime*
> *A Hufband parent languish out of time*
> *Confoling thoughts our faviour is the door*
> *To worlds of blifs where parting is noe more.*

764.   G. W.

In Memory of | *GEORGE WATSON* Esqr | who died the 3^d of
December 1800 | in the 83^d Year of his Age.

> *No folly wafted his paternal Store,*
> *No guilt, no fordid av'rice made it more:*
> *With honeft fame, and fober plenty crown'd,*
> *He liv'd and fpread his cheering influence 'round.*
> *Pure was his walk and peacefull was his end —*
> *We blefs'd his rev'rend length of Days,*
> *And hail'd him in the public ways,*
> *With veneration and with praife*
>   *Our Father and our Friend.*

It falls to the lot of but few people to leave such a reputation as that of Mr. Watson.
By his uprightness of character and uniform dignity of manners, he preserved the
respectability of his family to the grave, and we need no better testimonial of departed
worth, than to know that his fellow citizens, assembled in town meeting, recommended
the church bell to be tolled three hours on the day of his burial, a suspension of the
usual business in the town, the closing of shops and stores, and a display of flags at
half-mast on the shipping in the harbor. He was of an ancient and honorable family
and died in a ripe old age. Rev. Dr. Kendall attended his funeral services and
preached a sermon which was printed. Those who are familiar with North Street in
Plymouth, the place of his residence, will call to mind the great pleasure Mr. Watson
took in the cultivation of those fine linden trees at the front and rear of his house, and
under the shadow of whose limbs, and in the cool refreshing shade of which he spent
so many happy hours and days.

In person Col Watson was portly and well proportioned, his countenance noble
and placid, and his urbanity and courtesy were proverbial. He left three children:
Mary who married Elisha Hutchinson Esq., son of Governor Hutchinson of Massachusetts, and died in England before her father deceased. Sarah who married Mar-
tin Brimmer Esq, a merchant of Boston, and died in August, 1832. Elizabeth who
married Hon. Thomas Russell, a merchant of Boston. After the decease of Mr.
Russell, the widow married Sir Grenville Temple, and died in Rome about 1806,
leaving three children.

765.   In memory of | GEORGE STRAFFIN, | who was kill'd
with light- | ning in the Bay of Biscay | Jan. 10, 1801, | aged 32
y'rs. | *MARY S.* widow | of the above | died March 30, 1843, |
aged 73 y'rs. | Also their two sons, | *GEORGE*, died at sea |
July 7, 1824, | in the 26th year of his age ! | *ROBERT*, was lost
at sea | Jan. 1821, aged 21 y'rs.

766.   To the | memory of | Mr NATHANIEL DOTEN | who
died | March 12th 1801 | aged 60 | years.

767.   To | the memory | of | PENELOPE P. HAYWARD |
Daughter | of | Dr. NATHAN HAYWARD | and | JOANNA his wife
| who was born the 21th | and | died the 22th March | 1801.

768. In memory | of | Mrs LYDIA GOODWIN | Relict of |
Mr NATHANIEL GOODWIN, | Died | March 24th. 1801 | aged | 76
years.

769. This Stone | Consecrated | To the memory of | M^{rs}
ELIZABETH RIPLEY | Consort of | Capt NATHANIEL RIPLEY
| who died May 15th 1801 | In the 55 year of her | Age.

770. To the memory of | Mrs ELIZABETH KEMPTON |
wife of *Mr JOHN KEMPTON* | who died May 23th 1801 |
aged 82 years, | Alſo in memory of 6 | Children of Mr JOHN &
| Mrs ELIZABETH KEMPTON | viz JOHN & SAMUEL died
June 2th | 1757 aged 1 month NATHANIEL died | Aug^{ſt} 9th
1756 aged 13 years PRIſCILLIA | died Aug^{ſt} 15th 1760 aged 4
years SARAH | died Feby 23th 1770 aged 13 years SAMUEL
| died at ſea Aug^{ſt}. 1777 aged 22 years.

> *Beneath this monument lies Zion duft,*
> *Which in the refurrection of the juft,*
> *Shall rife in union to its head,*
> *And fit in Glory that fhall never fade.*

771. In memory of | ABIGALL THOMAS | DUNHAM
Daughter of | Mr WILLIAM and Mrs ELIZABETH DUNHAM his
wife | who died july 2 1801 | aged 9 years.

772. To the | Memory of | Wm MORTON | Son, to M^r |
DANIEL JACKSON | & Mrs REBECCA | his wife | Died July 9th |
1801 | Æ. 4 years & 6 months.

773. To | the memory of | Mrs JOANNA HOLMES |
Daughter of the late | Mr EPHRAIM HOLMES and | Mrs LUCY his
wife who died | Auguſt 12th A D 1801 in | the 22 year of her
age.

> *That Female Virtue which adornd thy bloom*
> *Friendship recalls & weeps upon thy tomb*
> *There fad remembrance drops a filent tear*
> *And chafte affection ftands a mourner there.*

774. In memory of 2 Children | of Doc^r STEPHEN and M^{rs}
| LUCY MERCY 1ſt a ſon | THOMAS J. MERCY who died |
Aug^{ſt} 17th 1801 aged 1 | year & 3 months. | 2^d a Daughter
MARY who | died Aug^{ſt} 19th 1801. | aged 2 years & | 11
months.

775. In memory of | Mrs HANNAH STEPHENS | Daughter of the late | Mr ELEAZER STEPHENS and | Mrs ELIZABETH his wife who | Died Augu^st 28th 1801 | In the 25th year of her | Age.

776. In | memory of | Mrs MARY TORREY | Daughter of the late | Deacon JOHN TORREY | who died ſep^r 19th | 1801 in the 45th year | of her age.

777. To | the memory | of | LEMUEL COBB ROBBINS | son of | Capt ANSEL ROBBINS | and HANNAH his wife | who died Oc^t 2^sd 1801 | aged 1 year & 10 days.

> *We have no Reason for to Moarn*
> *For gods will must be don*
> *He lent him for a Little space*
> *But sudden Call'd him home.*

778. To | the memory of | Mrs REBEKAH LEONARD | wife of | Mr WILLIAM LEONARD | who died | Oc^t 2th 1801 in the 32 | Year of her Age.

779. To | the memory | of | M^rs. HANNAH LUCAS | wife of | Capt LEVI LUCAS | who died—Octr 6th 1801 | in the 29th year of her age.

780. In memory of | Capt ANſELM RICKARDS | who died | of a malig^nant fever at | Martinico Oc^t 6th A D 1801 | in the 34th year of his age.

781. To | the memory of | SARAH TYLER BRECK | daughter of Mr MOSES | BRECK and Mrs MARY his | wife who departed | this life Octr 7th 1801 | aged 1 & 8 | months.

> *They die in jeſus and are bleſt*
> *how kind their ſlumbers are*
> *from ſufferings and from ſins releaſed*
> *and freed from every ſnare.*

782. To | The Memory of | LOIS DIMAN, | the much lamented Daugh^r | of Mr DAVID DIMAN | & Mrs LOIS his Wife; | who died Oct 8. 1801 : | In the 10th Year | of her Age.

> *When blooming youth is snatch'd away*
> *By death's resistleſs hand,*
> *Our hearts the mournful tribute pay,*
> *Which pity muſt demand.*

783. In memory of | LEMUEL BROWN | who died Oct^r
13th 1801 | aged 1 year 7 months | Alſo in memory of | SARAH
PALMER BROWN | who died Octr 5 1802 | aged 1 year 2
months | Children of | Mr LEMUEL BROWN and | Mrs SARAH his
wife.

784. To | the memory of | Mr LEMUEL NELSON | who
died Octr 30th | 1801 in the 30th | year of his | age.

785. To | the memory of | Mrs SARAH CHURCHILL |
wife of Mr BARNABAS CHURCHILL | Who Died Novemb^{er} 9th
1801 | in the 48th Year of her Age.

786. To | the memory of | Mrs MORIAH MENDIL | who
died Novr 22th 1801 | aged 80 years wife of | Mr JABEZ |
MENDIL.

Memento Mori.

787. In memory of M^{rs} | SELAH Wife of M^r | pELHAM
BRADFORD ſhe | Died Novr 29th 1801 | Aged 22 Years 1 month
| & 7 Days.

788. In | the memory of | Mr BENJAMIN BARTLETT |
who Died Decr 24th 1801 | aged 64 years | Likewise his late
Consort | JAMIMA BARTLETT | who | Died February 15th |
1808 | aged 66 years.

789. Here Lies | Buried the body of | JOSEPH DOTEN
Son of | Mr JOSEPH DOTEN and | Mrs ELIZABETH his wife |
Who Departed this life | Feb^{ry} 11th 1802 aged 2 | Years 7
months & 8 days.

790. To the memory of | Mr JOSEPH TRASK | who died
Feby 26th | 1802 aged 67 years, | Alſo in memory of 3 | Sons of
Mr JOSEPH & Mrs JERUſHA TRAſK viz. | JOSEPH & THOMAS
died | at ſea aged 23 years | WILLIAM aged 15 years.

God my redeemer lives, and often from
The skies, looks down and watches all my dust,
Till he ſhall bid it riſe.

791. In | memory | of | Mr ICHABOD | HOLMES Ju^r |
who Deceaſt | March 29th 1802 | in | the 44th year of his | age.

792. In | memory of | Mr SETH LUCE | who | Died May
6th 1802 | in the 58th year | of his age.

793. In memory of | Dr. JOHN GODDARD, | Surgeon of the U. S. frigate Boston, | dec^d in Gibraltar bay | June 15, 1802, | aged 32 years. | Also of his wife | GRACE HAYMAN, | dec^d Feb. 8, 1851, | aged 80 years. | And of | ABIGAIL OTIS, | dec^d Feb. 11, 1853, | in her 70th year.

794. To | the memory of | Mr SETH HARLOW | who | Died Jun 30th 1802 | in | the 65th years | of his age.

795. In | memory of | BENJAMIN DREW ye 3^d ſon | of BENJAMIN DREW Junr | and SOPHIA his Wife | Deceaſed July 8th 1802 | aged 1 year 7 months | and 2 days.

796. To | the memory | of | Mr DAVID BATES | who died | July 11th 1802 in | the 66th year of his age.

797. This | ſtone is erected | To the memory of | HENRY OTIS the ſecond | ſon of BARNABAS OTIS and | POLLY his wife who died | in the Iſland of Martinico | July 26^h A D 1802 aged 15 | years 5 months | and | 20 days.

798. Erected in memory | of | THOMAS DIKE ſon of | Capt ANTHONY DIKE | and MOLLEY his | wife who died in | Martinico July 26th 1802 | in the 18th year of | his age.

799. In memory of | Capt JOHN BIſHOP Junr | who departed this life | July 27 A D 1802 in | Dominica in the 24th year | of his Age. | Allso in memory of | GEORGE BISHOP who departed | this life Auguſt 1st 1802 in | Dominica in the Fifteenth | year of his age.

Short is the date of Sublunary Joys
The evening lowers soon as the sun beam^s riſe
Short is the uncertain life of helpleſs man
His days how Justly liken'd to a ſpan.

800. In | memory | of | Mr LEWIS LUMBER who departed | this life July 27th A D 1802 in | Dominica in the 24th year of his age | Allſo in memory of ELIZABETH LUMBER | who died Septr 13th 1802 in the 16th | year of her age.

Sleep silent dust till the Archangels sound
Bid soul & Body both unite again
And call thee forth from underneath the ground
To meet thy God with him to live and reign.

801. In | memory of | Mrs MARY DREW | Widow of | Mr JAMES DREW | who died Augt 29th 1802 | Aged 72 years.

802. To | the memory of | NANCY ATWOOD | Daughter of M^r | JOHN ATWOOD and | Mrs NANCY his wife | who died | ſeptr 7th 1802 | aged 1 year 1 | months 15 | days.

803. In memory of | GEORGE TAYLOR BACON | ſon of Mr GEORGE | BACON and M^{rs} BETſy his wife | who died Sep^r | the 8th 1802 aged 18 | months 8 & days.

804. In | memory of | DAVID WARREN | Son of | Capt DAVID WARREN | and | Mrs SALLY his wife | who died Sepr 12th 1802 | Aged 2 years 4 months.

Tis God who lifts our comforts high
And sinks them in the grave
He gives and blessed be his name
He takes but what he gave.

805. To the memory | of MARY B— | daughter o. | WILLIAM & M^{rs} | ANNA BRADFORD | who died Sept 17th | 1802 aged 1 year & 1 | month 1 day.

806. WILLIAM THOMAS, M. D. | Died Sept. 20, 1802, | Aged 84 years. | MERCY, | Daughter of | W^m & MERCY THOMAS | Died Nov. 1776, | Aged 17 years.

Dr. THOMAS was the son of William and Anne (Patershall) (Breck) Thomas; born in Boston 1718. He was a descendant in the sixth generation from William Thomas, a merchant adventurer, who came to America, from Yarmouth, England, in the "Marye and Ann," in 1637, and settled in Marshfield, Mass. He was an eminent physician, of extensive practice in Plymouth for upwards of fifty years. He was a member of the medical staff in the hazardous and successful enterprise against Louisburg in 1745, and at Crown Point in 1758. He was an active man in the struggles with the mother country during the Revolution. Soon after the first blow was struck at Lexington, in 1775, he, with his four sons, joined the first organized revolutionary corps. *Joshua* became *aide-de-camp* to General Thomas in the expedition to Canada in 1776, and, at the conclusion of peace, Judge of Probate for Plymouth County; *Joseph* was a captain of an artillery company; and *John* was on the medical staff, and upon the termination of the struggle settled at Poughkeepsie, in the State of New York, in the practice of his profession, where he died in 1818, leaving a son and one daughter. The other sons settled in Plymouth. A daughter married and settled in Charlestown, N. H.

He married, 1st, Mary Papillon, of Boston; 2d, Mercy Bridgham, of Boston; 3d, Mary Howland.

807. To | the memory of | EDWARD TAYLOR | DAVEE the ſun of | Capt SOLOMON DAVEE | and | Mrs JEDIDAH, who | died Sep^r | the 21th 1802 | aged 1 year 4 | months 18 days.

808. To | the memory | of | Mrs MERCY JACKSON | Consort of | Wm JACKSON E*/q*^r | Obiit | Septr 24th 1802 | Aged 39 years.

809. To the memory | of ELIZABETH TAYLOR | BREWSTER daughter of | Capt WILLIAM & M^{rs} | ELIZABETH BREWSTER | who died Sep 25th 1802 | aged 1 year 4 months | 17 days.

810. To | Perpetuate the memory | of | CHARLES HENRY BACON | Son of DAVID BACON | and Mrs. ABIGAIL his wife | who died September 26 1802 | in the Sixth year of his age.

In early life prepar'd for Death
Heaven call'd and I resign'd my Breath
Weep not dear Friends ; your tears dismifs
Nor wish me from the Realms of Bliss.

811. In | memory of | REBECKAH BARTLETT | daughter of | Mr JOHN BARTLETT and | Mrs REBECKAH his wife | who died Sepr 27th 1802 | aged 3 years & 2 months | & 17 days.

'Tis God who lifts our comforts high,
Or finks them in the grave,
He gives and bleffed be his name
He takes but what he gave.

812. In | memory | of | HARIOT BARTLETT | daughter of | Mr STEPHEN BARTLETT | and | Mrs POLLY his wife | who | died Sept 28th 1802 | aged 2 years.

813. In | memory of | DAVID TURNER *f*on of | Mr DAVID TURNER & | Mrs LYDIA his wife | who died *f*ept 29th 1802 | aged 1 year & 9 | months & 13 | days.

814. To | the memory of | Two Children of | Capt ELEAZER HOLMES & | M^{rs} BET*f*Y his wife | 1th a *f*on SAMUEL A | who died Sepr 29th 1802 | aged 9 months & 10 days. | 2^d a daughter ELIZA who | died June 25th 1803 aged | 3 years & 3 months & 19 | days.

Frefh in the morn the fummer rofe,
Hangs withar'd ere its noon,
We fcarce enjoys the balmy gift,
But mourn the pleafure gone.

815. To | the memory of | THOMAS BARTLETT | ſon of | Mr THOMAS & | Mrs RUTH BARTLETT | who died Septr 29th 1802 | aged 1 year 2 months & | 11 days.

> The wonce lov'd form now cold & dead,
> Each mournfull thought imploys.
> And nature weeps his comforts fled
> And withered all his joys
> But ceas fond nature dry thy tears
> Religon pints on high,
> And ever lafting ſpring appears,
> And joys that never die.

816. In | memory of | THOMAS PATY ſon of | Mr THOMAS PATY and | Mrs JERUſHA his wife | who departed this life | Oct 7th 1802 aged 2 years | 10 months and 20 days.

> And muſt thy children dye ſo ſoon.

817. To | the memory of | HANNAH C. LUCAS | Daughter of Mr | LAZARUS and Mrs | NANCY LUCAS who | died Octr 7th 1802 aged | 2 years & 28 days.

818. To | the memory | of | JOHN DICKſON | ſon of | Mr JOHN & | Mrs PHEBE DICKſON | who died | Octr 7th 1802 | aged 1 year 1 month & | 9 days.

> In early days away from us he flys,
> No more his pleaſing actions charmes our eyes.
> Gone but not loft I ſee him from afare.
> That ſublime part like a bright morning ſtar,
> A happy change from earth to ſure above,
> Now takes his dwelling in the realms of love.

819. To the memory of | PRICILLA DAVEA | Daughter of | Capt ROBART & Mrs | JERUſHA DAVEA who | died Octr 11th 1802 | aged 1 year 7 months | & 11 days.

> Babes rather caught from womb and breaft,
> Claim a right to ſing above the reft.
> Becaus their found that happy shore
> They never ſaw nor fought before.

820. ANNA MAY WETHRELL | Daughter of | THOMAS WETHRELL Jn^r | and NANCY his Wife | died Octo^r 12, 1802 | Aged 15 Months | and 16 days.

821. In | memory | of | Wm R. JACKSON | ſon of | W^m & MERCY JACKSON | Obiit | 12th Oct^r | 1802 | aged one year.

822. In | memory | of | Mrs RUTH BARTLETT wife of | Mr THOMAS BARTLETT | who Died Octr 14th 1802 | in the 22 year of her age.

Weep not for me, but weep for your selves.

823. To | the memory of | RICHARD HOLMES | Son of | Mr WILLIAM HOLMES | & Mrs HANNAH his wife | who died | October 15th 1802 | aged 2 years | 11 mounths & 12 days.

824. In | memory | of | WILLIAM S. HOLMES | Son of | Mr JOSEPH HOLMES | and | Mrs MARTHA his wife | who | died Oct 31th 1802 | aged 1 year and 4 months.

825. In memory of | ICHABOD SHAW HOLMES | Son of | Capt CHANDLER HOLMES & | Mrs PHEBE his wif | who died Novr 1st 1802 | aged 1 year 4 months.

The tender Parants have sc^arse time to wipe
Ther weeping eys loe heaven cauls and the other dies.

Alſo in memory of | CHANDLER HOLMES ther Son | who died Nov. 6th 1802 | Aged 4 year 10 months.

They ware Lovely & Pleasant in ther Life
And in ther Death ware not Devided.

826. JOANNA DAVIE, | wife of Capt ICHABOD | DAVIE, | died Nov. 3, 1802 ; | in the 31st year of her age.

827. Erected | in *Memory* of | *Twin Daughters* | of Capt *Thos* Atwood, | and *Mehetabel*, his Wife, | Born Nov. 2, 1802 : | Died Nov. 4, 1802. | Also | In *Memory* of *Darius*, Son | of Capt *Thos* Atwood and | *Mehetabel* his Wife who | Died Jan. 23, 1809 Aged 2 m^o & 8 days.

Here, here they lie! oh! could I once more view
Those dear remains; take one more fond adieu

Of th' work of God, their beauteous clay, which here
In infant charms so lovely did appear,
As tho' in nature's nicest model cast,
Exactly polish'd, wrought too fine to last —
By the same hand that wrought, again shall they arise
To bloom more gay more lovely in the skies.

828. To | the memory of | Mrs SARAH ROBBINS | Con-
ſort of | Mr JESSE ROBBINS | who died Novr 6th | 1802 in the
24th | year of her age.

> *Here lies intomb'd within this houſe of clay*
> *The mortal part of an engageing wife*
> *Whoſe virtue ſhone amid the blaze of day*
> *Whoſe kind affection ended with her life*
>
> *Till Gabriel's trumpet's animating found*
> *Bid foul and body meet and reunite*
> *Here reſt in ſilence in the vaulted ground*
> *Then meet thy God with rapture & delight.*

829. To | the memory | of | Mrs LUCY JACKSON | wife of
| Mr THOMAS JACKSON | who died | Novr 10th 1802 | aged 39
years.

> *The fainted partner and the friend fincere,*
> *The tendereſt parent, traveller, slumbers here*
> *Smote by the ſtorm with blooms and verdure crownd*
> *So falls the tree and ſpreads a fragrance round.*

830. To the memory | of HANNAH HUEſTEN | daughter
of | Mr WILLIAM & M^{rs} | MARY HUEſTEN | who died Novr 16th
| 1802 aged 2 years 2 | months & 15 days.

831. In | memory | of | Mrs LOIS WARREN | Conſort of |
Maj^r BENJ^n WARREN | Deceas^d Novr 19th 1802 | In the 53^d year
of her | Age.

832. In | memory | of | ANNA JACKſON | Daughter of |
W^m & MERCY JACKſON | Obiit | 27th Nov^r | 1802 | aged 3 years.

833. In | memory of | WILLIAM BATTLES | son of | M^{rs}
DEBORAH BATTLES | who died | Decem^b 12th 1802 | aged 2
months | & 18 days.

834. To the memory of | JANE BARTLETT | Daughter of Capt JAMES & Mrs MARY | BARTLETT who died Decr 24th | 1802 aged 2 years & 7 months.

> *My times of sorrow and of joy*
> *Great God are in thy hand*
> *My choicest comeforts come from thee*
> *And go at thy command.*

835. In | memory | of | Mr AMMAZIAH HARLOW | who | Departed this Life | December 25 1802 | In the 55 year of his | Age.

836. In memory of | Four Children of | Mr ZACHEUS KEMPTON | & SARAH his wife viz | *SALLY* aged 36 years | *CHARLES* aged 21 years | *WOODARD* aged 17 years | *ROBINSON* aged 2 years | they died between | 1802 & 1820.

> *Stop traveller and shed a tear*
> *Upon the fate of children dear.*

837. EPHRAIM WHITING, | Died in Jamacia | W. I. 1803 : | Aged 28 y'rs. | also | ELIZABETH, | widow of the late | EPHRAIM WHITING, | Died Sept. 27, 1855 ; | Aged 80 y'rs.

> *May their souls meet in heaven.*

838. To the memory of | THOS. LEONARD, | lost at sea, on a voyage | from Martinique to | Plymouth, Jan. 19, 1803, aged 32 yr's | Also his wife | SALLY | who died Dec. 22 1834, | aged 67 yr's.

839. Sacred | to the memory | of | CHARLES ROBBINS | Master Mariner | who died at | St. Pierre Martinique | Jan. 22, 1803, | aged— about 34 years, | Also to *MARY* his wife, | who died | Sept. 23, 1854, | aged 84 years.

840. To | the memory | of | Capt JOSEPH DOTEN | who | died at Guadaloupe | February 4th 1803 | in | the 33 year of his age.

> *Time on its wing conveys us home,*
> *To the mouldring ground whence we come:*
> *Prepare to meet the solemn call,*
> *When the last trumpet calls us all.*

841.   To the memory of | MARY TORREY daughter of |
Col JOHN & | Mrs ELIZABETH | TORREY who died | March 2d
1803 aged | 3 months & 21 | days.

842.   Erected | to perpetuate the memory | of two SONS | of
THOMAS & SARAH WETHRELL | Who died in the West Indies
| WILLIAM WETHRELL   Decd at St Thomas | March 23d
1803. | aged 22 years. | ISAAC WETHRELL | Decd at Mar-
tinico January 23d 1803 | aged 19 years.

> By foreign hands, thy dying eyes were closed
> By foreign hands, thy decent limbs compos'd
> By foreign hands, thy humble graves adorn'd
> By strangers honour'd, and by strangers mourn'd.

843.   In | memory of | two Daughters of Mr JOHN SILVES-
TERS | & LYDIA his wife | 1st ABIGAIL WASHBURN |
who died March 27th 1803. | aged 1 year 7 months | 2d ABIGAIL
WASHBURN who died Novr 28th 1804 aged | 1 year 3 months.

> Farewell vain world we bid adieu.

844.   To | the memory | of | Mrs RUTH NELSON | wife of
Mr EBENEZER NELSON | who died April 29th AD 1803 aged 69
| years.

845.   To | the memory | of Mrs LUCY HAMMATT | who
died | April 30th 1803 | Aetatis 77

> Composed in suffering, & in joy sedate,
> Good without show, for just discernment great.

846.   To | the memory | of Mrs ZERULAH CROMBIE |
Confort of | DEAn WILLIAM CROMBIE | who died May | 1st 1803
in the 66th | year of | her | age.

847.   In memory of | Mr ABNER HOLMES | who | died
May 26th AD. 1803 | Aged Twenty-five years | Also in memory
of | Mrs MARY HOLMES relict of Mr ABNER HOLMES | who
died April 17th 1804 | aged 24 years | and of their infant MARY
who died July 21th 1803 aged 4 months.

> What is this World—we saw this youthful pair
> Belov'd and happy—every prospect fair
> Now in the grave—but Kindred cease your sighs
> To them 'twas but the path to Christ above the skies.

848. In | memory | of | Mrs SARAH FAUNCE | wife of Capt BARNABAS FAUNCE | died July the 15th 1803 | in the 55th | year of her age.

849. To the | memory of | Mrs POLLY BARTLETT | Con-ſort of | Mr DAVID BARTLETT | who died July 22^d | 1803 in the 25th year | of her age. | alſo in memory of DAVID | ſoN of | Mr DAVID & Mrs POLLY | Bartlett who died Decr 30th | 1803 aged 1 year 2 months & 14 days.

> *Death like an over-flowing ſtream,*
> *Sweeps us away our life's a dream,*
> *An empty tale a mooring flower,*
> *Cut down and wither'd in an hour.*

850. To | the memory | of | Mrs REBEKAH HOLMES | Consort of | Capt ICHABOD HOLMES | who | died July 25th 1803 | in | the 75th year | of | her age.

851. To | the memory of | DAVID LEACH SON | of Capt FINNEY LEACH | and Mrs MERCY | his wife | who died Aug. 9th 1803 | Aged 2 months | and 8 days.

> *Wh^ere shall i go where shall i flee*
> *But to my loveing Saviours breast*
> *There within his arms to lie*
> *And safe beneath his wing to rest.*

852. In | memory | of | ESTHER COOPER | daughter of | Mr JOHN COOPER & | Mrs JERUSHA his wife | who died | Sep^t 9th 1803 | Aged 2 years & 2 months.

> *The infant smiles in lisping speach*
> *And in the grave in silence sleaps.*

853. To the memory | of GEORGE SAMſON | ſoN of | Mr GEORGE & | Mrs Patience Samſon | who died Sep^tr 15th | 1803 aged 1 year 7 months & 6 days.

> *Uncertain life how ſoon it flies,*
> *Swift as an hour how fhort the bloom,*
> *Like ſprings gay verdure once did rise*
> *Cut down ere night to fill the tomb.*

854. In memory of | LUCY TAYLOR COOPER | Daughter of | Capt. JOSEPH COOPER | and Mrs LUCY his wife | who died Septe^r 19th 1803 | Aged one year 5 months.

> *An emblem in this glass we see*
> *Of what we all must quickley be*
> *The infant has resigned its breath,*
> *Sleeps in the icy arms of death.*

855. To | Perpetuate the memory | of | Mr SAMUEL BAR-NES | who died | September 25th 1803 | in | the 23rd year | of | his age.

856. FATHER AND MOTHER | OLIVER KEMPTON | died Sept. 30th 1803 | on the Banks of Quereau, | in his 36th y'r | SALLY | his widow | died Feb. 18th, 1855, | Aged 84 years.

> *There is rest in Heaven.*

857. Also in memory of FANNY H | GARDNER daughter of Mr HARWOOD | & Mrs MEHETABEL GARDNER who | died Octr 6th 1803 aged 1 year 5 | months & 17 days.

The upper part of this stone is broken off.

858. In | memory of | JAMES CROMBIE | Son of | Mr CALVIN CROMBIE | & Mrs NAOMI | his wife | died October 9th 1803 | aged 1 year 10 months.

859. Sacred to the memory | of | Mrs PRISCILLA HAM-MATT | widow of | Capt ABRAHAM HAMMATT | & youngest daughter of the late | Doct^r LAZARUS LE BARON, | who departed this life | the 14th of Oct. 1803 | aged 50 years.

860. In memory | of | *Mr ELISHA DUNHAM* | who died | Novr 14th 1803 in | the 58 year of his | age.

861. To | the memory | of | G. W. & J. A. HAYWARD | twin Children | of | Dr N. HAYWARD | & | JOANNA his wife | who were born & died | 17th November | 1803.

862. To | the memory | of | Mrs REBECKAH | BART-LETT Con*f*ort of | Mr JOHN BARTLETT | who died | Dec^{br} 18th 1803 in the | 26th year of her age.

> *That female virtue wich adorn'd thy bloom*
> *Friendship recalls, and weeps upon thy tomb*
> *Their* *f*ad *remembrance drops a* *f*ilent *tear,*
> *And cha*f*te affection* *f*tands *a mourner their.*

863. In | memory of | THOMAS BRADFORD | Son of | Mr THOMAS BRADFORD | & Mrs MARY his wife | died Jan. 9th 1804 | aged 1 year | 1 month & 7 days.

864. WILLIAM BREWSTER | who died | Jan^ry 12th 1804 | in the | 34th year | of | his age.

'Twas thine to know the beft delights of life
A lovely off fpring and endearing wife,
At duty's call the rich-fraught bark didft guide
To distant climes on ocean's fwelling tide,
But now alas those blifs-ful scenes are o'er
Thy fafe return fhall cheer thy friends no more
Thy comfort mourns—with her we fympathife
And hope with Christ they'll meet in happier skies.

865. To | the memory | of | Capt WILLIAM CROMBIE | who died | Feb^ry 9th 1804 | in the 40th | year of his | age.

CAPTAIN CROMBIE, born in Plymouth, May 24, 1764, was the son of Deacon William and Zeruiah (Kimball) Crombie, of Andover, Mass., who removed to Plymouth about 1762, and for nearly forty years was Deacon of the church in Plymouth. He married Deborah, daughter of Samuel and Experience (Atwood) Jackson, of Plymouth.

866. To the memory | of | Doct^r STEPHEN MARCY | who died | March 24th 1804 | Aged 45 | years.

867. In memory of | WILLIAM BREWSTER | Son of | Capt WILLIAM BREWSTER | & Mrs ELIZABETH BREWSTER his wife | died April 5th 1804 | aged one year | 5 months & 13 days.

The father & the children dead
We hope to Heaven their souls are fled
The widow now alone is left
Of all the family bereft
May she now put her trust in God
To heal the wound made by his rod.

868. In | memory | of | Mrs NANCY DUNBAR | confort of | JOHN D. DUNBAR Esqr | Deceased | May 3^d 1804 | in | the 33^d year of her | age.

869. To | the memory of | PRISCILA HARLOW | daughter of | Mrs SETH HARLOW | and Mrs PRISCILA | his wife | who died | June 22nd 1804. | aged 3 months & 12 | days.

870. FANNY CROMBIE | daughter of | Mr CALVIN CROM-
BIE & | Mrs NAOMI his wife | Departed this life | June 25th AD
1804 | in the 8th year | of | her age.

> *As young as beautiful ! and foft as young*
> *And gay as foft ! and innocent as gay.*

871. Here was buried | the body of | ELIZABETH SYM-
MES | daughter of | Mr LAZARUS SYMMES | & POLLY his wife
| who | died July 21th 1804 | aged one year | 6 months | & 9
days.

> *Their rest in peace thou lovely*
> *Thier sleep in sweet repose*
> *From earthly parents thou art gone*
> *A better parent chose.*

872. Erected to the memory of five | Children of Capt AT-
WOOD DREW | & Mrs LYDIA DREW his wife, viz | LYDIA died
August 25, 1804, | aged one year 10 months. | ELIZA A.
DREW died Sepr 5, 1805 | aged one year 4 months, | LYDIA
W. DREW died Aprl 11, 1806 | aged 7 months, | WILLIAM
R. DREW died Octr 9, 1815 | aged 10 months. | ELIZA DREW
died Octr 17, 1817 | aged one year 6 month.

> *It is not the will of your father which is in heaven,*
> *That one of these little ones should perish.*
>
> > *Christ.*

873. This stone is placed here | To the memory of | Mr
ELKANAH WATSON | who Died Septr 7th 1804 | aged 73
years | Also CHARLES LEE WATSON his son | who died
16th of the same month | aged Eleven years.

874. In memory of | Mr ELKANAH CHURCHILL | who
was | drowned at Sea | October 7th 1804 | in the 27th year of his
age | Also in memory of | Mrs EUNICE his wife | who died
Novr 1st 18c3 | in the 24th year of her age.

> *Not blooming health nor beauty pleasing Charmes*
> *Can shield or save them from the Tyrants arms*
> *God in his Unerring wisdom had design'd*
> *A watery Grave to be my Tomb.*

875. In | memory of | FRANCIS COBB | Son of | WILLIAM COBB Esq. | & ELIZABETH | his wife | Died Oct 8th 1804 | aged 3 years | & 7 months.

876. To the memory | of | Majr BENJAMIN RIDER | who died | Octr 12th 1804 | aged 71 years,

877. In memory of | Miss GRACE COBB | Daughter of | Mr CORNELIUS COBB | & Mrs GRACE his wife | who | Died Octr 29th 1804 | in the 24th year of her age.

878. Here lies Inter'd the body of | Capt EDWARD MORTON | who Died | Novr 14th AD 1804 | In the 52 year of his Age | Likewise his late Consort | Mrs SARAH MORTON | who Died | Feb. 21 AD 1805 | Aged 49 years.

Healthful at Dawn, soft slumbers left his eyes,
" I've rested well," he said and in a moment dies !
Shock'd with the scene, with lingering grief opprest,
His consort met him, where the weary rest."

879. Consecrated to the memory of | Mr DAVID LOTHROP | who died November | 1804 in the 56 year | of his age | Also his Consort | Mrs BATHSHEBA LOTHROP | who died Oct. 1, 1817 | in the 63 year of her age.

880. To | the memory | of | Capt ELEAZER HOLMES | this | monument | is Erected | Obit | December 22 | 1804 | aged | 47 years.

881. this Stone | is Erected | To Perpetuate | the memory of | Mrs ELIZABETH HARLOW | Consort of | Capt JESSE HARLOW | who | Departed | this life | January 24th 1805 | in the 65 year | of her | age.

882. In | memory | of | HARVY CASWELL | son of | DANIEL CASWELL | and | CAROLINE | his wife | who | died Janay 26 | 1805 | Aged 4 years | and 2 months.

883. To | the memory | of | Miss SARAH COBB | who died | in Jany 1805 | aged | 59 years.

884. ANDREW FARRELL | of respectable connexions |
In Ireland | Aged 38 years, | Owner and Commander | of the
Ship Hibernia, | Sailed from Boston Jany 26, | And was wrecked
on Plymouth Beach | Jany 28 1805 : | His remains | With five of
seven seamen, | who perished with him, | Are here interred.

> " *O piteous lot of man's uncertain state!*
> " *What woes on life's eventful journey wait —*
> " *By sea what treacherous calms ; what sudden storms ;*
> " *And death attendant in a thousand forms.*"

885. In memory of | Mrs *POLLY DOTEN* Consort of |
Mr *THOMAS DOTEN* who Died | February 24th AD 1805 |
in the 25th year of her age | Also their Son an infant | who Died
February 9 aged 23 days.

> *Amidst the bloom of life*
> *The fondest joys decay*
> *And here in filence fleeps*
> *Till the grate rising day.*

886. To the memory of | Mrs DOROTHY BARTLETT |
Widow of | Mr JOHN BARTLETT | and Daughter to | Deacon JO-
SIAH CARVER, | who Died | March 11th 1805 aged 69 years.

> *Alas and has She gone and has She fled*
> *Gone to the Silent mansions of the dead*
> *Shes is gone we trust to join the joys on high*
> *With Saints and angels o'er the Starry sky.*

887. Consecrated | to the memory of | Mr SAMUEL JACK-
SON | who departed this life | March 27th 1805 | in the 74th
year of his age.

> *Let Earth dissolve, yon ponderous orb descend*
> *And grind us into dust, the soul is safe*
> *The man emerges mounts above the wreck*
> *As towring flame from nature's funeral pyre.*

888. In memory of | Mr JABEZ DOTEN | who Died | April
6th 1805 | In the 50th year of his age | Also in memory of | Four
infant Daughters of | Mr JABEZ DOTEN and Mrs HANNAH his
wife.

889. Consecrated | to the | Memory | of | Mrs MARY DYER | who died April 17th A D 1805 | aged 24th Years.

> *One thing is needful*
> *And Mary hath chosen that Good part*
> *Which shall not be taken away from her.*

890. This | Stone is Erected | to the memory of | M^{rs} RE-BEKAH FINNEY | Consort of | Mr JOSIAH FINNEY | the Eldest Daughter | of *Maj^r Benjⁿ Warren* | who Died June 4th 1805 | in the 37th year of her | age | Also to the memory of | their Son *JOSIAH* who | was born May 22 1795 | Died May 28, 1802.

891. In | memory of | Mrs LYDIA HARLOW | Consort of | Capt EZRA HARLOW | who | Died July 9th 1805 | in the 30th year | of her age.

892. In | memory | of | Mrs ABIGAIL FAUNCE | wife of | Capt BARNABAS FAUNCE | died July 15th 1805 | in | the 32^d year | of her age.

893. In memory | of | JERUSHA HARLOW | wife of | EPHRAIM HARLOW | who Departed this life | July 16th 1805 in the | 36 year of her age.

> *Death is A debt*
> *By nature due*
> *That i have paid*
> *And so must you.*

894. Erected | to perpetuate | the memory | of | Mrs MARY WESTON | Confort of | Captⁿ WILLIAM WESTON | who died July 28th 1805 | in the 69th year of her | age.

> *Can ftoried urn, or animated buft,*
> *Back to its manfion call the fleeting breath?*
> *Can honor's voice provoke the filent duft?*
> *Or flatt'ry footh the dull cold ear of death?*

895. In | memory of | MARY STETSON | Daughter of | Mr HERVEY STETSON | & Mrs MARY | his wife who | died Augt 10th 1805 | aged 1 year | 1 month | and 9 days.

896. In memory | of | Mr RUFUS GODDARD | who | Departed this life | August 26th 1805 | in the 29th year | of his age.

897. In | Memory of | Mr JOSEPH BRAMHALL | who | Departed this life | Septembr 17th 1805 | in the 62d year | of his age.

898. In memory | of | Mrs SARAH COVINGTON | Consort of | Capt THOMAS COVINGTON | who Died | Octor 19th 1805 1805 | aged 51st years.

899. This Stone | Is Erected to the | memory of | Mr JO-SEPH TRIBBELL | who Died | November 17th 1805 | in the 76 year | of his age.

900. This | Stone is Erected | To | the memory | of | Mr JOHN KEMPTON | who died April 18 1806 | in the 90 year of his age.

I ask them, whence their vict'ry came
They with united breath
Ascribe their conquest to the Lamb
Their triumph to his death.

901. In | memory of | Mrs ELISABETH STEPHENS | widow of the late | ELEAZER STEPHENS Deceasd | who Died April 30, 1806 | in the 71 year | of her age.

My flesh shall slumber in the ground
Till the last trumpet joyfull sound
Then bust the chains with sweet surprise
And in my saviours image rise.

902. To | The memory | of | Mr BARTLETT LE BARRON | who departed this life | June 24th 1806 | aged 67 years.

903. In | memory | of | MERCA TURNER | Daughter of | Mr DAVID TURNER | and Mrs LYDIA | his wife | who died July 10th | 1806 | aged 5 months.

904. In memory of | Mr WILLIAM LEWIS | who died July 15, 1806 | in the 30 year | of his age.

My flesh shall slumber in the ground
Till the last trumpets joyful sound
Then burst the chains with sweet surprise
And in my Saviours image rise.

905. In memory of | Mrs MERCY MORTON | wife of Mr SETH MORTON | who Died Aug 24 1806 | in the 72 year of her age.

My flesh shall slumber in the ground
Till the last trumpets joyful sound
Then burst the chains with sweet surprise
And in my saviour's image rise.

906. In | memory of | Mr JOSEPH HOWLAND | who | Died Sep^t 8th 1806 | in the 56 year of his age.

907. BETSY L. BARTLETT | Consort of Mr JESSE BART-LETT | Born Dec 25 1781 | and died | Sept 23 1806.

By this event a Husband is deprived
of his best Friend
Three children of an affectionate parent
A Mother of her only Child.

Farewell those Happy days that once I knew
Adieu my Friend I bid a Long Adieu
Till we united Shall that hand adore
That parted lovers on this Earthly shore.

908. In | memory of | Mr THOMAS FISH | who | Died September 29th | 1806 | in the 25th year of his | age.

909. In | memory | of | MARCIA LEACH | Daughter of | Capt FINNEY LEACH | and | MERCY his wife | born Febu^y 10th 1805 | died Octr 6th 1806.

God in his lovely word has said
Children were for his kingdom made
Then may we all to God submit
Who calls them home as he sees fit.

910. In memory of | LEWIS HARLOW, | who died | Oct. 10. 1806. | in the 35th. yr. | of his age. | HANNAH | widow of the above | died Aug. 3, 1848. | aged 72 years.

E'en as the Father willed,
The path of Life was trod :
Rest, for ye have fulfilled
The mission of your God.

> *Earth to its native earth,*
> *And dust to dust be given :*
> *But the pure spirit's birth*
> *Hath made it heir of Heaven.*

911.   Mrs BETSY HARLOW | Consort to Mr JOHN HARLOW, | was born Feb 22d 1786, | and Died Nov. 22d 1806 | This Stone—an unavailing | tribute of affection, | Is erected by her Husband | to her memory.

> *With her was crown'd my earthly blifs,*
> *Home was my Joy and Happiness*
> *But ah now soon Death's arrow flies!*
> *Depriv'd of her I love,*
> *On Christ alone my hope relies,*
> *We yet may meet above.*

912.   This stone is erected | in memory of DAVID HOLMES | son of DAVID & REBECCA HOLMES | who supported a good character | till a few days of insanity | which occasioned his | melancholy death Novr 23 | in the 32 year of his age | in the year Anno Domini 1806.

> *The tedious day the gloomy night*
> *Drew fast the bands of woe and grief*
> *Often bewilder'd in my sight*
> *I sought for death to find relief.*

913.   To | the memory of | Mrs BETHIAH CHURCHILL | wife | of | Mr ANSELL CHURCHILL | who died Decr 6th 1806 | in the 61st year of her age.

914.   In | memory | of | Mrs SALLY TORREY | Consort | of Mr JOSHUA TORREY | who Died Decr 7th 1806 | in the 44th year of her age.

915.   MRS. | EXPERIENCE. | wife of Dea. | JOSIAH ROBBINS. | born Sept. 22, 1789. | died Feb. 11, 1807. | PELLA MORTON | ROBBINS | born Feb. 3. 1807. | died March 3, 1811. | MRS. ANN G. | wife of Dea. | JOSIAH ROBBINS, | died Sept. 6, 1817 | Aged 29 years. | *JOSIAH ADAMS* died | Aug. 24. 1816, Æ. 7 m's. | ANN G. CUSHMAN | died Sept. 19. 1817 | aged 6 weeks. | MRS. REBECCA | JACKSON. | wife of Dea.

JOSIAH ROBBINS | died Oct. 19, 1850. | Aged 61 years | & 26 days. | REBECCA J. | ROBBINS | born Nov. 5, 1819. | died Jan 31, 1820. | ANN CUSHMAN | born Jan. 16. 1825. | died July 11, 1825.

916. In memory of | Mrs POLLY RIPLEY | Consort of | Mr LEVI RIPLEY | who died March 8 1807 | in the 34 year of her age | Allso their Child *LEVI* | died March 3 1807 | aged one year.

> *Here peaceful rest till Christ shall come*
> *To call the from beneath the ground*
> *His powerful voice shall rouse the Tomb*
> *With sweet salvation in the sound.*

917. In | memory | of | Mrs POLLY DILLARD | Consort | of | Mr BENJAMIN DILLARD | who | died March 1807 | in the 22 year | of her age.

918. In memory of | Mrs ABIGAL HOLMES | Consort of | Capt RICHARD HOLMES | who | died April 8th 1807 | in the 53 year | of her age.

919. In | memory of | ELIZABETH DIMAN | who departed this life | April 14th 1807 | in the 47 year of | her age.

> *Blessed are the dead*
> *That die in the Lord.*

920. In | memory of | Capt WILLIAM BARTLETT | who Departed | this life April 19 1807 | in the 79 year | of his age.

921. To | the memory of | Mr MOSES BRECK | who departed this life | May 1st 1807 | in the 40th year of his age.

> *Strangers & friends while you gaze on my urn*
> *Remember death will call you in your turn*
> *Therefore prepare to meet your God on high*
> *When he rides glorious through the upper sky.*

922. In memory of | Capt CORBIN BARNES | who was Drowned off the | Gurnet May 28, 1807 | aged 75 years, and his | Grandson *STEPHEN HARLOW* | in the 11th year of his age | Also *MRS. MARY BARNES* | who died May 9th, 1824 | in the 83 year of her age | widow of the above.

> *The withering age and Blooming youth*
> *Must yield to death; we feel this truth.*

923. In memory of | Capt THOMAS MATHEWS | who was born in | South Shields, England | Feby 17th 1725 died June | 1807 Aged 82 years | Also in memory of | Mrs DESIRE MAT-HEWS | his wife who died | September 15, 1807 | aged 75 years.

924. In memory of | Mrs. TABITHA PLASKET | who died June 10, 1807 | aged 64 years.

> *Adieu vain world I have seen enough of the*
> *And I am careless what thou sayst of me,*
> *Thy smiles I wish not;*
> *Nor thy frowns I fear,*
> *I am now at rest, my head lies quiet here.*

925. In memory of | Miss THANKFUL SHURTLEFF, | who died | July 10, 1807, | aged 57 years.

926. SACRED | to the memory | of | Doct^r ISAAC BAR-ROWS | who died July 19th, 1807 aged 27 years.

> *Oh the black cloud that shadows o'er his eyes*
> *Hangs there immoveable and never flies*
> *Fain would I bid the envious gloom begone*
> *Ah fruitless wish how are his curtains drawn.*

927. In memory of | Mrs HANNAH BARTLETT | the wife of | Mr NATHANIEL BARTLETT | who Departed | this life July 28 1807 | in the 40 year | of her age | Allso in memory of | Four children of | Mr NATHANIEL BARTLETT | & Mrs HANNAH BART-LETT | his wife.

928. In | memory of | LUCY STURTEVANT | Daughter of Capt WILLIAM STURTEVANT | and SALLY his wife | who died August 7th 1807 | aged 4 years | and 11 months.

929. In memory of | LUCRETIA ANN, | Born April 12. 1806. | Died Aug.st 10 1807 | *ELIZABETH MILLER,* | Born Sept'r 18 1810 | Died Feb.y 28 1811. | *BENJAMIN MARS-TON* | Born April 16, 1816 | Died March 26 1817 | Children of B. M. & L. B. WATSON.

930. In | memory of | Mrs JERUSHA TRASK | who Died Augt 20 1807 | in the 68 year | of her age.

> *Sins promisd joys are turnd to pain*
> *And i am drownd in Grief*

But my dear Lord returns again
He flies to my relief.
Seizing my Soul with sweet surprise
He draws with loving bands
Divine Compassion in his eyes
And pardon in his hands.

931. In memory of | THOMAS POPE son of | Cap THOMAS POPE | and PRISCILLA his wife | who Died Augst 31st 1807 | aged 7 years & three months.

The work of god that beautious cláy which here
In infant smiles so lovely did appear
As though in natures nicest model cast
Exactly polished wrought two fine to last
By the same powerfull hand again shall rise
To bloom more gay more lovely in the skies.

932. Sacred to the memory of | SAMUEL DICKSON son of | Mr SAMUEL DICKSON | and MARY his wife | who Died Sepr 10th 1807 | aged one year | 5 months & 22 days.

Receiv'd but yesterday the gift of breath
Now call'd to slumber in the armes of death

933. In memory of | AMELIA CHURCHILL | Daughter of Capt JOSEPH CHURCHILL | and MERCY his wife | died Sepr 12th 1807 | aged 7 months & 5 days.

The infant's bloom with morning smile
Did let the parent's hearts beguile
Faded in death now pale She lies
And fills the parents hearts with Sighs.

934. In memory of | LEAVITT RIPLEY | Son of | Capt NATHel RIPLEY | who died | Sepr 17th 1807 | in the 21st | year of his age.

The all surrounding heav'n the Vital air
Is big with Death.

935. I | am erected | by JOSIAH COTTON Esqr | in remembrance of RACHEL | his pious and Virtuous | Wife | who died Januy 17th 1808 | aged 50 years.

In belief of Christianity I lived,
In hope of a glorious Resurrection I died.

936. In memory of | Mrs SARAH TRIBBEL | widow to the late | JOSEPH TRIBBEL | Deceas'd | who died | January 14th 1808 | aged 75 years.

937. This monument | is erected in memory of | Mr JAMES BARTLETT Junr | who died | in the Island of Dominico | Feby 4th 1808 | in the 23 year of his age.

> *The time was once my youthful friends*
> *I liv'd & bloom'd like the*
> *The time will come tis hast'ning on*
> *When you shall fade like me.*

938. In | memory of | ELKANAH CHURCHILL | ſon of | Mr EPHRAIM CHURCHILL | and SALLY his wife | who died Apr^l 13th 1808 | aged 2 months | and 7 days.

939. This Monument | Erected by | Mr. *W^m. P. Ripley* | In remembrance of | Mrs *POLLY RIPLEY* | his Amiable wife | Who Died | May 5th 1808 | in the | 30th year of her age.

> *The Virtuous are truly happy.*

940. To perpetuate the memory of | Mrs SALLY ROBBINS, consort of | Mr WILLIAM R. ROBBINS | of North Carolina | who was born September 5. 1777 | and deceased May the 27 1808 | aged 31 years.

> *So fades the blooming flower*
> *Such and so withering are our early joys.*

941. Sacred | To the memory of | *ISAAC LOTHROP* Esq. | who departed this Life | the 25 of July 1808 | in the 75 year | of his age.

MR. LOTHROP was the son of Isaac and Priscilla (Thomas) (Watson) Lothrop, and was born in Plymouth, December 11, 1735, the eldest of five children, and, like his father, was a merchant, as well as Judge. He was appointed Judge of Probate for the county of Norfolk, which office he held till his death. The unbending uprightness of his conduct in his official capacity, the fidelity with which he discharged his duties, as well as his ability and gentlemanly bearing in all the works of life, will long be remembered with affectionate respect. He cherished with lively ardor a natural fondness for antiquity, and so exalted was his veneration for pious planters in New England, who first landed in Plymouth, that he delighted in tracing their every footstep, and the minutest circumstances of their history were treasured in his mind. He was one of the early members of the Pilgrim Society, and also one of the earliest members of the Humane Society.

"In his friendships he was steady, ardent and sincere; undisguised in his feelings, and removed from the least tincture of duplicity, his bosom was a sacred depository of confidential intercourse. If his prejudices were strong, they were invariably pointed at what he devoutly believed to be profligacy in principle, or dishonesty in practice. Such in fine was Mr. Lothrop's scrupulous integrity, such his thorough detestation of every species of iniquitous, or even temporizing procedure, that the inscription on the tombstone of his beloved father, would be an appropriate one for his own."—*Thacher.*

942. SILVANUS | TAYLOR BARTLETT | Son of | JAMES BARTLETT Junr | and SARAH his wife | died August 7th 1808 | aged 7 months | and 29 days.

943. To | the memory of | Mrs SARAH CARVER | who | Departed this life | August 12. 1808 | aged 64 years.

944. To | the memory | of | EDWARD W. HAYWARD | Son | of | Dr NATHAN HAYWARD | & | JOANNA his Wife | who was born the 18th | & | died the 19th of August | 1808.

945. In | Memory of | EXPERIENCE JACKSON | relict of | SAMUEL JACKSON | who died | August 23 1808 | aged 72.

946. In | Memory of | Mrs HANNAH DOTEN | Relict of | Mr JABEZ DOTEN, | who died | Septr 11th 1808 | in the 49 year of her age.

947. In memory of | Mr THOMAS BARTLETT | who departed this life | Sepr 17 1808 | in the 67 year | of his age.

948. Sacred | To the memory | of | ANNA LEWIS GOODWIN | Daughter of | Capt LEWIS GOODWIN | and Mrs ANNA his wife | who departed this life | September 26 1808 | aged three months | and 26 Days.

949. In memory of | Mrs SUSANNA LEONARD | wife of Mr WILLIAM LEONARD | who died Decr 14th 1808 | in the 45th year of her age.

Their infant EPHRAIM | BARTLETT LEONARD died Janu^y | 31st 1809 aged 7 months | and 14 Days.

950. Erected | to the *Memory* of | Mrs *MEHETABEL* Wife | of Capt *THO^s ATWOOD*, | who died Jan 14, 1809, | In the 38 year of her Age. | In early life, her feeble constitution | gave painful premonitions of her early | exit. She however, unexpectedly passed the | meridian of life, discharging, in a very | laudable manner, filial, parental & conjugal | duties. At length, the seeds of death were | planted in her vitals—she sickened, languished | and expired, in hopes of a blessed immortality.

> *Short is our longest day of life,*
> *And soon its prospect ends;*
> *Yet on that day's uncertain date*
> *Eternity depends.*

951.   Consecrated | to   the | Memory | of | Mrs   SARAH
KENDALL, | amiable consort | of | Reverend JAMES KENDALL,
| Who departed this life | Feby 13th 1809, | In the 33^d year of
her age, | Leaving to her surviving friends | The best consolation,
| The remembrance of her virtues | In life; | Her pious calm-
ness, christian resignation & triumphant hope | In death.

"Blessed are the dead who die in the Lord; yea saith the Spirit;
For they rest from their labors and their works do follow them."
Revelation.

Also | Their Infant, | ELIZABETH ; | who died Dec. 14th 1808
| aged 13 days.

"It is not the will of your Father which is in heaven,
That one of these little ones should perish."
Christ.

952.   Sacred | To the memory of | SUSANNA COBB | wife
of | JOHN K COBB | who died Feby 20th 1809 | in the 26 year of
her | age.

Here lies entomb'd within this house of clay
The mortal part of an engageing wife
Whose virtue shone amid the blaze of day
Whose kind affection ended with her life.

953.   In | memory of | Mr. ISAAC DOTEN | who died
March 6 | 1809 in the 74 year | of his age.

954.   In | Memory of | Mrs MARY DOTEN | who died
March 10 | 1809 aged 90 years.

955.   In memory of | Capt RICHARD BAGNELL, | who died
March 22, 1809, | in the 56th year | of his age.

Also *BETHIAH,* his wife | who died Jan 22, 1847, | in the
90th year | of her age.

956.   To the memory of | Mr EBENEZER NELSON | who
died June 29 | 1809 in the 86 year | of his age.

957.   In memory of | M^{iss} POLLY LOTHROP | Daughter of
| Mr DAVID LOTHROP | and Mrs BATHSHEBA | his wife | who
died July 12th 1809 | in the 32 year of her age.

958. This stone | is | erected | to the | memory | of | Capt
JESSE HARLOW | who died | Aug 20 1809 | aged sixty |
nine.

959. To | the memory of M^{iss} SALLY HOLBROOK |
Daughter of | Capt GIDEON HOLBROOK | and Mrs SALLY his
wife | who Died | August 29 1809 | in the 18 year of her age.

O youth whoe'er thou art stop read my death,
Consider well the God who holds thy breath
Remember too, e'er long you must appear
Before your judge your final doom to hear.

960. Sacred | to the memory | of LEWIS GOODWIN | Son
of Capt LEWIS GOODWIN | and Mrs ANNA his wife | who was
Born | and Died | September | the 2^d 1809.

961. Son of | Capt WILLIAM | and Mr^s ELIZABETH BREWSTER
| who died Sep^t 22^d 180– | aged 3 years 6 months | & 22 days.

Hush weeping parents and ye kindred dear,
Weep not for us nor shed a mournful tear,
Our bodys sleep within the silent dust
Our souls redeem'd are happy with the just.

This stone is broken.

962. In memory of | Miss LYDIA SHURTLEFF, | who died
| Octr 31, 1809 | aged 67 years.

963. THOMAS WETHERELL, | Born Dec 4th 1742, | Died
Dec 10th 1809.

964. Son of | Capt ELLIS BREWSTER | and Mrs NANCY his |
wife died Decr 13th 180– | aged 4 years.

He listen'd for a while to hear
Our mortal griefs then turn'd his ear
To angel harps and songs and cried
To join their notes celestial sigh'd and d'yd.

This stone is broken.

965. Sacred | to the memory | of | Mrs MARTHA BART-
LETT | wife of Mr SYLVANUS BARTLETT | who Deceased Dec
31 1809 | aged 83 years.

966. In memory of | Mrs SALLY HARLOW | Consort of |

Capt LAZARUS HARLOW | who died Jany 11 1810 | in the 56 year of her age.

> *Prepare me Lord for thy right hand*
> *Then come the Joyfull day*
> *Come Death and some celestial hand*
> *To bear my Soul away.*

967. In | memory of | Mrs MARY BROWN | the wife of *ROBERT BROWN* | who departed this life March 4 | 1810 in the 58 year of her age | Also in memory of two children | of *ROBERT BROWN* and MARY his | wife Viz WILLIAM died August 9th 1783 | aged 2 years | MARGARET died April 28th 1794 | aged 1 year.

968. In | Memory of | Cap ANTHONY DIKE | who died | March 14 1810 in the 60th | year of his age.

969. In | memory | of | LYDIA | youngest daughter | of | Reverend JAMES KENDALL, | who died March 21, 1810, | aged three years.

970. In | memory of | Mr ROBERT BROWN | who departed this Life | April 13 1810 in the 69 year | of his age | Also in memory of ROBERT | Son of ROBERT BROWN & | MARY his wife who died | at the City of Washington | October 14 1805 | aged 26 years.

971. Erected | to | the memory | of | Mrs. BETSEY TORREY | wife of | Col. JOHN TORREY | who died | April 15 1810 | Aged forty seven years.

> *"She pin'd in thought."*

972. H H | In memory of | Mr. HEMAN HOLMES, | who died | May 8th, 1810, | aged 45 years | and 10 months.

> *Those, who lov'd the living,*
> *And lament the dead,*
> *Pay their last tribute*
> *To thy gentle shade.*

973. In | memory | of | DEBORAH LUCAS | Daughter of | Mr ALDEN LUCAS | and Mrs DEBORAH | his wife | Died July 24th 1810 | aged 1 year & 8 days.

> *The infants soul has begat her clay*
> *We hope to heaven has wing'd away.*

974. In | memory of | *LUCY*, wife of | GEORGE BRAMHALL, & daughter of THO'S & and RUTH MORTON; | who died July 24, 1810, | aged 32 years & 10 mo. | Also *LUCY M* | daughter of GEORGE & | LUCY BRAMHALL: | died Feb. 6 1824 | aged 20 years & 5 mo.

975. To the memory of | Mr JESSE HARLOW | This stone is Erected | who Died August 4, 1810 | aged 50 years | in this Death his wife | Lost an agreeable Companion | his children | an affectionate Parent.

976. To | the memory of | Mrs JOANNA WHITE | wife | of | Captain GIDEON WHITE | who died September 23d | 1810 | in the 95th year of her age.

977. To the memory of | Mrs MARY HOLMES | wife of WILLIAM HOLMES 3d | and Daughter of | Capt ELIPHALET HOLBROOK | and MARY his wife | who departed this life | October 26th A D 1810 | aged twenty years | and nine months.

978. In | memory of | Mrs MARY BARTLETT | who died November 5 1810 | aged 89 year | and 9 months.

979. In memory of | Mr SAMUEL CHURCHILL | who died | Decr 15 1810 | aged 57 years. | He was a good neighbour, | a kind Husband, | a tender Parent.

980. In Memory of | SUSAN LOUISA, | youngest daughter of | DANIEL R. ELLIOTT Esqr, | deceased, of Waynesboro | Georgia. | She died January 16, 1811. | Aged 10 Months. | Leaving a Widowed mother, who | is consoled for the lofs of a lovely | Child by the afsurance that | "of such is the Kingdom of Heaven.

981. Mr CALVIN CROOMBIE | who | died Februy 26 1811 | in the 42 year | of his age.
This stone is broken and lies on the ground on the west end of the hill.

982. Sacred | To the memory of | Mr SAMUEL COLE | who departed | this Life March 18 | 1811 in the Eightieth | year of his age.

983. In memory of | WILLIAM DREW TUFTS | Son of |

JON^A & PRISCILLA TUFTS, | Born Novr 9 1791 | Died at the Island of Cuba | March 29 1811 | aged | Nineteen years.

> *"Green as the bay tree, ever green*
> *With its new foliage on*
> *The young, the healthful, have I seen*
> *I pas'd—and they were gone."*

984. ABRAHAM | Son of | WILLIAM HAMMATT | & ESTHER his wife | was born | 21st January A D 1811 | and died | 16th April following.

> *Of such is the Kingdom of God.*

985. this Stone is erected | to the memory of | Mrs FEAR BARTLETT | Late Consort of | Capt ISAAC BARTLETT | who died April 18, 1811 | in the 32 year of her age.

> *More worth and virtue seldom warm'd a breast*
> *Than hers who here lies undisturb'd at rest*
> *A tender mother and a faithful wife,*
> *Exemplary in every walk of life.*
> *Her infant children feel the chastening rod*
> *Her husband bows submissive—her spirit ascends to GOD.*

986. To | the memory of | NANCY WETHRELL | Consort of | THOMAS WETHRELL | who departed this life | April 23 1811 | in the 31 year | of her age.

987. In memory of | M^s THANKFUL STURTEVANT | Daughter of | Mr SILVANUS STURTEVANT | And Mrs HANNAH his wife | who died | April 24th 1811 | in the 18th year | of her age.

> *The time was once my youthful friends*
> *I lived and bloom'd like the*
> *The time will come, tis hastening on*
> *When you must fade like me.*

988. JANE | SAMSON BARTLETT | daughter of | JAMES BARTLETT Jr | & SARAH his wife | was born | July 11 1809 | & died April 25 | 1811.

989. In memory of | Mrs GRACE COBB | wife of | Mr CORNELIUS COBB | who | Died May 3. 1811 | in the 59 year | of her age.

990. In memory of | Mrs *HANNAH BURBANK* | the wife of | Mr NEHEMIAH BURBANK | who departed this life Aug. 7 1811 | in the 32 year of her age | Also their infant DANIEL TORREY | who died January 21 1805 | aged two months.

> *"Peace peace no murmur tis the will of God,*
> *"That GOD who orders all things for the best,*
> *"Tis ours to bow and kiss the afflicting rod,*
> *"Twas hers to seek the mansions of the blest."*

991. To | the memory of | CHARLES L. HAYWARD | Son of | BEZA HAYWARD Esq. | and EXPERIENCE his wife | who was born | January 21 1802 | & died August 17 | 1811.

992. Consecrated | To the memory of | Mrs PEGGY HOL-BROOK | wife of Mr JEREMIAH HOLBROOK | who departed this life | August 28 1811 aged 26 years | Her amiable Disposition | endeared her to her | friends and died lamented | by all who knew her.

> *Though harsh the stroke and most severe the rod*
> *Cease murmur cease it was a stroke from God.*

993. To | The memory | of | Mrs SARAH JACKSON | Relict of | THOMAS JACKSON Esq. | Obiit Octr 27th 1811 | Aged 78.

> *Although spar'd to life's utmost verge*
> *The tender Parent dies too soon*
> *For those who still survive.*

994. To | The memory of | Miss HANNAH CHURCHILL | Daughter of | Cap JESSE CHURCHILL and | Mrs ABIGAIL his wife | who died Nov. 6. 1811 | In the | 23 year | of her | age.

> *All you that do behold my stone,*
> *Consider how soon I was gone;*
> *Death does not always warning give,*
> *Therefore, be cautious how you live:*
> *Repent in time, no time delay.*
> *I in my youth was call'd away.*

995. Sacred | to the memory | of | Mr SYLVANUS BART-LETT who | Deceased | Nov. 16 in the year 1811 | Aged | 92 years.

996. In memory of | SUSAN MASON DUNHAM | Daughter of | Mr ISAAC DUNHAM | and Mrs BETSY his wife | who died Decr 1. 1811 | aged one year 11 months | and 10 days.

997. Sacred | To the memory of M^r | BARNABAS OTIS Junr who Died | at Sea May 18 1812 Aged 27 years | From inclination he commenced | traversing the Ocean in early life | and was attended by a series of uncommon | misfortunes and disasters on that | element until his death.

Cold is the breast, where pure affection flow'd.

998. In memory of | LUCY STURTEVANT | Daughter of | Mr SILVANUS STURTEVANT | and Mrs HANNAH his wife | who died July 4th 1812 | in the 17th year of her age.

Relations and my Parents dear
Mourn not for me I'm Sleeping here.
My Debt is paid now Death is free
Therefore prepare to follow me.

999. Sacred | to the memory | of ANNA HAMBLIN | Daughter of | HAMBLIN TILLSON | and SUSANNA his wife | who died July 4th | 1812 aged | 18 months 9 days.

So fades the lovely Blooming flower
frail Smiling solace of an hour
So soon our transient Comfor fly
and pleasure only blooms to die.

1000. In | Memory | of | Mr SAMUEL BATTLES | who died July 31 1812 | in the 78 year | of his | age.

1001. To the memory of | Mrs RUTH CHURCHILL | wife of Mr WILSON CHURCHILL | who died September 26, 1812 | in the 33 year of | her age.

Remember me as you pass by
As you are now so once was I
As i am now so you must be
Therefore prepare to follow me.

1002. In | Memory of | SALLY KEMPTON | died Decr 20, 1812. | in the 13, y. r | of her age. | Daughter of OLIVER & SALLY KEMPTON.

Here sleep dear daughter all alone
With aching hearts we leave thee
To the our sorrows are not known
Nor can our absence grieve thee.

1003. Consecrated | to the Memory of | Mrs. *ELIZABETH ATWOOD*, | amiable consort of | Capt THOˢ ATWOOD, | died April 11, 1813: | in the 31ˢᵗ Year | of her age.

The seasons as they fly
"Snatch from us in their course, year after year,
"Some sweet connection, some endearing tie.

1004. To | the memory of | Mrs ESTHER DAVEE | wife of | Mr SOLOMON DAVEE Juʳ | who | departed this life | August 8, 1813 | Aged | 22 years.

Here rests the patient sufferer tender wife
Partner of Joy of my life.
In the midst of life I am cut down
And here lie mouldering in the ground
To leave this world my friends and all
Willing to die when GOD doth call.

1005. This stone is | Consecrated | To the memory of | Mrs ANNA RIPLEY | Consort of | Mr Wᵐ P. RIPLEY | who departed | this life | Augᵗ 14 1813 | in the 38ᵗʰ year | of her age.

"Blessed are the dead, that die
In the LORD.

1006. In Memory of | Capᵗ ZEPHANIAH HOLMES | who died Sepʳ 13, 1813, | in the 47 year | of his age | Also their Children | RUFUS HOLMES | died August 5, 1799 | NANCY HOLMES | died October 13, 1802, | aged 2 years | & 22 days.

1007. Sacred to the memory of | Mrs MARY WILLIAMS wife of | Mr ELIAS WILLIAMS and Daughter | of Mr BARNABAS OTIS & POLLY his wife | died at King & Queen County | Virginia Oct. 3, 1813 aged 23 years | and was there interred & in March | 1817 her remains were taken from | that place and brought to Plymouth | and here deposited.

Too good the misries of this world to share
The hand of mercy took her from our sight
Releas'd from this abode of grief and care
Her gentle spirit sought the realms of light.

1008.   Erected | In Memory of | DARIUS | son of | Capt Thos Atwood, & Mrs. Elizabeth | his Wife | died Oct. 8. 1813. | Aged 11 Months | & 12 Days.

1009.   In memory of | Mr WILLIAM DOTEN | who died Octr 12, 1813, | in the 63 year of his age | Also his wife | Mrs JAIN DOTEN | died May 14, 1813 | in the 58 year of her age.

1010.   This Stone is Erected | to the memory of | Mr IVORY HARLOW, | who departed this life | November 2 1813, | in the thirtieth year | of his age.

> *Make Christ your friend who never dies,*
> *All other friends are vanity,*
> *Make him your life your end your all;*
> *Prepare for death that solemn call.*

1011.   In | memory of | PARNEY YOUNG | daughter of SIMEON | & MARY DIKE | who died Nov. 23 | 1813 Aged 1 year | & 9 months also | an infant.

> *Sleep on Sweet babes*
> *And take thy rest*
> *GOD call'd the home*
> *He thought it best.*

1012.   To | the memory of | Miss ELIZABETH WETHRELL | who | departed this life | January 5 1814 | in the 39 year | of her | age,

1013.   Sacred | to the memory of | two Children of Mr EBE-NEZER NELSON junr | and MARY his wife, | EBENEZER born & died | January 16. 1814, | LEWIS born Januy 3. 1818, | died April 18, 1820, | aged two years | three months | & 15 days.

1014.   In memory | of | Mr BEZA HAYWARD Jr | Son of BEZA HAYWARD Esq. | who was drowned in Plymouth Harbour | Feby 5. 1814: in the 22 | year of his age.

1015.   This Stone is erected | to the memory of | Mr NEHE-MIAH BURBANK, | who died February 8. 1814 | in the 37 year of his age.

> *'Tis GOD who lifts our comforts high,*
> *Or sinks them in the grave:*
> *He gives and (blessed be his name!)*
> *He takes but what he gave.*

Psalm   Verse 1st

133 G

vir   tue

1016. Erected for the memory | of | Capt. **LEVI LUCAS,** | who died | April 6. 1814 | AET. 46.

Behold, how good and how pleasant
for brethren to dwell together in unity.

1017. in memory of | JOHN HARLOW son of | Mr JOHN HARLOW, | & Mrs BETSEY his wife | who died August | 7 1814 aged 7 months & 3 day.

Frail tho endured the tie
The stronger band of grace,
Shall last when;
Death itself shall die.

1018. In | Memory of | SOPHIA DIMAN, | wife of | Dea^n JOSIAH DIMAN, | who died August 7, 1814, | in the 36 year | of her age.

Far from this world of toil and strife,
They'r present with the LORD
The labors of their mortal life
End in a large reward.

1019. JAMES | THOMAS BARTLETT | Son of | JAMES BARTLETT Jun | & SARAH his wife | was born May 1 1814 | and died | 31 August | following.

1020. In memory of | Mrs ELIZABETH CHURCHILL | wife of | Mr. SETH CHURCHILL | died Septr 5 1814 | in the 53 year | of her age.

1021. This | Stone is erected | to the memory of | Capt. JOHN VIRGIN, | who died | October 3 1814. | aged Forty Seven.

Protected by thy Saviour friend,
Whom wind & seas obey,
Here peaceful rest till time shall end
Then rise to endless day.

1022. Died | Mr. JOHN CHURCHILL | October 14 1814 | aged 39 years.

Death burst the revolving
Cloud and all was day.

1023. This stone is erected | to consecrate the memory of |
Miss MARY B. PERRY | daughter of Mr JOHN PERRY | and
Mrs RHODA his wife | who was born October 28 1793 | deceased
October 30 1814 | aged | 21 years & 2 days.

> *Come view the scene*
> *T'will fill you with surprise*
> *Behold the loveliest form in nature dies.*

1024. In | memory of | Deacon | WILLIAM CROMBIE,
| who lived & died | in the good mans hope | the 26 of Nov^r
1814 | in his 83 year.

1025. In | memory of | SILVANUS H. ROBERTS | son of
| Cap ROBERT ROBERTS | & ELIZA his wife who | departed this
life | January 13 1815 | aged 5 years | & 6 months.

1026. This Stone is erected | to the memory of | Capt ELI-
PHALET HOLBROOK | who died | Feb^{ry} 7 1815 | Aged 70
years.

> *What is the life of man, with all his cares,*
> *Tis like a shade which quickly disappears,*
> *But if that taper GOD allows to men;*
> *Continue burning threescore years and ten;*
> *Yet when 'tis spent and death puffs out its light,*
> *Is like a tale thats told or watch by night.*

1027. The remains | of | Mr DANIEL NICOLSON | who
was born March 11. 1796 | and who died March 6, 1815 | are
here | Intered.

1028. In | Memory of | JOHN W. HOWARD | Son of |
Cap JAMES HOWARD & Mrs HANNAH his | wife born March | 20
1815 | died April 2 1815.

> *He glanced into our world to see*
> *A sample of our misery."*

1029. This monument is erected | to the memory of | Cap
JEREMIAH HOLBROOK | who departed this life | April 18
1815 aged 31 years | Also in memory of | LUCY HOLBROOK
daughter | of JEREMIAH HOLBROOK and | BETHIAH his wife |
who died June 7 1817 aged 10 months.

1030.   In | memory | of | Hon^{bl} WILLIAM WATSON, | faithful in public trust, | in every relation | exemplary, | this stone is erected, | with grateful recollections, | of | his kindness and worth, | by | his surviving children. | Born May 6. AD 1730. O. S. | Died April 27 AD. 1815. | RESURGAM.

Mr. WATSON was the son of John and Priscilla (Thomas) Watson, was born May 6, 1730. Graduated at Harvard College in 1751. In 1775 was appointed by the Provincial Congress the first postmaster ever in the town. On the 28th of September, 1782, he was appointed Naval Officer of the Port of Plymouth. In 1789, again appointed by Washington as Collector, which office he continued till 1803. In 1790 he received a commission from Timothy Pickering as Deputy Postmaster of Plymouth, by authority of the United States. He married Elizabeth, daughter of Benjamin Marston of Manchester, by whom he had William, Elizabeth, who married Hon. Nathaniel Niles of Vermont, Benjamin, Ellen, who married Hon. John Davis.

1031.   To | the memory of | Capt NATHANIEL CARVER | who | Departed this life | April 30 1815 | aged 74 years.

1032.   In | remembrance of | Miss HARRIET WETHRELL | who | resigned this Life | May 7 1815 | aged 23 years.
     "*Calm be thy rest*
     Soft as the slumbers of a saint forgiven,
     And mild as opening gleams of promised Heavin."

1033.   In memory of | Mr. WILLIAM RICHMOND | who died June 7 1815 | in the 30 year of his | age.

1034.   Erected in memory of two | children of ZABDIEL SAMPSON Esq. | and Mrs. RUTH his wife. (viz) | ALGERNON SIDNEY, who died July 15, 1815, aged 6 years and 5 | months: and MILTON, who died | at New Bedford July 19. 1806 | aged 9 months.

1035.   *BATHSHEBA TRIBBEL*, wife of | *JOHN TRIB-BEL*, died July 24th, | 1815; in the 30th year of her age | *AL-BERT TRIBBEL*, died March | 30th 1817; in the 10th year of his age | *MARCIA TRIBBEL*, died February | 1st, 1818; in the 4th year of her age | *GUSTAVUS TRIBBEL*, died July | 5th 1821 : aged 2 years & 9 mon. | *LAVANTIA TRIBBEL*, died March | 9th, 1824; aged 2 years & 9 mon. | *CHRISTIANA D. TRIBBEL*, Died | December 2^d 1824; aged 19 years.

1036.   In | memory of | SYLVIA COOPER | Daughter of | JOSEPH COOPER Jun | & SYLVIA his wife | who died Octob^r 7. 1815 | aged one year & 2 months.

Though our fond hopes & schemes are crush'd
And with the laid beneath the dust,
Yet still we would not dare complain:
Our loss is thy eternal gain.

1037.   To the memory of | ELIZABETH DREW, | wife of
DEAC. LEMUEL DREW, | who died November 4, 1815. | Aged
67 years and 48 days.

"Blessed are the dead that die
in the Lord."

1038.   In memory of | Mrs THANKFUL BATES | wife of
Mr. DAVID BATES | who died | November 11. 1815 | in the 71
year | of her age.

1039.   This Stone | is Consecrated | to the memory of | Mrs
ELIZA CARVER | Consort of | Capt *JOSIAH CARVER* |
who died Novr 22 1815 | in the 43 year of her age.

Mourn not my friends, nought but my dust lies here
To be in Glory calls not for a tear.
Prepare for death, and then we all shall meet
In realms of Bliss, fruition all complete.

1040.   to the memory of MARY TILDEN | daughter of
BENJ^N & JOANNA WESTON | Born March 1 1813 | & died Nov
22 | 1815.

GOD in his holy word has said
Children were for his kingdom made.

1041.   Mrs | LYDIA CUSHING GOODWIN | died Decr 15th
1815 | aged 53 years. | WILLIAM GOODWIN Jr. | died at
Havana Decr 15th 1821 | aged 38 years. | WILLIAM GOOD-
WIN | died July 17th 1825, | aged 69 years. | SIMEON S.
GOODWIN, | died July 27, 1847, | aged 65 years.

WILLIAM GOODWIN, Senr., was the son of Nathaniel & Lydia (Le Baron) Goodwin, born in 1756, married Lydia Cushing, daughter of Capt. Simeon & Deborah
(Cushing) Sampson. He held the office of Assessor and Selectman of the town.
For many years was Postmaster, and was the first Cashier of the "Plymouth Bank"
from its organization till his death. He had a clear and discriminating mind, active
and intelligent, and was esteemed as a man of integrity and usefulness. Of his
children, his son Isaac, became a distinguished lawyer and antiquarian in Worcester,
where he died in 1832; Frederic, died at New Orleans in 1833; Hersey Bradford, was
ordained in the ministry at Concord, Mass.; Mary Ann, was the wife of Thomas
Russell; William, became a merchant and died as above.

1042. This stone is Erected | to the memory of | two Sons of Capt GEORGE BACON | and ELIZABETH his wife | Viz GEORGE T. BACON 2nd | who departed this life | Jany 11, 1816 in the 12 year of his age | Also NATHAN BACON who departed | this life Novr 7 1815 aged 13 months.

We have Buried three Blooming Flowers
Which ware nip^t in unexpected hours.

1043. Erected | In memory of | Mrs ABBIGAIL MARCY | wife of | Capt CHARLES MARCY | who died June 17th | 1816 in the 26 | year of her age.

1044. The memory of | Mr BENJAMIN MORTON | died April 9. 1816 | aged 53 years | Their Son JOSEPH MORTON | died August 24 1795 | aged 1 year | and 5 months.

1045. MICHAEL HODGE A. M. | graduate of | Harvard College, | formerly of Newburyport | Counsellor at Law, | died July 6th 1816. | Aged 36 years. | Genius and sensibility | Science, virtue and benevolence | adorned his life: | The tears of friendship and love | embalm his memory.

1046. WILLIAM BRADFORD | Born June 1, 1775, | Died July 25, 1816 | AE. 41. | Also his wife | NANCY, | Born Jan'y 28, 1775,—Died Jan'y 27, 1843, | AE. 68.

1047. In memory of | Capt. NATHANIEL ELLIS, | who died | July 30th, 1816, | in his 59th yr. | Also | of his Widow | JANE ELLIS, | who died | June 1st. 1851, | in her 87th yr.

1048. In memory of Four Children | of Mr SAMUEL ALEX-ANDER | and Mrs DEBORAH his wife. | viz SILVANUS P. ALEX-ANDER | died August 14, 1816: aged | one year and 7 months. SOPHRONIA ALEXANDER died | June the 3, 1818: aged one year and 3 months. | GEORGE ALEXANDER died | Sep 14, 1824: aged 9 months. | CHARLES ALEXANDER died Aug. 19 1826: aged Eight | months and 21 days.

1049. This | Stone is erected | in memory of | WM LE BARON Esqr | who deceas'd at Fairhaven | and their intered | the 23 day of October | in the year of our *LORD* | one thousand eight hundred & Sixteen aged 65 years.

1050. In | memory of | Miss PATIENCE C. TURNER, | Daughter of | Capt LOTHROP TURNER | and Mrs SUSAN his wife | who died Novr 10, 1816, | aged 15 years | and 9 months.

The pale consumption sure but lingering power,
Nip'd at an early date the tender flower;
She mark'd its near approach without a sigh
Mildly resign'd alike to live or die.

1051. In memory of | Mr BENJAMIN HARLOW 2d | who died | November 18th 1816 | aged 34 | years.

1052. Erected | In memory of | Mrs CHARLOTT MARCY | wife of | Mr JOSEPH MARCY | who died Decr 7th | 1816 in the 24th | year of her age.

1053. To the memory of | Mrs MERIAH M. JACKSON | the wife of | Mr WOODWORTH JACKSON | who died | December 25 1816 | aged 37 years.

1054. In | memory | of | Mr. TIMOTHY GOODWIN | who died January 24 | 1817 | in the 70 year of his age.

"I have walked in mine integrity
I have trusted also in the LORD."

1055. In Memory of | Miss *MATILDA,* | Daughter of Mr. DARIUS | and Mrs. MATILDA FULLER, | who died Feb. 17, 1817 | aged 17 years 8 months | and 7 Days.

Here lies the rose, sweet innocent!
Dear JESUS to her parents lent,
How soon he call'd a short adieu,
Dear child, we soon must follow you.

1056. Erected | In memory of | Mr JOSEPH MARCY | who died March 6th | 1817 in the 26 | year | of his age.

1057. In memory of | Mr JOHN OTIS, | who departed this life | March 27, 1817 in | the 74 year of his age, | Also in memory of | his Oldest Child | Mrs. TEMPERANCE COTTON, | Consort of Capt JOSIAH COTTON, | who departed this life | december 24, 1816 | in the 49 year of her age.

They Sleep in Death
But will arise in GLORY.

1058. In | Memory | of | Capt ICHABOD HOLMES | who was | Born February 17, 1725 | died April 10, 1817. | Aged 92 years.

1059. To the memory of | Mrs HANNAH BRADFORD, | Consort of | Mr EPHRAIM BRADFORD | died April 27, 1817 | in the 33 year of her age | Also their Daughter | ELENOR MORTON | died Septr 11, 1807 | aged 13 months.

1060. In memory of | Mrs. RUTH COBB | wife of | Mr. JOB COBB | died June 22 1817 | in the 70 year | of her age.

1061. In memory of | Capt ELLIS BREWSTER, | who died at Sea, | August 27, 1817, | in the 49 year | of his age.

1062. Sacred | to the memory of | PHEBE J BRAMHALL, | A native of Virginia | & wife of | BENJ BRAMHALL J^{un} | who died August 27, 1817 | Aged 21 years.

> *Possess'd of an amiable disposition,*
> *She endear'd herself to all around her.*
>
> *Weep not for her in her Spring time she flew*
> *To that land, where the wings of the soul are unfurl'd*
> *And now, like a star beyond evening's cold dew,*
> *Looks radiantly down on the tears of this world.*

1063. Erected | In memory of | ELIZABETH GALE | wife of | DANIEL GALE | and daughter of | EDWARD WINSLOW | of Duxbury | Died Sep 6, 1817, | aged 19 years.

> *As in Adam all die. even so in*
> *CHRIST, shall all be made alive.*

1064. In | memory of | LORENZO SIMMONS | Son of | Capt GEORGE SIMMONS | and Mrs MERCY | his wife who died | Septem 26 1817 | aged two years.

1065. In memory of | WILLIAM R. HOLMES, | Son of | WILLIAM HOLMES 3^d | & Mrs. BATHSHEBA his wife. | who died October 20, 1817, | Aged one year 6 months.

> *Our days are as the grass*
> *Or like the morning flower,*
> *If one sharp blast sweep o'er the field*
> *It withers in an hour.*

1066. In memory of | REBECCA BARTLETT | Daughter
of | ISAAC and REBECCA BARTLETT | who died November 14,
1817, | aged 4 years & 3 months.

> Behold a sweet and lovely Child
> Which one so fair serene and mild
> has bid the world adieu.
> To save the darling child from woe
> And guard her from all harm,
> From all the griefs you feel below
> I call'd her to my arms.

1067. In memory of | Mrs BETSEY PATY | wife of Mr.
EPHRAIM PATY | who departed this Life | December 31 AD 1817
| aged 30 years.

> Of this vain world she took her last adieu,
> The promis'd land was now within her view;
> With pleasure, she resign'd her mortal breath,
> And fell a willing sacrifice to DEATH.

1068. In | memory | of | Mrs LUCY GOODWIN | who died
January 28 | 1818 | in the 68 year of her age.

> "She opened her mouth with wisdom;
> And in her tongue was the law of kindness
> Let her own works praise her.

1069. In memory of | two children of ABRAHAM | and
PATIENCE DUNHAM, | ABRAHAM died May 10, 1818 | aged 2
years & 5 months, | ELIZABETH C. DUNHAM, | died May
11, 1818 | aged 4 years & 24 days.

1070. In memory of | Capt JAMES HOWARD | who de-
parted this Life | at St Martins | West Indies June | the 15, 1818
| aged 41 years,

> Life what a fleeting hour it is
> How swift our moments fly,
> Here to day we draw our breath,
> But soon we groan and die.

1071. In memory of | Miss MARY BARDAN, | Daughter
of | Mr GERSHOM BARDAN and | Mrs MARY his wife, | died June
18, 1818 | in the 19 year of her age.

Farewell bright Soul, a short farewell,
Till we shall meet again above
In the Sweet groves where pleasures dwell,
And trees of life bear fruits of Love.

1072. To the memory of LUCY WESTON | Consort of Capt HARVEY WESTON | who died July the 19, 1818, | aged 22 years 11 months & 5 days.

It is finished, yes
The race is run
The battle is fought
The victory is won.

Also to the memory of William | their Son who died Novr 26, 1817 | aged three months & 12 days.

So fades the lovely Blooming flower
Frail Smiling Solace of an hour
So soon our transient Comforts fly,
And pleasure only Blooms to Dye.

1073. In memory of | Mrs SUSAN BARTLETT | wife of | Mr. NATHANIEL BARTLETT | who died July 26 1818 | in the 24 year of her age.

Peace all our angery passions then
Let each rebellious Sigh
Be silent at his Sovering will
And every murmur die.

1074. To | the memory of | Mr CHARLES JACKSON | who departed this life | August 8, 1818 | aged 48 years.

1075. In memory of | Mrs MARY WHITING, | Consort of | Mr LEVI WHITING | who died Sep 28, 1818, aged | 40 years.

Alas! and has she gone and has she fled,
Gone to the silent mansions of the dead,
She is gone we trust to Join the Joys on high,
With saints and angels o'er the starry sky.

1076. In memory of | DEBORAH PAINE wife of | JOHN S. PAINE | died October 10, 1818 | aged 27 years | MARY BREWSTER PAINE | Daughter of JOHN S | and DEBORAH PAINE | died March 2, 1818 | aged 6 months.

1077. To | the memory of | Mrs LUCY JACKSON | widow of the late | CHARLES JACKSON Dec^d | who departed this life | October 15, 1818 | aged 50 years.

1078. This stone is erected | to the memory of | Mr SAMUEL SHERMAN, | who died Novem 8, 1818 | in the 67 year of his age.

> Hail glorious moon, auspicious day!
> When CHRIST shall wake the sleeping clay;
> When mould'ring dust shall rise and find,
> Salvation free for all mankind.

1079. In memory of | Mrs JOANNA MORTON | widow of the late | NATHANIEL MORTON deceased | who died November 14th | 1818 in the 86 year | of her age.

1080. Erected to the memory of | Mrs LUCY T. GLEASON wife of | Mr JAMES G. GLEASON died | November 23, 1818. | aged 18 years.

> Calm be thy rest,
> Till the last trump shall Sound,
> And then awake to sing the Glorious song
> Worthy the Lamb.

1081. This Stone is Erected | to the memory of | Mr GEORGE MORTON | who departed this Life | November 30 1818 | in the 60 year of his age.

1082. JAMES T. | son of JAMES | & SARAH BARTLETT, | was born Oct. 29, | 1818 | & died Dec 14, | 1818.

1083. To | the memory of | Genl. NATHANIEL GOOD–WIN | who | departed this life | March 8th 1819 | aged 70 years.

GEN. GOODWIN was the son of Nathaniel and Lydia (LeBaron) Goodwin; born 1748, married Molly, daughter of Thomas and Hannah (Woodworth) Jackson, 1769. His father was a merchant, and he was educated in the same line, under his father's care and discipline. He soon established a reputation for industry and perseverance. Upon the breaking out of the Revolutionary war, he was soon found in the army, entering the service in the office of Major of Militia, and was attached to Colonel Gerrish's regiment, and was located at Boston and Cambridge, to guard the conventional troops taken under Burgoyne at Saratoga. He was a Major in the expedition to Rhode Island in 1778. Afterwards promoted to the office of Brigadier, and later to Major-General of Militia, which office be retained till his death. For many years he represented the town of Plymouth in the General Court, and was also a magistrate, having the qualities of an impartial judge. In all the duties to which he was called he was assiduous and capable, and was held in the highest esteem for probity, integrity and other virtues.

By his first wife he had seven children. He married, 2d, Ruth, daughter of Rev. John and Ruth (Angier) Shaw of Bridgewater, 1782, by whom he had two children — Anne, who married Dr. Caleb Boutelle, and Ezra Shaw, who for twenty years was Pastor of the First Congregational Church in Sandwich, where he died Feby. 5, 1833.

1084. NANCY WINSLOW | Daughter of | Mr WILLIAM P. RIPLEY | & Mrs ANNA his wife | Born June 1. 1815 | died March 15 1819 | aged | 5 years & 9 months.

1085. This Stone | is Erected in memory | of Mrs PATIENCE WARREN | Consort of | Majr BENJAMIN WARREN | who died April 15 1819 | in the 69 year of her age.

Blessed are the Dead
That die in the LORD.

1086. Sacred | to the memory of | JOSIAH COTTON Esq | formerly Settled | in the ministry at Wareham | who was called from | this transitory scene | April 19: 1819 aged 71 years.

He deliver'd the poor that cried.
And those that had none to help them,
And caused the Widow's heart to sing for joy."

Job 29, 13.

1087. In memory of | Miss DEBORAH RICHMOND | who died May 29 | 1819 | aged 40 years.

1088. Capt THOMAS COTTON* | Born January 17th 1785 | Died in Havana | June 9th, 1819. | ROSSITER M. COTTON, | Born July 11th, 1798. | Died in Jackson Co | Louisiana Octr. 4th, 1817. | WILLIAM C. COTTON | Born April 17. 1804. | Died August 23, 1805 | Children of | ROSSITER & PRISCILLA COTTON.

1089. In memory of | Mr JOSEPH STURTEVANT | who died | July 6th 1819 | in the 28th year of his age.

Farewell my wife and children dear,
I leave you for a while:
For God has called and i must go.
And leave you all behind.

1090. In memory | of | Dr. CALEB BOUTELLE, | who died | September 2. 1819, | aged 35 years.

"He that believeth on me,
Though he were dead, yet shall he live."

* See number 583, page 63, *ante.*

1091. In | memory of | Capt RICHARD COOPER | who |
Departed this life | September 10. 1819: | aged 80 years.

1092. Sacred | to the memory of | MARY ELIZABETH, |
(dau. of CHARLES & ABIGAIL CHURCHILL) | who died Sept. 13.
| 1819: aged 6 weeks & 4 days. | Also NANCY, | (dau. of
THOMAS & MARY | CHURCHILL of Plympton) died Jan. 10. 1796:
| in her 16 year.

1093. In memory of | GEORGE T. BACON 3^d | son of
GEORGE BACON | and ELIZABETH his wife | who died Octr 11,
1819 | aged 2 years & 7 months | Also LEVERETT T. BACON |
who died July 1, 1823 | aged 6 weeks | and 3 days.

1094. Erected | to the memory of | Mrs NANCY B. JACK-
SON | widow of | Mr CORNELIUS S. JACKSON, | and daughter of
| Mr BENJAMIN CRANDON, | who died Novr 2, 1819 aged | 27
years & six months | Also | to the memory of | Mr CORNELIUS
S. JACKSON, | who died at Gaudalope | August 31 AD. 1815 |
aged 33 years.

1095. Erected | to the memory of | Miss MARY B. CRAN-
DON, | daughter of Mr BENJAMIN CRANDON, | and Mrs SUKEY
his wife | who departed this life | December 6 AD. 1819, | in the
15 year of her age.

1996. SALLY, | wife of | NATHANIEL HARLOW, | died Decr
7, 1819, | aged 44 y'rs. | Also three children, *viz.* | *SALLY*,
died Sept. 26, 1817, | aged 17 y'rs. | *SALLY*, died April 12,
1818, | aged 7 Mon. | CALEB BOWTEL, | died June 7, 1820, |
aged 9 Mon.

Their flesh shall slumber in the ground,
Till the last trumpet's joyful sound,
Then burst the chains with sweet surprise
And in their Saviours image rise.

1097. To | The memory | of | WILLIAM STURTEVANT
Esqr | who | Departed this | Life | Decem^{br} 15 1819 | aged 58
years.

1098. In memory of | Mrs. SUSANNAR BURGESS, | wife
of | Capt JOHN BURGESS Jn^r, | who departed this life | December
20, 1819, | aged 33 years & 5 months.

Thou lovely chief of all my Joys,
Thou Sov'reign of my heart,
How could I bear to hear thy voice
Pronounce the sound — depart.

1099. ISAAC LeBARON. | Born Jan. 1743 : | Died Dec. 1819 : | his wife | MARTHA HOWLAND, | Born Dec. 1739: | Died June, 1825.

1100. Erected | to the memory of | Miss SARAH CRAN-DON | Daughter of | Mr BENJAMIN CRANDON, | & Mrs SUKEY his wife, | who Departed this life | March 24 AD. 1820, | in the 23 year of her age.

1101. In | memory of | Mrs. ABIGAIL SYLVESTER | who | died June 20, 1820 | aged 88 years | wife of ABNER SYLVESTER.

1102. In memory | of | Capt. WILLIAM WESTON | who died | June 27, 1820. | in the | Ninetieth year of his age ;
Reader, Prepare to meet thy GOD.

1103. To | the memory of | Capt. THOMAS POPE. | who was born Novr. 1, 1770 | Died July 6, 1820 | in the 50 year | of his age.

1104. In | memory of | Mrs. PRISCILLA TUFTS, | wife of | Mr. JONATHAN TUFTS | who died | August 20, 1820, | aged 55 years.

1105. Erected | in memory of | Mrs. SYLVIA COOPER, | wife of Capt JOSEPH COOPER Ju^r | who died | September 29, 1820, in the 25 year of her age.
That once lov'd form, now cold and dead,
Each mournful thought employs,
And nature weeps, her comforts dead,
And wither'd all her joys.

1106. Sacred | to the memory of | Mr WILLIAM NELSON, | who died October 9 1820 | in | the 53 year of his age.
God my Redeemer lives,
And often from the skies,
Looks down and watches all my dust
Till he shall bid it rise.

1107.   EBER HALL, | lost at sea Oct. 11, 1820 | aged 29 y'rs. | ELIZABETH, | his wife | died Sept. 12, 1851,—aged 61 y'rs. | MARY, | their dau. | died Dec. 15, 1813, | aged 8 mo's & 26 d's.

Erected by their children.

1108.   Sacred | to the memory of | Capt RICHARD HOLMES | who died | October 22, 1820, | in the 76 year | of his age.

God, my Redeemer lives—
And often from the skies
Looks down and watches all my dust,
Till he shall bid it rise.

1109.   In | remembrance | of | Miss BETSEY RUSSELL | who | resigned this life | Novr 3^d 1820 | aged 30 years.

Heaven gives us friends to bless the present scene,
Resumes them to prepare us for the next.

1110.   In memory of | ABIGAIL W. KEMPTON | Consort of | ZACHEUS KEMPTON J^r. | who died Novem^r 26 1820 | aged 25 years | and 6 months.

God, my Redeemer lives—
And often from the skies
Looks down and watches all my dust
Till he shall bid it rise.

1111.   In memory of | two Children of WILL^M MOREY | and POLLY his wife viz | CORNEILUS died Decr 8. 1820 | aged one month & 23 days | MARY E. MOREY died March | the 20th 1823 aged one | year 5 months & 7 days.

1112.   In memory of | 3 children of | Mr JOHN B. CHANDLER | and M^rs. HANNAH his wife | viz. JOHN T. CHANDLER | died December 11th, 1820 | aged 6 months and 21 days | LUCY S. CHANDLER | died December 29th, 1820 | aged 5 years 11 months | and 13 days | HANNAH B. CHANDLER | died January 13th. 1821 | aged 4 years 6 months | and 13 days.

Their Souls are gone to Heaven we trust
God called them home he thought it best.

1113.   In | memory of | AUGUSTUS, Son of | ISAAC & LOIS TRIBBLE, | born July 5 | 1816 | died Decr. 20 | 1820.

1114. Sacred | to the memory of | Mr BENJAMIN DREW, | who died Decr. 22, 1820: | Aged 82 yr's. | also *DESIRE*, dau'tr | of BENJAMIN & ELIZABETH DREW, | who died Nov'r 15, 1815: | Aged 39 yr's. | and *SIMEON*, their son | who died Nov'r 1. 1815: | Aged 35 yr's.

> *What though this sad and gloomy hill contains*
> *Of Relatives and friends the loved remains,*
> *Yet in our breasts let cheering hopes arise,*
> *Again to meet in " mansions of the skies.*

1115. Erected | to the memory of | Mrs ABIGAIL LEONARD | wife of | Mr WILLIAM y LEONARD | who died Jany 4, 1821, | in the 48 year of her age.

> *Raised from the dead we live anew*
> *And justified by Grace*
> *We shall appear in Glory too*
> *And see our father's face.*

1116. To | the memory of | ISAAC EAMES COBB, | who | was born Jany 19, 1789 | and died Jany 14, 1821.

> *Possess'd he talents ten, or five or one*
> *The work he had to do that work was done*
> *Improv'd his mind, in wisdoms ways he trod,*
> *Reluctant died, but died resign'd to GOD.*

1117. In | memory of | Capt JOHN PATY, | who died | January 17, 1821, | in the 62 year of his age.

> *See smiling patience smooth his brow*
> *See bending angels downward bow*
> *To cheer his way on high,*
> *While eager for the blest abode*
> *He joins with them to praise the GOD*
> *Who taught him how to die.*

1118. In | memory of | Mr JONATHAN TUFTS, | who died | January 19, 1821 | aged 74 years.

1119. In memory of | Mr JOSHUA PERKINS, | who died, | February 9, 1821 | aged | 34 years.

1120.   Sacred | to the memory of | REBECCA BARTLETT
wife of | JOSEPH BARTLETT Esq. | who died | March 5th, 1821 |
aged 55 years.

> *This woman was full of good works*
> *And alms deeds which She did.*

1121.   In memory of | SARAH W. NELSON | Daughter of
| STEPHEN S and | EMILIA NELSON | who died Mar. 6 1821 |
Aged 3 years 3 months | and 24 days | Sweet flower soon
nip'd.

> *Be ye also ready.*

1122.   Erected in memory of | WILLIAM ATWOOD | Con-
sort of TEMPERANCE ATWOOD | who was drowned at Sea |
March 11, 1821 : aged 42 years | Also their Children | WILLIAM
ATWOOD Jr | died October 1. 1807: | aged one year | ISAAC
R. ATWOOD, | died March 24, 1814; | aged Four years. |
HENRY R. ATWOOD | died May 30, 1828: | aged sixteen
years.

1123,   CAPT. WM. FINNEY, | died at sea | April 4, 1821, |
aged 37 years. | And his wife | MARTHA, | died Aug. 4. 1856,
| aged 69 yrs. 8 mos.

1124.   Sacred | to the memory of | Miss *DESIRE HARLOW*
| who was born Sepr 27, 1797, | and died May 12 | 1821.

> *Dear hon'd spirit, if angels e'er bestow*
> *A thought on what is acted here below:*
> *With pitying eye this weak attempt survey,*
> *The last sad tribute which thy friend can pay.*

1125.   In memory of | Mr. LEVI WHITING, | who died
May 20, 1821, | in the 58 year | of his age.

> *Death but entombs the body*
> *Life the Soul*

1126.   In memory of | SARAH, | wife of LEMUEL BROWN |
who died | June 5th, 1821, | aged 46 years. | SARAH PALMER
| died June 30, 1807, aged 2 years & 7 months. | ANNE RICE |
died June 29, 1809, aged 11 years. | children of LEMUEL &
SARAH BROWN.

1127. In Memory of | Mrs. *DEBORAH*, wife of | Capt. ROBERT HUTCHINSON, | who died June 30th. AD. 1821, | Aged 28 y'rs. | Also their son *JOB B.* died | Sep^{t.} 29^{th,} AD. 1821. | aged 4 months.

Though justly in this vale below ;
A Husband's love she shar'd,
She with her babe was call'd to go
And leave this world of care.

1128. Father. | JOHN DICKSON, | Died July 13, 1821, | Aged 46.

1129. Erected | In memory of | Capt. BARTLETT SEARS. | who | departed this life | August 2, 1821, | aged 45 years.

The once loved form, now cold and dead,
Each mournful thought employs ;
And nature weeps, her comforts fled,
And withered all her joys.

1130. In Memory of | Mr. ICHABOD SHAW, | wno died Aug. 25, 1821, | aged 87 y'rs | also | PRISCILLA his wife | who died | July 24, 1824. | aged 84 y'rs.

1131, To | the memory of | ELIZABETH COBB, | widow of | ISAAC E. COBB, | who was born July 27, 1797, | and died Augu^t 28, 1821.

She is not dead, but sleeps to rise
An heir of glory in the skies,
With spirits pure, from flesh set free
T' enjoy a bless'd eternity.

1132. In | memory of | Mr BARNABAS CHURCHILL | who died | August 29, 1821, | in the 74 year | of his age.

1133. In memory of | NANCY E. LANMAN | Daughter of | NATHANIEL C. LANMAN | and NANCY his Wife | died Oct. 1st 1821 ; | aged 3 years | and 9 months.

Sleep on sweet child and take thy rest
For GOD has done as he thought best.

1134. In memory of | LUCIA ROBBINS | Daughter of | NATHAN B. ROBBINS | & LUCIA his wife | died October 1, 1821 | aged 1 year 9 months | and 19 days.

> *So fades the lovely blooming flower*
> *Frail smiling solace of an hour*
> *So our transient comforts fly*
> *Pleasure only blooms to die.*

1135.   In memory | of | Capt NATHANIEL RIPLEY | who died | October 23, 1821. | in the 80 year | of his age.

1136.   In memory of | CATHARINE LUCAS | Daughter of Mr ISAAC LUCAS | & CATHARINE his wife | died October 24. 1821 | aged 15 months & 24 days.

> *Christ said suffer little Children*
> *to come to me;*
> *and forbid them not*
> *for of such is the Kingdom of heaven.*

1137.   Here are interred | in adjoining graves, | the remains of | SARAH BRADFORD, | relict of | LeBARON BRADFORD | of Bristol Rhode Island, | Born June 29, 1754, | Died Nov. 10, 1821, | and of their son | LeBARON BRADFORD, | Born 1780 | Died Nov. 1846.

Mrs. SARAH BRADFORD was the daughter of Thomas and Mercy (Hedge) Davis of Plymouth, born 1754.

1138.   In | memory of | WOODWORTH JACKSON | who | died Novr 10, 1821 aged 47 years.

1139.   HENRY McCARTER, | died in Martinique W. I. | Jan. 7th 1822, | aged 34 yr's. | NANCY McCARTER | wife of the above | died Jan. 1st, 1827, | aged 34 yr's & 3 ms.

> *A living faith the soul sustains*
> *When death appears in dread array,*
> *It triumphs o'er our mortal pains,*
> *And points on high to endless day,*
> *Where happy ransomed spirits dwells*
> *The triumphs of the cross to tell.*

1140.   SILVANUS T. | son of JAMES | & SARAH BARTLETT | was born Feb. 2, | 1820; | & died April 14, | 1822.

1141.   In | memory of | MARY GODDARD | widow of | BENJAMIN GODDARD, | who died April 23 | 1822, aged 77 years.

1142. In memory of two children | of Isaac & Rebecca Bartlett. | An infant Son born June 6, | and died June 9, 1822; | *CALEB* born April 21, 1824; | and died July 24, 1826;

> *How sweetly sleeps the smiling flowers,*
> *Born but to blossom and decay*
> *O God! how solemn was the hour*
> *When their blest spirits fled away.*
>
> *May angels watch around their bed*
> *And JESUS his kind mercy show*
> *Till GOD shall bid their bodies rise*
> *And bloom where lasting lillies grow.*

1143. To the memory of | Mr. LEMUEL ROBBINS | who departed this life | July 28, 1822, in the 64 | year of his age | Also in memory of | Mrs MARY ROBBINS | his wife who departed this life | March 5 1821 in 62 | year of her age.

> *Ye living men, the tomb survey!*
> *Where you must shortly dwell.*
> *Hark! how the awful summons sounds*
> *In ev'ry funeral knell.*

1144. In memory of | Mrs. SUSANNA NICHOLS | wife of | Moses Nichols | who died Aug. 5, 1822. | in the 57 year | of her age.

> *Why do we mourn, why do we weep,*
> *For a departed friend,*
> *For she has left a world of wo*
> *And gone to a Just friend.*

1145. Erected | to the memory of | Miss *NANCY CHURCHILL* | dau of Mr John Churchill | and Mrs Nancy his wife | who died Aug. 21, 1822; | aged 14 years.

> *When spotless innocence resigns her breath,*
> *And beauty's faded in the armes of death,*
> *When youth's consigned to mingle with the dead*
> *How pungent are the tears survivors shed.*

1146. MARY JANE | dau. of Mr. John. | & Ester Kennady | who died Sept. 21. 1822. | aged 14 months.

So fades the lovely blooming flower,
Frail smiling solace of an hour,
So soon our transient comforts fly
And pleasure only blooms to die.

1147.   In memory of | Mrs MERCY CHURCHILL wife of |
Mr JOSEPH CHURCHILL who died | October 2. AD 1822. | in the
42 year of her age. | Also in memory of their children | ED-
WARD who died | January 8. 1809 | aged one year. | GEORGE
who died Oct. 21, 1811 | aged 3 months. | CHARLES THOMAS
who died | September 13. 1825 | aged 4 years & 5 months.

1148.   In | memory of | WILLIAM BISHOP, | who died |
Oct'r 13, 1822 : | aged 30 yr's.

"*His was the radiance of the risen day.*"

1149.   Erected | in memory of | Capt JOHN VIRGIN | who
died at Sea. | on his passage from | St. Ubes to Boston | Oct^r-
23. 1822 | in the 32 year of his | age.

Death but entombs the body
Life, the soul.

1150.   Erected | to the memory of | Miss JOANNA COTTON,
| Daughter of | JOHN COTTON Esq. | and HANNAH his wife, |
who died Novem^r 2, 1822 | aged 62 years.

1151.   Consecrated | in memory of | Mrs *ELIZABETH F.
RIPLEY* | Consort of | Mr *WILLIAM P. RIPLEY,* | who died
Decr 19. 1822, | in the 31 year of her age.

Forgive, blest shade! the tributary tear,
That mourns thy exit from a world like this ;
Forgive the wish that would have kept thee here,
And stay'd thy progress to the seats of bliss.

1152.   WILLIAM ROGERS Jr. | died Dec. 23d. 1822, | Aged
34 yr's. | JOHN ROGERS, | died Dec. 1st 1825, | Aged 27 yrs.
| ICHABOD ROGERS, | died March 18th 1854, | Aged 50 y'rs
& 10 Mon.

1153.   In memory of | LYDIA | widow of | BARTLETT LE
BARON, | who died | Jan. 1st. 1823. | aged 66 years.

Blessed are the dead
which die in the Lord.

1154. ELIZABETH | born Feb'y. 28, 1822, | died Jan'y 2, 1823 | SARAH NYE, | born Feb'y. 15, 1830, | died Dec. 18, 1837, | Children of BENJAMIN & | JOANN WESTON.

> *Thou art gone to the grave we no*
> *longer behold thee ;*
> *Nor tread the rough paths of the world*
> *by thy side:*
> *But the wide arms of mercy are*
> *spread to enfold thee:*
> *And sinners may die for the sinless*
> *has died.*

1155. In Memory of | JONATHAN STURGES, | Born April 8 1822, | Died Jan'y 20 1823. | Mrs. LUCRETIA WATSON, | wife of | Rev. H. B. GOODWIN | of Concord | Born Feb'y 15 1808. | Died Nov'r 11 1831. | Children of B. M. & L. B. WATSON.

1156. This stone is erected | to the memory of | Twin Children of | EPHRAIM FINNEY | and PHEBE his wife | who were born Oct'r 27, 1822 | ELIZABETH died March 10, 1823 | EZRA died September 14, 1823

> *My friends behold what death has done*
> *Taken these babes when they were young*
> *Prepare to live prepare to die*
> *Prepare for long Eternity.*

1157. Erected | to the memory | of | Capt. ATWOOD DREW, | who departed this life | May 10, 1823 | aged 43 years.

> " *Mourners forbear ; the ways of heaven are just,*
> *Afflicted mortals should belive, and trust,*
> *By a wise hand the universe is sway'd*
> *Which justly limits every life it made.*

1158. Consecrated | to the memory of | MARGARET J. WASHBURN | Consort to | Capt. GEORGE WASHBURN | who died | June 4 AD. 1823, | in the 32 year of her | age.

> *Rest! gentle Spirit: rest: thy toils are o'er:*
> *The place that knew thee knows thee now no more*
> *Cease mourners cease: sweet consolation dies,*
> *We part—but tis to meet in happier skies.*

1159. Capt | ELEAZAR MORTON | Died June 5, 1823, Æ.
69 y'rs | *JEMIMA* his wife died | Feb'y 26, 1823, Æ. 66 y'rs |
Also eight children. | *LAZARUS S.* was lost at Sea, | Dec. 1800.
Æ. 22 y'rs. | ELEAZAR Jr. WILLIAM, | ZEPHANIAH,
AMASA, | JEMIMA, JERUSHA, JANE.

1160. In | memory | of | JOHN T. CLARK, | Son of | JOHN
CLARK, 3ᵈ | & ABIGAIL his wife | who died Augt. 20, | 1823 |
aged 2 years.

1161. In memory of | THEADORE S. CARVER, Son | of
Capt. JOSIAH CARVER | and ABBIGAIL his wife | who died Sepr 5,
1823 | aged Three years | one month and twenty seven | days.

> *Suffer little children to come unto me*
> *And forbid them not.*

1162. In | memory of | Miss RUTH NELSON | who died |
September 13, 1823 | in the 64 year | of her age.

1163. In | memory of | Capt. *NATHL MORTON* | who died
| September 21 1823 | aged 39 years.

> *Why do we mourn departing friends?*
> *Or shake at death's alarms?*
> *Tis but the voice which Jesus sends*
> *To call them to his arms.*

1164. In memory of | FENELON T. BURGISS, | Son of
JOSEPH & | SALLY BURGISS, | who died Oct. 27. 1823, | aged 15
months & 19 days.

> *He's left a world of sorrow sin and pain*
> *Wish not to call him back to life again*
> *This lovely bud beginning to expand*
> *Was soon transplanted to that happy land.*

1165. In memory of | Mrs. SARAH R. KEMPTON | wife of |
Mr. ZACHEUS KEMPTON | who died January 31, 1824 | aged
Sixty one years | and Eight months.

> *Why do we mourn why do we weep*
> *For a departed friend*
> *For she has left a world of woe*
> *And gone to a just friend.*

1166. Sacred | to the memory of | Miss CAROLINE SAMP-
SON | dau. of Mr. GEORGE & | Mrs. HANNAH SAMPSON: | She
died | Feb^y· 5 1824. | aged 22 years. | 1 mo & 26 days.

" Her's was the mildness of the rising morn."

1167. In memory of | *SALLY*, dau'r of JOB & | HANNAH
CHURCHILL | died Feb'ry 16, 1824: | Aged 1 year & 2 mon's. |
Also | In Memory of | *SALLY* who died | April 2, 1823 : | aged
1 year & 5 mo's.

1168. In memory of | Mrs. SARAH HARLOW | wife of |
Mr SETH HARLOW | who departed this life | Feby 28, 1824 |
aged 82 years.

1169. In memory of | Mrs MERCY DILLARD. | Consort of
Mr BENJAMIN DILLARD. | who died | March 28, 1824 | aged 44
years.

1170. In memory of | REBEKAH MORTON | Daughter of
JAMES | & BETSEY MORTON | who died | June 15, 1824 | aged
four months | and 21 days.

For of such is the kingdom of heaven.

1171. In memory of | Mrs DEBORAH GAMMONS | wife of
| Mr BENJAMIN GAMMONS | who died | August 1st 1824 | aged
72 years.

Make Christ your friend who never dies,
All other friends are vanities,
Make him your life your all,
Prepare for Death that Solemn call.

1172. *PIRSES.* wife of ELIAB WOOD. | died Oct. 5th 1824,
| in the 38 y'r | of her age.

Let thy mercy, O LORD, be upon
us, according as we hope in thee,

1173. MERCY DOTEN | widow of NATHANIEL DOTEN, |
died Oct. 11th 1824, | aged 86 y'rs. | Also three Children of
| PRINCE & SUSAN DOTEN. | Viz. SAMUEL, died April 3. |
1825, aged 11 days. | SYLVANUS H. died Oct. 12. | 1825, aged
2 y'rs and 2 mon. | A Dau. died July 13th. | 1826: aged 3
hours.

1174. In | memory of | Mrs. EUNICE HOLMES | who died
Octr 16, 1824, | aged | 40 years.

> " *When holy friendship drops the pious tear,*
> " *And sacred garlands deck the hallowed bier,*
> " *Can bounteous heaven a greater solace give,*
> " *Than that which whispers, " friends departed live.*

1175. Sacred | to the memory of | Mrs. ELIZA DAVIS
Consort of | Mr JOSEPH DAVIS | & Daughter of JOSHUA | &
ELIZABTEH COLBY of | Newburyport | who died Novr. 8, 1824 |
aged 30 years.

1176. In | memory of | Mrs. SALLY BURGIS | Consort of
| Mr. JOSEPH BURGIS | who died | Decr 29, 1824 | aged 35 years.

1177. Mr. LEWIS WESTON, | died Jan. 22d, 1825, | aged
47 y'rs. | *Mrs. BETSEY*, his wife, | died Oct. 28th. 1851, | aged
73 y'rs. | Also Four Children Viz. | *HARRIET*, died Jan 10th,
1825 | in her 9th. y'r. | *LEWIS*, died Jan. 25th, 1838 | in his 16th
y'r. | *LEWIS*, died Sept. 21st 1800 | aged 17 Months. | *LEWIS*,
died May 8th 1802, | aged 2 months.

1178. In memory of | ELIZABETH OWEN | Daughter of
HENRY | and ABIGAIL HOLLIS, | died January 30, 1825. | aged
3 year & 5 months.

> *Alas her tuneful warbling breath,*
> *Is hushed forever hushed in death;*
> *And that still heart within the bier,*
> *Can feel not e'en a parents tear.*

1179. FREDERICK RUSSEL, | son of | F. & E. FREEMAN
| died | Feb. 1, 1825 aged 17 days.

1180. In memory of | JOHN T. JACKSON | Son of WOOD-
WORTH | & MERIAH JACKSON Dec^d | who died Feb 4, 1825 |
aged 11 years.

1181. In Memory | of | Mrs. RUTH GOODWIN | widow of
| Gen. NATH^L GOODWIN, | who died, Feb'y. 10. 1825 | Aged 79
years.

1182. Died of a Lingering | Distressing Sickness | Mr JOHN
BARTLETT | February 16, 1825 | in the 29 year | of his age.

O Death lover and friend
Hast thou put far from
His bere^aved Consort, and her
Acquaintance into darkness.

1183. Erected | In memory of | Mr. WILLIAM KEEN, |
who died | February 18. 1825, | aged 69.

This modest stone, what few vain marbles can
May truly say " Here lies an honest man:"
Calmly he look'd on either life, and here
Saw nothing to regret, or there to fear:
From Nature's temperate feast rose satisfied
Thank'd heav'n that he had liv'd, and that he died.

1184. In memory of | Mr. DAVID DREW | who departed
this life | April 16, 1825, | in the 48 year of his age. | Also three
children ·*Viz.* | LUCINDA died July 29, 1807 aged 4 mon. |
SOLOMON died April 6, 1813, aged 9 mon. | SOLOMON
AUGUSTUS died Feb. 15, 1821, | aged 8 months.

For those who throng the eternal throne;
Lost are the tears we shed:
They are the living — they alone:
Whome thus we call the dead.

1185. Erected in memory of | Dea. *LEMUEL DREW,* who
| with faith patience & Submission | to the will of God, died
May 24, 1825. | aged 80 years & 6 mo,s. | Also | *SARAH,*
dau,tr of LEMUEL and | ELIZABETH DREW, | died March 20,
1829: | aged 47 yr,s & 7 mo's.

We have fought a good fight,
we have finished our course,
we have kept the Faith.

1186. In | memory of | Mrs MARY COVINGTON | Con-
sort of | Capt THOMAS COVINGTON | died May 25 1825 | aged
65 years.

1187. Erected | In memory of | ALVIN M. GRATON, |
who was lost at Sea June | 4. 1825. Æt. 30 years. | Also MARY
D. GRATON, | who died January 5, 1840, | Æt. 41 years.

1188. In memory of | LYDIA CHURCHILL | wife of | BARNABUS CHURCHILL | died June 19 1825 | in the 65th year | of her age.

1189. In | memory of | JOANN WHITE | Daughter of | Capt GEOR^E SIMMONS | & MERCY his wife | died June 21st, 1825 : | aged 9 months | and 11 days.

1190. In memory of | JANE LEONARD | Daughter of | OLIVER & REBECCA WESTON | died July 12, 1825 | aged 2 years 6 months.

> *O may thy spirit wait*
> *The first at Heaven's gate*
> *To meet and welcome Me.*

1191. In memory of | Mr NATHANIEL HOLMES | who died | August 2, 1825 ; | aged Seventy eight | years.

> *His spirit gone and took its flight,*
> *To dwell in uncreated light,*
> *His body rest beneath the sod,*
> *Till call'd by his creator GOD.*

1192. CHARLES T. | son of JAMES | & SARAH BARTLETT. | was born Dec. 14, | 1824, | & died Aug. 2, | 1825.

1193. In memory of | Mrs MARY ROBERTSON | wife of | Capt DAVID ROBERTSON | and Daughter of | Capt DAVID CORNISH | and *MERCY* his wife | who died Aug^t· 12th: 1825 ; | in the 26 year of her age.

> *Her happy spirit sighed*
> *To leave these wastes of woe*
> *To Join the Ransom'd Church above*
> *And full fruition know.*

1194. LYDIA ALLEN BROWN | died Aug. 15. 1825, | Aged 11 yr's | & 6 mon.

1195. JOHN HOWLAND | Son of | WILLIAM & E. P. HAMMATT | of Howland | in the State of Maine | was born 14 Octr 1824 | and died | 15 August 1825.

1196. In memory of | MARY ELIZABETH | Daughter of | OLIVER WOOD & | ELIZABETH his wife | died Augt 22 1825 | aged 7 months | and 9 days.

1197. To the memory of | *ISAAC COAL* Son of | Mr ISAAC COAL and | Mrs SARAH his wife | who died Aug 28, 1825 | in the 17 year of his age.

> *Friends and Physicians could not save*
> *His mortal body from the grave*
> *Nor can the grave confine him here*
> *When CHRIST shall call him to appear.*

1198. Sacred | to the memory of | MARY ANN SAMPSON, | wife of | SCHYLER SAMPSON, | and daughter of AMASA, | and SARAH BARTLETT; | she died September 3rd 1825, | aged 26 years 11 months, | and 24 days.

> " *The virtuous are truly happy.*"

1199. In memory of | JOANN PERKINS, | Daughter of | STEPHEN PERKINS | & JOANN his wife | who died Sepr 10. 1825 | aged one year and 4 | months.

1200. Sacred | to the memory of | Mr PETER LANMAN | who departed | this life Sepr. 14, 1825 : | in the 66 year | of his age.

> *My Saviour shall my life restore,*
> *And raise me from my dark abode;*
> *My flesh and soul shall part no more,*
> *But dwell forever near my GOD.*

1201. Erected | to the memory of | JOHN BURBANK, | who died | Sept. 26th 1825, | in the 56th y,r of his age | Also *LYDIA*, | widow of the above | who died | March 20th 1842 | aged 70 years.

1202. To the memory of | ALVAN E. HOLMES | Son of ELLIS HOLMES, Jr | & CATHARINE his wife | died Octo^r 18, 1825 : | aged 2 years | and 11 months.

> *Sweet babe no more but seraph now*
> *Before the throne behold him bow*
> *His soul enlarged to Angel size*
> *Joins in the triumph of the Skies.*

1203. This stone is erected | to commemorate | Capt. THOM^S. COVINGTON, | who died | October 24, 1825, | aged 78 years.

1204. Here lies interred | the Body of | Madam PHEBE WATSON, | Relict | of GEORGE WATSON, Esq | died October 28, | 1825 : | aged 83 years | Her first Husband | was *JOHN SCOTT, Esqr·* | of *Newport* R. I.

1205. In memory of | SUSAN EDWARDS, | Dau of (JAMES) & LYDIA | WADSWORTH died Nov 22 | 1825 Aged 3 years | and 2 months.

> *Twere wrong in me, had I the power*
> *To call thy spirit back an hour.*
> *No thou wilt not return to me,*
> *But I ere long shall follow thee;*
> *O ever blest and happy one.*
> *Whose little pilgrimage was done.*

1206. In | memory | of | NANCY BARNES | Daughter of | JOSEPH BARNES, | & JANE his wife | who died Decr 5, | 1825 aged 4 years | & 5 months. | Also | ELLIS BARNES, who | Died Novr· 27. 1816 : | aged 1 year & 7 months.

1207. MARTIN BENSON | Died Dec. 8. 1825 | aged 6 years. | JULIANN. Died | Aug. 20, 1829 | aged 1 year. | Children of SETH | & BETHIAH THOMPSON.

1208. JOSEPH HOLMES, | died | Dec'r 9. 1825, | Aged | 48 yr's. | Also | MARTHA, his wife died | April 3, 1830, | Aged 53 yr's.

1209. In memory of | Mrs. SARAH CHURCHILL., | Consort of | Mr. ISAAC CHURCHILL, | who died | Dec. 28, 1825 | in the 69 year of | her age.

> *The grave is ready let me rest,*
> *No longer linger here oppressed:*
> *Cold, in the dust my perished heart may lie:*
> *But that which warm'd it once, will never die.*

1210. In memory of | Hon WILLIAM DAVIS | Born July 15, 1758 | Died January 5, 1826.

HON. WILLIAM DAVIS was the son of Thomas and Mercy (Hedge) Davis, born in Plymouth; a well known and highly respected merchant, as well as a valued member of the community. He was ardently devoted to the interests of his native town, and having been early called to engage in its municipal affairs, he entered into its duties assiduously. He never sought political distinction, and whenever called into public service it was with reluctance. He represented the town of Plymouth in the General Court as Representative, and in 1812 and 1813 was a member of the Executive Council; one of the Selectmen of the town for about thirty years; President of the Plymouth Bank, and at the time of his death was Vice-President of the Pilgrim Society, in which he was deeply interested. He was of cheerful temper, of social habits, faithful and discreet in the discharge of his public trusts, and displayed an energy and activity which served to animate and cheer others with whom he was associated, and his death caused a deep, heartfelt sorrow.

MR. DAVIS married Rebecca, daughter of Nathaniel and Rebecca (Jackson) Morton, of Plymouth, 1781, and had William, 1783: Nathaniel Morton, 1785; Thomas, 1791: Elizabeth, 1803, married Alexander Bliss; and George Bancroft. Mr. Davis was grandfather of Hon. William T. Davis, the historian of Plymouth.

1211. To the memory of | LUCIA W. ROBBINS | Consort of | NATHAN B. ROBBINS | who died Jan: 19, 1826 | aged 28 years.

> *Thus from thy kindred early torn*
> *And to thy grave untimely borne,*
> *Vanish'd forever from my view*
> *Thou partner of my youth adieu.*
>
> *Still, with my first ideas twined,*
> *Thine image oft will meet my mind,*
> *And, while remembrance brings thee near*
> *Affection sad will drop a tear.*
>
> *As in Adam all die, even so in CHRIST*
> *Shall all be made alive.*

1212. Erected in memory of | Mr. SETH RIDER, | who died Janu 21, 1826: | in the 82 year of his age. | Also in memory of | *Mrs. HANNAH RIDER* his | wife who died Sept. 26, | 1814: | in the 60 year of her age.

> *Our age to sev'nty years is set,*
> *How short the term! how frail the state!*
> *And if to eighty we arrive,*
> *We rather sigh and groan than live.*

1213. In Memory of | JOHN WATSON Esq. | Born Aug'st 26 1748, | Died Feb'y 1 1826. | also his Wife | Mrs LUCIA WATSON, | dau'tr of | BENJAMIN MARSTON Esq. | of Salem, | Born Feb'y 15 1748, | Died Oct'r 25 1793.

JOHN WATSON was the son of John and Elizabeth (Reynolds) Watson. He graduated at Harvard College, 1766; was one of the early founders of the Old Colony Club, in 1769, and the last surviving member of that association. He was the first vice-president of the Pilgrim Society, and succeeded Judge Thomas as president of the same, which office he held till his death.

Mr. Watson was the proprietor of "Clark's" Island, in Plymouth harbor, where he resided for forty years; a spot to which he was very much attached, affording to him many antiquarian associations, in which he delighted to indulge, and to recount to his family and friends.

By his first wife he had John, 1769; George, 1771; Sally Marston, 1772; Benjamin Marston, 1774; Lucia, 1776, married John Taylor; Daniel, 1779; William, 1783; Winslow, 1786, and Brooke. He married, 2d, Eunice, widow of Le Barron Goodwin and daughter of John Marston of Boston, and had Edward Winslow, 1797; Eliza Ann, 1799; Albert Mortimer, 1801.

1214. In memory of | Mr. WILLARD SEARS | who died | February 5, 1826: | in the 78 year | of his age.

> *What is the life of man with all his cares*
> *'Tis like a shade which quickly disappears.*

1215. In memory of | Mrs. DEBORAH PATY, | Relict of the Late | Capt· JOHN PATY, | who died Feby· 7. 1826: | aged 67 years.

> *Bless'd hour, when virtuous friends shall meet,*
> *Shall meet to part no more,*
> *And with celestial welcome greet,*
> *On an immortal shore.*

1216. Erected | to the memory of | THOMAS CHURCHILL | Consort of | MARY CHURCHILL, | formerly of Plympton | who departed this life | February 26, 1826; | aged 70 years.

1217. In Memory of | Mr JOB CHURCHILL | died March 23. 1826 | in the 39th year | of his age.

1218. Here lies buried | the Remains of | Mrs LUCY LOTHROP | Consort to | Doctor NATHANIEL LOTHROP | who died April 17. | 1826 in the 72 year | of her age.

1219. GEORGE. | died May 2 1826 Æt. | 4 days. Also | SALLY. | died Nov. 6. 1837. Æt. | 8 mo. 19 ds. Children of | DAVID & SALLY WARREN.

> *Weep not for us*
> *Our parents dear,*
> *While we the richest*
> *Blessings share.*

1220. Erected | to the memory of | Mr JOHN C. HOLMES | who | departed this life | May 17, 1826; | aged 28 years.

> *Lean not on earth; twill pierce thee to the heart*
> *A broken reed at best: but oft a spear,*
> *On its sharp point peace bleeds, and hope expires.*

1221. In memory of | Mrs REBEKAH BARNES | Consort of | Mr BENJAMIN BARNES Jʳ | who died June 10, 1826: | **in the** 55 year | of her age.

> *Hush our moans let all our tears be dry,*
> *Ere long our souls must quit their day, and fly*
> *To meet our friend in heaven, to part no more,*
> *And praise that GOD, we here on earth adore.*

1222. In memory of | Mr *ZOHETH CLARK,* | who **died** | June 12ᵗʰ, 1826; | in the 60ᵗʰ year | of his age.

> *Tis done he sleeps the sleep of death,*
> *Nor will he wake again,*
> *Till the last trumpets awful voice,*
> *Shall rend the grave in twain.*

1223. Erected | In memory of | Cap. RUFUS ROBBINS, | who died at New Orleans | July 4, 1826: aged 45 years. | **Also** in memory of | Mrs MARGARET ROBBINS | his wife | **who** died Januʸ 14, 1827: | aged 43 years.

1224. Erected in memory of | Capᵗ˙ ELLIS J. HARLOW, | who Departed this life | July 11. 1826: aged 33 years.

> *No nobler form has nature showed*
> *Than here has met an early blight,*
> *No fairer eye has ever glowed*
> *And beamed with intellectual Light.*
>
> *Yet scarce we mourn his manly form*
> *When once his nobler heart we view,*
> *In love so kind in friendship warm,*
> *In honor and devotion true.*
>
> *O grave! thy triumph all shall be,*
> *To guard awhile this precious dust,*
> *The LORD of life, is LORD of thee*
> *And thou shalt render back thy trust.*

1225. In memory of | SOLOMON HINKLEY | Son **of** | SOLOMON RICHMOND | and ANNA his wife | who died July **20** | 1826; aged one year | eight months and | twenty seven days.

1226. To the memory of | *CHARLES* son of TRUMAN | and EXPERIENCE BARTLETT | who died July 22. 1826: | aged 6 years & 7 mon.

> *The beauteous flower that charms the eye*
> *And decks the smiling plain*
> *With winter's blast does fade and die,*
> *But dies to bloom again*
> *Then why should sorrow wring thy brow*
> *Say mourner say why weepest thou.*

1227. Erected | to the memory of | *RICHARD FISHER* aged 31; | of *Salem,* | *JOHN JACOBS* aged 28; and | *WILLIAM WRIGHT* aged 21; | of *New York,* | who were drowned by the | oversetting of a | boat in Plymouth | Harbour Augt 9. 1826.

> *O time is a stream flowing rapidly onward,*
> *As life is advancing, we rush without fear*
> *On temptations rough sea, and pleasure's bland wave,*
> *Till we sink in its current, and reach the dark grave.*

1228. ELIZABETH DAVIE, | dau't. of Capt. ICHABOD & | JOANNA DAVIE, | died Aug. 15, 1826: | Æ. 25 yr's.

> *Farewell but not a long Farewell*
> *In heaven may I appear:*
> *The trials of my faith to tell,*
> *In thy transported ear,*
> *And sing with thee eternal strain:*
> *Worthy the lamb that once was slain.*

1229. In memory of | MARY ATWOOD COLLIER | daughter of | EZRA & MARY S. COLLIER | who died | August 28, 1826: | aged 10 months & 3 days.

> *" of such is the Kingdom of heaven."*

1230. In memory of SAMUEL BRADFORD | Son of SAMUEL BRADFORD | and LUCY his wife | died Sep 13, 1826; aged 2 years | and 3 months.

> *Death may the bands of life unlose*
> *But cant dissolve my love*
> *Millions of infant souls compose*
> *The family above.*

1231. In | memory of | Mrs. HANNAH COOPER | wife of Capt. RICHARD COOPER | who departed this life | September 23, 1826, | aged 82 years.

1232. In memory of | RUTH NELSON | Daughter of | GEORGE NELSON | and RUTH his wife | Died Sepr. 27 1826; | aged 6 months.

> Lovely babe thy days are ended,
> All thy painful days below,
> And thy spirit has ascended
> Where living pleasures ever flow.

1233. Erected | to the memory of | *ELEANOR HOWARD* Consort | of the late *JOHN HOWARD,* | who died Oct. 12. 1826: | aged 75 years. | Also to the memory of | Capt. JOHN HOWARD, | who was lost at Sea | March 1788; | aged 43 years.

1234. In memory of | HANNAH CURTIS PATY | Daughter of | Capt. WILLIAM PATY | and Mrs JANE his wife | who died Octr. 17, 1826: | aged 4 years and 6 mo.

> *Of such is the kingdom of heaven.*

1235. In memory of | Mr ASA JOYCE | who died | Nov. 5. 1826: | aged 57 years. | Mrs. LUCY A. JOYCE, | his wife | died July 24. 1852; | aged 81 years.

> *Blessed are the dead that die in the Lord.*

1236. In | memory of | GEORGE SAMPSON, | who died | Nov. 9. 1826, | in the 52 year of his age. | Also of | *PATIENCE* his wife | who died | Oct. 18, 1835, | in the 58 y'r | of her age.

1237. In | memory of | Capt *WILLIAM BARNES,* | who died Nover. 22, 1826, | in the 60th year | of his age.

> " *The year rolls round and steals away*
> *The breath which first it gave;*
> *What'er we do, where'er we be,*
> *We're trav'ling to the grave.*"

1238. In memory of | LOTHROP son of JESSE | and MARY L. HARLOW | who died | November 23, 1826; | aged 1 month | and 21 days.

> *So the lovely blooming flour*
> *Fades and withers in an hour*
> *So our transient comforts fly*
> *Pleasure only blooms to die.*

1239. In memory of | ELLIS J. HARLOW | Son of | Cap
ELLIS HARLOW and | Mrs JERUSHA his wife | who died Novem-
ber 24. 1826; | aged 17 months.

1240. Sacred to the memory of | Rev. ADONIRAM JUD–
SON, | who died Nov. 25, 1826, Æ. 75. A faithful | and devoted
Minister of Christ. | ELNATHAN JUDSON, M. D. | who died
at Washington City May 8, 1829, | Æ. 34 years. *ANN H. JUD-
SON*, his dau. | died May 30, 1832, Æ. 7 years. *ELLEN.* |
YOUNG. his wife, died Nov. 25, 1832, Æ. 30 y'rs. | ANN H.
JUDSON. | Missionary to Burmah, who died at | Amherst, B.E.
Oct. 24, 1826. Æ. 37 y'rs. | *ROGER W. JUDSON*, died May 4,
1816, Æ. 8 mo. | *MARIA E. B. JUDSON*, died April 24, 1827.
Æ. 2 y'rs 3 mo. *SARAH B. JUDSON*, missionary | to Burmah,
who died in the port of St. | Helena, Sept. 1, 1845, A.E. 42 y'rs.
| ADONIRAM JUDSON D.D. | Missionary of the American
Baptist | Missionary Union to the Burman | Empire, who died
at Sea, | April 12, 1850, Æ. 62 years. | *EMILY C.* widow of
ADONIRAM | JUDSON D.D. & Missionary to Burmah, | died June
1, 1854. Æ. 37 y'rs.

REV. ADONIRAM JUDSON was the first Pastor of the Third Congregational Society
of Plymouth, and was installed May 12, 1802. He was born in Woodbury, Conn.,
graduated at Yale College 1775, was pastor of a church in Malden from January,
1788, to September, 1701; in Wenham, Mass., 1792 to 1799.

In 1817 he, having changed his views and become a Baptist, was dismissed Aug.,
1817. He died in Scituate in 1826.

His children were Elnathan, who became a surgeon in the United States Navy;
Abigail, and Adoniram (born in Malden, August 9, 1788), who became a noted missionary at Burmah for about forty years. He graduated at Brown University 1807, Andover Seminary 1810. At one time he kept a private school in Plymouth, and was
the author of "Elements of English Grammar" and "Young Ladies' Arithmetic,"
published in 1808 and 1809. He was ordained February 6, 1812, and married, 1st,
Ann Haseltine, who died in 1826; 2d, Mrs. Sarah Boardman, in April, 1834, widow of
the late George Dana Boardman, also a missionary in India. She died September 1,
1845. 3d, Emily Chubbuck, well known as "Fanny Forrester," June, 1846. He published a sermon on baptism In 1812 and a Dictionary of the Burman Language in
1826.

See memoirs of his life by Francis Wayland, 1853; J. Clement, 1852; D. T.
Midleditch, 1854; Mrs. H. C. Conant, 1856, and W. Hague, 1851. Also Dr. James
Thacher, 1837, and W. T. Davis, 1883.

1241. MARY THOMAS, | widow of | Dr. WILLIAM THOMAS
| Died Dec. 4, 1826, | Aged 94 years.

Widow MARY THOMAS was the daughter of Consider and Ruth (Bryant) Howland, born 1732.

1242. In memory of | THOMAS S. SAUNDERS | Son of JOHN and | BETSEY SAUNDERS | Died Decr 22, 1826: | aged 2 years.

1243. In memory of | CONSIDER BRADFORD | Son of JAMES BRADFORD | and ELEANER his wife | who died December | 25, 1826; | aged 11 mo. & 17 days.

> *Short was thy stay sweet babe but this will give*
> *A longer space of heavenly life to live*
> *Yet with delight you drew your balmy breath*
> *And the first pain you seem'd to feel was death.*

1244. Erected | In memory of | Mrs HARRIOT DAVIE, | wife of Capt. ROBERT DAVIE, | who departed this life | January 12, 1827: | aged 28 years. | Also their Daughter | HARRIOT E. DAVIE, | died Jany. 20. 1827; aged | 4 years & 21 days.

> *Thus from thy kindred early torn*
> *And to thy grave untimely borne*
> *Vanish'd forever from my view*
> *Thou partner of my youth adieu.*

> *As in Adam all die even so in CHRIST*
> *Shall all be made alive.*

1145. In memory of | BETSEY M. JACKSON | daughter of WOODWORTH | and MERIAH JACKSON | who died | June 10, 1827; | aged 26 years.

1246. ELIZABETH, | wife of | WILLIAM ROGERS, | died June 14th. 1827. | Aged 58 y'rs.

1247. To the memory of | MERCY M. BRIGHAM, | Dau. of ANTIPAS BRIGHAM | and MERCY his wife | Died June 15. 1827. | aged 9 mo. and 5 days

> *Sleep lovely babe thy toils are o'er*
> *The choicest comforts of her parents*
> *That GOD of love has called her home*
> *Why do we weep why should we mourn.*

1248. E. D. | In memory of | Mr. ELIJAH DUNHAM | who died | Augt. 11th 1827, | aged 75 years.

My flesh, while buried in the dust,
Jesus shall be thy care,
These withering limbs with thee I trust
To raise them strong and fair.

1249.   SARAH DAVIE, | daut of Capt. ICHABOD & | JOANNA
DAVIE, | died Sept. 12. 1827 : | Æ. 29 y'rs.

While o'er these dear remains affection weeps,
A voice proclaims she is not dead but sleeps.
Jesus again descending from the skies
  Shall break her slumbers saying maid arise,
Then gently lead her to her father's feet,
  With kind command to give her angels meat;
Ascend in hope we wait the promised hour,
  Tis sown in weakness it is raised in power.

1250.   Erected | to the memory of | Mrs *SARAH LANMON*
| who departed | this life Sep. 18. 1827 : | in the 74 year of her
age.

Cold, in the dust, her perish'd heart may lie,
But that which warm'd it once, will never die!

1251.   In memory of | three Dau. of SAMUEL | & SALLY COLE,
Viz. | JANE R. | died Sept. 27, 1827, | aged 18 mo. | DE-
BORAH B. | died April 30, 1837, | aged 18 years. | CARO-
LINE E. | died Sept 13. 1842, | aged 20 years.

May we not meet in Heaven above
With love that has no trembling fears
In that dear home far far above
This land of tears.

1252.   JOANNA DAVIE, | daut. of Capt. ICHABOD & |
JOANNA DAVIE, | died Dec. 3, 1827 : | Æ. 28 y'rs.

Her rest is sweet in earth's cold arms,
  She mingles dust with dust;
On Jesus breast she leans her head,
  In firm unshaken trust,
Quickly she'll burst the bolted tomb;
  And rise in full unfading bloom.

1253. In | memory of | *DEBORAH*, Wife of | BENJAMIN THOMAS, | died Janu. 5, 1828, | aged 36 years. | Also their son JOSIAH. | died Jan. 13, 1828, | aged 1 year | & 3 months.

1254. In memory of | Mrs ELEANOR WOOD | wife of ELIAB WOOD | died Janu 28, 1828; | aged 35 years; | Also their Son | ISAAC L. WOOD | died June 26. 1828 | aged 5 months.

1255. Erected | to the memory of | Mrs SALLY C. CHURCHILL | wife of Mr OTIS CHURCHILL | who died Feb. 10, 1828; | in the 25 year of her age | Also their infant by her side.

How soon these well wrought frames decay,
How soon our pleasures fade away;
But at the LORD'S right hand on high,
Fair pleasures bloom that never die.

1256. JOSEPH TRIBBLE Jr | died March 13. AD. 1828. | Æt. 55 years. | MARY, widow of JOSEPH | TRIBBLE Jr. died Feb. 10, | AD. 1833 Æt. 58 y'rs. | Also their two sons | WM. died at Port au Prince A.D. | 1827. Æt. 23 y'rs. | ROBERT F. died at Savannah | AD. 1832. Æt. 21 y'rs.

1257. In memory of | RUFUS CHURCHILL | who died April 14, 1828; | in the 57 year | of his age | Also his child | who died Sepr. 12, 1799 | aged 5 months | and 11 days.

1258. ICHABOD HARLOW, | died | April 19, 1828, aged 47 yr's. | PATIENCE HARLOW, | died | Sept. 15, 1840, aged 61 y'rs. | GEORGE H. HARLOW, | died | Aug. 2. 1825, aged 2 y'rs. | ALBERT HARLOW, | died | May 12, 1833, aged 25 y'rs.

1259. Sacred | to the memory of | MARY S. HOLMES | who died May 12, 1828. | aged 2 years | Daughter of TRUMAN | & JENNETTE HOLMES.

1260. In memory of | Capt. LEMUEL BRADFORD | who died May 22, 1828; | Aged 77 yrs. | Also LYDIA, | wife of the above | died June 6, 1838; | aged 77 yrs.

1261. Sacred | to the memory of | RICHARD HOLMES. 2d | son of WILLIAM & HANNAH HOLMES, | who was drown'd in the Pacific Ocean | near the port of Lima | on the first of June 1828; | aged twenty two years | As brothers we adapt these lines | in testimony of respect | for those manly virtues | that adorn'd thy bloom.

The sad remembrance drops a silent tear,
Knowing thy worth when thou wast here.

1262. In | this sacred spot are | deposited the remains | of | Hon. ZABDIEL SAMPSON. | Faithful and assiduous in | public trust, amiable and | exemplary in private life; | the tears of friendship and | affection embalm his memory. | Born August 22. 1781 | Died July 19. 1828.

Hon. ZABDIEL SAMPSON, son of George and Hannah (Cooper) Sampson, was born in Plympton, August 22, 1781. In early life his aim was to receive a collegiate education. To this end he devoted all his time and best energies. It was while at work at the anvil that he did his best studying, carrying on both branches in the blacksmith's shop at the same time. He graduated at Brown University in 1803, and was the first person who received a liberal education, at any college, from the town of Plympton. He studied Law and was admitted to the Bar, and commenced the practice of his profession in Fairhaven, Mass. He next removed to Plymouth, where he passed the remainder of his life. He was often called to public office, and enjoyed the confidence of his fellow-citizens, having been chairman of the Board of Selectmen of Plymouth several years. In 1818 he was elected Representative to Congress, for one term of two years. In 1820 he was Collector of the Port of Plymouth, which position he retained with honor to himself till his death. It was his privilege to enjoy the special friendship of Daniel Webster, and it was through his agency mainly that the Act of Congress was passed allowing bounties to fishermen, in the form of a drawback of the duty on salt, which has done so much to encourage the fishing interests in Massachusetts.

He married Ruth, daughter of Capt. Ebenezer and Judith Lobdell of Plympton, October 18, 1804, by whom he had ten children.

1263. Sacred | to the memory of | Miss SALLY C. ROBBINS, | dau'r of Capt. SAMUEL & | MRS. SARAH ROBBINS ; | she deceas'd by a fall from | a chaise Aug. 14, 1828, | aged 25 years 5 mo's | and 10 days.

" Our home is in the grave:
Here dwells the multitude; we gaze around,
We read their monuments, we sigh, and while
we sigh, we sink."

1264. Sacred | to the memory of | Mr. JOSEPH JOHNSON, | who died Sept. 3. 1828, | aged 68 years. | Also | Capt. JOSEPH JOHNSON Jr. | who died Mar. 16, 1820, | aged 24 years.

1265. Here lies buried | the Remains of | Doctor NATHANIEL LOTHROP | who died | October 19, 1828 : | aged 92.

DR. LOTHROP was the son of Isaac, Esq , and Priscilla (Thomas) (Watson) Lothrop of Plymouth, and in the fifth generation of his respected ancestor, John Lothrop. He

graduated at Harvard University, at the head of the class of 1756. For many years **he was** the oldest person in the town, and survived all his old associates and companions, who were his joy and delight.

He left a legacy of five hundred dollars towards the completion of the Hall of the Pilgrim Society, in which he took a deep interest.

"He died in a good old age, an old man, and full of years, and was gathered to his **fathers.**"

He married Ellen, daughter of Noah Hobart.

1266.   To the memory of | Mrs. SARAH HARLOW | widow of | Cap. JESSE HARLOW | who died | November 22, 1828; | Aged 65 years.

1267.   Sacred | to the memory of | Mrs. CLARISSA | wife of | Mr. HENRY BARTLETT | who died Dec. 9. 1828; | Æt. 63, | Also | Mr. HENRY BARTLETT, | who died at sea March 14, 1817, | Æt. 48. | Also HENRY, their son | who was lost at sea | 1821: Æt. 28.

> *Though distant graves divide their dust,*
> *We hope in Christ they will meet at last.*

1268.   MARY A. | Dau. of JAMES | & SARAH BARTLETT, | **was** born Dec. 19, | 1825, | & died Jan. 13, | 1829.

1269.   Erected to the memory of | Miss FANNY ALEXANDER | Daughter of SAMUEL & | DEBORAH ALEXANDER who | Departed this life | January 25 1829; | aged 16˙years & 4 months.

> *Not beauty, youth, nor friends fond love could save*
> *The lovely victim from the cruel grave.*
> *Like a fair flower that faids in earliest bloom*
> *In life's bright morn she meet her early tomb.*
>
> *Oh! fare the well, dearest — thy spirit though gone*
> *Shall live in this desolate bosom alone.*
> *Till it burst in the splendor of weakness forgiven*
> *And glorious shine in the lustre of heaven.*

1270.   Erected | to the memory of | Mr EBENEZER NELSON. | who died Febr. 14. 1829; | in the 73 year | of his age.

E.   N.

> *Tis but at best a narrow bound*
> *Which heav'n allows to men;*
> *And pains, and sins run through the round*
> *Of threescore years and ten.*

1271. In | memory of | Capt JOSIAH COTTON. | who died
| March 7th 1829, | aged 76 years | Also in memory of | SARAH
D. COTTON. | died Oct. 14th 1826, | aged 19 years.

1272. In Memory of | WILLIAM son of WILLIAM | and
ELSEY BRADFORD | who died May 12. 1829: | aged 3 years 3
months | and 9 days.

> Bost not thyself of to morrow;
> For thou knowest not what a
> day may bring forth.

1273. To the | memory | of | SAMUEL DAVIS A.M. | who
died | July 10. AD. 1829 | in the 65th year of his age.

> From life on earth our pensive friend retires,
> His dust commingling with the pilgrim sires;
> In thoughtful walks, their every path he trac'd,
> Their toils, their tombs, his faithful page embrac'd,
> Peaceful, and pure, and innocent as they,
> With them to rise to everlasting day.

SAMUEL DAVIS, Esq., was the son of Thomas and Mercy (Hedge) Davis of Plymouth, born Mar. 5, 1765. Mr. Davis was truly an antiquarian, and few men within
our social circle possessed a greater fund of correct information relative to the character and circumstances of our primitive fathers. He contributed many articles of
historical interest concerning the towns in Plymouth County, to the Massachusetts
Historical Society's collection. He was, says the writer of an obituary notice, "the
man to whom the inquisitive stranger was, by all of us, promptly referred. There was
an accuracy and precision in the habit of his mind, that made all his minute and
curious information perfectly to be relied on. He was what the world would call a
man of leisure; but this leisure was no ignoble escape from thought; but was usually
exactly adapted to its full gratification. He loved the characters of the pilgrims. He
loved to trace out their original allotments, their first rude dwellings. He knew their
sons and daughters, their intermarriages, their changes of abode, the living branches
and the scions, that became new stocks in the most distant states. Of all these things
he made copious memoranda. It is easy to infer the moral traits of an intellectual
man, who, fond of history and biography, yet turned with disgust from the Cæsars, the
Charleses, and Napoleons, and for thirty years persevered with delight in learning the
minutest particulars of men like the pilgrims. The reader would be sure that he had,
in the proper use of the word, simplicity of mind; that he was unostentatious and
meek, and pure, and a lover of every age and clime. If he had peculiarities, they did
not arise out of disordered affections, or from bitter ingredients in the composition of
his mind; but were the natural growth of a life of celibacy, and seclusion of a mind
less forcibly acted upon than most others, by the events and prevalent passions of the
times he lived in."

The manner of his death was remarkable. Having walked out in the evening, he
retired to his chamber about ten o'clock, his usual hour, and made an entry in his
diary of the state of the weather. At breakfast time the next morning he was found
a corpse, his arms folded on his breast without any indication that departing life had
occasioned the least struggle, so tranquil was the end of his peaceful life.

(*Thacher.*)

1274. To | Perpetuate | the memory of | Mrs ABIGAIL BA—
CON | wife of | DAVID BACON Esq. | who died | July 19. 1829 |
in the 75 year | of her age.

1275. In | memory of | Cap. ROBERT DAVIE | who died | July 19, 1829, | aged 32 years.

> " Tis God that lifts our comforts high
> Or sinks them in the Grave:
> He Gives and blessed be his name,
> He takes but what he Gave.

1276. Erected | to the memory of | Mrs. MARY T ROLFE | who died July 30, 1829; | aged 26 years. | wife of | HORACE H. ROLFE.

> Blessed and holy is he that hath part
> in the first resurrection; on such,
> the second death hath no power:
>
> Rev. 20–6.

1277. CROSBY LUCE, | died Aug. 21, 1829; | Æ. 44 years. | Also | BETSEY, | his widow | died Sept. 10, 1854; | Æ. 65 years & 5 mo's.

1278. Erected | to the memory of | Mr. CROSBE LUCE. | died August 21, 1829; | aged | 44 years | Consort of | Mrs. BETSEY LUCE.

> C.   L.
>
> Our life is ever on the wing,
> And death is ever nigh;
> The moment when our lives begin,
> We all begin to die.

1279. In | memory of | Dea$^{n.}$ JOSIAH DIMAN, | who died | August 22$^{d.}$ 1829, | in the 63^d year | of his age.

> " They die in Jesus, and are bless'd;
> How kind their slumbers are
> From suffrings and from sins releas'd
> And freed from ev'ry snare."

1280. Sacred | to the memory of | BATHSHEBA NELSON | Consort of | WILLIAM NELSON. | died Sept. 12. 1829 | aged 56 years.

> Before thy face thy church shall live,
> And on thy throne thy children reign;
> This dying world shall they survive,
> And the dead saints be raised again.

1281. Departed this life | Sept. 30. 1829, | Aged 34 years, |
Mr GEORGE NELSON.

> *Gone to the resting place of man*
> *His long his silent Home*
> *Where ages past have gone before*
> *Where future ages come.*

1282. In | memory of | Mr DANIEL JACKSON | who died
| November 4. 1829, | aged 68 years.

1283. In | Memory of | Mr. WILLIAM DREW 2d | died
| Novr 7. 1829, | aged 45 y'rs.

> *Our life how short! a gleam, a sigh;*
> *We live & and then begin to die:*
> *But oh! how great a mercy this,*
> *That death's a portal into bliss.*

1284. JERUSHA TALBOT, | wife of | SAMUEL TALBOT. |
died Nov. 22, 1829: | Æ. 31 years.

> *When spirits from their cumbering clay,*
> *Ascend to heaven's bright shore,*
> *Our hoping hearts in triumph say:*
> *" Not lost, but gone before."*

JERUSHA. | their daughter | died Sept. 22, 1837: | Æ. 9
years & 4 mo's.

1285. In Memory of | BENJAMIN DEXTER | Son of BEN-
JAMIN & MARY | BULLARD. Died Jan'y | 20, 1830: aged 2 |
years & 5 months.

> *Let parents with thankfulness own,*
> *The encouragement Jesus has given;*
> *Be delighted to hear him declare,*
> *Of such is the kingdom of heav'n.*

1286. In | memory of | Mr. CORNELIUS COBB. | who die
Feb. 4, 1830 | aged 82 years | and 7 months.

> *An honest man the noblest work of GOD.*

1287. JAMES W. | died Feb. 10, 1830, | aged 2 months, |
MARY JANE | died Aug. 20, 1833, | aged 13 months. | Chil-
dren of CHARLES | & CORDELIA B. TUFTS.

1288. In memory of | Cap. NATHANIEL SYLVESTER. | who died | March 18, 1830, | aged 61 years. | Also his wife | ELSEY SYLVESTER, | who died | January 20, 1830, | aged 57 years.

Prepare to meet thy GOD.
This only can prepare the heart
For deaths surprising hour.

1289. Erected by Ezra Finney & wife | to the memory of | Dea. JOHN BISHOP. | who died March 26, 1830; | also his wife | ABIGAIL BISHOP, | who died March 24, 1830, | both buried in one grave. | he was Deacon of the Church | 34 years, & lived together | over 60 years.

1290. In | Memory of | WILLIAM P. G. DIKE | son of SIMEON & MARY DIKE | died April 13, 1830, | aged 25 years.

" Adieu a long adieu to all below
To death and Judgment I am call'd to go
My days though few have like an arrow fled
And now I'm number'd with the silent Dead.

Our God is love, his promises are sure:
Great is his Power, none can his wrath endure,
Oh! do not slight this Loud and solemn call,
And while you mourne for me make Christ your all."

1291. BETSEY THOMAS BARNES. | Consort of ISAAC BARNES Jr. who | died May 14, 1830, aged 33 years. | Also Their Children | *WINSLOW* died Oct. 10. 1825. | aged one year 6 mo. & 15 days. | *BETSEY WINSLOW* died Dec. | 21. 1825, aged 10 days. | *WINSLOW* died Sept. 6. 1828, | aged 13 mon.

1292. Miss ESTHER P. HOLMES, | died | June 3, 1830, | Aged 21 y'rs. | Also | ESTHER P. HOLMES | died | March 20, 1808 | aged 2 yr's.

1293. In | memory of | BEZA HAYWARD Esq. | who died | June 4th AD. 1830, | aged 78 years.

Hon. BEZA HAYWARD was the son of Nathan and Susanna (Latham) Hayward; born in Bridgewater, Mass., January 20, 1752; graduated at Harvard College in 1772; studied divinity, but never was settled. Much of his early life was spent in preparing young men for college and teaching school for the higher branches of education.

He represented his native town in the General Court; afterward elected Senator for Plymouth County, and afterwards became a member of the Executive Council. Patriotism, public virtue and love of order were eminent traits in his character. He possessed a peculiar tact for mathematical calculations, and was very reliable, in the results of his labors, when for months he was engaged on committees of valuation in the Legislature.

In 1808 he was appointed Register of Probate for the county of Plymouth, which office he sustained till his death. In all the public positions to which he was called he was much respected for probity, strict integrity and impartial justice, and under bereavement the virtues of meekness, humility and pious resignation were graciously exemplified in his demeanor.

He married, 1st, Abigail, daughter of Col. Briggs and Mercy (Wadsworth) Alden, of Duxbury, Mass., November, 1784, by whom he had John Alden, 1788, and Beza. His wife died 1800. He then married Experience, daughter of Ichabod and Priscilla Shaw, and widow of James Russell, of Plymouth, and had Charles Latham, John Shaw, and Susanna, 1805.

1294. BATHSHEBA   JAMES | wife   of | Capt WILLIAM HOLMES 3^d Mariner | and daughter to | Capt JOSEPH DOTEN Do | she was killed instantaneously | in a Thunder storm by the | Electrich fluid of lightning on | the 6th of July 1830, | aged 35 years and 26 days.

She was an affectionate Wife, a
dutiful Daughter, a happy Mother,
a kind and sincere friend. Alas
sweet Blossom short was the period
that thy enlivening virtues
Contributed to the Happiness of
those Connections: But oh how long
have they to mourn the loss of so
much worth and Excellence.

Fare well dear Wife untill that day more blest
When if deserving I with thee shall rest,
With thee shall rise with thee shall live above,
In worlds of endless bliss and boundless love.

1295.   CAROLINE E. BARTLETT, | Daughter of JOHN | & ELIZA BARTLETT, | died Aug. 4th, 1830. | aged 4 months.

again
The Babe shall live & bloom

1296.   Erected   in   memory   of | ROBERT   BARTLETT LEACH | Son of | Capt. FINNEY & Mrs. MERCY LEACH | who departed this life Sept. 12th, 1830. | aged 21 years. | Also four children of the same Viz | MARCIA died Oct. 25^{th,} 1813, aged 6 months. | REBECCA died May 4th, 1818, aged 10 weeks. | LOUISA died Oct. 17^{th,} 1818, aged 1 year & 11 mo. | GEO. EDWARDS died Dec. 22^{d,} 1820, aged 6 yrs. | and 1 month.

1297. Erected | to the | memory of | Miss. RUTH CRAN-
DON | daughter of | BENJAMIN & | SUKEY CRANDON. | who de-
parted this life | October 10, AD 1830 | in the 36th year | of her
age.

1298. WILLIAM THOMAS, | died Nov. 30, 1830, | Æt. 5
mo. 5 ds. | THOMAS, | died Jan. 25, 1844, | Æt. 17 ds. | HI-
RAM, | died March 7. 1845. | Æt. 2 y'rs 3 mo. | Children of
THs, and | MARIA P. TRIBBLE.

So fades these lovely blooming
flowers.

1299. Erected | In memory of | Capt, *JESSE TURNER,* |
who was lost at sea | on his passage | from Plymouth to W.
Indies | Dec. 5th, 1830, | in the 45th year of his age.

The kind husband and parent is gone,
But on the morn of the resurrection,
the sea shall give up its dead.

1300. Sacred | to the memory of | *MARGARET H.* wife |
of HENRY ROBBINS, | died Dec'r 27, 1830; | in the 31 yr. of | her
age.

In her tongue was the law of kindness.

Also three of their Children | HENRY AUGUSTUS, aged
1 yr 4 mo. | FRANCIS WILLIAM, | Aged 3 yrs 3 mo. |
MARGARET LEWIS. | aged 1 yr. 5 mo.

1301. In | memory of | Hon. WENDELL DAVIS. | who
died at | Sandwich | Dec'r. 30. 1830. | aged 54 years. | And is
here interred.

When I am gathered to my fathers
let me rest by the side of my kindred,
My trust is in GOD my Saviour.

HON. WENDELL DAVIS was the son of Thomas and Mercy (Hedge) Davis; born
February 13, 1776; graduated at Harvard College, 1796; admitted to the bar, 1799,
and settled in Sandwich, where he married Caroline Williams, daughter of Dr.
Thomas Smith, and had George Thomas, 1810, graduate of Harvard College, 1829,
who settled in Greenfield, Mass., in the practice of law, 1832, and was member of the
Massachusetts Senate 1840 and 1841, member of Congress 1851-53; Wendell Thorn-
ton, 1818, Harvard College, 1838, admitted to the bar, 1841, and several times member
of the General Court from Greenfield.

The father was Clerk of the Massachusetts Senate; afterwards Senator, also
Representative, from the town of Sandwich, and several years Sheriff of Barnstable
County.

1302. Erected | to the memory of | Mr. HORACE H.
ROLFE. | who died at Charleston | South Carolina | Feb'y 24,
1831, | Aged 30 years.

Blessed are the dead
who die in the Lord.

Also | MARY AUGUSTA ROLFE | died Nov. 1. 1831, |
aged 2 years & 4 months.

Of such are the Kingdom of Heaven.

1303. Erected | in | remembrance of | Colᵒ JOHN B.
BATES, | who died March 6, 1831, | aged 47 years. | Also
to ABBY WASHBURN | daughter of | JOHN B. & MARY
BATES | who died Oct. 3ᵈ· 1811, | aged 1 year.

1304. In | memory of | Mrs. POLLY OTIS, | the amiable
Consort of | Mr. BARNABAS OTIS, | who departed this life | April
25 1831, | in the 77 year | of her age.

" Yes, thou art gone, and we no more
Shall hold sweet converse here below;
But now we trust a brighter shore
Is thine beyond the bounds of woe."

1305. Erected | in | remembrance of | HULDAH JACK-
SON, | Consort of | HENRY JACKSON | died April 30, 1831, |
aged 53 years.

I now confide in Christ alone,
No other guide nor Lord I own;
Be glad my soul, rejoice and sing
He's both thy Saviour and thy King.

1306. Capt. | WILLIAM HOLMES 3ᵈ | who died | at Val-
paraiso | May 16, 1831, | aged 40 years.

He that giveth to the poor
lendeth unto the Lord.

Rest generous mortal, rest thy toils are ore,
Thy spirit's landed on that peaceful shore,
Where are no troubles or distress or pain,
But peace and happyness infinitely reign.

1307. In | memory of | ELIZABETH SAVERY | wife of |
LEMUEL SAVERY | who died | August 1, 1831 | aged 71 years.

Remember me as you pass by
As you are now so once was I,
As I am now you soon must bee
Prepare for death to follow me.

1308. Father & MOTHER | JOHN PERRY | died Aug. 19th 1831, | in his 64th y'r. | RHODA PERRY, | died July 10th 1855 | in her 83d. y'r.

Why do we mourn departing friends,
Or shake at death's alarms?
Tis but the voice that Jesus sends,
To call them to his arms.

1309. In | memory of | Capt CHANDLER HOLMES Jr | who died | October 4. 1831. | aged 27 years.

He spoke the meaning of his heart
Nor slandered with his tongue
Would scarce believe an ill report
Nor do his neighbour wrong.

1310. FRANCELIA | Daughter of DANIEL | & LYDIA RIDER | who died | Oct. 6. 1831, | aged 6 years | 8 mon. & 23 days.

1311. Erected | to the memory of | LUCY WESTON. | Daughter of | SETH & LUCY WESTON | late of Duxbury | who died Oct. 22, 1831, | aged 33 years.

Farewell, dear friend, a short farewell,
Till we shall meet again above,
Where endless joys and pleasures dwell
And trees of life bear fruits of love.

1312. In | memory of | NATHANIEL HUESTON. | who died Oct. 23. 1831. | in the 45 year | of his | age.

Where ere thy steps are bent,
Death hovers by thy side,
Thou knowest not what an hour
May to thy fate betide.

1313. SALLY. wife of ROBERT DUNHAM. | died Oct'r 29, 1831: aged 56 years. | ROBERT DUNHAM | died Jan'y 13. 1833: aged 54 years.

1314.   In memory of | THOMAS GOODWIN, | was lost at Sea. Oct. 1831, | Æ. 45 y'rs. | HEVERLAND T. GOODWIN | his son died | Jan'y 12. 1823, Æ. 6 mo. | DESIRE GOODWIN, his dau. died | April 30, 1823, Æ. 3 y'rs | HEVERLAND T. GOODWIN, | his son died | June 10, 1830, Æ. 3 mo. | CHARLES T. GOODWIN, | his son died | Feb. 7, 1831, Æ. 10 mo.

1315.   In | memory of | NANCY WILLIAMS, | a faithful (African) servant | in the family of | Rev. F. FREEMAN. | died Nov. 21. 1831, | aged 25 years.

"*Honour and shame from no condition rise:*
Act well your part; — there all the honour lies."

1316.   To the memory of | Capt. WILLIAM PERSONS | who died | Nov. 25, 1831, | aged 72 years.

A trew Patriot
& Hero of the Revolution.

1317.   Sacred | to the memory of | Mr *JAMES MORTON* 2ᵈ, | who died Dec'r 5, 1831 ; | aged 38 yrs. | Also | of *ABRA-HAM C.* | son of JAMES & BETSEY MORTON, | who died Nov'r 5, 1825 ; | Aged 7 yr's. | And of four deceased infant children.

Above life's scenes faith lifts her eye
To brighter prospects given,
Where rays divine disperse the gloom;
Beyond the confines of the tomb
Appears the dawn of heaven.

1318.   LOIS DIMAN | wife of | DAVID DIMAN | died Dec. 16, 1831, | in the 75 year | of her age.

Look down and view
The hollow gaping tomb:
This gloomy prison waits for you
When'er the summons come.

1319.   Erected | to the memory of | WILLIAM BARNES. | who died | Dec. 29ᵗʰ 1831, | aged 66 years.

"*Immortality o'ersweeps*
All pains, all tears, all times, all fears — and peals
Like the eternal thunders of the deep
Into my ears this truth — Thou liv'st forever."

1320. HANNAH PAINE, | Widow | died Jan. 3, 1832, |
Æ. 80 y'rs. | Also her Husband | STEPHEN PAINE, | died at
Liverpool, | N. S. 1794, | Æ. 48 y'rs.

1321. * LUCY, ANN | died Jan. 17, 1832, | aged 1 year. |
Daughter of | RUFUS & LUCY | W. CHURCHILL.

> *With equal voice, in unknown Worlds,*
> *Old men and babes appear.*

1322. To | ROSELIA L. | daur of JOSEPH | & JANE BARNES
| who died | Febr 2. 1832, | in the 23 year | of her age.

> *An affectionate child*
> *and sincere christian.*

1323. In memory of | Mr. EBENEZER DAVIE, | who died
Feb. 10, 1832, | aged 56 years & 11 mo's. | GEORGE DAVIE,
| son of the above, was | drowned at sea. Aug. 11. | 1831, aged
18 years.

> *Seize mortal ! seize the transient hour;*
> *Improve each moment as it flies:*
> *Life's a short summer man a flower,*
> *He dies, Alas ! how soon he dies..*

1324. THOMAS NELSON | died Feb. 17. 1832, | aged 66
y'rs. | *ABIGAIL,* his wife | died March 10, 1838, | aged 71 y'rs.
| Also *MARTHA,* their Dau. | died July 15, 1839, | aged 45
y'rs.

1325. BENJAMIN F. | son of BENJAMIN | & ALICE DUN-
HAM | died March 2, 1832, | aged 14 days.

1326. Erected | in memory of | MARY ANN, | dau. of |
NATHL & LYDIA GOODWIN, | died April 7. 1832, | aged 26 y'rs
& 6 mo. | Also their Son | EDWARD J. GOODWIN, | died in
Havana | March 16. 1828. | aged 24 yrs. & 6 mo.

1327. Erected | to the memory of | EZRA CHURCHILL, |
who departed this life | April 11, 1832, | in the 27th year | of his
age.

---

* This stone lies on the ground.

Life's but a moment, friend repress
thy tear,
My second life's begun an endless
year;
You soon like me while in your
youth may fade,
Seek then a house above with
hands not made.

1328. In memory of | Capt ANDREW BARTLETT, | who
died | May 6. 1832, | aged 67 yrs. & 5 mo. | Also ELIZABETH,
| widow of the above | who died | July 9. 1844. | aged 73 yrs. &
4 mo.

When we at Death must part,
How keen how deep the pain,
But we shall still be joined in heart,
And hope to meet again.

1329. Erected | to the memory of | Mrs BETSEY BART-
LETT, | wife of | Mr ELEAZER S. BARTLETT | who died | May
9, 1832, | in the 25th year | of her age.

My soul, my body I will trust
With him, who numbers every dust,
My Saviour, faithfully will keep
His own — their death is but a sleep.

1330. In | memory of | Mrs. LOIS ROBBINS | wife of |
Mr. WILLIAM ROBBINS | who died | May 26th 1832, | in the 68th
year | of her age.

1331. In | memory of | Mrs. MARY HUESTON | wife of
| Mr. WILLIAM HUESTON | who died May 30th 1832 | in the 74
year | of her age.

My soul my body I will trust
With him who numbers every dust;
My Saviour faithfully will Keep
His own — their death is but a sleep.

1332. In memory of | WILLIAM TRIBBLE, | who was |
born Jan. 2. 1783, | died June 14. 1832.

1333. In | Memory of | Mr. THOMAS POPE, | who died |
July 20, 1832., | aged 23 years.

Unveil thy bosom, faithful tomb,
Take this new treasure to thy trust:
And give these sacred relics room
To slumber in thy silent dust.

No pain, no grief, no anxious fear
Invade thy bounds: no mortal woes
Can reach the peaceful sleeper here
While angels watch its soft repose.

1334. died Aug 4th, 1832. | GEORGIANA MINERVA | daug. of C. J. & C. W. | WARREN aged 14 Mon.

Here sleep, dear daughter,
all alone, thee:
With aching hearts we leave
To the our sorrows are not
known thee.
Nor can our absence grieve

1335. OUR FATHER WHICH ART IN HEAVEN
ANTIPAS BRIGHAM | died | August 6, 1832, | Aged 33 years.

1336. In Memory of | JAMES H. HOWARD, | who returned to his friends | from Eastport, Me, June 2 | after an absence of several | years on account | of feeble health, | died Aug'st 7, 1832.: | Æt. 24 yr's & 9 mo's.

His mind was tranquil and serene,
No terrors in his looks were seen,
His saviour's smiles dispell'd the gloom,
And smooth'd his passage to the tomb.

1337. Mrs SARAH R. BARSTOW | wife of | Mr. ICHABOD W. BARSTOW | and Daughter of | Mr JOHN & Mrs. MARY CLARK, | who died | August 15th, 1832, | aged 36 years.

Sweet spirit dear, a sad farewell
Till we shall meet again,
The place where happy souls do dwell,
Is free from toil and pain.

Great were her suffrings mighty GOD
We heard her groan and die.
But Jesus Christ's most precious blood
Was shed on Calvary.

1338.   LYDIA ALLEN BROWN | died Aug. 20. 1832 |
Aged 6 y'rs.

1339.   In memory of | Deac. LOT HARLOW | died Sept.
10th 1832 | aged 64 years. | MARY, Relict of Deac. LOT HAR-
LOW, | died Sept. 21st 1832, | aged 62 years. | STEPHEN
HARLOW, their Son | died Dec. 23d 1831, | aged 25 years.

1340.   In memory of | CYRUS COLE, | Son of the | Rev.
TIMOTHY | & SUSAN COLE, | who died | Sept. 28, 1832, | aged 4
weeks.

1341.   In | memory of | Mr. JAMES MORTON, | who died |
Oct'r 19, 1832, | aged 58 years.
The eye of him that hath seen me
Shall see me no more.

1342.   In memory of | JANE, | daughter of | WILLIAM &
SARAH STURTEVANT, | who died Nov. 8, 1832 : | aged 38. | Also
of her sister | HANNAH, | wife of THOMAS J. LOBDELL, | who
died & was entombed | at Boston Oct. 3. 1818 : | aged 22.

1343.   Sacred | to the Memory of | EPHRAIM BARTLETT,
| who was born Feb'y 19, 1809 | died Dec'r 3, 1832.
There is a calm for those who weep,
A rest for weary pilgrims found;
And while the mouldering ashes sleep
Low in the ground,
The soul of origin divine,
God's glorious Image freed from clay
In Heaven's eternal sphere shall shine
A star of day.

1344.   Erected | In memory of | Capt. ZEACHUS BARNES.
| who Departed this life | December 26. 1832, | aged 34 years.
Oft as the bell with solemn toll,
Speaks the departure of a soul,
Let each one ask himself, am I,
Prepared, should I be called to die."

1345. Capt. | WILLIAM HOLMES | died Jan'y 3. 1833, | aged 65 years. | HANNAH. widow of | WILLIAM HOLMES, died | Feb. 22. 1854. Æ. 87 y'rs. | Also Miss POLLY HOLMES, | died April 2. 1849, | Æ. 69 y'rs.

1346. To the memory of | Mrs. BETSEY JOHNSON, | wife of | Mr. JOSEPH JOHNSON, | who departed this life | Jan. 15, 1833, | aged 63 years.

The grave is ready let me rest
No longer linger here oppressed
Cold in the dust, my perished heart may lie
But that which, warm'd it once, will never
die.

1347. In memory of | Miss CHARLOTT BARNES, | who died | Feb. 22, 1833, | in the 60th year | of her age.

I call that legacy my own,
Which Jesus did bequeath
Twas purchas'd with a dying groan
And ratified in death.

1348. In memory of | ELIZABETH, | wife of the | Rev. FREDERICK FREEMAN, | who died | March 12, 1833, | aged 33 yrs. | Leaving her husband and | five children to deplore | their loss, and cherish the | dear remembrance of | her worth.

" Her children rise up and call
her blessed; her husband also
and he praiseth her."

Rev. FREDERICK FREEMAN was son of Nathaniel Freeman, of Sandwich, Mass.; was settled as Pastor of the "Third Church" in Plymouth, 1824; dismissed in May, 1833. Mr. Freeman was the author of the History of Cape Cod, published in two volumes in 1858.

1349. In memory of | ISAAC SAMPSON, | who died May 7, 1833: | Aged 42 yr's. | Also *ISAAC,* | Son of ISAAC & ELIZABETH | SAMPSON died Dec'r | 11, 1833: | Aged 3 yr's & 8 mo's.

" How vain is all beneath the skies,
How transient every earthly bliss,
How slender all the fondest ties,
That binds us to a world like this."

" Then let the hope of joys to come
Dispel our cares and chase our fears,
If God be ours we're travelling home,
Though passing through a vale of tears."

ISAAC SAMPSON (the father) was the son of Benjamin and Priscilla (Churchill)
Sampson, of Kingston, Mass.; b rn December, 1789; married Elizabeth, daughter of
William and Elizabeth (Drew) Sherman, of Plymouth, January 1, 1822, and had three
children—Elizabeth, George and Isaac. He was a dry goods merchant in Plymouth.

1350.   Departed this life | May 24, 1833: | in the 74th, yr.
of her age | Mrs. REBECCA RUSSELL, | Relict | of JONATHAN
RUSSELL, | late of Barnstable.

1351.   In | memory of | Miss DRUSILLA GOULD, | late of
Franklin, | (Mass.) | who died | May 31 1833, | aged 64 years.

1352.   Died | June 20. 1833 | Aged 15 years & 7 mon. |
EBENEZER NELSON. | Died | Sept. 13. 1826 | Aged 2 years.
| LYDIA NELSON | Children of LEMUEL & | BATHSHEBA
BRADFORD.

1353.   In memory of | *ADALINE*, daug. of | *Mrs. BETSY
E.* and | Capt. ROBERT HUTCHINSON | died June 28th. AD. 1833,
| aged 10 months. | *GEORGE W.* their son | died Feby. 27th.
AD. 1835 | aged 5 years | 6 months. | Also | their two infants.

Here in this low and grassy bed
Brothers and Sisters dear are laid,
*Cold Death has nipp'd them in the bu*ᵈ
And they are gone to rest with God.

1354.   In memory of | SARAH, | daughter of | WILLIAM &
SARAH STURTEVANT. | who died | July 7. 1833; | aged 33.

1355.   Erected | to the memory of | Mr. HENRY HARLOW
| who died | July 15, 1833, | in the 51 year. | of his age.

1356.   BATHSHEBA. | the affectionate wife of | ANSEL H.
HARLOW, and dau'tr of | Capt Wᴹ HOLMES 3ᵈ she died | Aug'st
11 1833: aged 20 yr's.

Behold, I shew you a mystery; we shall not all
sleep, but we shall be changed.
In a moment, in the twinkling of an eye,
at the last trump; for the trumpet shall
sound, and the dead shall be raised
incorruptible, and we shall be changed
                                        St. Paul.

1357. Erected | In memory of | *PAMELIA*, wife of | SAMUEL ROBBINS Jr. | who died Sept'r 5, 1833: | Aged 50 yr's. | Also their Sons, | EDWARD, died Nov'r 5, 1802 | Aged 5 mo's. | ADONIRAM, died March 16, | 1815: aged 6 mo's. | LEWIS F. died Feb'y 14, 1824 | Aged 11 mo's.

" *As we have borne the Image of the earthy,*
we shall also bear the Image of the heavenly."

St. Paul.

1358. In memory of | *JAMES P.* son of | PHILIP & NANCY TAYLOR, | who died Oct. 6, 1833, | aged 11 years | & 6 mon.

So fades the lovely blooming flower,
The smiling solace of an hour
So soon our transient comforts fly,
And pleasure only blooms to die.

1359. WILLIAM DUNHAM, | Born Oct 13, 1764; | Died Oct. 8, 1833; | Æ. 69 years.

Our life is ever on the wing,
And death is ever nigh:
The moment when our lives begin,
We all begin to die.

1360. In Memory of | Mr. THOMAS MORTON, | who died Oct. 15, 1833, | in the 77 year of his age. | Also his Son *THOMAS.* | who died at Sea on a | Passage from Savannah | to Philadelphia | July 14, 1815, | aged 18 years.

1361. REBECCA T. | Dau. of JAMES | & SARAH BARTLETT, | was born Dec. 31 | 1828, | & died Oct. 23, | 1833.

1362. MARY HARLOW | Daughter of | W. & M. B. SYL–VESTER | died October 31, 1833 | aged 3 months.

1363. MARTIN L. | died Nov. 1. 1833. | Æ. 4 y'rs. | CHARLES A. | died Jan. 13, 1847. | Æ. 4 mo's. | Children of MARTIN | and PHEBE BENSON.

Parents cease your bitter weeping
Although chastened by the rod,
For thy Children now are sleeping
In the bosom of their God.

1364. In   memory   of | LYDIA   ANN. | Daughter   of |
CHARLES & LYDIA WESGATE | who died Nov. 14, 1833 | aged 5
y'rs & 3 mon.

> Our daughter rests beneath the sod.
> Our hearts are with her there,
> Her spirit it hath gone to GOD,
> To dwell forever there.

1365. GEORGE SCHUYLER | son of SCHUYLER and |
SARAH T. SAMPSON, | died Nov'r 22, 1833; | aged 12 mo. &
24 ds.

> " This lovely bud, so young so fair,
> Call'd hence by early doom,
> Just came to show how sweet a flower
> In paradise would bloom."

1366. Erected | to the memory of | Mr. LEMUEL SIM-
MONS, | who died Dec. 11, 1833, | in the 85 year of his age. |
And | *Mrs. ABIGAIL*, his wife | died Oct. 2. 1817, | in the 66
year of her age.

> Their happy spirits onward rise
> To yon blest world above the skies.
>
> Come children view this place of rest
> Prepare and be forever blest.

1367. In memory of | Four Children of Capt. | EPHRAIM &
MARTHA PATY, | *Viz.* | *CORDELIA.* died Dec. Dec. 14, | 1833,
aged 2 y'rs 2 mon. & 19 days. | *SETH*, died Dec. 23. | 1833, |
aged 4 y'rs 2 mon. & 11 days. | *ELVIRA.* died Jan. 4. | 1834, |
aged 6 y'rs 4 mon. & 24 days. | *GEO. WINSLOW*, died Jan. 12,
1834, | aged 8 yrs. & 3 months.

1368. Erected | to the memory of | LEMUEL B. CHURCH-
ILL, | who died Dec'r 30, 1833: aged | 23 yr's 2 mo's and 17
days. | Son of HEMAN & JANE CHURCHILL. | Also | six children
viz | *HEMAN*, died Oct'r 1, 1802 Aged | 3 years & 11 mo's. |
JANE, died June 11, 1808: Aged | 7 years & 3 mo's. | *HE-
MAN*, died April 26, 1808: Aged | 2 years & 5 mo's. | *JANE
H.* | died April 26, 1812; Aged | 2 years 3 mo's and 25 days. |
two Sons in their infancy.

Sweet is the thought, the promise sweet,
That friends, long-severe'd friends shall meet;
That kindred souls, on earth disjoined,
Shall meet, from earthly dross refined.
Their mortal cares and sorrows o'er
And mingle hearts, to part no more.

1369. Erected | to the Memory of | NATHAN G. CUSH-
ING | who died Jan. 22, 1834, | in the 31st year | of his age.

No take me to your side, ye loved
Ye lost, yet once again —
To bear no more what I have borne
Nor be as I have been —
For rest, for rest, O give me room
And give me rest within the tomb.

1370. WILLIAM WALLACE | Son of | E. & M. A.
HOLMES, | died Feb'y 2. 1834 | aged | 1 yr. 10 mo's & 17 days.

Peaceful be thy slumbers
Thou darling of our love;
But thou art safe and happy,
In heavenly bliss above.
Thy troubles are all ended —
Thy pains, thy sufferings done;
Thy parents still will love thee,
Thou dear; thou only son. *

1371. MARY ANN, | dau'tr of SOLOMON and | MARY A.
SYLVESTER, died | Feb'y 3, 1834: | Aged 8 y'rs & 3 mon's. |
SOLOMON, died Oct'r | 8, 1825: Aged 13 mo's. | *FANNY*,
died March 24, | 1830; Aged 8 mo's.

She heard a voice we all must hear
Which said, no longer stay,
She saw a hand we all must see,
Which beckoned her away.

1372. GEORGE PERKINS, | died Feb. 6. 1834, | in the
54th y'r of his age.

---

* These lines are on the back of the stone.

" Receive O earth, his faded form,
In thy cold bosom let it lie;
Safe let it rest from every storm
Soon must it rise no more to die."

1373. Sacred | to the memory of | SYLVESTER DAVEE, | who died | Feb'y 15. 1834: | aged 28 years.

" Accept lov'd friend a lingering last farewell!
Long shall thy manly worth in memory dwell,
Taught by the example thy short life has giv'n,
O, may we wisely live, prepar'd for heaven."

1374. MASSENA FRANCIS | son | of | ANSIL & MIRIAM | C. HOLMES. | died Feb. 19, 1834, | aged 17 mon.

" Ere sin could blight, or sorrow fade,
Death timely came with friendly care,
The opening bud to heaven conveyed:
And bade it Bloom forever there.

1375. Erected | in memory of | *ELIZABETH,* wife of | Capt. JESSE TURNER, | died March 18th 1834, | in the 45th yr. of her age.

Farewell lov'd friend tho' neath the cold green sod
Thy form reposes, we will hold the dear,
Oft will we visit thy still small abode
And o'er thy ashes drop a silent tear.

1376. MARY HELEN, | died March 20. | 1834, | aged 3 yr's & 4 mon. | Dau'tr of | S. & M. W. BRAMHALL.

1377. In memory of | *BETSEY* daug. of | NATHANIEL & BETSEY | F. HOLMES | who died March 26, 1834 | Æt. 3 yrs. 9 mo. & 19 days.

Short sudden was the gale
That wafted her to rest,
Awhile the waves empetuous rush'd,
A moment tossing and twas hush'd.

1378. Erected | to the memory of | Capt. THOMAS AT-WOOD, | who Departed this life | April 23, 1834, | in the 65 year | of his age.

1379. Rev. | JAMES H. BUGBEE, | Preacher of the | Gospel of Christ, | Pastor of the | First Universalist | Society in | Plymouth, Died | May 10, 1834: | Aged 31 years.

Mr. BUGBEE was ordained as pastor of the First Universalist Church in Plymouth Dec. 22, 1826, the day of dedication of their new house of worship.

1380. Sacred | to the Memory of | Capt. JOHN FAUNCE, | who departed this life | June 19, 1834: | aged 46 years.

> *Gone to the resting place of man*
> *His long his silent home*
> *Where ages past have gone before*
> *Where future ages come.*

1381. In memory of | LEMUEL SAVERY | who died June 23, 1834, | Æt. 42 years. | Also his two children | CORDELIA B. | died Oct. 9, 1818, | Æt. 1 year 9 months. | ANN. M. | died Sept. 14, 1836, | Æt. 2 years 3 mons.

1382. Erected | In memory of | *SARAH*, wife of | JOSEPH R. PECKHAM | who died | June 29. 1834, | in her 34 yr.

1383. MARY ANN. | died July 3. 1834, | aged 3 yrs. and 4 mo. | ROBERT, | died May 5, 1833, | aged 3 mo. & 21 days. | Children of ROBERT | & ANN COWEN.

> *Let little children come to me*
> *Our blessed Saviour said:*
> *And to his arms on wings of love*
> *Their spotless souls have fled.*

1384. LORRAIN H. | Dau. of LUKE P. | & STELLA LINCOLN | died Aug. 31, 1834 | aged 1 year | & 8 mon.

1385. This Stone | Is Erected | in memory of | Dea. JESSE HARLOW | who departed | this life | Sept'r 3, 1834: | aged 42 years.

> *With silent steps he meekly trac'd the way,*
> *To the bright realms of love his wish'd abode,*
> *Nor did he ask a moments longer stay,*
> *When the last summons call'd his soul to God.*

1386.　MARY, | wife of | NATHANIEL DOTEN | died Sept. 23, 1834 | in the 59 y'r | of her age.

> *Thus fell the wife most kind*
> *The partner dear*
> *The tender parent*
> *And the friend sincere.*
>
> *In such an hour as ye think*
> *not the Son of man cometh.*
>
> **Matt.**

1387.　Erected | in memory of | three Children of | GEORGE & POLLY | WESTON. | LYDIA H. WESTON, | died Oct, 1, 1834. | aged 17 yrs. 3 mo. | JAMES H. WESTON, | died Feb. 2. 1830 | aged 1 yr 3 mo. | GEORGE WESTON Jr. | died Feb 2, 1823, | aged 5 days.

> *Our dearest friends, when death shal*
> *At once must hence depart;　call.*
> *In heaven, we hope to meet them all*
> *And never, never part.*

1388.　REBECAH. | Daug. of SIMEON | & MARY DIKE, | died Oct. 15. 1834, | aged 8 years | & 9 mon.

> *She heard a voice we could not hear*
> *Which said no longer stay,*
> *She saw a hand we could not see,*
> *Which beckon'd her away.*

1389.　In | Memory of | Mrs. EUNICE, | widow of | ELIJAH DUNHAM, | died Oct'r 31, 1834, | in the 78 y'r. | of her age.

> *Her happy soul we trust is with her GOD*
> *While all of earth now rest beneath the sod*
> *Till that blest morn shall burst the parting ski—*
> *When JESUS voice shall bid the dead arise.*

1390.　Erected | to the Memory of | WILLIAM MORTON, who died Nov. 2, 1834, | in the 32d. year of his age | And to | HENRY MORTON | who died March 3, 1840, | in the 25th year of his age.

To weep for those with heart sincere,
And on their graves to drop the tear,
Revives their memory — calls from the tomb
Their life, their love, their early doom.
Yet while we weep, we can rejoice,
In those who make a heaven their choice.

1391. JOANNA. | Relict of | ISAAC SYMMES, | died Dec. 14.
1834, | in the 81st year | of her age.

Tis GOD who lifts our comforts high
Or sinks them in the grave
He gives & blessed be his name
He takes but what he gave.

1392. In | Memory of | Mr. WILLIAM HUESTEN | who
died | Dec. 25. 1834 | aged 79 years.

Fled from the rageing storms of time,
And wafted to a smoother clime.

1393. In memory of | SARAH | wife of | Capt SAMUEL
ROBBINS; | who died | Dec. 31, 1834, | aged 76 years.

1394. CLARISSA, | wife of | SAMUEL ELLIOT, | died Jan.
27, 1835, | aged 39 years. | Also | an Infant Son.

1395. In memory of | *PRISCILLA*, wife of | LEMUEL SIM-
MONS, | who died March 1. 1835: | in the 42 yr. of her age |
Also | their infant son | who died | Jan'y 26, 1823: | aged 3
days.

1396. AMASA BARTLETT. | Born June 23. 1763, | Died
March 3, 1835. | SARAH TAYLOR, | Relict of | AMASA
BARTLETT, | Born June 29, 1767, | Died April 13, 1849.

1397. In memory of | Capt. JOSEPH BARTLETT | Born
June 16, 1762, | Died March 4 1835, | Also to his five Sons, |
JOHN, | JOSEPH, | SAMUEL, | BENJAMIN, | and AUGUS-
TUS.

1398. Miss ELEANOR MORTON | Daughter of | EDWARD
& SARAH MORTON | died March 6, 1835, | aged 40 years &
1 Month.

1399. MARY | wife of | Benjamin Ballard, | died **March** 9, 1835 | Aged 31 years.

> *Why do we mourn departing friends,*
> *Or shake at death's alarm,*
> *Tis but the voice that Jesus sends,*
> *To call them to his armes.*

1400. Sacred | to the memory of | *LUCIA*, wife of | Thomas Somes, of Boston | and dau'tr of the late | Capt. James Russell, who died | March 22, 1835: aged 47 yr's. | Also in memory of | *JAMES RUSSELL* son of the | late Capt James Russell, who | was lost at sea, May 12, 1819: | aged 29 yr's.

1401. In memory of | Deacon SOLOMON CHURCHILL | who died at Perry, Ohio | April 10, 1835, | aged 73 years : | And of | *ELIZABETH*, his wife, | (whose remains rest here) | deceased Oct. 26, 1811, | aged 45 years.

1402. REBECCA T. | daughter of Charles | & Abigail Churchill. | departed this life | May 12. 1835, | aged 1 **year** 10 months | & 19 days.

1403. BETHIAH | widow of | Jeremiah Holbrook, | died | May 26, 1835; | aged | 48 yrs. | Also | two infant children.

1404. In Memory of | LOTHROP TURNER, | who departed this life | June 16, 1835 | aged 73 years.

1405. MARY, | widow of | THOMAS CHURCHILL, | died July 12, 1835, | aged 76 y'rs.

1406. In | Memory of | SUKEY CRANDON, | wife of | Benjamin Crandon | who died July 16, 1835, | in her 67 y'r.

1407. EMELINE P. | wife of | William B. Cooper | died Aug, 9. 1835, | aged 20 years | and 8 mon.

> *A partner's withered hope is here*
> *Here friendship gives its faithful tear.*

1408. THOMAS MARSH, | died Sep'r 16, 1835; | Aged 61 yr's. | *WARREN*, son of the | above died at Sea Aug'st | 25, 1828: Aged 21 yr's. | *MARCY*, | dau'tr of the above | died Sept'r | 3, 1813; | Aged 9 mo's.

1409. In Memory of | POLLY. | widow of the late | DAVID HOLMES, | who died Sept. 19, 1835, | aged 56 yr's & 9 mo.

Dearest mother thou hast left us,
Here thy loss we deeply feel,
But tis GOD that hath bereft us,
He can all our Sorrows heal.

Yet again we hope to meet thee,
When the day of life is fled,
Then, in heaven, with joy to greet thee,
Where no farewell tear is shed.

1410. In memory of | *BETSEY*, consort of | JOHN HARLOW Ju^r | who died | Sept. 22. 1835, | in her 44 year. | Also MARY L. aged 1 year & 10 mo's; | and JOHN H. aged 7 mo's. | children of the above.

A husbands care: a husbands love,
Could not save her from the grave:
With thy children sweetly rest
And learn the anthems of the blest.

1411. In memory of | BENJAMIN M. WATSON Esq. | Born Nov. 15. 1774, | Died Nov. 12. 1835.

1412. In | memory of | Mr. JOHN BURBANK Jr. | who died | Nov. 30th, 1835, | aged 40 years.
" Behold I die, but GOD.
shall be with you."

1413. In memory of | ANN L. BOUTELLE. | who died Dec. 5, 1835, | Aged 16 yrs. | Also | ELLEN G. BOUTELL, | who died Sept. 3, 1823. | Aged 6 yrs. | Also | NATH. G. BOUTELL, | who died at Lexington | Sept. 26, 1816, | aged 1 yr & 3 mon.

1414. In memory of | Mr. JOB COBB, | died | Dec. 13, 1835: | in the 91st. yr. | of his age.

1415. Dr. ZACHEUS BARTLETT | Born Sept. 20, 1765 | Died Dec. 25, 1835. | HANNAH BARTLETT | Born Aug. 21. 1777, | Died June 21, 1858.

1416. HELEN AUGUSTA, | dau'tr of ANN | and WILLIAM
DREW 2d. | died | Jan'y 24, 1836: | Aged | 4 yr's & 4 mo.

> *Transplanted from the woes to come*
> *To heaven's immortal bower,*
> *Through all eternity to bloom,*
> *A sweet and fadeless flower.*

1417. CHARLES R. | son of | R. & E. FLEMMONS, | who
died In Taunton | Feb. 5. 1836, | aged 3 yrs. 10 mon. | & 18
days.

> *When from our eyes such loveliness is torn*
> *Tis not for them but for ourselves we mourn.*

1418. JAMES BRADFORD, | died March 1, 1836. | aged
49 yrs. | *SARAH*, their Dau. | died Oct. 19, 1832, | aged 2 y'rs
& 7 mon.

> *Earth, guard what here we lay in holy trust,*
> *That which hath left our home a darkened place,*
> *Wanting the form, the smile, was veiled in dust,*
> *The light departed with our fathers face;*
> *Yet from thy bonds undying hope springs free;*
> *We have but lent our father unto thee.*

1419. In | memory of | ISAAC, Son of | ISAAC & LOIS
TRIBBLE, | born July 26, | 1830, | died April 12, | 1836.

1420. Miss MARY ANN SEARS | died April 17, 1836, |
in the 20 year of her age. | HIRAM R. | died April 28, 1815, |
aged 19 mon. | Children of ELEAZER & | POLLY SEARS.

> *Farewell a short farewell,*
> *Till we shal meet again above*
> *In the sweet groves where pleasures dwell*
> *And trees of life bear fruits of love.*

1421. Erected | in memory of | MARY A. N. | Daugh. of |
JOSEPH & JANE BARNES | who died | April 18, 1836, | in her 7
year.

> *Sh's gone! I trust the God who gave,*
> *Has laid this fair flower in the grave—*
> *To pass beyond that narrow bourne:*
> *And join the choir before his throne.*

1422. In | memory of | Mrs. *SALLY* | Consort of | Capt.
WILLIAM BARNES, | who died | April 19, 1836, | Aged 59 y'rs.

Fled from the raging storms of time,
And Wafted to a smoother clime.

1423. Erected | in memory of | *Capt. LEWIS GOODWIN*
| who died April 26. 1836, | aged 53 yrs. | also | of *LORENZO*;
son of | LEWIS & ANNA GOODWIN, | who died Oct. 1. 1818,
aged 2 Mon.

What is our life — Tis but a moment lent;
A transient lease of earthly troubles given.
And, what is death. — Tis but a summons sent,
To call us from this tenement to Heaven.

1424. In memory of | BENJAMIN HOLMES, | died May 7,
1836, | aged 61 years.

1425. In memory of | Mr. ANSEL BARTLETT | died May
26. 1836, | aged 58 years. | Also | ANSEL BARTLETT | son of
the above | died in Bremen | Nov. 24, 1831, | aged 24 years.

1426. The remains | of | Mrs. ESTHER JACKSON, | wife
of | Wᴹ JACKSON Esqr | Rest here | Decᵈ June 1ˢᵗ, 1836 | aged
71.

1427. ANN ELIZABETH, | died July 24ᵗʰ, 1836, | Aged 3
y'rs & 7 mon. | GEORGE, | died April 19ᵗʰ, 1839, | Aged 3 y'rs
& 5 mon. | Children of JOHN & | BETSEY ANN EDDY.

1428. In Memory of | Mrs. *PHEBE.* | Consort of | CHAND-
LER HOLMES, | who died July 26, 1836, | aged 65 y'rs.

Blessed are the Dead who Die in the LORD.

1429. HARRIET FRANCES | dau. of ROBERT & | FANNY
DAVIE, | died | Aug. 4. 1836, | aged 7 yrs. 6 mo.

1430. Erected | in memory of | Mrs. MARY BARNES, |
wife of Capt Z. BARNES, | who departed this life | Oct'r 20 1836,
| aged 38 y'rs.

The months of affliction are o'er,
The days and the nights of distress,
We see her in anguish no more —
She's gained her happy release.

1431. In memory of | *HANNAH*. the virtuous | and amiable consort of Silvanus | Harlow, who after a distressing | illness of 6 months, which she | bore with unexampled forti- | tude, Untill exhausted natu | re compell'd her to say, I must | give up. | Departed this life Nov. 1, 1836. | aged 48 yrs & 19 d's.

> *Crop'd like a flower she wither'd in her bloom*
> *And flattering life had promis'd years to come*
> *The years she liv'd, in virtues path she trod*
> *But now her spirit sought to meet her god*
> *In realms of bliss, where joys eternal reign*
> *Devoid of care, and uncontroll'd by pain.*

1432. SALLY, | the wife of | Daniel Churchill, | died Nov. 3. 1836, | in the 60 y'r | of her age.

1433. This stone is Erected | As an unavailing tribute, | of respect and humanity | By the Children, | To *Mrs. HANNAH*, | wife of Mr. Jesse Harlow, | who Departed this life | November 18, 1836, | Aged 72 years & 6 months.

> *Her husband knew her worth*
> *Her children knew it well.*

1434. Erected | in memory of | JOSEPH CHURCHILL, | who Sailed from Boston | Nov. 1836 | in the Brig Plymouth Rock | of Plymouth, | Bound to Rochelle in France | and sup— posed Foundered | at Sea, aged 54 years. | Also to his Children | *JOSEPH LEWIS*, died at | sea on board the Brig | Andros- coggin of Portland | Aug. 1842, aged. 37 yrs. | *MARCIA GOODWIN*, | died May 2, 1839, | aged 22 years.

1435. ELISHA | Son of Elisha & | Betsey Waterman. | was Drowned | in Murdock's Pond | Dec'r 10, 1836, | aged 9 yrs & 4 mos.

1436. Sacred | to the memory of | Capt. SAMUEL C. DAVEE, | who died | at St. Thomas | Dec. 30, 1836, | aged 41 years.

> *Midst strangers in a foreign land*
> *Thou to thy Maker yield'st thy breath*
> *Thy generous heart, thy open hand*
> *Are silent in the arms of Death.*

Thy Partner on life's dreary waste
Weeps for thy loss, Oh! how severe,
And to thy memory, constant pays
The contrite heart, the silent tear.

1437. Erected | to the memory of | BATHSHEBA BRAD-
FORD | Dau'tr of LEMUEL & | BATHSHEBA BRADFORD | died
Jan'ry 15, 1837, | in the 22 y'r | of her age.

Ah, art thou gone, is thy short journey o'er
O lovely child, shall we not see thee more
Thy soul has gone to everlasting rest,
To dwell with Christ and be forever blest;
We'll not repine nor wish thee back again
To this dark world of trouble and of pain
Nor will we murmur at the hand divine,
That took our daughter Lord, for she was Thine.

1438. Erected | to the memory of | BETSEY T. DAVEE. |
dau'tr of JOHNSON, and | PHEBE DAVEE, | died Jan'y 23, 1837 |
Aged | 10 yr's and 9 mo's.

" We miss her in the hour of wo,
For then she tried to cheer,
And the soothing words of the pious child
Could dry the mourner's tear.

Even when she erred, we could not chide
For though the fault was small,
She always mourned so much and sued
For pardon from us all.

She was too pure for earthly love
Strength to our hearts was given
And we yielded her in her childhood's light,
To a brighter home in heaven.

1439. In | this sacred spot are | deposited the remains | of |
Mrs. RUTH L. SAMPSON | relict of | Hon. ZABDIEL SAMPSON :
| born April 10. 1784 | died Feb. 16, 1837.

1440. In | Remembrance | of | Miss MERCY RUSSELL, |
who | resigned this life | March 2, 1837, | aged 50 y'rs.

1441.   In memory of | ELISHA LAPHAM, | died March 8, 1837: | aged 19 yrs. 6 mo. | *ELIZA ANN,* died Nov. 17; | 1821: aged 10 mo. | *ELIZA ANN,* died | Nov. 20. 1823: | aged 1 yr. 2 mo. | Children of ELISHA & MARY LAPHAM.

> *Farewell farewell we could not bid thee stay*
> *From sin and sorrow soon thou art call'd away*
> *But O forgive this agony of heart,*
> *Tis hard dear children hard with thee to part.*

1442.   In memory of | *ESTHER,* wife of | OTIS CHURCHILL, | who | died March 8th. 1837; | in the 39th yr. | of her age.

> *The months of affliction are o'er,*
> *The days and the nights of distress,*
> *We see her in anguish no more,*
> *She has gained her happy release.*

1443.   WILLIAM ALFRED | son of WILLIAM & MARY B. SYLVESTER, | died | March 9. 1837, | aged 29 ds.

1444.   Erected | In memory of | Mr. BARNABAS HOLMES | who died March | 20, 1837. | aged 81 years.

> *By temperance governed and by reason taught,*
> *The path of peace and pleasantness he sought;*
> *With competence and length of days was blest,*
> *And cheered with hopes of everlasting rest.*

1445.   In Memory of | SUSANNA TURNER, | wife of LOTHROP TURNER, | who departed this life | May 15, 1837, | aged 70 y'rs.

1446.   ADRIANNA, | dau. of WILLIAM & | MARY CHURCH-ILL, died | May 15, 1837 Aged | 5 y'rs 3 m's & 11 ds. | also a female Infant | died Dec'r 12, 1834: | aged 19 days.

1447.   Sacred | to the memory of | Mr. JOSEPH BARNES, Jr | who died | May 38, 1837, | in the 49 y'r of his age.

> *" Youth oft times healthful and at ease,*
> *Anticipates a day it never sees,*
> *And many a tomb like this aloud,*
> *Exclaims: prepare thee for an early shroud."*

1448.   In memory of ICHABOD SHAW. | who was born. | November 14, 1769, | and died July | 26, 1837.

1449. In memory of | Mr. THOMAS JACKSON Jr. | who died | August 8, 1837: | aged 80 years.

1450. In memory of | Mrs. ZILPAH FAUNCE, | Consort of | Capt. BARNABUS FAUNCE | died Sept. 17. 1837. | in the 75 y'r | of her age.

1451. In | Memory of | WILLIAM ELLIS, 2d. | aged 22 years | who was Drown'd | in Plymouth Harbour | by the up-seting | of a Boat, | Sept. 24, 1837.

He was much respected by all who knew him.

1452. In memory of | Mrs. SARAH M. JACKSON, | widow of | THOMAS JACKSON Jr. | who died | Sepr 27th, 1837: | aged 76 years.

1453. MARTHA T. | Dau'r of ELISHA | & BETSEY WATER-MAN | died Nov. 7, 1837, | aged 4 y'rs | and 4 mon.

1454. In | Memory of | Miss MERCY HARLOW, | died | Nov. 9. 1837, | in the 60 y'r | of her age.

She died in hope, She died in faith
A life of suffering o'er
She smiling met the shafts of death
And lives to die no more.

1455. In memory of | Mr. NATHANIEL BRADFORD, | who died Nov. 24, 1837, | in the 90th. year of his age. | Also *RE-BECCA*, his wife | died June 15, 1838, | in the 85th. year of her age. | *ELIZABETH*, their dau. | died Oct. 1800, aged 6 yrs | *NATHANIEL*, their son | died in New York | June 11, 1830, aged 55 yrs.

1456. NAOMI, | died Dec. 7, 1837, | aged 9 mo. | & 18 ds. | HORACE, | died March 4, | 1841 | aged 6 mo. & 9 ds. | Children of | EDWARD & JULIA | SEYMOUR.

1457. SUSAN BRADFORD | wife of | HAMBLIN TILLSON, | departed this life | December 11, 1837. | in the 58th year | of her age.

Her Children arise up and call her blessed.

1458. Sacred | To the memory of | Mrs. MARY LANMAN | Widow of | Mr. PETER LANMAN | who died Jan. 5, 1838, | aged 73 y'rs.

1459. Sacred | to the memory of | JAMES MORTON | who
died | Jan. 18, 1838, | aged 31 y'rs.

> *'Tis but at most a short farewell,*
> *We bid to those we fondly love,*
> *Soon death will summon us to dwell*
> *With them, in brighter speres above.*

1460. NATHANIEL E. | son of | ALBA & HULDY | WOOD
| died Jan. 19, | 1838 | aged 2 mo's.

1461. Erected | to the memory of | Mrs. LYDIA RIDER |
widow of | Mr. WILLIAM RIDER, | died March 2, 1838 | in the
80 year of her age.

> *I now confide in Christ alone*
> *No other guide nor Lord I own*
> *Be glad my soul rejoice and sing*
> *He's both thy Saviour and thy King.*

1462. In memory of | Miss MARY THACHER | who died
| March 3. 1838, | aged 81 years.

1463. Erected to the memory of | HENRY HOLLIS, | who
died Mar. 9, 1838, | aged 45 years.

1464. In memory of | NATHANIEL THOMAS, | born |
Nov. 22, 1756: | and died | March 21, 1838.

1465. REBECCA W. MOORE, | wife of | Rev. JOSIAH
MOORE, | and the last | of the daughters of | WILLIAM STURTE-
VANT Esq. | died of Consumption, | at | Duxbury, April 7th, |
1838: | aged 33 years.

1466. Sacred | to the Memory of | ANGELINE. | dau'tr of
TRUMAN | and EXPERIENCE BARTLETT | died April 24, 1838: |
Aged 20 y'rs.

> *Weep not for her, whom the veil of the tomb*
> *In life's happy morning hath hid from our eyes,*
> *Ere sin threw a blight o'er the spirit's young bloom*
> *Or earth had profaned what was born for the skies.*

1467. In memory of | *LYDIA*, wife of | JACOB T. MOR-
TON, | who died | May 15, 1838, | aged 53 years, | Also 3 Chil-
dren | 2 Daughters & 1 Son.

1468. AMY ALLEN, | Daughter of JOHN & | LUCY BUR-
BANK, | died June 6th. 1838, | aged 2 years.

> " As the sweet flower that scents the morn
> But withers in the rising day:
> Thus lovely was this infants dawn,
> Thus swiftly fled its life away."

1469. Mrs. NANCY CHURCHILL | widow of | Mr. JOHN
CHURCHILL, | died July 11, 1838, | in her 54th year. | Also
their Son *JOHN*. | died May 15, 1806 | aged 11 mon.

> Yet again we hope to meet thee,
> When the stay of life is fled,
> Then in heaven with joy to greet thee
> Where no farewell tear is shed.

1470. *DORCAS*, wife of | EPHRAIM MORTON, | died | June
12, 1838: | in the 54th yr. | of her age. | Also | their dau'tr |
DORCAS, died, | Oct'r 16, 1806: | Aged 3 yr's.

1471. MARY EDWARDS, | died | June 12, 1838: | aged 2
y'rs 8 mo, & 2 ds. | WILLIAM THOMAS, | died | May 10.
1838: | aged 3 weeks & 3 ds. | Children of WILLIAM | & SUSAN
S. MOREY.

> See the lov'ly blooming flowers,
> Fades and withers in an hour,
> So our transient comforts fly,
> Pleasurs only bloom to die.

1472. In memory of | DEBORAH C. DAVIE | who died |
July 13. 1838. aged | 25 years. 5 mos | & 27 days.

> She winged her way to realms above,
> Where all is light, and life, and love,
> Forever with her Savior blest,
> Her home His bosom, there to rest.

1473. In memory of | Capt. SAMUEL | ROBBINS, | who
died | July 27, 1838, | aged 86 years.

1474. Erected | in memory of | Mrs ANNA GOODWIN |
wife of | Capt. LEWIS GOODWIN. | died Aug, 7, 1838. | in the 59
yr | of her age.

> *Cease then to murmur; — know that God is just;*
> *And learn this truth; for, it is His decreeing;*
> *Though dust must mingle with its mother dust,*
> *The Spirit flies to Him who gave it being."*

1475. JOSEPH THOMAS, | born Jany. 8th, 1755, | died August 10th, 1838 : | Captain of Artillery | during the War of the | Revolution.

1476. CHARLES FIELD | Born Jan. 14. 1804, | Died Aug. 22, 1838.

1477. SARAH ANN ELIZABETH | dau of WILLIAM & | SARAH NELSON, | died Sept. 8th, 1838 : | aged 1 year & 6 mo.

> *Thus fades a parents hope,*
> *The carnal turns to clay;*
> *In dust the soul no more will grope,*
> *But bloom in endless day.*

1478. EUNICE, | Relict of the late | JOHN WATSON, | Born. Feb. 5. 1759, | Died Sept. 14, 1838, | ELIZA ANN, | Dau. of the above, | Born March 28, 1799, | Died Sept. 14. 1847.

1479. ABNER F. | Son of NATH'L & | BETSEY D. FREEMAN | Died Sep. 1838 | aged 3 years.

1480. ABIGAIL ROGERS | died Oct. 7. 1838, | aged 86 y'rs | Consort of | SAMUEL ROGERS | who died at Sea | July 1795, | aged 42 y'rs.

1481. In memory of | Mrs. NATHAN HOLMES, | who died | Nov. 3. 1838; | in the 63d. yr. | of his age.

> *" Now he resides where Jesus is*
> *Above this dusky sphere;*
> *His soul was ripen'd for that bliss,*
> *While yet he sojourn'd here."*

1482. MARY W. | daughter of | Mr. JOSEPH B. & Mrs. MARY D. LOTHROP. | died | Nov. 15, 1838: | aged 6 ms. 13 ds.

> *Though hard for us to spare the now*
> *God saw the here opprest;*
> *And sent his angel down to earth*
> *To bring the hence to rest.*

1483. MARIA THOMAS | daughter of | *THOMAS* and | MARIA P. TRIBBLE, | died Novr. 25, 1838. | Æt. 17 y'rs 16 days.

> *Calm be the spot, where her form*
> *Now reposeth:*
> *May the friends who so loved*
> *Revisit the grave.*
> *And feel — though the cold sod*
> *Her ashes encloseth:*
> *She lives in the presence of him*
> *Who can save.*

1484. To | the memory of | Mrs. SARAH STURTEVANT, | widow of | WILLIAM STURTEVANT Esq'r | departed this life | Dec'r 5; 1838, | aged 69 years.

1485. In memory of | PRISCILLA, | wife of JOHN DAVIE: | who died | Dec. 10, 1838, aged | 19 years & 10 mo^{s.} | JOHN L. DAVIE, | their son, died Jan. 20, 1839, aged | 5 mo^s & 20 days.

1486. Sacred | to the memory of | Dea. JOSHUA TORREY | who departed this life | Dec. 22. 1838, | aged 71 years.

> *In faith and hope he trod the heavenly way,*
> *To meet the Saviour in the realms of day.*

1487. Erected | to the memory of | WILLIAM WESTON, | who departed this life | Decem. 28th, 1838, | aged 82 years. | Also *MARY*, his wife | departed this life | March 7th, 1843, | aged 83 years.

1488. In memory of | two children of CHA'S | & MARY R. WHITTEN, | JOSEPH W. | died Jan. 3. 1839, | Æ. 10 mo. | EDWARD W. | died April 6, 1849, | Æ. 5 y'rs 6 mo. 4 ds.

1489. ELIZA | wife of | ALBERT G. GOODWIN | died. | Jan. 16th 1839: | aged 39 years.

1490. In memory of | Mr. JOSEPH BARNES | who died | Jan. 28. 1839, | aged 75 y'rs.

1491. HEZEKIAH B. REED, | Died | Feb. 10, 1839, | Æ. 42 y'rs 8 mo. | Also his Infant daughter | EUNICE.

> *Our life is ever on the wing*
> *And death is ever nigh."*

1492. In | Memory of | Capt. *JAMES COLLINS* | died Feb. 17, 1839, aged 90 y'rs.

1493. OBED   KEMPTON | died | February 24. 1839: | Aged 24 years. | OBED W. KEMPTON | died June 17, 1855 : | Aged 16 years.

1494. Erected | to the memory of | Mr. BENJAMIN BAG-NELL | who died | March 8, 1839, | in the 47 year | of his age. | Also *ELIZABETH.* | dau. of BENJAMIN & | LUCY BAGNELL, | died Jan. 26, 1834, | aged 4 years & 8 mon.

1495. GRACE | wife of | ELLIS HOLMES, | died March 30. 1839 | aged 71 years. | Also *POLLY*, their Dau. | died Sept. 7. 1813. | aged 22 mon.

1496. Erected | to the memory of | Capt. SOLOMON DA-VEE, | who died | May 31, 1839, | in the 79 year | of his age.

> *An Honest Man, is the noblest work of GOD.*

1497. Dau. & Moth. | In Memory of | MEHITABLE P. LYNCH, | who died June 5, 1839, | in the 29 y'r | of her age. | also | MEHITABLE P. SMITH, | who died April 22. 1826, | aged 44 y'rs.

> *Our flesh shall slumber in the ground,*
> *Till the last trumpets joyful sound,*
> *Then burst the chains with sweet surprise,*
> *And in our Saviour's image rise.*

1498. In memory of | THOMAS BURGESS, | who died | June 11, 1839, | in the 51 year | of his age.

1499. ELIZABETH | Widow of | SAMUEL CHURCHILL, | died July 7th 1839, | in the 83d year | of her age.

1500. BETSEY | Daughter of JOHN & | LUCY BURBANK, | died Aug. 18th, 1839, | aged 10 years & 1 mo.

> *Her mothe's hopes of earthly joys are flown;*
> *Oh! who can tell her grief so 'reft and lone!*
> *Her lovely daughter, late her sole delight,*
> *For whom she lived, no more can bless her sight.*

1501. In memory of | *NANCY*, wife of | BENJAMIN HOLMES 2d, | died | August 29th, 1839. | in the 27th yr. | of her age.

1502. Sacred | to the memory of | GEORGE MORTON, | Son of | JAMES & BETSEY MORTON | who died Sept. 14, 1839, | Aged 18 years.

> *Brother thou art gone above — thy*
> *precious soul has flown,*
> *Where tears are wiped from every*
> *eye, and sorrow is unknown:*
> *And when the Lord shall summon*
> *us, whom thou hast left to mourn*
> *May we, untainted by the world*
> *meet at our Father's throne.*

1503. *WILLIAM JACKSON* Esq'r | Born July 14, 1763, | Died Oct'r 22, 1836, | aged 73.

> *Here rests an affectionate Parent*
> *A sincere friend & Christian.*

1504. BETSEY | wife of | ELIAB WOOD, | died Oct. 23, 1839, | in the 49th y'r | of her age.

1505. Erected | to the memory of | Capt FINNEY LEACH, | who departed this life | Novr 5th, 1839, | in the 65 year | of his age.

> *Forever, O Lord, thy word is settled in Heaven.*
>
> Scrip.
>
> *Tread lightly o'er this sacred ground,*
> *A resting place for mortal man*
> *Free from all care which earth abounds,*
> *For this short life is but a span.*
>
> *Stop! view your bed of earthly clay*
> *And think how soon your race is run,*
> *Prepare yourself without delay,*
> *For soon must be your setting sun.*

1506. In Memory of | MARTHA L. TURNER | wife of | DAVID TURNER | who departed this life | Nov. 6. 1839, | aged 29 yrs.

> *Farewell? thou sainted one, farewell!*
> *Though death each earthly tie hath riven,*
> *With heavenly hope our bosoms swell,*
> *That we shall meet again in Heaven.*

1507. ABIGAIL T. SAVERY, | wife of | THOMAS SPIN-
NEY, | of Boston Mass, | Obit Nov. 7, AD. 1839, Aged 42. |
Also In memory of her son | ROBERT HUNTRESS SPINNEY, | who
died in | New Orleans, on the 14 of | August 1843, aged 22.

1508. In memory of | Mrs RUTH HOLMES, | wife of | Mr.
NATHAN HOLMES, | who died Nov. 15. 1839, | in the 63d. yr |
of her age.

> " *Thrice happy souls, who're gone before*
> *To that inheritance divine!*
> *They labor, sorrow, sigh no more,*
> *But bright in endless glory shine.*"

1509. In memory of | LYDIA | Widow of the late | WIL-
LIAM KEEN, | died Dec. 7ᵗʰ 1839, | aged 72 y'rs.

> *But no, I would not call the hence —*
> *For thou art with the blest,*
> *And oh, may I prepare to be*
> *A sharer in thy rest.*

1510. WILLIAM DREW | Born Sept. 21, 1779. | Died Dec.
16, 1839.

1511. MARY HOLMES | dau. of | WILLIAM R. and | MARY
ANN COX, | died Dec. 23. | 1839 aged 7 mo. | and 9 ds.

1512. LYDIA H. | dau of AMERICA | & ELIZA ROGERS died
| Jan. 17th, 1840, | aged 2 yrs. & 1 mo.

> *Cease thy regrets, fond parents cease,*
> *Thy infant dwells in joy and peace,*
> *Tis free from care, grief and pain;*
> *To her thy los, is perfect gain.*

1513. ELIZABETH ANN | HAYWARD, | daughter of NA-
THAN & JOANNA | HAYWARD, | died Feb. 3, 1840, | aged 35
years.

1514. Erected | to the memory of | Miss NANCY HAR-
LOW | who died | Feb. 3. 1840, | in the 55 year | of her age,

1515. In memory of | *LUCY*, wife of | SAMUEL BRADFORD,
| died Feb. 10th. 1840, | in the 44th yr | of her age.

Farewell my friends and kindred dear,
Farewell my children too,
Farewell my husband near and dear,
I bid you all adieu.

Blessed are the dead who die in the LORD.

1516. *BRIDGHAM RUSSELL* Esq. | died March 29th **1840**: | aged 47 years.

The many exelencies of his
character in public and private
life — endeared him to an extensive
acquaintance, who will long
cherish his virtuous memory.

Blest thought! he is not lost
But gone before us.

1517. ALMIRA JUDSON, | dau of JUDSON | & ALMIRA RICE, | died | April 27, 1840. | aged 5 years 4 mo.

The loved one sleeps she sleeps serene,
In the dark bosom of the tomb,
And the pale moon with trembling beam,
Is gliding bright its dreary gloom.

1518. In memory of | NATHANIEL CLARK, | who died April 28, 1840, | aged 75 years. | Also | ABIGAIL CLARK, | wife of the above. | died Nov. 18, 1817, | aged 54 years.

1519. In | memory of | Mrs. MARY COLLINS | widow of | JAMES COLLINS | who died | May 28th, 1840, | aged 83 years.

1520. CORDELIA B. | wife of CHARLES TUFTS, | died June 20, 1840; | Aged 32 years. | CHARLES HENRY, | Son of CHARLES & | CORDELIA B. TUFTS, | died July 15, 1841; | Aged 2 years.

1521. In memory of | LYDIA, | wife of EBEN^R DAVIE, | who died | June 29, 1840, aged | 63 years. | NATHANIEL C. DAVIE, | their son, died at Amsterdam, | Oct. 6. 1839. | aged 19 years, 10 mos & 6 days.

1522. *ELEANOR*, wife of | JAMES BRADFORD, | died | July

29. 1840, | aged 43 yrs. | *WILLIAM*, their son | died Oct. 24, 1836, | aged 9 yrs.

> *But thou, O heaven, keep, keep what thou hast taken,*
> *And with our treasure keep our hearts on high:*
> *The spirit meek and yet by pain unshaken,*
> *The faith, the love the lofty constancy —*
> *Guide us where these are with our blessed flown;*
> *hey were of thee, and thou hast claimed thine own.*

1523.   REBEKAH | Relict of | NOAH GALE, | Died | Aug: 10. 1840, | Æt. 86. | NOAH GALE, | Lost in a storm on | Block Island | Nov. 1806. Æt. 49.

> *Rest in peace.*

1524.   MARY B. | dau. of | SOLOMON & ANNA | RICHMOND, died | Aug. 14th, 1840, | aged 7 mo & 5 ds.

1525.   SUSANNAH W. | wife of | IGNATIUS PIERCE Jr. | died Aug. 24. 1840, | aged 22 years. | Also their Son | died July 26, 1838.

> *A husbands care a husbands love*
> *Could not save her from the grave*
> *With thy child now sweetly rest*
> *And learn the anthems of the blest.*

1526.   In memory of | NANCY D. PAULDING | who died | Aug. 27, 1840, | aged 43 years.

> *Christ my Redeemer lives*
> *And often from the skies*
> *Looks down and watches all my dust*
> *Till he shall bid it rise.*

1527.   JANE WIGHT | Dau. of BRADFORD L. | & NANCY BATTLES, | died Sept. 4, 1840, | aged 4 years | and 5 Months.

1528.   LUCY | Daughter of | Capt. IGNATIUS | & BETSFY PIERCE | died Oct. 16, 1840, | aged 18 years.

> *My flesh shall rest beneath the ground*
> *Till the great trumpets joyful sound*
> *Then i'll awake in glad surprise*
> *And in my Saviours image rise.*

1529. In | memory of | Mrs. LUCY WESTON, | who departed this | life Oct. 16, 1840, | in the 84 year | of her age.

Blessed are the dead who die in the
LORD.

1530. Sacred | to the Memory of | Mr. SOLOMON RICHMOND, | who died | Oct. 16th 1840: | aged 58 yr's.

1531. GEORGIANA. | dau. of | NATHANIEL & | JANE BURGESS, | died | Oct. 18, 1840, | aged 7 yrs. 3 mo.

1532. In | memory of | MARGARET JAMES, | wife of | Capt. THOMAS BARTLETT, | who died | Oct. 23d. 1840, | aged 65 years.

1533. *He that wounds can heal.*
Sacred to the memory of | Capt. *EZRA HARLOW*, who died | suddenly Oct. 27th, 1840, aged 68 yrs.
Our loss is his gain, though the body lies mouldering bene | ath this sod, the Spirit has gone to God, there to receive the | reward of all his labours of love, he lived a life of self denial that | he might releive the distres'd, though dead he lives forever more, | O glorious hope, O bless'd abode I shall be near and like my God, | O the depth of the riches both of the wisdom and knowled | ge of God! how unsearchable are his judgments: and | his ways past finding out!

I leave the world without a tear,
Save for the friend I hold so dear
To heal her sorrows, Lord! descend,
And to the friendless, prove a friend.

The sick the pris'ner, poor and blind,
And all the sons of grief,
In him a benefactor found —
He loved to give relief.

Tis love that makes religion sweet
Tis love that makes us rise,
With willing minds and ardent feet,
To yonder happy skies.

1534. In | memory of | Mr. THOMAS JACKSON | who died | Nov. 10, 1840, | aged 86 years.

1535.   MARY B. | wife of WM. NICKERSON, | died Nov. 18.
1840: | aged 37 years. | MARIA H. | died Oct. 3. 1826: | Æ. 1
day.

WARREN M.	MARIA A.
died Mar. 8. 1830:	died June 21, 1832:
Æ. 2 days.	Æ. 2 mo's & 22 days.

Children of WILLIAM & MARY | NICKERSON.

1536.   HEMAN CHURCHILL, | died Nov. 22. 1840. | in his
69 yr. | Also *JANE*, his widow, died April 2. 1848. | in her.
73 yr.

" *Why do we mourn departing friends,*
Or shake at death's alarms?
Tis but the voice that Jesus sends,
To call us to his arms."

1537.   JERUSHA, | wife of | CHARLES L. FAUNCE | died |
Dec. 5th, 1840, | aged 26 years.

She hath gone to that radiant shore,
Where the bowers are mansions of rest;
Where weeping for ever is o'er,
And the spirit for ever is blest.

1538.   JAMES BARTLETT, | Born Aug. 7. 1760, | Died
Dec. 22, 1840.

1539.   This stone is erected | by her surviving connexions, |
to perpetuate the memory of | HANNAH WHITE, | daughter of
GIDEON and JOANNA WHITE, | who died January 3, 1841. | aged
93 years. | Her long pilgrimage on earth | was ennobled by the
practice of the duties | of Christianity. | cheered by its hopes, |
and sustained by its faith.

1540.   To the Memory of | Mr. LEMUEL COBB, | who died
| Jan'y 4th, 1841, | in the 66th, y'r | of his age.

That manly virtue, that adorned thy bloom,
Friendship recalls and weeps upon thy tomb,
The sad remembrance drops a silent tear,
While chaste affection stands a mourner here.

1541.   EXPERIENCE, | wife of TRUMAN BARTLETT, | Born
April 5th, 1780: | Died Jan. 11th. 1841, | STEPHEN, Son of
TRUMAN & | EXPERIENCE BARTLETT | died at Buenos Ayres |
Dec. 16th. 1840: | aged 38 years.

1542. Erected | to the memory of | PHEBE C. | wife of | THOMAS BARTLETT 2ᵈ· | who died Jan. 25, 1841. | aged 29 years.

> *Farewell my husband near and dear,*
> *Farewell my children too,*
> *Trust in GOD for happiness,*
> *And wisdoms paths persue.*

1543. HULDY | wife of | ALBY WOOD, | died March 3, 1841, | aged 48 years.

1544. ANSEL HOLMES | Consort of | MIRIAM C. HOLMES, died March 3d, 1841, | aged 38 years. | Also their Son *ANSEL* | died Sept. 11ᵗʰ, 1840. | aged 3 months.

1545. Sacred | to the memory | of | RIZPA NICHOLS, | wife of MOSES NICHOLS, | who died March 4, 1841, | aged 84 years.

1546. In memory of | WILLIAM H. JEWETT, | who died | March 31, 1841, | in the 26 year | of his age.

1547. LEMUEL F. | Son of L. T. & | LYDIA ROBBINS, | died May 1 1841, | aged 3 years | & 3 mon.

1548. *SARAH*, relict of | THOMAS MORTON, | died | May 22, 1841, | aged 81 years. & 9 mos.

> *My Saviour summons me away,*
> *A brighter world to see,*
> *Although a while behind you stay,*
> *Weep not, weep not for me.*

1549. Erected | to the memory of | Capt. JOHN CLARK, | who died | May 30, 1841, | aged 74 years.

> *Hark! the sad sound, that spirit bright has fled,*
> *That once bright form lies numbered with the dead,*
> *He was a tender husband, father, dear,*
> *Come, all who knew him drop a social tear.*

1550. CAROLINE JACKSON | died | June 5. 1841, | aged 48 years.

1551. In | memory of | BETSEY S. | Wife of | ELIAB WOOD Jr. | who died | June 13. 1841, | aged 25 years.

1552. In memory of | JOHN DAVIE, | who died | June 27, 1841 aged | 32 years 11 moˢ | & 15 days.

1553. Erected | in memory of | RICHARD HOLMES, | Born Sept. 7. 1777, | died July 4, 1841.

Hear what the voice from Heaven proclaims
For all the pious dead;
Sweet is the savour of their names
And soft their sleeping bed.

Far from this world of toil and strife,
They're present with the Lord;
The labors of their mortal life
End in a large reward.

1554. In memory of | Mrs. PATTY WESTON, | who died | July 27, 1841, | aged 78 years. | THOMAS WESTON, | son of Capt. COOMER and | Mrs. PATTY WESTON | died at St. Pierres | Martinique, | Dec. 10. 1808, | aged 20 years.

1555. PHINEAS PIERCE | died Aug'st 10th 1841, | aged 37 years. | Also | REBECCA JANE. | Daugh'r of PHINEAS | & DORCAS M. PIERCE, | died Sep'r 8th, 1833, | aged 4 years.

1556. THOMAS BARTLETT, | Born March 10, 1776, | Died August 18, 1841, | LUCIA, | daughter of TRUMAN | and EXPERIENCE BARTLETT, | Born July 4, 1813, | Died October 3, 1841.

1557. Erected | to the memory of | Miss SARAH WHIT- MARSH, | of Boston, | who died | Sept. 19th. 1841, | in the 64th y'r. | of her age.

She was beloved by all who knew her
Worth.

1558. In | memory of | BENJ. CRANDON Esq, | who died Sept. 28, 1841, | in his 78th | year.
He was appointed Inspector of the Customs of Duxbury, | under the administration of Gen. Washington, | and held the office of Dep. Collector and Inspector of | Plymouth, untill April 20ᵗʰ, 1841, having held | the office under every President of the | United States.

1559. Sacred | to the memory of | JANE | wife of FRED-
ERICK | ROBBINS: | who died Oct. 11, 1841, | aged 38 y^s, 1 mo.
| and 11 days. | HANNAH HARLOW | dau. of the above, died
May | 27, 1838, aged 1 y^r, & 11 days.

When the Christian's race is run,
Tho' low she slumbers in the ground,
Her virtues, like the setting sun,
Shall shed a heavenly lustre round.

1560. CATHARINE, | Daug. of NATHANIEL | & BETSY
HARLOW, | died Nov. 30th. 1841, | Aged 11 y'rs 2 mon. | & 28
days.

1561. HARRIET N. | Daugh. of ELEAZER | & POLLY SEARS.
| Died Dec. 29th, 1841, | Aged 19 years.

From the grave so dark & drear
Thoughts of comfort rise,
Our darling Sister is not here
She lives beyond the skies.

1562. In | memory of | Miss. ESTHER HOLMES | who
died | Jan. 6. 1842, | aged 32 yrs.

1563. Erected | to the memory of | Mr. NATHAN REED.
| who died | January 12, 1842, | in the 78 y'r | of his age.

So man lieth down, and riseth not:
till the heavens be no more, they shall
not awake, nor be raised out of their sleep.
JOB, 14, 12.

1564. Sacred | to the memory of | Mrs. ABIGAIL, | wid. of
the late Rev. | ADONIRAM JUDSON | who died | Jan. 31. 1842,
aged | 82 years.

Her hope was in the Gospel of our
Lord and Saviour Jesus Christ. She
felt the balm and efficacy of those lea-
-ves which are for the healing of
the nations.
A guilty weak and helpless worm,
On thy kind arms I fall;
Be thou my guide and righteousness,
My Jesus and my all.

1565. NANCY CARVER, | Dau. of BENJ. & | JOANNA WES-
TON, | died March 18, 1842, | in the 27 y'r | of her age.

> Could our fond gaze but follow where
> thou art,
> Well might the glories of this world
> Seem naught,
> To the one promise given the pure
> in heart.

1566. ZERUAH THOMAS, | Born in | Middleboro' | Died
in Plymouth | March 23, 1842, | Aged 52 years.

1567. In memory of | Mr. SAMUEL ELLIS, | who died |
April 2. 1842 | aged 49 years.

1568. Sacred | to the memory of | ISRAEL HOYT, | who
died | May. 6, 1842, | aged 53 yrs. | Also BETSEY M. dau. | of
ISRAEL & RUTH | HOYT, died | Jan. 6. 1824, | aged 3 yrs. 7 mo.

1569. Erected | to the memory of | Mrs. LUCY MARCY; |
wife of the late | Dr. STEPHEN MARCY, | who died June 13, 1842
| aged 83 years.

> " Servant of GOD well done;
> Rest from thy loved employ;
> The battle fought: the victory won,
> Enter thy Master's Joy."

1570. ELIAB WOOD | died June 14, 1842 | in the 57 year |
of his age.

> For our hearts shall rejoice
> in him, because we have
> trusted in his holy name.

1571. HARRIET ELIZABETH | dau. of WM. & H. M. |
ATWOOD, died | June 29, 1842, | aged 3 yrs 4 mo.

> Yet, O child beloved, while my loss i mourn,
> Not a tear is shed for thee;
> For thy soul uncaged has fled to its home,
> In a world of purity.

1572. HENRY O. | died July 27th. 1842. | aged 4 mon. & 19
days. | HENRY O. | died Sept. 4th 1843. | aged 2 mon. & 5
days. | CLARIBEL T. | died Dec. 29th 1844, | aged 4 years &
17 days. | Children of HENRY O. | & BETHIAH STEWARD.

Jesus : aid suffer little children,
and forbid them not, to come unto
me, for of such is the kingdom of
heaven.

1573. WILLIAM H. | died Aug. 2, 1842; | aged 1 y'r & 1 mo. | CHARLES B. | died Oct. 4, 1849; | aged 5 mo's & 15 d's. JAMES S. | died Feb. 2, 1854; | aged 14 y'rs & 6 mo's. | Children of THADIUS & | MARY A. FAUNCE.

By agels borne they fly to rest,
We know 'tis well nay more 'tis best;
When we our Pilgrim path hath trod,
We hope to meet them all with God.

1574. MARCIA, | born December 16, 1840, | died August 2, 1842, | ANDREW, | born March 7, 1839, | died July 9, 1845, | SOPHIA GORDON, | born March 15, 1833, | died September 20, 1845. | Children of JACOB & JOANN JACKSON. | Also *LA-VANTIA*, | born June 14, 1831, | died September 23, 1851.

1575. ELIZABETH S. | died | Aug. 4. 1842, | aged 2 mo. & 7 ds. | REBECCA F. | died Oct. 6. 1847, | aged 2 yrs & 9 mo. | Children | of EBENEZER S. | & REBECCA GRIFFIN. | GEORGE W.) 14 mo. | *Innocence.*

1576. Erected | to the memory of | Miss POLLY BURBANK | who died | Aug'st 23d 1842, | aged 70 years.

1577. Erected | in memory of | LYDIA GOODWIN, | Consort of | NATH'IEL GOODWIN, | died Aug. 29. 1842, | in her 74th year.

1578. In memory of | *MRS. LUCY* wife of | Capt. JOSEPH COOPER, | who died. Oct. 13. 1842, | aged 70 years.

1579. NATHANIEL CARVER, | died Oct. 18, 1842, | aged 78 yrs. | JOANNA CARVER, | died April 10, 1842, | aged 76 yrs. | NATHANIEL CARVER Jr. | died Oct. 2, 1823, | aged 32 yrs. | *BETSEY*, his wife | died Sept. 23, 1814, | aged 27 yrs, | *NANCY*, his wife | died Feb. 22, 1826, | aged 30 yrs. | *NANCY* | dau. of NATHANIEL | & NANCY CARVER. | died Sept. 2. 1824, | aged 13 mo. | STEPHEN, | died March 14, 1790, | aged 45

ds. | NANCY, | died Sept. 24, 1798, | aged 1 yr. & 8 mo. |
NANCY, | died Nov. 27, 1814, | aged 14 yrs, & 9 mo. | MARY,
| died Nov. 10. 1811, | aged 3 mo. | Children of | NATHANIEL
& JOANNA | CARVER.

1580. "HAVING A DESIRE TO DEPART AND TO BE WITH
CHRIST." | Sacred | to the memory of | Dea. WILLIAM P.
RIPLEY, | who died Nov. 10. 1842; | aged 67 years. | A friend
of the oppressed | and enslaved.

> *The poor will cherish his memory,*
> *The widow and the fatherless shall*
> *call him blessed.*
>
> *His life was gentle, and serene his mind,*
> *His morals pure, in every action just,*
> *A husband dear, and as a parent kind;*
> *As such he lies lamented in the dust.*
> *While weeping friends bend o'er the silent tomb,*
> *Recount his virtues and his loss deplore,*
> *Faith's piercing eye darts through the dreary gloom,*
> *And hails him bless'd where tears shall flow no more.*

1581. In memory of | JOHN ALEXANDER, | who died |
Dec. 5, 1842, | Æt. 32 y'rs 27 ds. | Also his daugh. GEOR-
GIANNA, | Æt. 14 mo.

1582. MARY W. | Daughter of the late | ZEACHEUS & MARY
| BARNES, | died Dec. 11th, 1842, | aged 14 years.

> *Think of that bright world where I*
> *No more shall suffer pain,*
> *And of that Haven where all of us*
> *May hope to meet again.*

1583. MARY SOPHIA BROWN | aged 21 | died Dec. 19,
1842.

> *"Blessed are the pure in heart."*

1584. WILLIAM BRADFORD | Born June 1, 1775, | Died
July 25, 1816, | Ae. 41. | Also his wife | NANCY, | Born Jan'y
28, 1775, | Died Jan'y 27, 1843, | Ae. 68.

1585. ESTHER DOTEN | widow of | EDWARD DOTEN, |
died Jan, 27, 1843, | aged 67 years. | Also their son *LEWIS*, |
died Feb'ry 27, 1839. | aged 26 years.

1586. In memory of | Mrs. LYDIA COTTON, | widow of | Capt. JOSIAH COTTON, | died Jan. 28th 1843, | aged 63 yrs.

1587. In | Memory of | SAMUEL COLE. | who died | April 1st, 1843, | aged 62 years.

> *Yes thou art gone and we no more*
> *Shall know thy dwelling here below,*
> *But yet we trust a brighter shore*
> *Is thine beyond the bounds of woe.*

1588. EUNICE STURTEVANT, | died May 10, 1843: | aged 15 years. | SAMUEL DREW, | Was lost at Sea Feb. 1, 1837: | aged 18 years. | Children of PERKINS & | ELIZABETH RAYMOND.

> *That gentle one has passed away*
> *No more to roam with us below:*
> *And gone to realms of brighter day,*
> *Where storms of woe shall ceas to flow,*
> *Where'er our eyes do chance to fall,*
> *We find some relic left behind*
> *That will her feeble form recall*
> *And bring her peaceful voice to mind,*
> *Then we'll not wish her back again,*
> *But think she's happy now on high:*
> *No more to strive with earthly pain,*
> *No more to weep & groan & die,*
> *And as we ne'er can meet below,*
> *Our only wish & prayer shall be*
> *That when far hence we're called to go*
> *We may in heaven her spirit see.*

1589. In Memory of | PHEBE SOULE, | wife of | J. RUSSELL DIKE, | who died | May 16, 1843, | Æ. 24 y'rs. | Also their son RUSSELL R. | Æ. 3 mo. 11 days.

1590. Erected | to the memory of | SIMEON DIKE, | who died | June 4th 1843, | aged 62 y'rs.

> " *Sleep dearest Husband, while above thee*
> *Flows the sad and silent tear;*
> *Oft at eve shall those that love thee,*
> *Weep and pray unnoticed here.*"

1591. Erected | to the Memory of | ELIAS COX, | who died | June 8, 1843, | in the 71 y'r | of his age.

1592. MARY ELLEN. | Dau. of | WILLIAM H. & | MARY S. MORTON, | died June 23. | 1843 | aged 10 weeks.

1593. LYDIA ANN, | dau. of JOSHUA | & LYDIA STANDISH | died July 1. 1843 | aged 3 yrs. & 8 mo.

1594. In | memory of | Mrs. LUCY, | widow of | Mr. THOMAS BURGESS, | who Departed this life | July 5th 1843, | aged 58 y'rs.

1595. In memory of | MARY, | Consort of | LEWIS CHURCH-ILL, | died July 19. 1843, | aged 32 y'rs. | Also two Children | STEPHEN, aged 1 y'r. | STEPHEN, aged 3 mo.

1596. LUCRETIA, | wife of | JOHN PIERCE | and consort of CYRUS B. PHILLIPS, | died Sept. 8, 1843, | in the 46th. yr. | of her age.

1597. In | memory of | CYNTHIA BARTLETT, | widow of | JOHN BARTLETT 3d. | who died | Sept. 11th, 1843, | aged 47 years.

> She died in hope, she died in faith
> A life of suffering o'er
> She smiling met the shafts of death
> And lives to die no more.

1598. Erected | In memory of | CHARLES ALWIN, | GRA-TON | son of ALWIN M. & MARY D. | GRATON, | who died Oct. 10, 1843, | Æt. 19 years 6 mo.

1599. Mrs. BETSEY, wife of | DAVID BRADFORD, | died Nov. 26. 1843. | aged 46 yrs. 4 mo. | Also 5 children | DESIRE H. died | July 28, 1825, aged 19 mo. | ANDREW J. died | June 10, 1833, aged 18 mo. | LYDIA H. died | Aug. 9. 1834, aged 8 mo. | LYDIA H. died | Sept. 27, 1837, aged 2 yrs. 2 mo. | DAVID L. died | Aug 31, 1838, aged 17 yrs. 4 mo.

> Rest sweetly, dear Wife and lovely Children until morning;
> Then will the Archangel, with his shrill trumpet,
> Burst thy tomb; and cause thee to spring into Life Eternal,
> Sparkling with brightness.

1600.   In memory of | JAMES BAXTER, | who died | Dec. 11, 1843, | aged 52. | and three of his children. | ABNER MORTON | died Aug. 29, 1826, | aged 3 ; | CHARLES HOMER | died Aug. 29, 1843, | aged 8 ; | ANN ELIZABETH | died Dec. 29, 1844, | aged 15 years.

1601.   In memory of | Capt. CHANDLER HOLMES, | who died | Jan. 14th, 1844, | in the 72 year | of his age.

1602.   In memory of | Miss MARY FAUNCE | died Feb. 1, 1844, | aged 61 yrs.

1603.   MARIA, | died Feb. 12, 1844, aged 15 y'rs & 8 mo's.

> *She bid farewell to all below*
> *To dwell among the just,*
> *And thus resigned her youthful form*
> *To Slumber in the dust.*
>
> *To parents, brothers, sisters dear,*
> *She speaks in tones of love,*
> *I shall meet you all again*
> *In realms of bliss above.*
>
> *When every tear is wiped away,*
> *From all our weeping eyes,*
> *When the last trumpets joyful sound*
> *Shall echo through the skies.*

JOHN, died Jan. 10. 1819, | aged 1 yr & 11 mo's. | *JACOB,* died May 16, 1823, | aged 1 y'r & 8 mo's. | *JACOB,* died Aug. 16. 1825, | aged 1 yr & 1 mo. | Children of | JOHN & LYDIA NICKERSON.

1604.   In | memory of | ISAAC DREW, | who departed | this life | March 2ᵈ 1844, | aged 54 years | & 6 mon.

> *Precious in the sight of the Lord*
> *is the death of his saints.*

1605.   Erected | in memory of | SETH MORTON, | who died | April 12th. 1844. | in the 70th. year | of his age.

1606.   In memory of | Miss SARAH TUFTS, | who died | April 18, 1844, | aged 49 years.

1667.   In memory of | JAMES THACHER, M. D. | a surgeon in the army during | the war of the Revolution ; | after-

wards, for many years, | a practising physician | in the county
of Plymouth; | the author of several historical | and scientific
works: | esteemed of all men | for piety and benevolence, | pub-
lic spirit and private kindness. | Born February 14, 1754, | Died
May 26, 1844. | Also of | SUSAN THACHER, | for 57 years,
his pious | and faithful wife. | who died May 17. 1842, | aged 86
years.

1608. MARY ANN, | wife of | MENDAL PIERCE, | died June
2, 1844, | in her 25th yr. | Also their dau'tr | ANN ELIZA-
BETH, | died Jan. 22, 1844, | aged 5 mo. 15 ds.

Behold the righteous marching home,
And all the angels bid them come,
While Christ the judge, their joy proclaims
Here comes my saints I know their names.

1609. WILLIAM ROGERS | died June 16th. 1844, | Aged
77 y'rs | & 6 mo.

1610. Here lies the body of | HANNAH | widow of the late
| THOMAS NICHOLSON | of this Town and daughter | of the late
JOHN OTIS | of Barnstable, | who died in Boston | June 23, 1844,
| aged 76 years.

1611. MARY, | widow of | GEORGE MORTON, | died Sept.
4, 1844, | aged 88 yrs. | Also | HANNAH WITHERELL, |
died Jan. 18, 1834. | aged 94 yrs.

1612. WILLIAM NELSON, | Son of | J. & M. S. PIERCE,
| died Sept. 18, 1844 | aged 18 mo.

Dear little babe thy
months were few,
And suffering was
thy lot below:
But Jesus' call thou
hast obeyed,
And left this world
of sin and wo.

1613. In memory of | DANIEL GODDARD, | who died
Oct. 30, 1844, | in his 73 year | Also | *LEMUEL,* his Son |
died in South America 1842. | in his 37 year.

1614. In memory of | two children of | SAMUEL M. & | HARRIET B. WHITTEN, | Viz. *SAMUEL*, died | Dec. 24th, 1844, | in his 4th yr. | HARRIET B. died | Aug. 15th 1838. | aged 3 weeks.

Twise deaths keen shafts have smitten here
Spoiling what nature holds most dear,
Fond parents faint not GOD reproves
And chastenes oft where most he loves.

1615. In memory of | Mrs. *SARAH.* widow | of JOHN WARLAND | of Cambridge | who died | Feb. 9. 1845, | aged 85 yrs.

1616. PATIENCE C. HOLMES, | daugh. of | NATHAN & RUTH HOLMES, | died April 1, 1845, | in her 24 y'r.

Shed not for her the bitter tear,
Nor give the heart to vain regret;
Tis but the casket that lies here,
The gem that fill'd it sparkles yet.

1617. WILLIAM BROWN Esq. | died May 9, 1845, | in the 61st y'r | of his age. | Also three Children Viz. | *LYDIA*, died Sept 28, 1809, | aged 9 weeks. | *WILLIAM*, died Sept. 14, 1813, | aged 3 y'rs & 2 mon. | ABIGAIL ALLEN, | died Sept. 28, 1813, | aged 1 y'r & 5 Mon.

1618, AMERICA PIERCE, | died May 9, 1845; | aged 77 years. | MARGARET DREW, | his wife | died Sept. 15. 1806; | aged 35 years.

1619. In memory of | SUSAN H. ALLEN, | wife of | JAMES H. DREW, | who died | May 22, 1845, | aged 38 years.

1620. ELIZABETH F. | died | Sept. 4, 1845, | aged 23 yrs. | LEWIS O. | was lost at Sea | Oct. 3. 1841. | aged 17 yrs. | BARNABAS L. | died | June 5, 1838, | aged 3 yrs. & 5 mo. | Also 4 Infants, | Children of | LEWIS & BETSEY HARLOW.

1621. LUCIA R. | dau. of NATHAN B. | & LUCIA W. ROBBINS, | died Sept. 7, 1845, | in the 22 yr. | of her age.

1622. ELKANAH CHURCHILL | died Oct. 7, 1845; | in his 37 years.

> *Look here my friends and read your doom.*
> *For you are hast'ning to your tomb.*

1623. FANNA A. | Daughter of | Mr. HENRY H. | Mrs. MERCY M. | ROBBINS, | Died Oct. 9. 1845 | aged 2 yrs, 10 Mo's.

1624. In memory of | LEMUEL BROWN | who died | Nov. 19th. 1845 | aged 73 years.

> *The dead how sacred.*
> Young.

1625. BARNABAS A. BROWN, | died Jan. 6. 1846 | in in the 27 y'r | of his age.

1626. JOHN PERRY, | died Jan. 6. 1846, | aged 49 yrs. | Also two children of | JOHN & RUTH PERRY, | Viz | LEWIS, died Feb. 1, 1843, | aged 2 yrs. & 2 Mon. | LEWIS, died Feb. 17. 1846, | aged 3 yrs & 4 Mon.

> *The graves of all the saints he bless'd*
> *And soften'd ev'ry bed*
> *Where should the dying members rest,*
> *But with their dying Head.*

1627. In | memory of | *SARAH*, widow of the | late THOMAS JACKSON, | who died Jan. 30. 1846, | in her 70th year.

1628. | Erected | to the memory of | JOHN B. CHANDLER | who died | March 4, 1846, | aged 61 yrs. | Also his wife | *HANNAH*, | died Nov. 5, 1845, | aged 58 years.

> *Into thine hand, O GOD of truth,*
> *Our spirits we commit.*

1629. BETSEY | widow of | WILLIAM TRIBBLE. | born Sept. 8, 1789, | died April 24, 1846, | *FRANCIS*, their son | died | Feb. 14, 1830 | aged 5 mo.

1630. In | memory of Miss MARY COLLINS | died June 14th, | 1846. | aged 60 y'rs

1631. CHARLES THOMAS, | son of JAMES M. | & PHEBE ATHERTON, | died Aug. 7, 1846, | aged 2 yrs. & 4 mo.

1632. ALMIRA E. | Dau. of SILAS H. | & ALMIRA A. BURT, | died Aug. 16, 1846, | aged 6 mo. | & 16 d's.

Adieu sweet babe a short farewell,
The Saviour Calls — with him to dwell.

1633. CHARLES BROWN, | died Sept. 20, 1846, | in the 25ᵗʰ y'r | of his age. | Also *CHARLES*, | Son of CHARLES & CHARLOTTE ANN BROWN, | died Jan. 29ᵗʰ, 1853, | aged 5 y'rs & 11 Mo.

Why am I left alone.

1634. Erected | to the memory of | CHARLES BRAD-FORD, | Lost at Sea | Sept. 1846, | Aged 25 yrs. & 8 Mon. | Also | HANNAH E. BRADFORD, | Died March 23ᵈ 1854 | Aged 21 years.

Our Saviour summons us away,
A brighter world to view,
Although awhile behind you stay,
Weep not — weep not for us.

1635. WILLIAM F. MANTER | died Oct. 30, 1846; | aged 19 y'rs & 6 mo's, | WINSLOW MANTER | died Dec. 7, 1835; | aged 7 y'rs. | LUCY E. MANTER | died Oct. 25, 1837; | aged 6 y'rs. & 10 mo's. | LUCY M. MANTER, | died Sept. 7, 1842; | aged 13 mo's. | Children of | Wᴹ· & LUCY B. MANTER.

1636. In memory of | ESTHER SHAW | Widow of the Late | ICHABOD SHAW, | who died Nov. 1. 1846, | in the 78 yr. | of her age.

1637. Erected | to the memory of | Capt. THOMAS PATY | who died Nov. 26, 1846, | aged 73 years. | Also his Grandson THO'S P. HARLOW | who was lost at sea Sept. 1848, | Æ. 25 years.

Blessed are the dead who
die in the Lord.

1638. SOUTHWORTH SHAW, | Born | July 28, 1775, | Died | January 18, 1847 | aged 71 years, | 5 moˢ· 21 days.

1639. In memory of | Mrs ANN BROWN | widow of | Mr. LEMUEL BROWN, | Born: 14ᵗʰ March 1783, | Died 28ᵗʰ Janʸ· 1847.

1640. Erected | to the memory of | THOMAS DAVEE, | son of JOHNSON and | PHEBE DAVEE, | died Feb, 12, 1847, | Æ. 5 years. | *Innocence.*

1641. SUSAN BARTLETT | died | Feb. 18, 1847. | aged 52 yrs.

1642. In memory of | REBECCA DAVIS | relict of | Hon. WILLIAM DAVIS | Born December 30, 1762, | Died April 1, 1847.

1643. In Memory of | Susan C. wife of | | ICHABOD T. HOLMES, | who died | April 14, 1847, | Æ't 31 y'rs 4 mo's.

Her soul has gone to Heaven we trust,
God called her home he thought it best.

1644. ABIA, | widow of | Capt. WILLIAM PEARSON | died April 21, 1847. | aged 84 years.

1645. In memory of | PHYLANDER SAMPSON, | who died May. 18, 1847, | Æt. 36 years. | Also two children of PHYLAN-DER | and SARAH A. SAMPSON, | SARAH E. died April 18, 1845, | Æt. | 4 y'rs 3 mo. ALBERT L. died May 6, 1845, | Æt. 6 y'rs 2 Ho.

Calm be the spot where their forms now repose,
May the friends who so loved them revisit the grave,
And feel, though the cold sod their ashes enclose,
They live in the presence of him who can save.

1646, *BETSEY M.* wife of | LLOYD KEITH | of Bridge-water, | and dau, of | ISRAEL HOYT | of Plymouth. | Died June 7, 1847, | in the 22d· yr, | of her age.

God lent us the flower: and now doth reclaim
The exotic in radiant bloom:
In love from our Father, the reaper, Death, came
And exhaled the spirit's perfume.

The casket is all that is left us below:
The gem that it bore, lives above;
While mem'ry its incense, around us doth throw,
As we guard this dear spot with our love.

1647. Erected | to the memory of | POLLY S. | wife of | THOMAS DIMAN, | died Aug. 22d· 1847, | aged 42 y'rs & 5 mon. | Also | two of their Children | POLLY S. | died Oct. 11. 1835 | aged 2 mon. & 11 Days. | MARY H. | died Nov. 31st. 1838. | aged 9 mon.

1648. Erected | in memory of | PHEBE FINNEY, | wife of Capt. EPHRAIM FINNEY, | died | Sept. 26, 1847, | aged 64 yrs. & 7 mo.

1649. Sacred to the memory | of | NICHOLAS H. DREW | who died | October 21, 1847. | aged 41 years.

> " *The righteous hath hope in his death,*"
>
> *Thou art gone to thy rest dear Husband,*
> *Whilst I am left to mourn;*
> *And travel on in sorrow,*
> *And trouble here alone*
>
> *But again I hope to meet thee*
> *When the ills of life are fled:*
> *And in Heaven I hope to greet thee,*
> *Where no farewell tear is shed.*

1650. In memory of | Mrs. BETHIAH, | relict of the late | Capt, | ZEPHANIAH HOLMES, | who died Oct. 25, 1847, | in her 69 y'r.

1651. In memory of | Mrs. | POLLY DIMAN, | Consort of the late Dea. JOSIAH DIMAN, | died Nov. 15, 1847, | aged 71 years.

> *So Jesus slept; — God's dying Son*
> *Pass'd thro' the grave, and bless'd the bed;*
> *Rest here, blest saint, till from his throne*
> *The morning break, and pierce the shade.*

1652. Died | 17th *Nov.* 1847, | Capt. | AMERICA BREWSTER, | aged 74 yrs.

1653. Erected | in memory of | Miss LUCY WESTON, | who died | Jan. 1. 1848, in the | 63 yr. of her age.

1654. In memory of | ICHABOD DAVIE, | Born Nov. 11, 1771. | Died April 4, 1848.

> *Affection to thy cherished memory rears*
> *This stone — a tribute poor to worth like thine:*
> *But Faith alone can check her flowing tears,*
> *And point to realms of peace and joy divine,*
> *Where thy pure spirit dwells, which earth could not*
> *enshrine.*
>
> *Blessed are the dead who rest in humble hope.*

1655. In memory of | JOSEPH HOLMES, | who died |
July 4. 1848, | Æ. 60 y'rs 3 mo. | & 20 days.

Calm be the spot where his form now repose,
May the friends who so loved him revisit the grave,
And feel, though the cold sod his ashes enclose,
He lives in the presence of him who can save.

1656. Erected | to the Memory of | BETSEY DAVEE, |
dau. of the late | Capt· SOLOMON DAVEE | Born July 25, 1787, |
Died Aug. 18, 1848, | in her 62 year. | *Meekness.*

1657. WILLIAM | JOHNSON, | son   of | JOHNSON   & |
MARY B. BROWN, | died Sept. 12. 1848. | Aged 8 mon.

1658. In memory of | THOMAS DAVIS | son of | WILLIAM
& REBECCA DAVIS, | Born April 3. 1791 | Died Sept. 14, 1848.

1659. In memory of | Five children of JAMES | & MARY
BURNS, | Drowned at Manomet Point | Nov. 20th, 1848, |

> *ELLEN*,   Aged 11 years.
> *CATHARINE*   "   9 y'rs.
> *HENRY*   "   7 y'rs.
> *MARY*   "   5 y'rs
> *ROSE*   "   3 y'rs.

From the Sch'r Welcome Return.

Requiescant in Pace.   Amen.

1660. SALLY K. | wife of | JAMES KENDRICK, | Died Dec.
15, 1848, | aged 27 yrs. | Also an Infant Daughter.

Rest, kind Mother & Companion rest,
Thy cares are all o'er,
O may we meet in Heaven above,
And there to part no more,

1661. In memory of | MARY, | wife of | DANIEL GODDARD,
who died | Dec. 30. 1848, | in her 52 yr. | Also | DANIEL, |
their son who died | Sept. 28. 1821, | aged 16 mon.

1662. JOHN NOONNEN. | Died Dec. 31, 1848, | aged 52
y'rs. | & his son WILLIAM H. | Died March 19, 1855, | aged 19
y'rs | 2 mo.

Tis God, who lifts our comforts high,
Or sinks them in the grave;
He gives — and blessed be his name?
He takes but what he gave.

1663.   MARY L. | dau. of JESSE | & MARY L. HARLOW, |
Born Aug. 18, 1829, | Died Jan 18: 1849,

Spring will revisit us.
Summer appear,
Brown autumn follow
With winter so drear,
But Mary no more
Thy smile and thy voice
Blend freely with ours;
The zest of our joys,
Bright was thy blooming,
Swift thy decay
E'en as a flower
Thy life passed away.

1664.   Erected | to the Memory of | JEDIDAH DAVEE, |
widow of the late | Capt. SOLOMON DAVEE, | Born July 25, 1763,
| Died Jan. 19, 1849, | in her 86 year.
Our Mother.

1665.   AUGUSTA GRATON | died Feb. 27, 1849, | aged 4
y'rs 6 Mo. | Daughter of | WILLIAM S. & | HANNAH HOLMES,

Step Lightly round th
is holy spot. For one of
Christ's Lambs is Sle
eping here.

1666.   AMBROSE E. | son of | WILLIAM & BETSEY | NICK-
ERSON, | Died Feb. 27. 1849: | aged 4 y'rs. & 4 mo's.

1667.   GEORGE M. | Son of GEORGE | M. & LYDIA N. |
COLLINS, | died | March 11, 1849, | Æ. 5 mo. 7 ds. | *Innocence.*

1668.   In memory of | SARAH B. dau. of | L. T. & LYDIA |
ROBBINS, who died | March 19, 1849, | Æ. 6 years.

1669.   BETHIA, | wife of | THOMAS B. BARTLETT, | died |
March 24, 1849, | aged 42 years.

1670. In memory of | LYDIA   JACKSON, | dau. of |
THOMAS JACKSON Esq. | & SARAH his wife. | born April 8, 1758,
| died March 27, 1849.

> *The mortal remains are deposited here,*
> *but the spirit has returned to God who gave it.*

1671. MARGARET HODGE | and | BENJAMIN GLEA-
SON | Children of | GEORGE and LYDIA A. | RAYMOND, | April
1849.

1672.   *The fathers have eaten*
>   *sour grapes, and the*
>   *children's teeth are set*
>   *on edge.*

ANN L. | died April 2, 1849, | aged 3 y'rs & 1 Mo. | Dau. of
THOMAS | & MARY J. CHURCHILL.

>   *O who would cling to earth*
>   *When a brighter Sphere*
>   *awaits us.*

1673. In memory of | MARY ELLEN, | dau. of | LEAVITT &
MARY | W. FINNEY, | who died | April 20, 1849, | Æ. 3 y'rs
11 mo's.

> " *Tis God, who lifts our comforts high,*
>   *Or sinks them in the grave;*
>   *He gives — and blessed be his name!*
>   *He takes but what he gave.*

1674. Erected | in memory of | MERCY, | widow of | WIL-
LIAM BARNES, | who died | April 21, 1849, | in the 79 y'r | of
her age.

1675. MARY EDWARDS, | Daughter of | WILLIAM H. &
| MARY S. MORTON, | died May 14, | 1849, | aged 2 y'rs 6 mo.
| and 16 days.

1676. In memory of | MARIA P. | wife of | THOMAS TRIB-
BLE, | who died July 16, 1849, | Æ. 44 y'rs | 5 mo. & 16 ds.

1677. In memory of | DANIEL GODDARD Jr. | who died
| Aug. 1, 1849, | in his 53 year.

1678. In memory of | ISAAC LE BARON, | born March 11, 1777, | died Jan. 29, 1849. | of MARY DOANE | his wife— born July 19, 1787. | Died June 18, 1863. | And of their children | ISAAC FRANCIS, | Born Oct. 29, 1814. | Died June 28, 1816. | FREDERIC, | born Feb. 28, 1816. | died July 5, 1851. | MARY JANE, | born Aug. 12, 1817. | died Nov. 28, 1855. | ISAAC, | born Dec. 6, 1819, | died Dec. 24, 1853.

1679. CEPHAS A. | Son of | DAVID C. & LOUISA S. | HOLMES, | Died Feb. 11, 1849 | Aged 9 years.

1680. ABBY JANE. | Daughter of | CAPT. WILLIAM & | SARAH JANE ATWOOD, | died Feb. 22, 1849 | aged 6 Mon.

1681. CAPT. | WILLIAM HOLMES | died Jan. 3, 1833, | aged 65 yrs. | HANNAH, widow of | WILLIAM HOLMES, died | Feb. 22, 1854, Æ. 87 yrs.
Also MISS POLLY HOLMES, | died April 2, 1849, | Æ. 69 y'rs.

1682. In Memory of | two children of CHAS. | & MARY R. WHITTEN, | JOSEPH W. | died Jan. 3, 1839, | Æ. 10 mo. | EDWARD W. | died April 6, 1849, | Æ 5 y'rs 6 mo. 4 ds.

1683. SAM'L. W. BAGNELL, | died June 18, 1849, | aged 62 years. | LOIS | his wife. | died Dec. 20 1820, | aged 32 years.

1684. CAPT. EPHRAIM PATY, JR. | Died | in California, July 24, 1849. | Aged 43 yrs. | WILLIE A. | Died Feb. 30, 1847. | Aged 13 mo's 12 d's. | SARAH C. | Died Aug. 19, 1850. | Aged 14 y'rs 9 mo's. | WILLIE A. | Died Sept. 5, 1850. | Aged 13 mo's 23 d's. | LIZZIE F. | Died July 11, 1860. | Aged 10 y'rs 7 mos. | Children of | CAPT. EPHRAIM JR. & | SARAH C. PATY.

1685. JOSEPH STURTEVANT | died Nov. 3, 1849. | aged 35 y'rs & 3 Mon. | Also three children of | JOSEPH & MARCIA STURTEVANT, | viz. | JOSHUA P. died Aug. 23, 1842, | aged 5 Mon. & 24 days. | JAMES T. died Jan. 14, 1845, | aged 1 year

& 7 Mon. | MARCIA ANN, died Sept. 15, 1746, | aged 1 year
& 18 days.

> *Then shall the dust return to the earth*
> *As it was : and the spirit shall return*
> *Unto God, who gave it.*

1686.   Erected | to the memory of | SAMUEL HARLOW, |
who died | Nov. 30th, 1849, | aged 73 yrs.

1687.   MARGARET H. | wife of | SAMUEL N. DIMAN, |
Died Dec. 8, 1849, | Aged 32 yrs. | and 6 Mon.

> *Rest, sleeping dust, in silence rest,*
> *In the cold grave that Jesus blest;*
> *In faith and hope we lay thee there,*
> *Safe in our Heavenly Father's care.*

1688.   In memory of | NANCY, | wife of | BENJAMIN DIL-
LARD, | who died | Dec. 22d, 1849, | in her 67 yr.

1689.   In | memory of | CAPT. THOMAS BARTLETT, |
who died | Dec. 30, 1849, | in the 80th year | of his age.

1690.   GEORGE | RAYMOND JR. | Drowned | at Billing-
ton Sea | Jan. 12, 1850, | aged 45 years.

1691.   HENRY, | Son of PHILLIP | & ELIZABETH SMITH, |
died, Jan. 30, | 1850, | aged 3 mon. | & 8 days.

1692.   In Memory of | MARIAH, widow of | BENJAMIN
HOLMES, | who died | April 13, 1850, | Æ. 75 y'rs 4 mo's.

> *Thrice happy souls who're gone before,*
> *To that inheritance Divine,*
> *They labor, sorrow, sigh no more,*
> *But bright in endless glory shine.*

1693.   MISS SUSAN | W. HOLMES, | Died April 29,
1850 | aged 43 years.

1694.   CAPT. | JOHN BURGESS, JR. | born March 26,
1785, | died May 4, 1850.

The anchor's dropt — the sails are furled!
Life's voyage now is o'er;
By faith's bright chart he has gained that world
Where storms are felt no more.

1695. In memory of | ELIZABETH A. wife of | SILVANUS HARLOW, | Born Oct. 28, 1812 | Died June 4, 1850, | Æ. 37 y'rs 7 mo. & 7 days.

We mourn who loved her here,
And who that knew her ne'er could fail to love,
Yet we would dry the tear,
And strive to meet her in the world above.

Also their dau. ELIZABETH A. | Died Jan. 13, 1842, | Æ 3 weeks & 2 ds.

With chastened heart we'll strive to bear
Submissive to God's will,
'Tis He that gives, 'tis He that takes,
And we will bless Him still.

1696. In this town | June 7, 1850, | MARY ALLERTON | dau. of SAM'L & REBECCA | SAMPSON | Æ 3 y'rs 10 mo.

1697. HANNAH ELLIS, | wife of | JOSEPH W. BURGESS, | oied Aug. 11, 1850, | in her 34th year. | Also 4 infant children.

Mourn not for her, ye who below
Beneath th' afflictive stroke are
bending,
For your loved one has gone to know
A bliss above which has no ending.

1698. HAMBLIN TILLSON | departed this life | August 16, 1850, | in the 70th year | of his age.

The memory of the just is blessed.

1699. In Memory of | ELIZABETH C. | dau. of SILVANUS and | ELIZABETH H. CHURCHILL, | who died | Aug. 27, 1850, | Æ. 11 y'rs 1 mo. | Also 4 Infant sons | WILLIAM C. 1822, | WILLIAM C. 1829, | Twins 1833.

1700.   In memory of | JOHN C. | Son of | STEPHEN D. &
LYDIA W. DREW, | Died Sept. 10, 1850, | Æ. 11 Months.

1701.   MARIA SHAW | wife of | SOUTHWORTH SHAW,
Born | March 20, 1778, | Died | October 5, 1850; | aged 72
years | 6 mos. 15 days.

1702.   SARAH, | Widow of | CAPT. | AMERICA BREW-
STER, | died Dec. 22, 1850, | aged 75 y'rs.

1703.   CATHERINE BRIDGHAM, | daughter of | CHARLES
and | ABIGAIL CHURCHILL, | age 11 years, | Dec. 31, 1850.

1704.   EBENEZER DREW, | Died | Jan. 6, 1851, | Aged
77 y'rs. | DEBORAH | his wife | Died April 15, 1844, | Aged
72 y'rs.

1705.   In memory of | MOSES HOYT, | died Jan. 23d
1851, | aged 71 y'rs. | Also two Sons Viz. | MOSES, | died in
Peru, Ill. | Oct. 3rd 1838, | in his 30th yr, | OTIS, | died Jan.
19, 1851, | in his 28th yr.

1706.   In | memory of | REBECCA, | Consort of | DANIEL
JACKSON, | deceased January | 24th 1851, | aged 90 years | &
10 Months.

1707.   In | memory of | EXPERIENCE, | widow of the
late | BEZA HAYWARD, ESQ. | who died | March 4th, 1851, |
Aged 88 years | & 8 Months.

1708.   In | memory of | WILLIAM TAYLOR, | aged 47 |
Born in London | April 25, 1804, | Died in Boston | June
27, 1851.

1709.   GEORGE | AUGUSTUS, | son of SIMON R. | & JANE
E. BURGESS, | died July 31, 1851, | Æ. 9 y'rs 3 mo's.

1710.   In memory of | LYDIA, | Widow of | EBENEZER
NELSON, | who died | Oct. 21st, 1851, | aged 87 years.

1711.   BETSEY P. | died Oct, 25, 1851, | in her 19th y'r. |
HELLEN | died Sept. 4th, 1847, | aged 7 years. | LOUISA S. |

died Sept. 12, 1847, | aged 3 years. | Children of EDWARD & | SALINA DOTEN.

'Tis the blest hope that they shall meet
Their daughters in the skies;
And with their friends, shall
Jesus greet—
That lamb-like sacrifice.

1712. LEWIS W. PERRY, | died Oct. 30, 1851, | in his 28th y'r. | Also LEWIS F. | son of LEWIS W. & | CHARITY S. PERRY, | died March 29, | 1852.

1713. In memory of | CAPT. | JOSEPH COOPER, | who died Nov. 25, 1851, | aged 82 years.

1714. JANE, | widow of | NATHANIEL THOMAS, | died Dec. 22d, 1851, | in her 81st y'r. | Also | NANCY | their Daughter | died Jan. 18th, 1821, | aged 18 y'rs.

1715. Our Father & Mother | Have gone to Rest. | LAZ-ARUS SYMMES | Died Dec. 25, 1851, | Aged 70 y'rs. | Also his wife | MARY, | Died Dec. 4, 1863, | Aged 79 y'rs.

I am the ressurrection and the life, he that believeth in Me
though he were dead, yet shall he rise.

1716. Father & Mother | JOAB THOMAS, | Born | May 20, 1782, | Died March 20, 1852. | LOIS THOMAS | his wife, | Born April 4, 1782, | Died June 2, 1870.

"Father, I will that they also whom thou hast given me, be
with me where I am."
"Forever with Jesus."

1717. SARAH T., | Daughter of | WILLIAM & C. B. | BISHOP, | Died Apr. 3, 1852, | Aged 3 mo's.

1718. MARY BARTLETT, | widow of | JAMES BART-LETT, | Born May 19, 1759, | Died April 9, 1852.
NOTE.—See No. 1538.

1719. 🝫 LOUISA, | Dau. of | DAVID C. & LOUISA S. | HOLMES, | Died Apr. 13, 1852, | Aged 17 yrs. 3 mos.

1720. CURTIS F., son of | CURTIS & HARRIET | HOYT, who died | July 1, 1852, | Æ 2 y'rs, 8 mo.

> *Because thy smile was fair,*
> *Thy lips and eyes so bright:*
> *Because thy cradle care*
> *Was such a fond delight;*
> *Shall love with weak embrace,*
> *Thy Heavenward flight detain ?*
> *No ! angel, seek thy place*
> *Amid yon cherub train.*

1721. In memory of | LYDIA W., | wife of | STEPHEN D. DREW, | who died | Aug. 28, 1852, | Æ. 41 y'rs, 5 mo.

> *My hour has come, I lay me down,*
> *With the dark grave in view ;*
> *And, hoping for a heavenly crown,*
> *I bid the world adieu.*

1722. EUNICE B. | Daughter of ELEAZER | & POLLY SEARS, | Died Sept. 14, 1852, | Aged 27 years.

> *Rest sleeping dust in silence rest*
> *In the cold grave that Jesus blest,*
> *In faith and hope we lay thee there*
> *Safe in our Heavenly Father's care:*
> *O, may we hear thy warning given*
> *Prepare to die and go to Heaven.*

1723. ERECTED | In memory of | BATHSHEBA, | widow of the late | CAPT. BARTLETT SEARS, | who departed this life | Sept. 25th, 1852, | aged 74 years.

1724. In Memory of | BETHIAH, | wife of | HENRY O. STEWARD, | who died | Oct. 1, 1852, | Æ. 35 y'rs 1 mo. | & 25 days.

1725. WILLIAM T. | Son of HARVEY & | OLIVE L. RAYMOND, | died Nov. 12, 1852, | aged 2 y'rs & 4 mo's.

> *Parents and Friends*
> *Weep not for me,*

Nor ov'r this Bodey mo
urn,
Soon, soon you'll meet
With me Again;
when Christ shall
call you home.

1726. ELIZABETH | Wife of | EDWARD BURT, | died | Nov. 13, 1852; | Æ. 54 y'rs & 2 mos.

1727. CAPT. ANSELM RICKARD, | Died | at Martinico, | Oct. 6, 1801, | Aged 34 y'rs. | MARGARET | his wife | Died Nov. 21, 1852, | Aged 81 y'rs, |

1728. JOHN WILLIAMS | Born March 4, 1800; | Died Nov. 23, 1852. | ELIZA ANN, | Born June 30, 1829; | Died April 6, 1830. | JOHN, | Born July 3, 1831, | Died Sept. 8, 1831. | children of | JOHN & ELIZA WILLIAMS.

1729. LYDIA A. | dau. of | ELKANAH & LYDIA | CHURCH-ILL, | died Dec. 17, 1852; | aged 15 y'rs. & 3 mo's.

Her youthful hopes were like the morning flower,
Cut Down at noon and withered in an hour;
But hopes more fair, and bright than youth or health can give
Rise in immortal bloom beyond the grave.

1730. In memory of | MRS. REBECCA HARLOW, | Relict of | CAPT. EZRA HARLOW, | Born Jan. 5, 1795, | Died Dec. 18, 1852.
"There is rest in Heaven."

1731. In memory of | CHARLES | son of CHARLES & | LUCY NELSON, | died Dec. 31, 1852, | in his 20th y'r.

He died in hope, he died in faith,
A life of suffering o'er;
He smiling met the shafts of death,
And lives to die no more.

Also an Infant Daughter.

1732. In memory of | LEMAN L. | Son of | STEPHEN D. & | LYDIA W. DREW, | Died Jan. 24, 1853, | Æ 6 Months.

1733. MALACHI DREW, | Died | Feb. 22, 1853, | Aged 78 y'rs.

1734. ANNABELLA, | daughter of JACOB | & DEBORAH B. SWIFT, | died Feb. 27 1853, | aged 17 months.

Ere sin could blight or sorrow fade
Death came with friendly care
The opening bud to Heaven conveyed
And bade it blossom there.

1735. HARRIET L. WATSON, | Died in Boston, Mar. 24, 1853, | Æ 68 yrs. | Grant to her oh Lord | we beseech thee, eternal rest. | Her husband | WINSLOW WATSON, | Died at sea, Dec. 17, 1816, | Æ 30 yrs.

THEIR AFFECTIONATE CHILDREN PLACE THIS STONE TO THEIR MEMORY.

1736. JEROME W. | died May 6, 1853; | aged 16 yrs. & 6 Mo. | MARY E. | died Sept. 22, 1846. | aged 1 y'r & 10 Mo. | children of | WILLIAM & LYDIA | C. PURINGTON.

Those buds were plucked before half blown,
Because there Maker called them home.

1737. This | stone is erected | to the memory of | MRS. PRISCILLA WESTON, | who died May 30, 1853; | aged eighty-six years. | Her first husband was | CAPT. JOHN VIRGIN.

1738. In memory of | MRS. A. M. E. KIKEET. | who died | June 10, 1853. | Æt. 44 yrs.

1739. ALLEN C. SPOONER | Born | March 9, 1814, | Died | June 28, 1853. | SUSAN L. SPOONER, | Feb. 25, 1814. | May 5, 1880.

1740. ERECTED | to the Memory of | PATIENCE COX, | Widow of the late | ELIAS COX, | Who died July 14, 1853, | in the 81 y'r of her age.

1741. LUCY D. BARTLETT, | Widow of | Capt. Joseph
Bartlett, | Died | July 30, 1853, | Aged 75 y'rs.

1742. LIZZY RYAN, | Aged 2 yrs. | & 8 Mon. | died |
Aug. 1st, 1853.

1743. GEORGE WASHBURN, | Son of George and |
Priscilla Washburn, | Died in Montgomery, | Alabama,
Sept. 4, 1853, | Aged 25 y'rs & 6 mo.

The only son of a Widow'd Mother.

1744. HENRY ERLAND, | Born in Devonshire, Eng. |
Mar. 7, 1798, | Died Sept. 6, 1853.

His virtues will embalm his memory.

1745. In memory of | MARY H. | Dau. of Charles | &
Lydia N. | Whitten, | who died | Sept. 12, 1853. | Æ. 3 mo.
7 ds.

1746. WILLIAM RANDALL, | died Nov. 23, 1853; |
Æ. 60 y'rs 3 mo's & 16 d's. | Also his two sons, | GEORGE, |
died Sept. 17, 1835; | Æ. 12 y'rs & 9 mo's. | CHARLES, |
died Aug. 30, 1851; | Æ. 25 y'rs & 10 mo's.

Blessed are the dead who die in the Lord.

1747. In memory of | DEBORAH, | wife of | Samuel
Alexander, | died Dec. 20, 1853, | Aged 68 y'rs, | 8 months

" There is rest in Heaven."

1748. REBECCA ELLIS, | Died Jan. 11, 1854. | Aged 50
years | & 9 Months. | NATHANIEL ELLIS, | Lost at Sea,
Dec. 6, 1812, | Aged 21 years | & 11 Months.

1749. JOHN OSGOOD | died | Jan'y 31, 1854, | Æ. 25
y'rs 9 mo. | & 3 days.

1750. Erected in memory of | EPHRAIM PATY, | who
died Feb. 9, 1854; | aged 70 y'rs & 10 mo's . | Also his son |

GEORGE WINSLOW, | who died at sea | July 14, 1853, | aged 19 yrs. & 5 mo's.

> " *Blessed are the dead who die in the Lord,*
> *And their works do follow them.*

1751. NATHANIEL BARNES, | died Feb. 20, 1854; | aged 60 years. | His daughter | BETSEY G. ELLIS, | died Dec. 9 1848; | aged 27 years. | NATH'L BARNES JR. | died Feb. 7, 1854, | aged 25 years.

1752. GRANVILL S. | Died Dec. 20, 1852, | Aged 19 y'rs. 5 mo's. | EDWARD P. | Died March 18, 1854, | Aged 16 y'rs 7 mo's. | REBECCA J. | Died Oct. 10, 1851, | Aged 10 mo's | Children of GRANVILL & | REBECCA D. GRIFFIN,

> *Gone, but not forgotten.*

1753. WILLIAM ROGERS JR. | died Dec. 23d, 1822. | Aged 34 yrs. | JOHN ROGERS, | died Dec. 1st, 1825. | Aged 27 yrs. | ICHABOD ROGERS | Died March 18th, 1854. | Aged 50 yrs. & 10 Mon.

1754. HARVEY H. RAYMOND | Born | Sept. 19, 1809 | Died | March 18, 1854.

1755. In memory of | MRS. LUCY, | wife of | BENJAMIN BAGNELL | who left us | Apr. 19, 1854, | Æ 61 yr's & 9 ms.

> " *There shall be no more death, neither shall*
> *there be any more pain: for the former*
> *things are passed away.*"

1756. WINSLOW M. | Died Aug. 3, 1853, | Aged 10 mo's. | ANN E. | Died May 26, 1854, | Aged 10 yrs. 11 mo's. | Children of | JOHN R. & BETSEY B. | DAVIS.

1757. ELIZABETH, | widow of | WILLIAM DUNHAM, | Born Mar. 20, 1770; | Died July 20, 1854; | Æ. 84 y'rs & 4 mo's.

When the Christian's race is run,
Though low she slumbers in the ground;
Her virtues like the setting sun,
Shall shed a heavenly lustre round.

1758. In | memory of | SALLY HALL, | who died | Oct. 8th, 1854, | Aged 63 yrs. | Also | NATHAN HALL, | who died | Feb, 12th, 1854, | Aged 25 yrs.

1759. In | memory of | ELLIS HOLMES, | died Oct. 18, 1854, | in his 88th yr.

1760. Erected | in memory of | JACOB SWIFT, | Died Nov. 1, 1854, | Aged 43 years | and 5 mon.

1761. Erected | to the memory of | JERUSHA PATY, | widow of the late | THOMAS PATY, | who died Dec. 29, 1854, | aged 81 years.

The love that seeks another's good,
In her did warmly burn,—
Oh, let us imitate that love,
Nor ask for her return.

1762. KATE C. | Wife of | HARRISON FINNEY | Died Jan. 1, 1855, | Aged 30 y'rs. | HARRISON K. | their son | Died Apr. 22, 1853, | Aged 2 y'rs. 2 mos.

1763. LEMUEL BRADFORD, | died | March 1, 1855, | aged 66 years.

Calm be the spot where his form now repose,
May the friends who so loved him revisit his grave,
And feel though the cold sod his ashes enclose,
He lives in the presence of one who will save.

1764. Sacred | to the memory of | DANIEL CHURCH-ILL | who departed this life | March 2, 1855, | aged 83 years.

1765. BETSEY, | wife of | WILLIAM NICKERSON, | died

Mar. 19, 1855, | Æ. 36 years & 8 mo's. | CHARLES H. | their son died Mar. 4, 1853 ; | Æ. 4 y'rs. 6 mo's. & 17 days.

A bitter cup the angel gave,
  To her, a mother aud a wife;
She drank, death was not in the wave,
  To her it was eternal life.

Beyond the dark and swelling flood,
  She vanished from our yearning sight;
The radiant gate of Heaven inclosed,
  And welcomed home the child of light.

1766. In memory of | ELIZABETH | daughter of | THOMAS NICOLSON | born in Plymouth July 11, | 1777, | died in Boston, Apr. 20, 1855, | Æ. 77 years.

1767. In | memory of | HANNAH S. BARTLETT, | who died | Apr. 20th, 1855, | Aged 65 years.

Faithful in life.

1768. MANLY M. | son of DR. E. & | HARRIET W. | WEBSTER. | died May 28th, | 1855. | Æ. 3 Mon. & 22 d's.

1769. BETSEY ROBBINS, | Died March 22, 1839, | Aged 51 years. | SALLIE CURTIS. | Died Sept. 10, 1839, | Aged 11 years. | JESSIE ROBBINS. | Died June 3, 1855, | Aged 74 years.

1770. In | memory of | ELON S. | Daugh't of ROBERT & | KEZIAH D. SWINBURN, | who died | July 27, 1855, | Aged 10 y'rs. & 6 d'ys. | Also an infant Son.

For thee this heart shall beat,
  For thee these tears shall flow;
And thy fond name I'll repeat
  When sad with many a woe.

1771. LYDIA, | Widow of | GEORGE RAYMOND JR. | Died Aug. 13th, 1855, | Aged 47 y'rs 6 mo.

1772. JOHN E. | died | Sept. 7, 1854, | Æt. 10 mo's. 12 d'ys. | JOHN E. | died | Aug. 23, 1855, | Æt. 4 weeks. | Children of | ELLIS T. & | JANE LANMAN.

1773. LOUISA SAVERY | Wife of | DAVID C. HOLMES. | Died | Sept. 4, 1855, | Aged 45 yrs. 6 mo.

1774. In memory of | HANNAH J. GOODWIN, | daughter of JOHN & | HANNAH GOODWIN, | who died | Sept. 6, 1855, | Aged 81 years.

1775. HORACE JACKSON, | Died | in Norfolk, Va. | Sept. 9, 1855; | Æ. 27 years & 5 mo's.

1776. EPHRAIM WHITING | Died in Jamacia | W. I. 1803; | Aged 28 yrs. | also | ELIZABETH, | widow of the late | EPHRAIM WHITING, | Died Sept. 27, 1855, | Aged 80 y'rs.

May their Souls meet in heaven.

1777. JOHN BATTLES | born Feb. 26, 1778, | died Sept. 29, 1855. | ELIZABETH, | his wife | died Sept. 29, 1800 | aged 23 yrs. 5 mo's. | LYDIA, | wife of | JOHN BATTLES, | died Apr. 20, 1865, | aged 86 yrs. 3 mos.

NOTE.—See No. 755.

1778. In memory of | JAMES SULLIVAN, | who died | in Plymouth | Oct. 6, 1855, | aged 22 y'rs.
A native of County | Cork, Ireland, Parish | of Castletownsend.

1779. In memory of | SALLY, | Widow of the late | SAMUEL COLE, | Died Oct. 23d, 1855, | in her 73d. year.

For I know that my Redeem | er liveth, and that he shall stand at the latter day upon the earth.—(Job 19; 2–5.)

1780. JOHN CHASE | Died | Dec. 15, 1855, | Æ. 74 years. | ABIGAIL, | His wife | Died Sept. 17, 1872, | Æ 89 yrs. 4 mo's.

1781. In Memory of | GIDEON H. Son of | ISAAC & LOIS TRIBBLE, | Born March 3, 1813, | Died Dec. 19, 1855, | aged 42 y'rs. 9 mo's, | and 16 days.

1782. SAMUEL R. | Scn of | S. R. & R. F. | DICKSON |
Died Jan. 13, 1856, | Aged 21 yrs. 8 mos. | 19 days.

1783. In memory of | AMASA ROBBINS, | who died |
Jan. 28, 1856, | aged | 33 yrs. 10 mons. |
" The casket lies
beneath the sod but Heaven
claims the gem.

1784. TIMOTHY BARRY, | died Feb. 5, 1856; | Æ. 58
yrs. 2 mos. & 25 dys.

Fare thee well; though woe is blending
With the tones of earthly love.
Triumph high and joy unending,
Wait thee in the realms above.

MARIA BARRY, | died Apr. 12, 1824, aged 2 dys. | TIMOTHY
BARRY JR. | died Dec. 29, 1836, aged 7 wks. & 4 ds.

1785. In Memory of | RUTH G. | Born Sept. 26, 1852, |
Died Feb. 22, 1856. | RUTH G. 2d | Born March 2, 1856, |
Died Sept. 12, 1856, | Children of ICHABOD | T. & RUTH
HOLMES.

1786. In Memory of | LYDIA DELANO | who died Mar.
22, | 1856, | aged 52 yrs. 4 mos. | & 22 days.

TO OUR SISTER.

A marble monument marks the spot
And these words on it are graven,
Though her body lies here in the still church-yard
Our sister lives in Heaven.

1787. MARY E. | daughter of JAMES & | DEBORAH KEN-
DRICK | died Mar. 29, 1856, | Æ. 2 y'rs. 10 mos. | & 13 days.

1788. ELIZABETH B. | only daughter of | BRIDGHAM &
BETSEY F. RUSSELL, | died May 7, 1856; | aged 27 yrs. &
3 mo's.

May her dear memory serve to make
Our faith in goodness strong.

1789. MARIA T. JACKSON, | Died | May 18, 1856, | aged 52 years. | Also LAVANTIA, | born June 14, 1831, | died September 23, 1851.

She was the daughter of JACOB and JOAN JACKSON.

1790. DEBORAH, | wife of | JAMES KENDRICK | Died | June 11, 1856, | Aged 27 years.

" When Christ who is our life shall
appear, then shall ye also appear
with him in glory."

1791. OLIN E. | son of | DR. ERVIN & HARRIET W. | WEBSTER | passed onward | Aug. 28, 1856 aged | 4 years, | 4 mo. & 20 days.

1792. ERVIN WEBSTER, M. D. | PASSED ONWARD | Aug. 28, 1856, | aged | 28 years, 2 months & | 28 days.

1793. JERUSHA T. TALBOT, | wife of | SAMUEL TALBOT, | Died Sept. 8, 1856; | Æ. 54 years.

Peace to thy soul; no more shall earth
Thy spirit pure oppress;
No more shall sorrow waste thy frame,
For thou hast gone to rest.

NANCY E. | their daughter, | died Apr. 22, 1838, | aged 19 mo's.

1794. MARIA TILLSON | Daughter of | HAMBLIN & SUSAN B. | TILLSON, | Born July 24, 1822, | Died Sept. 23, | 1856.

1795. LUCY B. | wife of | WILLIAM MANTER, | died Dec. 3, 1856, | Æ. 48 yrs. & 5 mo's.

1796. Erected | In memory of | NATHANIEL GOODWIN, | died Feb. 13, 1857; | in his 87 year.

1797. ELIZABETH J. | wife of | WILLIAM A. PERKINS, | died March 5, 1857, | aged 35 years. | PRISCILLA, | died July 30, 1851, | aged 16 years. | PELLA M. | died March 25, 1853, | aged 28, years. | Daughters of JOSEPH & ELIZA HOLMES.

1798. OUR MOTHER | PHEBE J. BARNES, | Died |
April 20, 1857 | Aged 58 y'rs 2mo. |
Holy thoughts cluster about thy name.

1799. DAVID N. | son of DAVID & | MARY ANN CRAIG |
died May 24, 1857, | in his 8th yr.

> *Suffer little Child*
> *ren to come unto*
> *me and forbid th*
> *em not, for of suc*
> *h is the kingdom*
> *of Heaven.*

1800. FREDERICK JACKSON, | Born | May 19, 1791; |
Died June 27, 1857.

1801. JOHN L. MORTON, | died July 22, 1857; | Æ. 68
years and 9 mos. | SALLY, | his wife, died Oct 6, 1810; | aged
20 years.

> *No more can we their forms behold,*
> *Which now in death lie lifeless—cold;*
> *But may we meet when life is o'er*
> *And dwell at last on Canaan's shore.*

JOHN B. MORTON, | died Mar. 6, 1811; | aged 1 year & 3
mos.

1802. MOTHER | MARY W. | Wife of | EDWARD L. DO-
TEN | Died July 30, 1857, | Aged 27 y'rs 6 mo's.

"Blessed are they that mourn, for they shall be comforted."

1803. AN INFANT, | son of ISAAC B. | & HARRIET A. |
KING, died | Aug. 27, 1857, | aged 10 weeks.

1804. FATHER | CHANDLER ROBBINS, | Born | Jan.,
1793, | died | Oct., 1857.

" The memory of the just is as a shining light."

1805. LITTLE | CHARLIE, | son of J. A. & | N. E. DUN-
HAM, | died Oct. 5, 1857, | aged 8 mo. 17 ds.

1806. CAPT. WM. STEPHENS, | died at Matanzas, Oct. 15, 1857 | Æ. 46 yrs. 9 mo's & 20 dys. | AUGUSTA FRANCES | daughter of Wm. & JANE STEPHENS, | died Aug. 4, 1854 | Æ. 3 yrs. 6 mos. & 17 days.

> *Though distant from us thou wast called*
> *Beneath a tropic sun*
> *To hear thy Master call for thee,*
> *Yet, Lord! Thy will be done.*
>
> *We mourn as those who have a hope,*
> *For death to thee was gain;*
> *In habitations of the blest,*
> *Thou wilt forever reign.*

1807. JACOB JACKSON | born January 9, 1794, | died October 22, 1857. | JOANN HOLMES | His wife | born January 23, 1803, | died January 2, 1879. | MARCIA, | born December 16, 1840, | died August 2, 1842. | ANDREW, | born March 7, 1839, | died July 9, 1845. | SOPHIA GORDON | born March 15, 1833, | died September 20, 1845. | Children of JACOB & JOANN JACKSON.

1808. ALPHEUS RICHMOND | died Aug. 30, 1858, | Æ. 76 years, 3 mos. | ABBIGAIL, | his wife | died Nov. 30, 1857. | Æ. 73 years, 6 mos. | ALPHEUS RICHMOND, JR., | was lost at sea, | Mar. 18, 1854, | Æ. 47 years 4 mos.

1809. ROBERT D. TALBOT, | Born May 13, 1834, | Died Dec. 2, 1857.

> *His was an early summons to the tomb,*
> *But though so brief, his life was not in vain;*
> *God does not call his children home too soon;*
> *For such, " to live is Christ, to die is gain."*

1810. HATTIE S., | Daughter of TIMOTHY | & MARIA BARRY, | Died Dec. 30, 1858; | Æ. 15 years 2 mo. | & 19 days.

> *Thy gentle spirit passed away*
> *Mid pain the most severe ;*
> *So great we could not wish thy stay*
> *A moment longer here.*

> *Thou minglest now in that bright throng*
> *Around the eternal throne,*
> *And join'st the everlasting song*
> *With those before thee gone.*

1811. In memory of | LUCY MAYHEW, | daughter of |
THOMAS NICOLSON, | Born in Plymouth, July 28, | 1778 | died
in Boston Jan. 22, 1858, | Æ. 79 years.

1812. NABBY, | Widow of | WILLIAM BROWN, ESQ., |
Died Feb. 8, 1858; | in the 74th year of | her age.

1813. Sweetly fell asleep in | Jesus, Feb. 17, 1858, | ELIZ-
ABETH ABBY | only dau. of OTIS & | ELIZABETH B. WRIGHT,
| Aged 11 y'rs, 11 mo., 2 ds.

> *The once loved form now cold in death,*
> *Each mournful thought employs;*
> *And nature weeps her comforts fled,*
> *And withered all her joys.*
>
> *Hope looks beyond the bounds of time.*
> *When what we now deplore,*
> *Shall rise in full immortal prime*
> *And bloom to fade no more.*

1814. MOTHER | PHEBE DICKSON | Died February
26, 1858, | Aged 81

1815. In memory of | NANCY H. SYMMES | died March
15, 1858. | Æ. 71 y'rs, 4 mo. | & 13 days.

> *Say why should friendship grieve for those*
> *Who safe arrive on Canaan's shore,*
> *Released from all there hurtfull foes,*
> *They are not lost but gone before.*

1816. OLIVE W. GRIFFIN | Died | May 21, 1858.

1817. JOHN NICKERSON, JR., | Died | May 31, 1858. |
Aged 39 years | 9 mo's.

When a few short years have fleated,
When our work on earth is done,
May our circle all unbroken,
Find with thee in Heaven our home.

1818. FATHER | MERRICK RYDER, | Died | June 8, 1858. | Aged | 68 y'rs, 9 mo's.

1819. MARY, | Wife of | ABNER PIERCE, | Died | Aug. 25, 1858, | Aged 33 years | ALSO | An infant daughter.

1820. ELLIS BARNES, | Died | in Whatcom, | Washington Territory, | Aug. 29, 1858, | Aged 35 y'rs.
An affectionate Son and Brother.

1821. PRESCILLA WASHBURN, | Wife of William Drew, | Born Dec. 7, 1786, | Died Sept. 21, 1858.

1822. In Memory of | ISAAC J. LUCAS, JR., | Born Feb. 20, 1830, | Died Oct. 17, 1858, | Aged 28 y'rs 8 mo.
Mark the perfect man, and behold the upright, for the end of that man is peace—Ps. 37 : 37.

1823. POLLY MORTON, | Died | November 4, 1858, | Aged 73 7ears.
Dearest sister, we will meet thee
In that land where all is blest;
There where sorrows never enter,
We will dwell forever blest.

1824. FATHER & MOTHER | Sacred | To the memory of | CAPT. GEORGE BACON, | who was drowned at Sea, | on a voyage from Hamburg, | to New York, | Sept. 6, 1826, Æ. 53 years. | ELIZABETH, | his widow, died | Jan, 6, 1859, | Æ. 79 y'rs & 4 months.
There is rest in Heaven.

1825. DEA. | JOSIAH ROBBINS | died Jan. 30, 1859, | Aged 72 years 10 mo.
See No. 915 Ante.

1826. ABRAHAM JACKSON, | Born | November 29, 1791, | Died | February 6, 1859; | Æ. 67 years.

1827. REBECCA, | wife of | NATHAN REED, | Died | March 2d, 1859, | Aged 81 y'rs & | 9 mo's.

" The memory of the just is blessed."

" The reapers are the angels."

"AS A SHOCK OF CORN IN HIS SEASON."

1828. REV. JAMES KENDALL, D.D., | Ordained 1 Jan. 1800, | Died 17 March, 1859, | Aged 89 Years.

FOR SIXTY YEARS MINISTER OF THE FIRST PARISH IN THIS TOWN.

" My peace I give unto you."
" The gift of God is Eternal life."

1829. EMMA CORDELIA, | daughter of | CHARLES & CORDELIA B. | TUFTS, died Mar. 19, 1859, | aged 22 y'rs.

1830. ALICE A. NEAL, | Dau. of Samuel | and | ALICE A. BROWN, | Died April 7, 1859, | Aged 29 y'rs, 7 mo's, 2 d's.

1831. REV | AURIN BUGBEE, | Born | Sept. 12, 1808, | Died | April 14, 1859.

1832. ELIZABETH FAUNCE, | widow of the late | Capt. BARNABAS FAUNCE, | died Apr. 23, 1859; | Æ. 85 years.

"Blessed are they who die in the Lord."

1833. LUCIA W. | wife of | WILLIAM H. | MORTON, | died May 4, 1859 | aged 25 years, | & 4 mos.

" Oh! why should we in anguish weep."
" She is not lost, but gone before."

1834. SARAH ELIZABETH, | daughter of | CHARLES & CORDELIA B. | TUFTS, | died July 3, 1859, | aged 24 yrs.

1835. WILLIAM H ROGERS | Died | July 12, 1859 | aged 23 yrs. 5 mos. | Only son of | A. B. & ELIZA ROGERS.

1836. In memory of | DAVID HARLOW, | who died | July 22, 1859; | Æ. 60 years, 6 mos.

Dear as thou wert, and justly dear,
We will not weep for thee;
One thought shall check the starting tear,
It is that thou art free.

1837. Sacred | to the memory | RUTH | widow of | ISRAEL HOYT, | died Aug. 10, 1859, | aged 60 y'rs. 4 mos. | & 6 days.

1838. MARY H. | died Sept. 12, 1853; | Æ. 3 mos. & 7 days. | WILLIE BRADFORD | died Sept. 4, 1859; | Æ. 3 weeks & 2 days.

1839. PHILLIP, | Born Jan. 20, 1855 | Died Sept. 22, 1859, | Æ. 4 y's.

1840. ABIGAIL, | widow of | HENRY HOLLIS, | died Sept. 27, 1859; | aged 63 yrs.

" Whosoever liveth and believeth in Me shall never die."
—*John, II, 26.*

1841. PRISCILLA˙COTTON, | widow of | JOSIAH COTTON | Born Sept. 30, 1760, | Died Oct. 4, 1859.

1842. REBECCA, | wife of | JACOB TINKHAM, | Died | Oct. 17, 1859. | Æt. 76.

·"Blessed are the dead, that die in the Lord."

1843. GEORGE W. TALBOT, | Born December 29, 1838 | Died November 1, 1859.

"A good boy."

1844. FATHER & MOTHER. | CAPT. IGNATIUS PIERCE | Died | Aug. 24, 1853, | aged 68 years. | BETSEY, | his wife, | Died Nov 30, 1859, | aged 73 years.

" Blessed are the dead who die in the Lord.

1845. In Memory of | MARY A. B., | wife of | IRA ALLEN, | and dau. of DAVID & | SALLY C. WARREN, | died Dec. 31, 1859, | aged 29 y'rs. 1 mo. 16 ds.

1846. WINSLOW M. TRIBBLE | died Jan. 5, 1860; |
Æ. 49 years & 1 mo.

Also three of his children: | MARSTON W., | died Dec. 2,
1858; | Æ. 25 years & 2 mos. | HORACE G., | died Nov. 7,
1859; | Æ. 21 years & 4 mos. | CHRISTIANA D., | died Sept.
22, 1837; | Æ. 1 year & 25 days.
Eternal upward progression is the destiny of all in Spirit life.

1847. IDA LIZZIE, | dau. of THOMAS & ELIZABETH R.
SPEAR, | died Jan. 23, 1860 | Æ. 3 years & 4 mos.

1848. NATHANIEL HOLMES JR., | died Aug. 29, 1805 ;
in the 31st year of his age. | ELIZABETH HOLMES, | his
widow | died Jan. 30, 1860; | Æ. 86 y'rs, 7 mos. & 8 days, |
BETSEY C. HOLMES, | their daughter | died Feb. 26, 1848 ; |
in the 48th year of her age.

1849. OUR | HATTIE | Aged 7 years. | LITTLE CLARA |
Aged 3 years, 8 mos. | Children of WILLIAM & SUSAN A. WES-
TON, | died Feb. 22, 1860.
TREASURES IN HEAVEN.

1850. FATHER & MOTHER | ISAAC TRIBBLE, | Born July
31, 1789, | Died Feb. 16, 1865. | LOIS TRIBBLE, | Born Dec.
14, 1788, | Died Mar. 31, 1860.

1851. MARY A., | wife of LEWIS HALL | died Apr. 27,
1860; | Æ. 43 & 6 mos.
" Blessed are the dead who die in the Lord."

1852. NATHANIEL SPOONER | died at sea | Mar. 9,
1817; | aged 31 years. | LUCY W. SPOONER, | his wife |
whose remains lie beneath, | died in Plymouth, | April 29,
1860; | aged 77 years.

1853. WHITTEN. | LYDIA N. | wife of | CHARLES WHIT-
TEN, JR., | called home, | Apr. 30, 1860; | Æ. 30 years.
Thou still art dear, though numbered with the dead.

1854. LUISE, | daughter of | VALENTINE & CAROLINE ZAHN, | died May 31, 1860; | Æ. 2 y'rs & 3 mos.

1855. JOHN KING, | died June 1, 1860; | Æ. 78 years & 5 mos. | POLLY, | his wife | died Jan. 10, 1847; | Æ. 62 years & 9 mos.

1856. GEORGE E. CHASE | died 1824; | Æ. 15 years. | WILLIAM CHASE | died 1830; | Æ. 23 years. | SAMUEL R. CHASE | died Aug. 21, 1849; | Æ. 20 years & 7 mos. | HENRY CHASE | died July 1860; | Æ. 43 years. | SONS OF JOHN & ABIGAIL CHASE.

—I. H. S.—

1857. In memory of | ANN | wife of | JOHN CASSADY, | who died | July 20, 1860; | in her 77th year.

1858. CAPT. DAVID BRADFORD | Born April 28, 1786; Died July 22, 1860.

1859. In memory of | CURTIS HOYT. | Died Aug. 3, 1860. | Aged 42 yrs.

" I am the resurrection and the life."

1860. MARY BROWN | died Aug. 16, 1760; | aged 71 years, 6 mos & 22 days.

1861. SONNY B.

Lent, but not given;
To bud on earth
And bloom in Heaven.

HORACE B. JENKS | Died Oct. 1, 1860, | Aged 3 y'rs, 3 mos, 21 ds.

1862. PHEBE, | wife of | JAMES G. GLEASON, | died Oct. 10, 1860; | aged 70 yrs. 1 mo.

Dear is the spot where our loved ones sleep,
And sweet the strain which angels pour;
O, why should we in anguish weep?
They are not lost,—but gone before.

1863.   JULIA ANN | died Sept. 4, 1842; | Æ. 3 y'rs & 7 mos. | NATHANIEL T., | died June 25, 1853; | Æ. 19 mos. | ALMIRA W. | died Mar. 6, 1855: | Æ. 11 weeks. | LAURA W. | died Mar. 7, 1858; | Æ. 19 mos. | LAURA A. | died Oct. 13, 1860; | Æ. 8 mos. | CHILDREN OF JAMES & ALMIRA SEARS.

1864.   MARY T. BACON | died Nov. 12, 1860. | Aged 50 yrs. 10 mos.

1865.   LYDIA DREW | widow of—CAPT. ATWOOD DREW | Born Jan. 7, 1782; | Died Jan. 3, 1861.

> *We mourn for her; we still do weep;*
> *No more we'll see her here;*
> *In Jesus she doth sweetly sleep;*
> *Why shed for her a tear?*

1866.   BATHSHEBA BRADFORD | wife of | LEMUEL BRADFORD | died Jan. 22, 1861; | aged 68 y'rs. 10 mos. & 12 days.

> *Dear as thou wert, and justly dear;*
> *We will not weep for thee;*
> *One thought shall check the startling tear;*
> *It is, that thou art free.*

1867.   GEORGE STEWARD | Died Feb. 13th 1861; | Aged 28 years.

1868.   ANNETTE C. | daughter of JOHN E. | & MERCY H. MORRISON, | died Mar. 26, 1861; | aged 2 y'rs, 2 mos. & 10 days.

> *Sleep, dear Nellie, sleep,*
> *Till Jesus bids thee rise;*
> *Then may we also be prepared*
> *To meet thee in the skies.*

1869.   MARY A. LUCAS, | wife of | ISAAC J. LUCAS, JR., | Died Apr. 8, 1861; | aged 28 years 5 mos.

1870.   OUR MOTHER. | BETSEY MORTON | died June 11, 1861; | aged 64 years.

Dear mother, you have soared away
To dwell in everlasting day,
Up to the shining courts above,
To enjoy your Saviour and your God.

1871. OUR MOTHER. | REBECCA, | widow of | WILLIAM ROGERS, JR. | died June 19, 1861 ; | Æ. 70 years & 2 mos.

1872. CLARISA A. | Wife of | GEORGE F. GREEN, | died Aug. 7, 1861 | aged 25 years 4 mos.

1873. CHARLIE IRVING | Son of J. D. | & E. B. BAXTER | fell asleep Aug. 8, 1861 ; | aged 1 year, 9 months & 12 days.
Our dearly loved one will not be forgotten.

1874. IN MEMORIAM. | SARAH [BRINLEY] | wife of SAMUEL NICOLSON; | born in Boston May 23, 1798; | died in Cambridge Sept. 9, 1861.
Beloved and lamented.

SAMUEL NICOLSON, | son of | THOMAS & HANNAH [OTIS] | NICOLSON | born in Plymouth, | Dec. 2, 1791, | died in Boston, | Jan. 6, 1868.

1875. SYLVANUS ROGERS | Born Nov. 24, 1798 | Died April 20, 1860 | Æ. 62 yrs & 7 mos. | JANE ROGERS, | his wife | Born Jan. 12, 1800 | Died Sept. 15, 1861 | Æ. 61 y'rs & 8 mos. | Also their daughter | JANE F. | born Jan. 54, 1824, | died Sept 12, 1825 | Æ. 1 year, 8 mos.
There is rest in Heaven.

1876. MOTHER | Died Oct. 1861 | Aged 43.

1877. MRS. SARAH SHERMAN | Died | Dec. 20, 1861, | Aged 76 y'rs, 1 mo. | 2 days.

1878. CHARLOTTE T. | Wife of ASA KENDRICK | died July 14, 1862; | aged 62 years 6 mos. | REUBEN R. KENDRICK | died Mar. 18, 1862; | aged 24 years. | MARY B. | wife of REUBEN R. KENDRICK | died May 2, 1862; | aged 22 years. | ELIZABETH F. | daughter of ASA & | CHARLOTTE T. KENDRICG | died Jan. 19, 1858; | aged 17 years 9 mos.

1879. ELLEN M. | daughter of SAMUEL B. | & CAROLINE
REMAND | sweetly fell asleep with | Jesus, May 25, 1862; |
Æ. 10 y'rs, 8 mos. & 2 d'ys.

> *Thy gentle spirit passed away*
> *Mid pain the most severe ;*
> *So great we could not wish thy stay*
> *A moment longer here.*

1880. In memory of | NATHANIEL BARTLETT, 2ND. |
Died | June 23, 1862; | aged 56 years & 6 mos.

1881. NANCY RIPLEY, | wife of | WILLIAM P. RIPLEY, |
Died Aug. 16, 1862, | Aged 83. yrs.

*She trusted in the mercy of the Lord: and now rejoices in his
salvation.*

1882. In memory of | LOIS COLLINS, | born May 20,
1787, | died Aug. 23, 1862, | Æ. 75 years, 3 mos. & 3 days.

1883. SUSAN THACHER, | Wife of | WILLIAM BARTLETT
| died August 25, 1862, | Œ. 68 years.

1884. EDWARD BURT | died July 6, 1861; | Æ. 66 y'rs
& 10 mos. | THOMAS B. | Son of EDWARD & | ELIZABETH
BURT, | died at | Harwood Hospital, | Washington, D. C. | Oct.
31, 1862; | Æ. 23 yrs & 9 mos. | A member of Co. E, 29 Reg.
Mass. Vols.

1885. CAPT. JOSEPH W. COLLINGSWOOD | Co. H, 18th
Reg. Mass. Vols. | wounded at the battle | of Fredericksburg,
Va. | Dec. 13, 1862; | Died Dec. 24, 1862, | Aged 41 years.

> *He who gives his life for his country,*
> *gives his own, but for a higher life.*

1886. HENRY S. HOLMES, | Died | Dec. 19, 1862 | Aged
3 y'rs, 1 mo. 28 ds.

1887. SAMUEL A. | Son of ANTONIO & | SARAH C.
FRANK, | Born May 4, 1849; | Died Jan. 12, 1863.

He was our best loved one
Kindly and gentle ever
Death early claimed his own,
We can forget him never.

1888. WILLIAM S. RUSSELL, | Born Jan. 11, 1792. | Died Feb. 22, 1863.

1889. SARAH FRENCH, | Only daughter of | JOHN B. & SARAH A. F. | RUSSELL, | died Mar. 13, 1863; | Æ. 3 years, 7 mos. 26 days.

> *She has gone to heaven before us,*
> *But she turns and waves her hand.*
> *Pointing to the glories o'er us,*
> *In that happy spirit land.*

1890. ALFRED C. FINNEY, | a member of | Co. E, 5th Reg. Mass. Vols. | died at Newbern, N. C. | Mar. 13, 1863; | Æ. 21 years, 6 mo. 24 days.

> *" Drop a kind tear for the soldier that's gone,*
> *For 'tis manly to weep for the brave."*

1891. IN MEMORY OF | CAPT. ROBERT COWEN | who died Mar. 30, 1863; | Æ. 62 years & 10 mos.

1892. IN MEMORY OF | LYDIA BRADFORD, | Born Jan. 25, 1795, | Died Apr. 14, 1863. | ALSO OF | CORNELIUS BRADFORD, | who died at New Orleans, | Aug. 16, 1824. Æ. 31 years.

1893. THOMAS H. GIBBS, | Co. A, | 3 N. Y. Reg't. | Died Apr. 29, 1863. | Æ. 17 y'rs 8 mos.

1894, In memory of | SARAH | wife of | ROBERT SEARSON | & daughter of DENNIS | & SARAH DELEANY. | Born June 6, 1832; | Died May 3, 1863.

> *I will remember thee love when*
> *many have forgot, and may you*
> *rest in peace with God.*

1895.   OUR MOTHER—GONE HOME. | PHILA H. | Wife of | DR. ISAAC HATCH, | Died | May 14, 1863; | aged 56 years, 9 months.

1896.   FREDERIC HOLMES, | Lieut. 38, Mass. Vol. Infantry, | aged 28 years, | was killed June 14, 1863, | while leading his men to | the assault on the enemy's | works at Port Hudson, La.

His memory | shall not be less green, nor | heroic virtues less honored, | that his body lies amid the ruins | of the Rebellion he gave his life to destroy.

1897,   CAPT. GEORGE SIMMONS | died July 26, 1863; | aged 81 years. | MERCY SIMMONS | his wife | died Nov. 29, 1858 | aged 75 years.

1898.   LIEUT. HORACE A. JENKS, | Co. E. | 29 Reg't Mass. Vols. | Died at Milldale, Miss. | July 26, 1863. | Aged 30 years.

Though not upon the Battlefield
He breathed his latest breath
For freedom and for country, still
He died a hero's death!

Promoted from the ranks below
To join the ranks on high,
In bleeding hearts he loved and left,
His name shall never die.

1899.   WILLIAM BARTLETT | Died | July 30, 1865, | aged 77 years.

1900.   GEORGE E. WADSWORTH, | of Co. E. 29th Mass. Reg., | died | at Crab Orchard, Ky. | Aug. 31, 1863; | Aged 35 y'rs 8 mos.

" So calm, so constant was his rectitude
That, by his loss alone, we know its worth,
And feel how true a man has walked
With us on earth.

1901. THOMAS W. HAYDEN, | of Co. E., 29 Mass. Vol's. | Died | at Crab Orchard, Ky. | Sept. 4, 1863. | Aged 33 years | & 2 mo's.

A precious sacrifice for freedom.

1902. CAROLINE A. | Wife of | NELSON P. PERRY, | & daughter of JUDSON | & ALMIRA RICE, | Born Mar. 5, 1831, | Died Sept. 5, 1863.

A beloved wife, an affectionate daughter and a
true friend. May she find rest in heaven.

1903. WILLIAM | Son of | ICHABOD & MARY | MOREY, | Died Oct. 13, 1863, | Aged 27 y'rs 1 mo. | 18 days.

The pains of death are past,
Labor and sorrow cease ;
And his life's warfare closed at last,
His soul now rests in peace.

1904. HANNAH J. WASHBURN | daughter of ISAAC J. | & CATHERINE LUCAS | Died | October 17, 1863 ; | Æ. 36 years 6 mos.

1905. In Memory of | CAPT. GEORGE WESTON | who died Nov. 28, 1844, | Aged 54 years | MARY | his wife | died Oct. 23, 1863 | aged 72 years, 3 mo's.

See No. 1387, Ante.

1906. LEMUEL SIMMONS | Died | Dec. 6, 1863 | aged 73 years | 4 months.

He was universally beloved and respected ;
honest and upright, with a cheerful and
pleasant manner, and a kind benevolent
heart. To know him was to esteem him.

1907. JOHN H. BRADFORD | Born | July 14, 1780, | Died | Dec. 7, 1863.

1908. ANN ELIZA, | daughter of JOHN | & BETSEY ANN EDDY, | died Dec. 31, 1863 ; | aged 16 y'rs, 9 mo. | 16 days.

1909. JOHN B. BARLOW | Died Jan. 8th, 1864, | aged 2 yr's and 8 months.

1910.   ELIJAH J. WESTON | died Jan. 14, 1864; | aged 30 years, 6 mos.

> *I trust my blood was spilled for thee,*
> *Who shed thy precious blood for me,*
> *Here lies a husband and a father,*
> *Who was kind and gentle ever.*
> *Death early claimed thee,*
> *We shall forget thee never.*

Also our gentle child | JOHNNY C. | Son of ELIJAH J. & | SUSAN WESTON, | died Aug. 12, 1863 ; | Æ. 1 year, 8 mos, 5 days.

> *They were dearly loved on earth by us all.*
> *I trust now they are loved in heaven.*

1911.   HENRY F. EDDY | Co. E. | 29 Mass. Regt. | Died Jan. 20, 1864 | Aged 23 y'rs 2 m's.

1912.   MARY T. BARTLETT | Daughter of | JAMES & MARY BARTLETT, | Born Jan 11, 1784, | Died Feb. 15, 1864.

1913.   ELISHA C WHITTEN, | Died | March 4, 1864, | Aged 23 y'rs 2 mo's | 14 days.

> *"Blessed are the dead which die in the Lord."*

1914.   ALBERT R. ROBBINS | Co. E. | 29 Mass. Regt. | Died Mar. 5, 1864 | aged 22 y'rs 5 m's | 23 days.

1915.   In memory of | GEORGE COOPER, | who died | April 29, 1864; | Æ. 66 years 8 mos.

1916.   JAMES T. DEVINE | Died May 8, 1864 | Aged 2 yr's 5 mos 21 days.

1917.   OUR MOTHER. | ABAGAIL T. | Widow of | THOMAS GOODWIN, | died May 11, 1864; | aged 77 years.

1918.   Erected in memory of | MARTHA | Wife of | EPHRAIM PATY, | who died May 12, 1864, | aged 69 yrs, 5 mos, | 16 days.

> *Asleep in Jesus.*

1919. JOHN B. ATWOOD | Died | May 12, 1864, | aged 60 y'rs.

1920. JOHN K. ALEXANDER | Co. E. 29 Mass. Vols. | Died at | Fredericksburg, Va., | May 12, 1864, | aged 28 y'rs.

> *And underneath the evergreen*
> *Away from grief and care,*
> *Alone beneath its leafy screen*
> *They laid a loved one there.*

1921. MOTHER | SALLY DREW | Born | May 7, 1782; | Died | May 17, 1864.

1922. HOMER BRYANT | Co. E. | 23 Mass. Regt. | Died | June 6, 1864 | Aged 45 years.

1923. ELIJAH RICKARD | Died | July 22, 1864, | Aged 80 y'rs.

> *"Let me die the death of the righteous and let my last end be like his."*

LUCY RICKARD, | Died April 3, 1863, | Aged 70 yrs.
> *"Precious in the sight of the Lord is the death of his saints."*

1924. In Memory of | SETH W. EDDY, | a member of | Co. H. 58th Regt. Mass. Vols. | who died | Aug. 13, 1864; | aged 27 years | and 8 days.

WILLIE O. | Son of SETH W. | & FRANCES M. EDDY, | died Mar 5, 1859; | aged 4 mos.

> *Bloom brightly sweet roses*
> *Bloom brightly above*
> *The mound that encloses*
> *The form that we love.*

1925. LUCIE S. | Wife of | CHARLES W. JOHNSON | died Aug. 19, 1864; | Æ. 21 yrs 6 mos & 6 d.

> *We shall meet with these our loved ones,*
> *That were torn from our embrace,*
> *We shall listen to their voices,*
> *And behold them face to face.*

Also | JAMES H. | GRACE D. | & ELLA P. | children of
JAMES J. | & NANCY G. PAULDING.

1926. In memory of | MRS. LUCRETIA BURR WATSON
| widow of | BENJAMIN M. WATSON, | Born at Fairfield, Conn.,
Nov. 21, 1781, | Died at Plymouth, Aug. 29, 1864.

1927. Erected | to the memory of | JOSHUA SAWYER, |
who died | Sept. 10, 1864; | Aged 33 years.

> *To this lone spot I love to stray,*
> *Where sleeps the dust of that dear one*
> *Who fled so soon from earth away,*
> *Ere yet his life was scarce begun.*
>
> *O lowly spot! O husband dear,*
> *I almost envy thee thy bliss;*
> *O, gladly would I leave earth's care,*
> *For such a resting place as this.*

1928. OUR FATHER, | JOHN HARLOW, | Born | Sept. 15,
1777, | Died | Sept. 5, 1864.

1929. GEORGIE |

> *God called thee home,*
> *He thought it best.*

Son of | F. W. & A. W. | RICKARD, | Died Sept. 22, 1864, |
aged 6 mo's 14 d's.

1930. ROBERT McLAUTHIN | Co. B. | 14 Mass. Regt. |
Died Oct. 13, 1864 | Aged 20 y'rs 6 m's 3 days.

1931. ISAAC DAVIE | Died | Oct. 29, 1864, | Aged 75
y'rs | 8 mo's.

> *"Which hope we have as an anchor*
> *of the soul, both sure and steadfast*
> *and which entereth into that*
> *within the vail.*

1932. In memory of | CHARLES WADSWORTH, | of Co.
B. 39th Mass. Reg. | who died | a Prisoner of war | at Salisbury
N. C. | Nov. 10, 1864; | aged 31 y'rs 4 mos.

Who shall offer youth and beauty,
On a Nation's shrine,
With a loftier sense of duty,
Or truer heart than thine.

1933. ANNA M. BARTLETT, | Born | January 31, 1771; | Died | November 20, 1864.

" *Asleep in Jesus.*"

1934. SARAH B. | Born Feb. 22, 1850, | Died Dec 15, 1864.

The above inscription is on a small stone in the Robbins Lot.

1935. OUR MOTHER. | LYDIA STANDISH, Died | Dec. 27, 1864, | aged 44 y'rs 4 m's | 14 days.

1936. JOHN D. HAMROSA | Died Dec. 30th, 1864, | aged 1 month.

1937. CATHERINE HOWLAND | Wife of | Isaac J. Lucas, | Born July 17, 1800; | Died Jan 18, 1865, | Æ. 64 y'rs 6 mos.

Also three children | CATHERINE H., LEWIS F. | & GEORGE W.

1938. BRIDGET CASSIDY, Born Jan. 2d, 1864 | Died Feb. 19, 1865, aged 1 yr 1 mo 17 ds.

1939. HANNAH, | dau. of | david & Eliza S. | harlow. | died march 2, 1865 | Æ. 26 years 7 mo's.

Lone are the paths and sad the hours,
Since thy loved spirit's gone,
But Oh! a brighter home than ours,
In Heaven is now thine own.

1940. EMMA FRANCES, | Dau. of | ELLIS & MELINDA | ROGERS, | died March 6, 1865, | aged 16 y'rs, 4 m's, | & 6 days.

Our dear one is gone to the land where no care
Can ever approach her or trouble her there
Her Saviour has called her to enter the fold
Prepared for the righteous as promised of old.

1941. LIZZIE G. DIMAN, | died | May 7, 1863, | aged 25 y'rs, 1 mo. 1 day.

HATTIE A. DIMAN, | died Feb. 8, 1864, | aged 21 y'rs 9 mo's | 5 days.

MIRIAM G. DIMAN, | died Apr. 9, 1865, | aged 18 y'rs 5 mo's, | 9 days.

A sleep in Jesus.

1942. GEORGE F. | Son of FRANCIS H. & | SARAH J. P. ROBBINS, | died Apr. 20, 1865 ; | aged 1 year 8 mo. | & 21 days.

Also an | an infant daughter.

1943. FATHER | WILSON CHURCHILL, | died | April 21, 1865, | aged 85 y'rs 2 mos.

1944. MOTHER. | LUCY DELANO | Wife of | MERRICK RYDER, | died | April 28, 1865, | aged | 70 y'rs, 9 mo's.

1945. In memory of | ANN T. COWEN, | who died May 16, 1865, | Æ. 57 years 11 mos. | & 9 days.

1946. LILLY R. MORTON, | Wife of | JOHN L. MORTON, | died | May 17, 1865 ; | Æ. 74 years.

Dear as thou wert, and justly dear
We will not weep for thee ;
One thought shall check the starting tear,
It is, that thou art free.

1947. WM. H. SHAW, | Co. E. | 32 Mass. Regt. | died Aug. 6, 1865, | aged 35 y'rs.

1948. LOVICA T. McGLATHLIN, | Born | Sept 28, 1780, | died | Aug. 28, 1865.

We shall meet beyond the River.

1949. MARTHA T. | dau. of | CHARLES & LUCY | NELSON,
| died Sept. 8, 1865, | Aged 25 yrs. | 7 mo's.

> *Rest, blessed spirit, rest.*
> *Life's fitful fever's o'er,*
> *Earth's circle numbers one the less*
> *But heaven, one seraph more.*

1950. LYDIA W. ELLIS, | Wife of | SAMUEL ELLIS, |
Died Sept. 8, 1865 | Aged 71 yrs.

1951. VALENTINE DITMAN | *Died* | Oct. 14, 1865, |
Aged 39 y'rs, 5 m's, | 24 days.

1952. In memory of | MRS. JEAN PATY | Wife of | CAPT.
WM. PATY. | Died Nov. 2, 1865, Æ. 68 years.

1953. ELLA MARIA. | Only daughter of | ZOETH & RE-
BECCA M. | CLARK, | died Dec. 17, 1865, | aged 14 y'rs, 4 m's
| & 1 day.

> *And lo! above the dews of night*
> *The vesper star appears;*
> *So faith lights up the mourner's heart*
> *Whose eyes are dim with tears.*
>
> *Night falls, but soon the morning light*
> *Its glorie shall restore;*
> *And thus the eyes that sleep in death*
> *Shall wake to close no more.*

1954. ELLEN, | Wife of | WILLIAM H. RICHMOND | died |
Dec. 21, 1865, | aged 43 y'rs.

WILLIAM H. | their son | died July 24, 1872, | aged 27 y'rs
3 mo's, | 6 days.

WILLIAM H. RICHMOND | died | January 19, 1864; |
aged 49 years 7 mo's.

> *"Just as I am without one plea,*
> *But that thy blood was shed for me*
> *And that thou bidst me come to thee*
> *O lamb of God, I come."*

1955. HANS WITTE, | Died Jan. 10, 1866, | Aged 46 yrs, 9 mos, 26 ds.

1956. BETSEY FARRIS RUSSELL, | Wife of | BRIDG-HAM RUSSELL, | Died March 3, 1866. | Aged 72 years.

A devoted wife, a fond mother, a kind and sympathizing friend to all in distress or affliction.

1957. SALLY, | Wife of | CAPT. JOSEPH WRIGHT, | Died March 21, 1866, | Aged 63 yrs. 7 mo.

1958. BETSEY HARLOW, | *Died* | March 27, 1866, | Aged 53 years. | BENJAMIN HARLOW, | *Died* | Aug. 18, 1846, | Aged 35 years.

"Blessed are they that mourn, for they shall be comforted."

1959. PRISCILLA, | wife of | GEORGE RAYMOND, | Died | Apr. 6, 1866, | Aged 81 y'rs, 6 mo's.

" Jesus saith, Becaus I live, ye shall live also."

1960. HANNAH T. | his wife | died Apr. 8, 1866, | Aged 76 years. | Wife of JOB CHURCHILL.

1961. ELIAS E. COX | Son of | ELIAS & ELIZA COX | *Died* | April 8, 1866, | Aged 27 years, 6 mos. | 28 days.

So near perfection in his early day,
Why should we weep to see him snatched away;
To see him reach at once the immortal prize,
And rise triumphant to his native skies.

1962. BETSEY, | Wife of | NATHANIEL HARLOW, | *Died* | April 23, 1866, | Aged 77 years.

" Heaven is my home."

1963. FRANK C. | Son of | T. S. & E. T. ROBBINS. | Passed away | June 14, 1866. | Aged 17 y'rs 11 mos.

Loving and loved—his life to ours
Was like the sunshine from above.
His sudden call from unseen powers,
Makes him immortal in our love.

THOMAS S. ROBBINS | Died | May 16, 1861. | Aged 43 y'rs, 4 mo's | 16 days.

> *He suffered many weary years.*
> *" To him the grave no victory had*
> *and death no sting."*

FRANKIE L. | Son of | T. S. & E. T. ROBBINS, | Born Feb. 15, 1846. | Died Dec. 20, 1847.

> *" Weep not for those*
> *Who sink within the arms of death,*
> *'Ere yet the chilling wintry breath*
> *Of sorrow o'er them blows."*

1964. MARY D. | Dau. of | WILLIAM & JANE | STEPHENS, | Died July 24, 1866, | Æ. 21 y'rs. 8 mos.

> *Cold is that form once filled with youthful bloom;*
> *It sleeps, alas! within the lonely tomb;*
> *Commingling with the dust, it wears away,*
> *Companion only for its fellow clay;*
> *But that ethereal spark of " heavenly flame*
> *Too strong to live within its earthly frame.*
> *Has winged its flight, we trust to realms above,*
> *Forever to enjoy a Saviour's love."*

1965. NANCY HOLMES, | Wife of | NATHANIEL HUESTEN | Born | June 30, 1791, | Died | Sept. 4, 1866.

> *" Blessed are the pure in heart, for they shall see God."*

1966. SOPHIA B. | Wife of | PELHAM WHITING, | Died Sept. 4, 1866, | Aged 41 years.

1967. WM. HEMMERLY, | Died Sept. 21st, 1866 | Aged 31 yr, 6 months.

1968. In memory of | our Mother | ELIZABETH | widow of | the late THOMAS ATWOOD, | Born in Truro, June 30, 1778. | Died in Fairhaven, Nov. 2, 1866. | Aged 88 y'rs, 4 mo's, 3 d's.

1969. OUR MOTHER. | ZORADAY T. | Wife of | CAPT. T. E. CORNISH, | Died Nov. 10, 1866, | Aged 61 years.

1970. TENIA. | Gone home loved one. | bouquet. | But we shall meet again. | ALBERTENIA L. | Dau of | L. W. & E. A. WHITTEN, | Died Dec. 24, 1866, | Aged 12 y'rs, 8 mos, | 18 days.

1971. MAGDALENA BUERKE | Died Jan. — 1867. | Aged — yrs 6 mos.

1972. WM. T. NICKERSON, | Son of WILLIAM & MARY NICKERSON | Died Jan. 11, 1867 | Aged 29 y'rs, 9 mos, | 22 days.

1973. MISS ABBY BARTLETT, | Died | Jan. 22, 1867. | Aged 72 y'rs, 6 mos.

" There is rest in Heaven."

1974. PETER J. DEVINE, | Died Feb. 13, 1867. | Aged 9 mos. 5 days.

1975. HARRIE W. | Son of | H. & F. M. HOLMES, | Died April 10, 1867. | Aged 1 year, 4 mos. | 14 days.

'Tis Jesus speaks: " I fold," says he,
These lambs within my breast;
Protection they shall find in me,
In me be ever blest.

1976. JAMES BURNS. | MARY | Wife of | JAMES BURNS, | Died | April 17, 1867, | Aged 54 yrs.

Requiescant in peace. Amen.

1977. JAMES BARTLETT | Died | June 17, 1867, | Aged 64 y'rs, 1 mo.

1978. GEORGE F. SNOW, | Died | July 22, 1867, | Aged 31 y'rs, 3 mo's.

" Therefore be ye also ready; for in such an hour as ye think not the Son of Man cometh."

1979. BENJAMIN F. BATES | Co. E. 29 | Mass. Regt. | Died June 17, 1867. | Aged 30 yrs, 10 m's. | 29 days.

1980. REUBEN HALL, | Died | Aug. 30, 1867, | Aged 53 y'rs. 4 mo's.

Dear Husband, dear father, now sweetly at rest,
United forever with those that are blest,
Now an angel in heaven before the white throne,
Praising God for His goodness in taking thee home.

We miss that sweet smile and loving caress,
So fondly bestowed on those you loved best,
But that smile is now sweeter and the love is more strong
And the angels in chorus have joined your glad song.

1981. GEORGE F. HEMMERLY, | Died | Sept. 7, 1867 | Aged 2 yrs, 10 mos.

1982. EMMA M. | Dau. of | S. S. & R. M. HOWLAND | Died Sept. 15, 1867 | Aged 15 y'rs, 12 ds.

Affection lives beyond death's dark and withering will.

EMMA. | GONE FROM US | THE CHILD WE LOVED.

1983. In memory of | NANCY DAVIE, | Born Oct. 30, 1785, | Died Oct. 10, 1867.

1984. IN MEMORY OF | MARY C. | wife of | GEORGE COOPER, | died Nov. 3, 1867, | Æ. 70 years 10 mos.

1985. JULIA. | JULIA S. SHAW, | Died | Nov. 29, 1867 | Aged 17 y'rs, 6 mo's | & 7 days.

1986. FATHER & MOTHER | CAPT. LEWIS FINNEY, | Lost at sea, | Sept. 1818, | Aged 39 y'rs. | ELIZABETH, | His widow | Dec. 2, 1867, | Aged 80 y'rs, 3 mos.

1987. In memory of | MY MOTHER | HARRIET T. | Widow of | SAMUEL J. JONES, | died Dec. 19, 1867, | Aged 62 years, | & 2 mo's.

Beloved and lamented.

1988.   CHARITY S. | Wife of | STEPHEN D. DREW, | Died Jan. 25, 1868, | Aged 41 y'rs.

1989.   LUCY COTTON JACKSON, | Wife of | CHARLES BROWN, | Died Feb. 9, 1868 | aged 69.

How sweet to think of peace at last,
And feel that death is gain.

1990.   PELHAM FINNEY, | Died | Feb. 12, 1868, | Aged 56 yrs. 7 mos. | WILLIAM H., | PELHAM W., | CLARA, | ALMIRA J., | Children of | PELHAM & MARY A. FINNEY.

1991.   MARY REIDLE, | Died | Feb. 14th, 1868, | Aged 33 years.

1992.   MARGE CALLHAN, | Died | Feb. 25, 1868, | Aged 61 y'rs.

My work is with my God.

1993.   HANNAH WESTON, | Died | March 22, 1868, | Aged 82 y'rs, 4 mo's.

1994.   PARTED BELOW. — UNITED ABOVE. | SARAH HOLMES, | Died | April 1, 1868, | Aged 86 years.

1995.   ANSEL HOLMES, | Died | April 2, 1868, | Aged 90 y'rs, 11 mo's, | 21 days. | FATHER. | PARTED BELOW.

1996.   ASA A. WHITING | Died | April 29, 1868, | Aged 55 y'rs, | 9 mos.

" The gift of God is eternal life."

1997.   WILLIE & GEORGIE | Sons of | CAPT. WM. & SARAH J. ATWOOD. | WILLIAM PERLEY, | Died May 26, 1868. | Aged 18 y'rs, 1 day. | GEORGE HERBERT, | Supposed to have been | lost at sea, | Aug. 2, 1867, | Aged 14 y'rs, 11 mo. 1 day.

1998.   HELEN. | HELEN M. SHAW, | Died | June 29, 1868, | Aged 18 y'rs, 1 mo. | & 7 days.

1999. CATHARINE REIDLE, | Died | Aug. 17th, 1868 | Aged 6 months.

2000. ZEPHANIAH BRADFORD, | Died | Sept. 1, 1868 | Aged 69 y'rs, 1 mo. | 17 days.

2001. ANTOINETTE, | Wife of | FRANKLIN B. HOLMES, | died Sept. 25, 1868, | aged 39 y'rs 2 mo's.

Waiting on the other shore.

2002. SAMUEL D. BALLARD, | died | Sept. 27, 1868, | aged 41 yrs 8 mo.

I know he waits beside the gate,
For us to come, our child and me;
He'll meet us when life's day grows late,
And we, too, cross the billowy sea.
Yes, we shall meet in the land above,
For heaven is light, and "God is love."

2003. BETSEY, | Widow of | WILLIAM ELLIS, | died Oct. 19, 1868, | aged 93 y'rs 3 mos.

WILLIAM, | Their son | Drowned | Sept. 24, 1837, | aged 22 years.

2004. GEORGE S., 2nd. | Lost at sea | Dec. 15, 1868, | aged 19 y'rs 3 mo's.   MARY H. | died Nov. 22, 1868, | aged 24 y'rs 18 d's.

Children of STEVENS & HELENA C. ELLIS.

2005. CAPT. ROBERT HUTCHINSON. | died | Dec. 27, 1868, | aged 80 y'rs.   DEBORAH, | His wife | died June 30, 1821, | aged 28 y'rs.

"Even so, Father; for so it seemed good in thy sight."

2006. LUCRETIA, | Wife of | CAPT. OTIS ROGERS, | died Jan. 10, 1869, | aged 40 y'rs 29 d's.

The memory of thy name, dear one,
Lives in my inmost heart,
Linked with a thousand hopes and fears
That will not thence depart.

2007. SARAH, | Wife of | LEWIS PERRY, | & dau. of | DAVID & SALLY DREW, | died Jan. 10, 1869, | aged 65 y'rs 9 mo's.

> *Yet, ah—and let me lightly tread—*
> *She sleeps beneath this stone,*
> *And would have soothed my dying bed,*
> *Aad wept for me when gone.*

2008. MARY REITER, | died | Feb. 11th, 1869 | aged 12 yrs 6 mos.

2009. SUSAN WESTON, | died | Feb. 27, 1869 | aged 55 yrs 7 mos. | 14 days.

> *"The memory of the just is blessed."*

2010. Our Father | JOSHUA PRATT, | died March 17, 1869, | aged 87 y'rs 5 mo's.   Also his wife | ELENER BOYSE, | died May, 1829, | aged 45 y'rs.

> *God calls our loved ones, but we lose not wholly*
> *What he has given.*
> *They live on earth in thought and deed as truly*
> *As in heaven.*

2011, Our Mother | MARY A. | Wife of | JOSHUA PRATT, | Died March 25, 1869, | aged 55 y'rs 5 mo's. Also three infant children.

> *It hath heard the angel welcome,*
> *Met the friends who've gone before,*
> *Robed itself in light and beauty*
> *On the radiant spirit shore.*
> *There it lives to watch and guide us,*
> *On our path to shed a light*
> *Walk an angel form beside us,*
> *Through the shadows of the night.*

2012. WILLIAM FINNEY | died | Apr. 13, 1869, | aged 61 yrs 6 mos.

2013. DAVID TURNER. | Died May 14, 1869, | aged 66 yrs | 4 mos.

"When Christ, who is our life, shall appear, then shall ye also appear with him in glory."

2014. In memory | LYDIA W. SIMMONS | died | Feb. 6, 1864, | aged 37 y'rs 10 mo's.   GERSHOM SIMMONS, | died May 21, 1869, | aged 54 y'rs.   IRAETTA | their dau. | died Apr. 22, 1862, | aged 1 y'r 7 mo's.

2015. BENJ. BATES, | died | Dec. 21, 1868, | aged 60 y'rs | MARTHA | his wife | died May 29, 1869 | aged 58 y'rs. | | BENJ. F. | their son | died June 17, 1867, | aged 30 y'rs 10 mo's | 29 days.
Gone but not forgotten.

CHRIST IS OUR VICTORY, EVEN HERE.

2016. SUSAN E. WADSWORTH, | died | July 7, 1869. | aged 38 y'rs.

2017. JESSE H. TURNER, | died | July 14, 1869, | aged 53 yrs.

2018. HENRYETTA MILLER, | Born | in Germany, | July 22, 1807, | died June 13, 1869.

2019. CAROLINE | Infant child of | CONRAD & MAGDALINE | SHADE. | died July 29 | 1869.

2020. REBECCA A. BARTLETT, | Daughter of | JAMES, & MARY BARTLETT, | Born Aug. 3, 1798, | died Aug. 2, 1869,

2021. SOPHRONIA ALEXANDER | NICKERSON, | died | Sept. 4, 1869, | aged 50 y'rs 4 m's. | 12 days.
Meet me in Heaven.

2022. SAMUEL L. ALEXANDER | Died | Sept. 21, 1869, | Aged 69 y'rs.

2023. JOAN BRADFORD | Wife of | Wm. Nickerson, | Died | Oct. 13, 1869, | Aged 61 y'rs, 1 mo. | & 11 days.

> *And those dear eyes have shown through tears,*
> *But never looked unkind,*
> *For shattered hopes and troubled years,*
> *Still closer seemed to bind*
> *Thy pure and trusting heart to mine,*
> *Not for thyself dids't thou repine,*
> *But all thy husband's grief was thine,*
> *My beautiful, my wife.*

2024. OUR | WILLIE |

"*Thy will be done on earth as it | is in Heaven.*

WILLIAM L. WESTON, | Died Oct. 31, 1869, | aged 21 y'rs 6 mo's, | 15 days.

2025. ANSELM RICKARD, | Died | Nov. 20,1869, | aged, 71 years.
CYNTHIA, | his wife | Died March 6, 1867, | aged 72 y'rs.

2026. ELIZABETH S. | Dau. of | Benj. & Lucy | Bagnell | died Dec. 21, 1869, | aged 32 y'rs 9 mo's.

2027. HIRA BATES, | Died | Jan. 13, 1870, | aged 50 y'rs 6 mo's 29 days.

2028. EBENEZER N, BRADFORD, | Killed on Rail road, | at Copetown, Canada, | Jan. 28, 1870.

> *He giveth his beloved sleep.*

On back of stone is the following: Born Oct. 31, 1836.

2029. In memory of | PRISCILLA TUFTS | died | April 9, 1870 | aged 72 years.

2030. In memory of | OUR MOTHER | MARY ANN, | Widow of | George W. Callaway, | died Apr. 20, 1870, | aged 65 y'rs. 9 mo's | 16 days.

Though I walk through the valley of the shadow of death I will fear no evil; for thou art with me, thy rod and thy staff they comfort me.

2031. My Husband | CAPT. ALBERT HOLMES | died |
June 4, 1870, | aged 48 years.

> Lifes uncertain, death is sure,
> Sins the wound, and Christ the cure.

2032. FATHER & MOTHER | JOHN BARTLETT | Died |
June 12, 1870, | aged 71 y'rs.   CAROLINE | His wife |
Died May 31, 1846, | aged 46 years. | Gone Home.

2033. FATHER | CAPT. COOMER WESTON, | died July
7, 1870, aged 85 y'rs 8 mo's.

2034. WILLIAM E. BARNES, | Died | Aug. 27, 1870, |
Æ. 34 yrs 8 mo's | 15 days.

> God calls our loved ones, but we lose no wholly
> What He hath given;
> They live on earth, in thought and deed, as truly
> As in his Heaven.

2035. BETSEY HOBART. | died Aug. 29, 1870, aged 78
y'rs. | & former wife of | JOSHUA PERKINS | who died Feb.
9, 1820, | aged 34 y'rs.   And their children | BETSEY M. |
died Nov. 16, 1837, aged 26 y'rs.   JAMES A. | died Nov. 22,
1840, aged 26 y'rs.   CHARLES T. | died June 8, 1842, aged
24 y'rs. | Gone before.

2036. PRINCE DOTEN, | died | Nov. 11, 1870, | aged 89
years. | He has gone to the land of the blest.

> We shall meet beyond the river.

2037. HORACE. | HORACE, | Son of IVORY L. & RE-
BECCA B. HARLOW. | Died Nov. 29, 1870, | Aged 23 y'rs 3
mo's.

2038. NANCY K. | Wife of LEWIS PALMER, | Died Dec. 14,
1870, | aged 52 yrs. 11 mos. | & 6 ds.

> WEEP NOT.
> Sweet was her life—exceeding sweet,
> To deeds of kindness given;
> A rounded life — by love complete
> And bearing her to heaven.

2039. WM. BREWSTER BARNES, | Died | Dec. 14, 1870, | Aged 59 y'rs 10 m's.

An affectionate Husband and Father.

2040. DAVID C. HOLMES | Died | Dec. 21 1870 | Aged 69 years.

2041. CHARLES TUFTS, | Born July 29, 1803. | Died Jan. 22, 1871.

Blessed are the dead which die in the Lord.

2042. BETSEY HAYWARD | Wife of | MICHAEL HODGE, Died Feb. 27, 1871, | Aged 84 y'rs 8 mo's.

2043. SAMUEL ALEXANDER, | Died | March 30, 1871 | Aged 91 y'rs, 2 m's, | 23 days.

Blessed are the dead who die in the Lord.

2044. JACOB T. MORTON | Died | May 4, 1871, | Aged 8? yrs. | LYDIA, | HIS WIFE | Died May 15, 1838, | Aged 53 years.

2045. THOMAS COLGAN, | Born in | King's Co., Ireland, | Nov. 6, 1825, | Died Sept. 11, 1871. | JOHN, | Son of | THOMAS & ANN COLGAN, | Died Dec. 12, 1861, | Aged 4 y'rs.

May they rest in peace.

2046. MARTHA HOLMES, | Died | Oct. 17, 1871, | Aged 90 yrs 3 mo's | 12 days. | MOTHER. | UNITED ABOVE.

2047. MARY T. HOLMES. | Died | Oct. 21, 1871, | Aged 95 y'rs, 5 mo's | 19 days.

Blessed are the dead which die in the Lord.

2048. JAMES H. BURNS, | Locomotive | Fireman, killed at | his post of duty, | during the inundation | of Rowley Marshes, | Nov 15, 1871. | Son of JAMES & | MARY BURNS. | 21 yrs. 6 mo's.

Erected by the Eastern R. R. Co.

2949. In memory of | LYDIA, | wife of | DANIEL GODDARD | died | Dec. 9, 1861, | Aged 65 y'rs. | 4 mos.

2050. HARRIET OTIS, | Wife of | ABRAHAM JACKSON, | Died Jan. 21, 1873 | Æ. 74.

2051. CHARLES A. | Son of | EDWARD & SALINA | DOTEN, | Died Mar. 23, 1872, | Aged 23 y'r 2 mo's.

2052. MERCY, | His wife | Died April 10, 1872, | Aged 96 y'rs. | *Wife of Capt. Seth Morton.*

2053. CATHARINE, | Wife of | JAMES T. PAULDING | Died May 7, 1872, | Aged 46 y'rs, 6 mos.

2054. JAMES KENDRICK | Died | May 18, 1872, | Aged 51 y'rs, 10 mo's, | 18 days. | HATTIE B. | Died Feb. 22, 1864 | Aged 3 days. | Dau. of JAMES & ELEANORE KENDRICK.

Rest, kind Husband and Father, rest,
Until the trump of God shall sound.
When thou shall be raised to glory,
Immortality and eternal life,
To dwell with God, and thy loved of earth,
To part no more.

2055. SARAH DREW | Wife of | ABBOT DREW | Died | May 18, 1872, | Aged 54 yrs, 1 mo.

2056. REBECCA CHURCHILL, | died | Sept. 15, 1872; | aged 84 y'rs, | 11 mo's.

Not slothful in business; fervent in Spirit, serving the Lord.—Romans XII, II.

2057. JOHN B. WILLIAMS | Died | Oct. 9, 1872, | Aged 35 years.

2058. LUCY, | Wife of | IVORY HARLOW, | Died Oct. 18, 1872, | Aged 88 y'rs, | 10 mo's.

2059. MOTHER. | BELINDA T. | Wife of | DANIEL H SEARS, | Died Oct. 21, 1872, | Aged 58 y'rs, 2 mo's. | 15 days.

2060. MERCY B. LOVELL. | Wife of | LEANDER LOVELL, | Born April 22, 1796 | Died Nov. 6, 1872.

2061. MERCY STURTEVANT | Died | Nov. 12, 1872, |
Aged 78 y'rs, 5 mo's, | 15 days. | MERCY A. | Her dau. | Died
July 19, 1839, | Aged 23 y'rs, 3 mo's.

2062. JOHN KING, JR., | Feb. 4, 1873, | Aged 63 'yrs |
7 mos.

2063. MARTHA T. | Died Feb. 18, 1872. | Aged 19 y'rs
3 mo's. | NELLIE F. | Died Jan. 21, 1873, | Aged 11 y'rs, 5
mo's. | WILLIE B. | Died Sept. 18, 1860, | Aged 4 y'rs, 2 mo's.
WILLIE L. | Died Aug. 10, 1855, | Aged 11 mo's. | Children
of THOMAS & M. A. COLLINGWOOD.

> *Dear Children gone to rest,*
> *On Canaan happy shore;*
> *And we hope to meet again,*
> *Where parting will be no more.*

2064. FATHER & MOTHER. | WILLIAM C. GREEN. |
Died Oct. 18, 1846, | Aged 40 yrs. | MARCIA C. | his wife |
Died Mar. 9, 1873. | Aged 78 y'rs, 6 mo's.

> *Why do we mourn departed friends,*
> *Or shake at death's alarms.*
> *'Tis but the voice that Jesus sends,*
> *To call them to his arms.*

2065. ICHABOD SHAW, | Died | March 20, 1873, | Aged
69 years. | MARY SAMPSON, | Wife of ICHABOD SHAW |
| Died May 18, 1851, | Aged 47 y'rs. | MARY ELIZABETH
| Died June 23, 1858, | Aged 27 y'rs. | REBECCA BART-
LETT, | Died April 16, 1859, | Aged 25 y'rs. | Daughters of
ICHABOD | & MARY S. SHAW.

2066. SAMUEL B. RAYMOND, | Died | April 3, 1873, |
Aged 43 y'rs, 5 mo's, | 23 days.

> *Husband, thou art gone to rest,*
> *Thy sins are all forgiven,*
> *And saints in light have welcomed thee,*
> *To joy the shares of Heaven.*

2067. ALLEN HATHAWAY | Co K. | 99 N. Y. Regt. | Died June 3, 1873 | Aged 71 y'rs 20 d's.

2068. LEMUEL D. HOLMES, | Died | June 4, 1873, | Aged 75 y'rs 4 mo's. | POLLY, | his wife | Died Sept. 13, 1866 | Aged 65 y'rs 1 mo. | MARY E. | their dau. | Died Dec. 30, 1832, | Aged 4 y'rs 2 mo's.

2069. MRS. LYDIA KEYES, | Died | Nov. 18, 1861, | Aged 89 y'rs. | MISS LYDIA KEYES, | Died June 30, 1873, | Aged 75 y'rs.

2070. SALLY C. ERLAND | Widow of | HENRY ERLAND, | Died Sept. 30, 1873, | Aged 78 y'rs 3 mo's. | 13 days.
Entered into rest.

2071. ELLIS ROGERS | Died | Nov. 27, 1873. | Aged 64 y'rs & 6 mo's.

2072. SUSAN | Wife of | Prince Doten | Died Jan. 25, 1874, | Aged 86 y'rs.

2073. FATHER & MOTHER | LEONARD SNOW, | Died | March 7, 1874, | Aged 76 y'rs, 5 mo's. | MARIA, | His wife | Died Sept. 30, 1870, | Aged 72 y'rs, 11 mo's.
"When Christ who is our life shall appear, then shall ye also appear with Him in glory."

2074. RUTH | Wife of | JOHN PERRY, | Born Feb. 24, 1811, | Died June 18, 1874.
Safe in the arms of Jesus.

2075. FATHER & MOTHER | JABEZ SWIFT, | Died | March 14, 1865, | Aged 47 y'rs, 6 mo's. | LUCY B. | His wife | Died July 2, 1874, | Aged 54 y'rs, 10 mo's.
Loved ones we shall meet and rest
Mid the holy and the blest.

2076. BETSEY HOLMES, | Died | Sept. 5, 1874, | Aged 86 y'rs, | 5 mo's.
Died in Faith.

2077. In memory of | ANN GOODWIN BOUTELLE | who died | Oct. 2, 1874, | Aged 89 y'rs.

" Jesus said unto her, I am the resurrection and the life."

2078. ABIGAIL, | Wife of | CHARLES CHURCHILL, | Died Nov. 8, 1874, | Aged 77 y'rs, 5 mo's. | 3days.

2079. HUSBAND. | LEWIS H. WHITTEN, | Died | Nov. 24, 1874, | Aged 43 y'rs, 7 mo's.

Waiting on the other shore.

2080. LUCY, | Wife of | CHARLES NELSON, | Died Nov. 26, 1874, | Aged 69 y'rs, 11 mo's.

2081. MARIA S. DIMAN, | Died | Jan. 15, 1875, | Aged 38 y'rs, 8 mo's. | 23 days.

Asleep in Jesus! blessed sleep!
From which none ever wake to weep.

2082. ADELINE W. | Wife of | FREEMAN W. RICKARD, | Died Jan. 18, 1875, | Aged 49 y'rs. 18 d'ys.

She has gone to heaven before us,
But she turns and waves her hand,
Pointing to the glories o'er us
In that happy spirit land.

2083. SARAH J. | Died | Feb. 5, 1875, | Aged 66 y'rs, | Daughter of | CAPT. | SOLOMON DAVEE.

2084. ANTONIE FRANK, | Died Feb. 19th. | A. D. 1875, | Aged 67 years.

2085. EUNICE, | Wife of RUFUS CHURCHILL, | Died | March 25, 1875, | Aged | 97 y'rs, 11 mo's.

2086. LYDIA L. CHURCHILL, | Died | April 28, 1875, | Aged 81 y'rs.

2087. EMMA E. | Dau. of | WILLIAM & JANE | STEPHENS, | Died Sept. 11, 1875, | Æ 21 y'rs, 7 mo's, | 20 days.

The memory of thy loveliness
Shall round our every pathway smile,
Like moonlight where the sun has set,
A sweet and tender radiance yet.

2088. DANIEL DEACON, | Died | March 13, 1842, | Aged 51 y'rs. | POLLY T. | His widow | Died Sept. 28, 1875, | Aged 82 y'rs. | SUSAN A. | Their daughter, | Died May 22, 1836, | Aged 3 y'rs.

2089. HUSBAND. | BENJAMIN GODDARD, | Born | March 3, 1813, | Died Oct. 15, 1875. | ANN E. GODDARD, | Born Sept. 1, 1841, | Died Aug. 3, 1842.
Beloved ones rest in peace.

2090. THOMAS T. JACKSON, | Born | Sept. 11, 1798. Died | Jan. 4, 1876.

2091. IRVING B. | Son of | H. & F. M. | HOLMES, | Died Jan. 21, 1876, | Aged 3 y'rs, 4 mos.

2092. NANCY B. | Dau. of | ELIZABETH & WILLIAM | ROGERS, | Died Feb. 3, 1876 | Aged 69 y'rs, 7 mos. | 4 days.

2093. KATIE B. | Daughter of | WILLIAM & C. B. | BISHOP | Died Apr. 2, 1876, | Aged 15 y'rs, | 10 mos.

2094. MEHITABLE HOLMES | Born | March 2, 1811, | Died | May 9, 1876.
Safe in the arms of Jesus.

2095. In memory of | ELIZABETH H. CHURCHILL | Died June 22, 1876, | Æ. 77 y'rs, 9 mos, |
He raiseth up the soul and lighteneth the eyes:
He giveth health, life, and blessing.

2096. NANCY F. | Wife of | JOHN A. MORSE, | Died July 9, 1876, | Aged 65 y'rs, | 22 days.

2097. EDWARD W. WATSON | Born on | Clark's Island, | Dec. 17, 1797, | Died Aug. 8, 1876.

2098. REBECCA RUSSELL | Died | Aug. 26, 1876, | Aged 76 y'rs, 1 mo. | 12 days.

2099. FATHER & MOTHER. | ABRAHAM T. DUNHAM, | Died | Aug. 23, 1847, | Aged 60 y'rs | PATIENCE, | his widow | Died Sept. 23, 1876, | Aged 73 y'rs, 9 mos.

2100. LEWIS PERRY | Died | Oct. 11, 1876, | Aged 78 y'rs, 7 mo's.

> *Jesus can make a dying bed*
> *Feel soft as downy pillows are,*
> *While on his breast I lean my head,*
> *And breath my life out sweetly there.*

2101. BEULAH SIMMONS | Died, | Nov. 28, 1876, | Aged 74 y'rs, 2 mos. | 28 days.

2102. SALLY C. | Wife of | DAVID WARREN, | Died Feb. 13, 1877, | Aged 75 y'rs, 9 mo's, | 6 days.

2103. OLIVE FAUNCE, | Wife of | PELEG FAUNCE, | Died March 22, 1877, | Aged 77 years.

> *At Rest.*

2104. JOSEPH B. WHITING, | Died | July 2, 1877, | Aged | 36 y'rs, 4 mo's.

2105. WIFE. | LUCY, | Wife of | BENJAMIN GODDARD, | Born Jan. 10, 1814, | Died July 24, 1877.

> *Gone home to enjoy the promised rest.*

2106. MINERVA, | Wife of | SAMUEL W. BAGNELL, | Died Dec. 8, 1877, | Aged 82 y'rs, 4 mo's, | 8 days.

2107. ISAAC J. LUCAS, | Born | July 3, 1797, | Died Dec. 20, 1877, | Aged 80 y'rs, 5 mo's, | 17 days.

> *Trusting in Jesus.*

2108. ELIAS COX, | Died | Jan. 20, 1878, | Aged 79 y'rs, | 11 mo's.

2109. WILLIAM SWIFT, | Co. E. | 29 Mass. Regt. | Died Feb. 18, 1878, | Aged 52 y'rs.

2110. In memory of | SILVANUS CHURCHILL, | Died March 2, 1878, | Æ. 81 y'rs, 8 mo's.

> *I will bind up that which is broken and strengthen that which is weak.*

2111. ELIZA A. WILLIAMS, | Died | May 5, 1878, |
Aged 45 y'rs, | 9 mo's.

2112. In memory of | MRS. POLLY BARTLETT, | Wife
of | ANSEL BARTLETT, | Died June 23, 1878, | Aged 95 y'rs,
9 mo's.

2113. MERCY C. | Wife of | SAMUEL ELLIOT, | Died |
July 8, 1878, | Aged 71 y'rs.

2114. HARRISON FINNEY, | Died | July 27, 1878, |
Aged 64 y'rs 4 mo's, | 11 days.

2115. HANNAH. | Widow of | NATHANIEL BARNES, |
Died Aug. 12, 1878, | Aged 83 y'rs, 7 mo's, | 33 days.
At Rest.

2116. LEVONZO D. BARNES, | Co. B. | 3 Mass. Regt. |
Died Aug. 30, 1878, | Aged 62 y'rs, 1 mo.

2117. JOHN S. PAINE, | Died | Sept. 29, 1878, | Aged 89
y'rs, 7 mo's, | 24 days. | SUSAN B. | Dau. of JOHN S. & |
SUSAN W. PAINE, | Died Oct. 19, 1835, | Aged 4 mo's.

2118. PELEG FAUNCE, | Dea. First | Baptist Church. |
Died Oct. 3, 1878, | Aged 80 years.
In hope.

2119. FREDDIE A. | Died | March 20, 1858, Æ. 15 mo's |
MINNIE S. | Died | Jan. 28, 1862, | Æ. 7 mo's & 14 d's. |
EZRA C. | Died Sept. 1, 1862, | Æ. 7 yrs, 4 mo's. | & 22 d's.
| Children of DANIEL, | & SUSAN E. CURRIER.

> *Treasures to their parents given*
> *Planted on earth to bloom in Heaven.*

EZRA CHURCHALL | Died | April 11, 1832, | In his 28th
year. | SUSAN A. | his wife | died Oct. 18, 1878, | Æ. 70 yrs, 3
| 7d's. | DANIEL CURRIER. | SUSAN E. | Wife of |

DANIEL CURRIER | & daughter of EZRA, & SUSAN A. CHURCH-
ALL | Died April 18, 1864, | Æ. 32 yrs, 11 d's.

Although her earthly sun has set,
Its light shall linger round us yet,
Pure—radiant—blest!

2120. BETSEY, | Widow of | MOSES HOYT, | Died Jan. 3,
1879, | Aged 88 y'rs. 4 mos. | CROSBY, | their son | Died
Sept. 23, 1857, | Aged 42 y'rs.

2121. ADDIE | Dau. of | ABBOTT & BETSEY | DREW | Died
Feb. 15, 1879, | Aged | 37 y'rs. 6 ms. 20 ds.

2122. LEANDER LOVELL, | Born, | March 9, 1799, |
Died | Oct. 1, 1879.

2123. EDWARD SOUTHWORTH | Died | Feb. 7, 1863, |
Aged 93 y'rs. 5 mos. | 20 days. | RUTH B. | His wife | Died
May 8, 1879. | Aged 101 y'rs. 10 mos. | 13 days.

2124. SALLY H. | Wife of | ZEPHANIAH BRADFORD | Died
Oct. 24, 1879, | Aged 81 yr's. 1 mo. | 23 days.

2125. WILLIAM K. | Son of | WILLIAM & BARBARA |
HEMMERLY, | Died in Boston, | Feb. 8, 1880, | Aged 23 y'rs,
4 mo's, 11 days.

2126. ABIGAIL, | Widow of | CAPT. JOHN VIRGIN | whose
earthly life | closed Feb. 13, 1880, | Aged 87 y'rs, 7 mo's |
16 days.

" Blessed are the pure in heart."

2127. ZILPAH, | Wife of HENRY RICKARD, | Died May 8,
1880, | Aged 50 y'rs, 9 mo's, | 18 days.

Divided below, United above.

2128. MOTHER, | MARY A. | Wife of | LEAVITT FINNEY |
Died | Aug. 5, 1880. | Aged 65 y'rs, 8 mo's, | 29 days.

Not lost blest thought but gone before,
Where we shall meet to part no more.

2129. IRENE HARLOW, | Dau. of | ELLIS & MELINDA | ROGERS, | Died Aug. 16, 1880, | Aged 25 y'rs, 4 m'os, | 24 da's.

Resting, sweetly resting.

2130. JAMES T. PAULDING, | Co. B. 3 Mass. Regt. | Died Aug. 19, 1880. | Aged 59 y'rs.

2131. RUBY F. | Wife of SAMUEL R. DICKSON, | Died | Aug. 25, 1880, | Aged 68 y'rs.

2132. NANCY HOLMES, | Wife of | JAMES COX. | Born Feb. 17, 1803, | Died Sept. 13, 1880.

2133. FRANKLIN B. HOLMES, | Died | Oct. 23, 1880, | Aged 55 y'rs, 9 mo's, | & 22 d'ys.

2134. REBECCA D. | Wife of | GRANVILLE GRIFFIN, | Died | April 9, 1881, | Aged 72 years, 24 d'ys.

Gone but not forgotten.

2135. ANN, | ANN M. WESTON, | Died | Aug. 3, 1881, | Aged 68 y'rs, 2 mo's.

2136. CHARLES CHURCHILL, | Died | Oct. 9, 1881, | Aged 89 y'rs, 29 d'ys.

2137. RHODA C. DAVIE, | Died | Oct. 11, 1881, | Aged 86 years, | 1 mo's.

Rest for the toiling hand,
Rest for the anxious brow,
Rest for the weary wayworn feet,
Rest from all labor now.

2138. GEORGE H. DREW, | Born | Oct. 21, 1808, | Died Nov. 23, 1881, | Aged 73 y'rs, 1 mo, | & 2 d'ys.

2139. REV. ISAAC WETHRELL, | Son of | THOMAS & NANCY [SHAW] | WETHRELL, | Born in Plymouth, October 24, 1806, | Died in Boston | November 30, 1881.

Requiescat in pace.

2140. ABBOT DREW | Died | Dec. 3, 1881, | Aged | 80 y'rs. 8 mo's, 18 ds.

2141. HUSBAND. | FREEMAN W. RICKARD, | Died | Jan. 21, 1882. | Aged 67 y'rs, | 9 mo's, 10 ds.

2142. HANNAH. | HANNAH D. BOURASSO, | Died | Feb'y. 20, 1882, | Aged 73 y'rs, 3 mo's, | & 19 d'ys.

2143. CAROLINE A. PERRY, | Daughter of | PELEG & OLIVE FAUNCE, | Died March 2, 1882, | Aged 48 years, 9 mo's.

WITH CHRIST.

2144. KEZIAH D. | Wife of | ROBERT SWINBURN, | Died Mar. 26, 1882, | Aged 77 y'rs. 4 mos. | & 11 d'ys

MOTHER

"Dear wife and mother."
To us you have done your duty,
Now lie here and rest,
It was God's will to take you from us,
For he knew what was best.

2145. SALLY BRADFORD. | Daughter of | NATHANIEL & REBECCA | BRADFORD. | Died April 19, 1882 | Aged 99 y'rs 3 mos. | 11 das.

"She was the last of the sixth generation in direct descent from the Pilgrim Governor."—WILLIAM BRADFORD.

2146. ANSEL H. HARLOW. | Born | Dec. 1, 1804, | Died | May 21, 1882.

2147. FATHER | DANIEL H. SEARS | Died, Sept. 1, 1882. | Aged 71 y'rs. 5 mos. | 12 days |

2148. MELINDA. | Widow of | ELLIS ROGERS. | Died | Sept. 13, 1882 | Aged 67 y'rs, 5 mos. 24 ds.

At Rest.

2149. SUSAN W. PAINE, | Born | Aug. 8, 1804, | Died | Dec. 16, 1882. | Aged 78 y'rs. 4 ms. | 8 days.

2150. ELIZA H. CLARK, | Dau. of | the Late CAPT. JOHN | & MARY ROBERTS CLARK, | Died Dec. 23, 1882. | Aged 78 y'rs, 1 mo, | & 10 d'ys.

"*I am the Resurrection and the Life.*"

2151. JOSEPH HOLMES, | Co. F. | 32 Regt. Mass. Vols. | Died Mar. 7, 1883, | Aged 59 y'rs, 4 mo's, | 7 days.

2152. 1860 | MORTON. | CATHARINE B. | Wife of | SETH MORTON | Died | July 8, 1883, | Aged | 77 years 1 mo.

2153.   "*Oh for the touch of a vanished hand*
          And the sound of a voice that is still."

LUCY N. [MORTON] | the beloved wife of | EDWARD HATHAWAY | Born in Carver, | Aug. 15, 1821, | Died Aug. 11, 1883. | Æ 62 y'rs, 11 mo's, 27 ds.

> "*Turn those dear eyes,*
> *Once so benignant to me, upon mine,*
> *That open to their tears such uncontrolled*
> *And such continued issue.   Still awhile*
> *Have patience ; I will come to thee at last.*
> *A few more prayers, a few more tears,*
> *And the long agony of life will end,*
> *And I shall be with thee.   If I am wanting.*
> *To thy well being, as thou art to mine*
> *Have patience, I will come to thee at last.*

2154. Parted below, United above. | PRISCILLA [WHITING,] | the affectionate wife of | EDWARD HATHAWAY, | Born in Bucksport, Me. | October 22, 1818, | Died June 29, 1842 ; | Æ 23 y'rs, & 9 mo's.

> "*Farewell dear wife, until that day more blest*
> *When if deserving, I with thee shall rest ;*
> *With thee shall rise, with thee shall live above,*
> *In worlds of endless bliss and boundless love.*

2155. *I love thee.* MARY B. C. | wife of | JAMES MORTON | Died Sept. 12, 1883, | Aged 66 years, | 11 mo's.

I lean o'er thee my Best Beloved,
My heart on thy heart lay,
I lean o'er thee and do weep,
For the time to come for us to meet.

2156.   SAMUEL TALBOT, | Died | Sept. 28, 1883, | Aged 88 y'rs, 2 mo's, | 14 days.

2157.   CAPT. HARVEY WESTON, | Died | July 7, 1876, | Aged 84 years. | SALLY C. | His wife | Died Oct. 21, 1883, | Aged 83 years. | SARAH E. | Their Dau. | Died May 12, 1858, | Aged 18 years.

2158.   ADONIRAM J. HOLMES. | Co E. | 32 Regt. Mass. Vols. | Died Nov. 15, 1883, | Aged 68 y'rs, 3 m's, | 6 days.

2159.   LUCY EMILY | Dau. of | Benj. & Lucy Bagnell, | Died Jan. 2, 1884, | Aged 61 y'rs, 4 mo's.
He giveth his beloved sleep.

2160.   SETH MORTON, | Died | Jan. 6, 1884, | Aged | 86 years 1 mo.

2161.   WILLIAM NICKERSON | Died | January 15, 1884 | Aged 79 y'rs. 11 mo. | 11 days.
At Rest.

2162.   Father & Mother | JACOB HOWLAND | Died | June 3, 1876, | Aged 82 y'rs. 8 mos. | SALLY, | His wife | Died Jan. 20, 1884, | Aged 88 y'rs. 4 mos. | Also, | WILLIE | LIZZIE | WILLIE.

2163.   ABIGAIL BROWN JUDSON. | born in March 21, 1791, | died in Plymouth, Jan. 25, 1884.

See ante, pages 156 and 205. Miss Judson was the daughter of Rev. Adoniram and Abigail (Brown) Judson, born in Malden, Mass., and was sister of Rev. Adoniram Judson, D.D., missionary to Burmah.

2164.   Husband, | K. of P. | JOHN W. PERRY. | Died Feb. 9, 1884. | Aged 45 years. | 5 mos.

2165.   ELIZABETH, | Wife of | Isaac Sampson | Born | June 19, 1795 | Died | February 22, 1884.

2166. ELIZA O. | Wife of | ELIAS COX, | Died Feb. 24, 1884 | Aged 81 y'rs. 4 mo's. | 11 days.

2167. CATHERINE B. | Wife of | WILLIAM BISHOP | Died | July 16, 1884, | Aged 57 y,rs 3 m'os.

2168. JOHN A. GOODWIN | Died at Lowell, Sept. 21, 1884. | aged 60 years.

Hic non corpus sed illi locus carissimus.

See No. 1041, ante. HON. JOHN ABBOTT GOODWIN was son of Isaac and Eliza (Hammett) Goodwin, born 1824, and resided in Lawrence, Mass., where he was editor of a newspaper. Removed from that city to Lowell, Mass., in 1854, and was connected with the well known paper called *Vox Populi*, also editor of the *Lowell Courier*. Represented the city of Lowell in the Legislatures of 1857, 1859, and was Speaker of the House in 1860 and 1861. Postmaster at Lowell from 1861 to 1874, besides filling other local offices. He was deeply interested in historical studies, and has given to the public the results of his labors in his work entitled, "The Pilgrim Republic," an excellent work on the early history of the Old Colony, for which he had a special adaptation. He died at Lowell, Mass, Sept. 21, 1884, universally respected by those who knew him, and lies buried on this hill, which he took a great interest in.

2169. WILLIAM WESTON | Born | July 19, 1819, | Died | Oct. 18, 1884.

2170. PRISCILLA D. WASHBURN, | Daughter of | GEORGE and PRISCILLA WASHBURN, | Died Dec. 31, 1863; | Aged 33 y'rs. & 11 mo. | PRISCILLA | Wife of | GEORGE WASHBURN | Died March 7, 1885, | Aged 81 y'rs.

2171. FATHER. | LEAVITT FINNEY. | Died | June 3, 1885, | Aged 72 y'rs. 4 mos. | 29 days.

No pain, no grief, no anxious fear
Can reach the peaceful sleeper here.

2172. NATHANIEL DOTY | Died | Dec. 9, 1872, | Aged 63 y'rs. 2 mos. | JOANNA | His wife | Died | Sept. 5, 1885, | Aged 59 y'rs. 10 mos.

2173. JOHN T. HALL | June 6, 1819. | Sept. 21, 1885 |
I shall be satisfied, when I awake with thy likeness.

2174. FANNY EDDY, | Widow of | CAPT. ROBERT DAVIE | Born | Aug. 11, 1804, | Died | Oct. 16, 1885.

2175. RICHARD BAGNELL, | Died | March 4, 1868, | Aged 67 years. | LYDIA, | His wife | Died Dec. 10, 1885, | Aged 85 years.

2176. JOHN R. DAVIS, | Died | Dec. 28, 1885, | Aged 73 y,rs, 10 m's, | 10 days.
He died in the hope of a glorious reserrection.

2177. REBECCA W. | Widow of | Capt. Joseph W. Collingwood, | Died Oct. 29, 1886, | Aged 70 y'rs, 11 mo's, | 4 days.
" Her children shall rise up and call her blessed."

2178. SETH Mc GLAUTHLIN, | 1812—1869. | Priscilla, | His wife | 1813—1886.

2179.   WIFE.
*No sin, no grief, no pain,
Safe in my happy home.*
EMELINE A. | Wife of | Lewis H. Whitten. | Died | Jan. 13, 1887, | Aged 54 y'rs, 4 mo's, | 15 days.

RUSSELL.

2180. On the top of this hill, not far from the monument of Governor Bradford, may be seen a granite boulder, brought from the pine hills of "Manomet," on which is neatly cut the following inscription:

THOMAS RUSSELL,

BORN,

Sept. 26, 1825,

DIED,

Feb, 9, 1887.

Hon. Thomas Russell, was the son of Thomas and Mary Ann (Goodwin) Russell, of Plymouth, born September 26, 1825. His early home was on Leyden Street, the first street of the Pilgrim Fathers, and here he received his earliest impressions of the trials and endurance of the founders of New England, and commenced early in life to honor the history of their lives in which he always took a lively interest. From early boyhood he was of a lively turn of mind, quick, bright and active, and a good scholar, receiving his education in the excellent schools which his native village afforded; he entered Harvard College at an early age, from whence he graduated in 1845, with high honors. He studied law at Harvard Law

School, and in the office of Hon. Jacob H. Loud at Plymouth, till 1847, when he became a resident of Boston, and was a member of the Suffolk bar. Although a citizen of another municpiality he never ceased to remember the town of his nativity, and was active in promoting the interests of her citizens, and the historical associations connected with the old mother town. He was chosen president of the Pilgrim Society in 1879, to succeed Hon. William T. Davis, and retained that position till his death. He was also instrumental in having inscribed upon the rock on Clark's Island the words, " On the Sabboth day wee rested," in remembrance of the first Sabbath spent on the shore by the Pilgrims.

Judge Russell did not practice his chosen profession long, for in 1853, at the early age of 27 years, Governor Boutwell appointed him Judge of the Municipal Court of Boston, a position which he filled with such general satisfaction that, in 1859, Governor Banks selected him as a proper person for Associate Justice of the Superior Court, where he remained until 1867. It was while he occupied the judicial chair of this court that he displayed those traits of firmness in his convictions and good judgment which were prominent characteristics belonging to him as a magistrate. Among the many good things the judge did while in the fearless discharge of his duties was the record he made in putting down garrotting in the streets of Boston. His sentence to the extent of the law was so promptly given that a reign of terror soon followed among all who were disposed to commit crimes of that nature, the influence of which has lasted to the present time. In 1866 he resigned his position on the bench to become collector of the port of Boston, which position he held until 1874, when he resigned, and was soon after appointed by President Grant Minister Resident at Caracas, Venezuela, where he remained till March, 1878. In 1879 he represented Boston in the Massachusetts Legislature, and became an influential and useful member of that body.

In June, 1879, he was appointed by Governor Talbot Railroad Commissioner, a position he filled, as chairman of the board, at the time of his death. Besides the foregoing, he occupied many other positions of honor and trust. In 1878 he was President of the Emigrant Savings Bank, and was an Overseer of Harvard College, a Trustee of the State Reform School and the Nautical School Ship, and during the war was a Draft Commissioner, and was intensely loyal to the Union, and always looked after the interests of the soldier, prompt and patriotic in all his acts.

Judge Russell was of a kindly disposition, genial temperament, and had many social traits that won for him hosts of friends; of much original wit and humor, a wonderful conversationalist, full of varied information acquired by extensive reading.

His humanity was large, and his love of liberty was such that it was not strange that we find him identified with such men as Garrison, Phillips, Andrews, and others in the Anti-Slavery cause, and a leader in the Free Soilers' ranks. Upon the occasion of the visit of General Grant to Plymouth, it was Judge Russell's privilege, as President of the Pilgrim Society, to receive the General, and place in his hand the sword of Captain Myles Standish.

He saw the bright side of life, and enjoyed it. He was, indeed, eminent as specialist, jurist, statesman, and orator. Among his best efforts as a public orator was the occasion of the obsequies of General Grant, August 8, 1885, by Post 76, G. A. R. "which was an eloquent, appropriate and fitting eulogy upon the great Chieftain." His last public address was upon the occasion of the Anniversary of the Pilgrim Society at a dinner at which Hon. James Russell Lowell was present, December 21, 1885.

He was a member of Mt. Lebanon Lodge, A. F. and A. M., Boston, and had spoken at a great many assemblies, and was well known in political, judicial and social circles of Boston, as well as throughout the State. His death took place February 9, 1887, at his home, 20 Hancock Street, in Boston, and in accordance with his oft repeated desire to be buried on Burial Hill, his request was granted.   B. K.

2181. LUCY MARCY, | Died | Feb. 20, 1887, | Aged 92 y'rs, 9 mo's.

2182. MIRIAM C. [HOLMES] | His wife | May 7, 1810, | Feb. 27, 1887.
Wife of Ansel Holmes.

2183. ELIZA, | Wife of | John Williams, | Born | Aug. 16, 1808, | Died | March 23, 1887.

2184. CHARLOTTE S. | Wife of | Sam'l. L. Alexander | Died | April 9, 1887, | Aged 83 years.
At Rest.

2185. JAMES COX, | Born | July 23, 1803. | Died | April 22, 1887.

2186. BETSEY CROCKER, | Dau. of | Benj. & Lucy | Bagnell, | Died Sept. 6, 1887, | Aged 62 y'rs, 7 mo's.
My trust is in the Lord.

2187. MARY B. COOPER, | Died | Dec. 3, 1887, | Aged | 77 y'rs, 8 mo's.

2188. Alice. | ALICE BRADFORD, | Daughter of | Samuel & Rebecca Sampson, | Nov. 2, 1844, | Dec. 26, 1885. | Father. | SAMUEL SAMPSON, | Feb. 22, 1818, | Dec. 27 1887.

2189. SARAH M. HOLMES, | Born | Oct. 6, 1805, | Died | March 11, 1888.

2190. SUSAN S. | Wife of | William Weston, | Born | Oct. 7, 1819, | Died | May 26, 1888.

2191. CAPT. | GEORGE ALLEN | Born | Feb. 2 1806, | Died | June 5, 1888.

The following inscriptions are on a solid granite monument recently erected.

2192. JOSIAH A. | ROBBINS, | 1823 — 1885. | JOHN BRIGGS, | 1855—1866. | JOSIAH THOMAS | 1857, — 1868. | WALTER JACKSON, | 1870 — 1873. | Sons of | JOSIAH A. & R. W. | ROBBINS.

2193. FATHER. | WILLIAM COLLINGWOOD. | 1790,— 1866. | MOTHER. | ELEANOR COLLINGWOOD. | 1794, — 1884. | Children of | WILLIAM & ELEANOR | COLLINGWOOD. | WILLIAM JR. | 1818 — 1878. | JOHN. | 1818 — 1818. | MARY. | 1819—1820. | ROBERT S. | 1836—1860.

In near proximity to the last mentioned lot, is a broken marble headstone on which we read

LT. JOHN B. COLLINGWOOD. | Died in h—

2194. ELLIS D. BARNES, | 1831— 1888. | WILLIAM T. BARNES, | 1868—1889.

Beside the last monument is a small marble with "LITTLE LIZZIE" upon it.

2195. ELIZA C. | Wife of | ASA PIERCE | Died | Feb. 1, 1890. | Aged 69 y'rs, 6 m's | 7 days.

At Rest.

2196. MARTHA B. | Wife of | JOHN B. ATWOOD. | Died. | Jan. 28, 1891. | Aged 81 y'rs.

See No. 1919, page 251.

2197. JANE, | Wife of | ELLIS T. LANMAN. | 1825—1891.

In this lot are two polished granite blocks, on one of which is JANE LANMAN, 1825 — 1891, | on the other is JOHN E. 1854. — JOHN E. — 1855.

2198. BETSY ROGERS | Widow of | WILLIAM NICKERSON | Died | Mar. 3, 1891, | Aged 71 y'rs, 8 mos.

At Rest.

2199. BENJAMIN HARLOW, | Died, | Aug. 8, 1846, | Aged 33 years.

Blessed are the pure in heart,
For they shall see God.

2200. MOTHER. | SUSAN, | Wife of WILSON CHURCHILL, Died Jan. 31, 1848, | Aged 54 y'rs, 4 mos.

2201. CHARLES, | Son of | GEO. & PRISCILLA | RAY-
MOND, | Died | March 19, 1822, | Aged 16 y'rs.

2202. CAPT. JESSE TURNER, | ELIZABETH H. | His
Wife |
On the back of this marble tablet is the following inscription :
CAPT. JESSE TURNER | Lost at Sea | on passage from |
Plymouth to W. India, | Dec. 5, 1830, | Aged 48 y'rs. | ELIZA-
BETH H. | His wife, | Died Mar. 18, 1834, | Aged 45 y 'rs.
This marble is a thick gothic top, and is near the monument of Gov. Bradford, to
the west of, and near the main path.
[See page 167, No. 1299, and page 180, No. 1375, and page 263, No. 2017.

2203. JAMES JORDAN, | Drowned | in Smelt Pond, | June
25, 1837, | Aged 27 y'rs. | Buried on the day | he was to have
been | married.

2204. SAMUEL N. HOLMES, | Died | July 10, 1840, |
Aged 84 y'rs, 8 mo's.
He rests from his labors.

2205. HANNAH BURT | Wife of | LABAN BURT | Died
April 21, 1832, | Aged 43 y'rs, 9 mo's. | LABAN BURT |
Died Nov. 13, 1842. | Aged 60 y 'rs, 2 mo 's, 7 da 's. | ANSON
L. BARNES, | Died Oct. 6, 1836, | Aged 21 y'rs, 6 mo's.
" *For if we believe that Jesus died and rose again, even so them
also which sleep in Jesus will God bring with him.*"

2206. CHARLOTTE A. | Daughter of | ABBOTT & BETSEY
| DREW, | Died July 5, 1843, | Aged 5 y'rs, 10 m's, 18 d's.

2207. BETSEY CHURCHILL, Wife of ABBOTT DREW |
Died | Mar. 2, 1848. | Aged 43 y'rs.

2208. WILLIAM NELSON | Died | Nov. 16, 1848, | Aged
3 y'rs, 9 mo's. | Son of | I. & M. S. PIERCE.
See No. 1612, page 212.

2209. MISS MARY HARLOW | Died | Nov. 17, 1848, |
Aged 86 y 'rs.

2210. WILLIAM A. JOHNSON, | Died | 1854.
The above inscription is on a wood tablet.

2211. GEORGE Le BARON RAYMOND, | Died Jan. 24, 1860. | Æ 27 y'rs.

2212. DAVID DIMAN, | 1794—1861. | ABIGAIL B. DIMAN, | 1800—1843. | ABIGAIL N. DIMAN, | 1819—1860.
The above inscriptions are on finely polished granite blocks, on the right of the path leading from the church to the summit of the hill.

2213. CORPORAL | THOMAS COLLINGWOOD, | CO. E. 29 Reg. Mass. Vol. | Died at Crab Orchard, Ky. | Aug. 31, 1863, | Aged 32 y'rs, 9 mo's, | 21 days.

Why do we mourn for dying friends,
Or shake at deaths alarms,
Tis but the voice that Jesus sends,
To call them to his arms.

2214. BEULAH, his wife | Died Nov. 19, 1863, | Aged 89.
Wife of Daniel Goddard.

2215. JERUSHA T. | Wife of | CAPT. ALBERT HOLMES | Died Jan. 30, 1864, | Æ 37 years, 5 mos, 25 days. | CARRIE CLIFTON, | Died April 9, 1861, | Æ 3 years, 10 mos, 16 days. | CHARLES EDWARD. | Died March 31, 1857, | Æ 2 years, 8 mo's. | ALBERT HENRY. | Died April 7, 1845, | Æ 4 mo's, 25 days. | Children of | ALBERT & JERUSHA T. | HOLMES.

2216. OUR FATHER. | WILLIAM BARNES. | Died | April 31, 1865, | Aged 70 y'rs 4 mo.
How sweet and ever green thy memory.

2217. HENRY RICKARD | Died | Dec. 18, 1867, | Aged 36 y'rs, 10 mo's, | 20 days.

2218 GEORGE RAYMOND. | Died | May 23, 1868, | Aged | 85 y'rs, 10 mo's.

2219. ALBERT B. | Son of | JAMES & ELEANOR | KENDRICK.
Called from earth to bloom in Heaven.

The following may be found on the back of the marble :

Died | May 26, 1874, | Aged | 1 y'r, 6 mo's 28 d's.

2220. ANNA ELIZABETH. | Wife of | WM. M. BARNES, | Dau. of | CAPT. GIDEON HOLBROOK | Died | Oct. 27, 1881 | Aged 59 y'rs, 7 mo's, 4 ds.

2221.   DEARLY LOVED ONE !
              Jesus called thee home
              to adorn a brighter sphere.

ANNA FRANCIS BARNES, | died June 4, 1860, | aged 8 y'rs, 9 mo's, 15 d's.

In the same enclosure with the last, on a small marble block, is a small lamb couchant, and "LITTLE WILLIE" on the same in front, also,

"WILLIE H. BARNES," | Died Aug. 16, 1850, Æ 10 mo's, 11 d's.

Another small neat marble tablet, on which is "LITTLE LIZZIE," is in the same enclosure.

2222. GOODWIN TOMB | MRS. LYDIA CUSHING GOODWIN. | died Dec. 15th, 1815. | aged 53 years. | WILLIAM GOODWIN, Jr., | died at Havana, Dec. 15th 1821, | aged 38 years. | WILLIAM GOODWIN, | died July 17th, 1825, | aged 69 years. | SIMEON S. GOODWIN, | died July 27, 1847, | aged 65 years. | ISAAC GOODWIN. | died at Worcester, Sept. 10, 1832, | aged 46 years. | JOHN A. GOODWIN, | died at Lowell, Sept. 21, 1884, | aged 60 years.

See No. 2168, page 279.   No. 1041, page 126.

2223. DARLING | ALMA MAY. | Daughter of | J. S. & M. B. | BUTLER | Died Dec. 17, 1888, | aged 9 y'rs, 2 mo's
              Her heart was folded deep
                  in ours.

2224. OUR | FATHER, | SAMUEL ELLIOT. | June 12, 1801 | Aug. 3, 1890.

2225. MARY T. BACON, | Died Nov 12, 1860, | Aged 50 y'rs 10 mo's. | BETSY BACON, | Died Jan 23, 1891, | Aged 82 y'rs, | REBECCA BACON, | Died Mar. 27, 1891, | Aged 78 y'rs. | Daughters of | CAPT GEO. & ELIZABETH | BACON.

The above inscriptions are on a handsome polished granite tablet.

2226. RUTH C. HOPKINS, | Died | July 7, 1891. | Aged | 83 y'rs, 18 mo's, 20 days.

> *" Rest in peace, thou gentle spirit*
> *Throned above —*
> *Souls like thine with God inherit*
> *Life and love."*

2227. ELIZA ANN | and | ELIZABETH THACHER. | children of WILLIAM | and | SUSAN T. BARTLETT.

This lot is on east brow of the hill, with granite posts and iron rail.

2228. TWINS. | ALBERT B. | & BETSEY J. HARLOW | Æ 5 months.

The above is inclosed with a white painted fence, on the east slope of the hill, and the inscription is on a marble scroll tablet.

2229. MOTHER. | NANCY, | Wife of | WM. STEPHENS.

By the side of the above is a marble tablet, on the top of which is " FATHER." On the front is WILLIAM STEPHENS. Situated on the east slope of the hill near the Jackson lot.

2230. FATHER & MOTHER. | WILLIAM C. NYE. | BETSEY NYE. | ANN H. NYE.

Arise, let us go to our Father.

LUCY NYE died June, 1844. | WILLIAM NYE died Feb. 25, 1849. | WILLIAM C. NYE died June 5, 1807. | BETSEY NYE died Feb. 10, 1819. | ANN H. NYE died Mar. 13, 1834.
The above deaths are from the Town Records.

2231. PAULDING. | CLARIBEL, | ALLIE B, | FRANCES A. | HERBERT S. | SYLVANUS S.

In this lot are two marb'e headstones, one marked " FATHER," the other " MOTHER," and each of the foregoing names has a separate marble tablet.

2232. PHEBE, | Wife of | CAPT. THOMAS FARMER. | Aged 40 y'rs.

2233. ELKANAH BARNES. | CYNTHIA D. BARNES.

These inscriptions are at the southwest side of the hill, near to the boundary line.

In the lot of WILLIAM KEEN at the westerly end of the ground, may be found two wooden tablets, having on them the names " WILLIAM " and "JOANNA."

MEMORANDUM

Of Odd and Broken Stones found in Various Portions of the Ground, the Inscriptions of which are Copied as Found.

Child of CAPT. ELLIS BREWSTER. Dec. 13, 180—
Child of CAPT. WILLIAM BREWSTER. Sept. 22, 180—
To the memory of, JERUSHA BARTLETT, wife of JOHN BARTLETT, no date.

————RIDER—29, 1767, in his 95th year.
On the Town Records we find Joseph Rider died Oct. 29, 1766.

REBECKAH dau. of JABEZ & EXPERIENCE HARLOW died May 10—
JOHN HARLOW. Died Mar. 10, 17—in his 73 year.
CALEB COOK. Died Feb. 5, 17½ in his 72 year.
ELIZABETH PHILLIPS. Died Jan. 5, 17— in her 10th year.
MRS. ELIZABETH TILLSON—CAPT. EDWARD TILL-SON,—foot stones.
JOB MORTON 1761.
ELIZA ANN & ELIZABETH T. Children of WM. & SUSAN T. BARTLETT.
ELISHA MORTON, died Oct. 23, 172— in his 15th year.
MRS. ABIGAIL DREW, wife of NICHOLAS DREW—Died— 17—
LYDIA wife of NICOLAS DREW Decd.—173—
BARNABE, son of BENJAMIN MORTON Nov. 7, 17—4 aged 10 days.
JOHN GODDARD, died Feb. 3, 174—aged 33 years.

A small fragment of stone has the following only,
—43d year of her age.

BAR— | of MR.— | —DUNHAM. | at the age | on April.—
also a son still— | —side.

GED. A. BOUT— | 15 months.

The front of this stone is split off.— Probably this was *Boutelle.*

There are several stones with initial letters only which were foot stones like the following:

E. T.—M. J. T.—J. T. R.—W. H. J.—W. H. J.—T. F. and J. CURTIS, 1767, on a footstone.

LIST OF RECENT BURIALS

On the Hill without Headstones or Monuments.

ABIJAH DREW. March 26, 1888. Aged 85 years.

NANCY BATTLES. May 9, 1888. Aged 75 years, 7 mos.

ALMIRA H. CHURCHILL. May 10, 1888. Age 63 years 9 months.

BETSEY E. FINNEY. June 29, 1888. Aged 80 years, 10 montns, 11 days.

MERCY H. MORRISON. July 8. 1888. Aged 49 years, 11 months.

GEORGE W. BASSETT. Oct. 29, 1888 Aged 30 years, 6 months.

THOMAS BASSET. Dec. 11, 1888. Aged 80 years, 1 month.

SYLVANUS S. PAULDING. Dec. 16, 1888. Aged 76.

IVORY LEWIS HARLOW. Dec. 17, 1888. Age 79 years, 4 months.

SARAH R. FINNEY. Jan 17, 1889. Aged 57 years 17 days.

ROBERT SEARSON. April 3, 1889. 54 years 3 m.

JOHN S. STURTEVANT. Apr. 26, 1889. 79 y'rs 2 m.

PELLA M. ROBBINS. June 4, 1889. Aged 77 y'rs. 3 months.

LUCY T. COOPER. Nov. 25, 1889. Aged 83 years, 11 months.

MARY R. WHITTEN. Dec. 17, 1889. Aged 78 years.

REBECA B. HARLOW, widow of Ivory L. Harlow, Aged 98 years, 9 months.

REBECCA BATTLES. Mar. 15, 1890. Aged 80 years, 4 months.

MARY WINSLOW RUSSELL. Widow of William S. Russell. April 3, 1890. Aged 91 years, 4 months and 6 days.

JANE STEPHENS. Oct. 24, 1890. Aged 76 years, 4 months 9 days.

ASA N. KENRICK. Nov. 9, 1890. Aged 75 years, 11 months, 10 days.

LORENZO W. WRIGHT. Nov. 23, 1890. Aged 33 years, 6 months.

LYDIA S. WADSWORTH. Feb. 18 1891. Aged 94 years, 1 month.

MEMORIAL LIST

OF SOLDIERS WHO SERVED THEIR COUNTRY, IN THE ARMY OR NAVY, AND
WHOSE REMAINS ARE NOW BENEATH THE SOD OF BURIAL HILL.

ALEXANDER, JOHN K.
ALLEN, CHARLES B.

BARNES, WILLIAM E.
BARNES, LEVONZO D.
BARNES, ELLIS D.
BATES, BENJAMIN F.
BRADFORD, EBENEZER N.
BRYANT, HOMER
BURT, THOMAS B.

COLLINGWOOD, JOHN B.
COLLINGWOOD, JOSEPH W.
COLLINGWOOD, THOMAS

EDDY, SETH W.
EDDY, HENRY F.
ELLIOT, SAMUEL

FINNEY, ALFRED C.

GIBBS, THOMAS

HOLMES, FREDERIC
HOLMES, JOSEPH
HOLMES, ADONIRAM J.
HAYDEN, THOMAS W.

HATHAWAY, ALLEN
HOLBROOK, ELIPHALET

JENKS, HORACE A.

MCLAUGHLIN, ROBERT

MOREY, WILLIAM

NICKERSON, WILLIAM T.

PAULDING, JAMES T.
PERRY, JOHN

ROBBINS, ALBERT R.
ROBBINS, FRANK C.
ROBBINS, JOSIAH T.
RICKARD, HENRY
RAYMOND, SAMUEL B.

SHAW, WILLIAM H.
SNOW, GEORGE F.
SWIFT, WILLIAM

WADSWORTH, GEORGE E.
WADSWORTH, CHARLES
WILLIAMS, JOHN B.
WHITING, JOSEPH B.

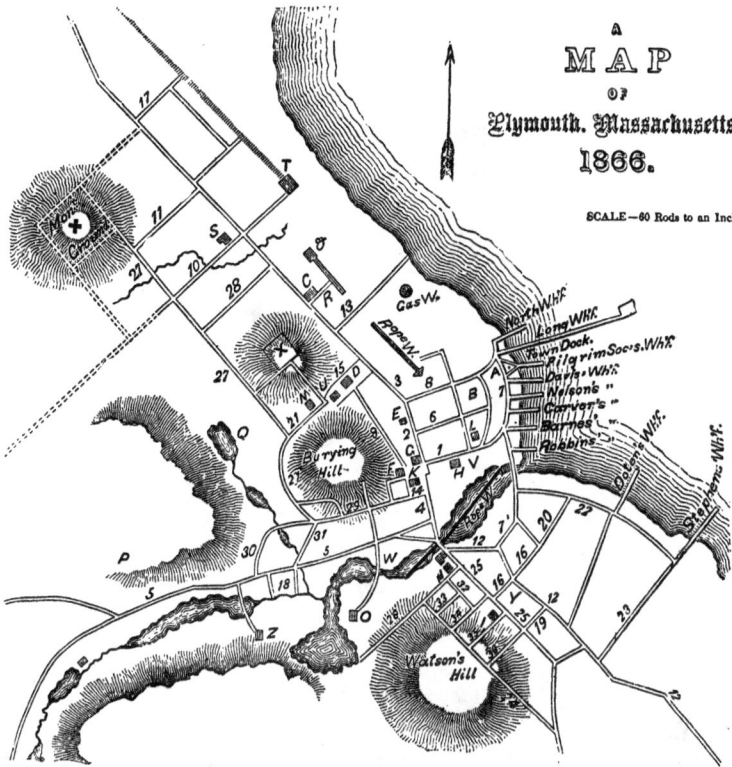

A
MAP
OF
Plymouth, Massachusetts.
1866.

SCALE—60 Rods to an Inch.

References to Public Buildings, &c.

A — Forefathers' Rock and Canopy, at the head of Pilgrim Society's Wharf.
B — Cole's Hill, first Bur'l G'd of the Pilgrims.
C — Pilgrim Hall.
D — Court House.
E — Banks.
F — First Church of Plym'th, and the First Congregation'l Ch'ch in America.
G — Church of the Pilgrimage.
H — Baptist Church.
I — High School.
K — Town House.
L — Universalist Church.
M — Methodist Church.
N — Episcopal Church.
O — Alms House.
P — Cemetery.
Q — Murdock's Pond.
R — Drew Place.
S — Samoset House.
T — Railroad Station.
U — Grammar School.
V — Place where the First House was built by the Pilgrims, called Common House, twenty feet square.
W — Pilgrim Spring.
X — Reservoir.
Y — Training Green.
Z — Rolling Mill and Nail Factory.
& — Line Factory.

References to Streets. &c.

1. Leyden Street.
2. Main Street.
3. Court Street.
4. Market Street.
5. Summer Street.
6. Middle Street.
7. Water Street.
8. North Street.
9. School Street.
10. Samoset Street.
11. Cushman Street.
12. Sandwich Street.
13. Howland Street.
14. Town Square.
15. Court Square.
16. North Green Street.
17. Lothrop Street.
18. Willard Place.
19. South Green Street.
20. Commercial Street.
21. Russell Street.
22. Union Street.
23. Fremont Street.
24. Mayflower Street.
25. Pleasant Street.
26. Robinson Street.
27. Prospect Street.
28. Vernon Street.
29. High Street.
30. Edes Street.
31. Bartlett Street.
32. Sagamore Street.
33. Massasoit Street.
34. Jefferson Street.
35. Franklin Street.
36. Washington Street.

A DESCRIPTIVE LIST

OF TOMBS, MONUMENTS, ENCLOSED LOTS, INSCRIPTIONS OF
SPECIAL INTEREST, ETC.

ENTRANCE TO BURIAL HILL.

As we ascend by the path leading from town square, on the right hand, are several granite block front tombs with iron doors, over which are marble caps, with the following names upon them. The first one belongs to the town. The others in order are FINNEY, BARNES and STEPHENS. In the centre of the tombs is a marble tablet having "A. D. 1833" upon the same.

On the left hand, as we pass up the hill in the rear of the First Church, are several other tombs, upon which are the names of HEDGE, DAVIS, SPOONER and WARREN; further on is the tomb of EPHRAIM PATY—1856.

On the right hand, or north side of the concrete path, is the monument of FREDERIC HOLMES, 1863. (See No. 1896, page 248.)

On the easterly brow of the hill, a short distance away on the right, is an obelisk in marble, nine feet in height, on the top of which is a Bible; the whole enclosed with an iron fence and be-

longing to the family of DEA. JOSIAH ROBBINS.   (See No. 915,
page 108, and No. 1825, page 199.)

Next to the last named is a lot enclosed by a low wood fence,
and having marble and slate stones, belonging to the family of
BRIDGHAM RUSSELL.   (See No. 1516, page 199.)

ABRAHAM JACKSON'S lot is enclosed by an iron fence, and
contains marble stones, a little to the north of the ROBBINS
monument.   (See No. 1826, page 240.)

Almost to the top of the ascent is a marble shaft eight feet
high, on which is inscribed BATTLES, enclosed by a granite
border.   (See No. 1777, page 233.)

FAUNCE GRAVESTONE.

We next notice an old slate
stone at the grave of ELDER
THOMAS FAUNCE, quite ne.r the
path, worthy of attention.   (See
No. 1777, page 233,)

At the junction of the main
path at the top of the hill is a lot
fenced with wood, belonging to
the COWAN family.   (See No. 1891,
page 247, and No. 1945, page 254.)

A short distance further on is a
neat marble monument about 4
feet high, with HOWLAND on its
base.   (See No. 1982, page 259.)

Following the main path in a
northerly direction, on the right
we come to the grave of JUDGE THOMAS RUSSELL, which is
covered by a huge bowlder brought from the "Pine Hills of
Manomet."   (See No. 2180, page 290.)

Adjoining to the last named is the tomb
of the Russell family, having a horizontal
marble slab supported by four stone col-
ums, on which are the following inscriptions: JOHN, CHARLES, NANCY and MARY
RUSSELL.   (See No. 757, page 86.)

RUSSELL TOMB.

A few feet distant from the Judge Russell monument to the
eastward may be seen the white marble obelisk erected several
years since to commemorate the memory of GOVERNOR WIL-
LIAM BRADFORD, the second Governor of Plymouth Colony.
This shaft is about eight feet in height, and is situated in a most
prominent position on the hill, commanding a full view of the
town below, the harbor and the bay, and has become a central
attraction for many thousands of visitors to the resting place of
the pilgrims.

Here multitudes have gathered under the shadows of the beautiful elm and larch trees, and lingered to contemplate in their minds the wintry scenes of 1620. This is the central point of interest on the hill. (See No. 1, page 1.)

From this last monument, following the path northerly on the right, we read the names of BRADFORD, BARNES, BARTLETT, COOPER, DOTEN, HOLMES, SAMPSON, SHURTLEFF and SYLVESTER, while those on the left are BRADFORD, COBB, JACKSON, MORTON, RICKARD, TRIBBLE and WETHERELL. The last named is enclosed by an iron fence and is near to the main path.

At the junction of the main path with the north path leading to the westerly entrance of the ground may be seen a solid granite monument about 5 feet high, on the front of which is a panel in bronze commemorating the memory of one of Plymouth's late well-known physicians, DR. ZACHEUS BARTLETT. (See No. 1415, page 185.)

In the MORTON enclosure, on the north-easterly slope of the hill is a marble monument 4 feet high, having on the same, neatly cut, a chain in a circle, with "Parted Below, United Above." (See No. 1833, page 240.)

At the northerly end of the main path is a double base granite monument, having an octagon shaft about ten feet in height, on which are the names of CHURCHILL and CURRIER. (See No. 2119, page 273.)

In a wooden fence enclosure in the northeast section, on a polished granite block, is the name of ELLIS D. BARNES. (See No. 2194, page 283.)

At the extreme north part of the hill may be found the following names: BARNES, BARTLETT, BRADFORD, BREWSTER, BROWN, CHURCHILL, CLARK, COOPER, COLLINGWOOD, CURRIER, GLEASON, GOODWIN, GRIFFIN, HALL, HUESTON, HOLMES, NELSON, PERRY, RAYMOND, RICHMOND, RIPLEY, ROBERTS, SHAW, STEPHENS, TRIBBLE, WHITTEN and WOOD.

In memory of
Mrs. Tabitha Plasket.
who died June 10,1807.
aged 64 years.

Adieu vain world I have seen enough of thee
And I am careless what thou sayst of me;
Thy smiles I wish not,
Nor thy Frowns I fear,
I am now at rest my head lies quiet here.

Passing from the monument of Dr. Bartlett in a south-westerly direction, a short distance on the right hand, are two slate stones marking the graves of JOSEPH and TABITHA PLASKET, at which visitors would do well to pause, and read the quaint inscriptions on the same. (See No. 655, page 72, and No. 924, page 110.)

Adjoining the last-mentioned graves is a polished granite monument, 5 feet high, enclosed by a substantial iron railing and stone corners. This lot belongs to the well-known family of JOHN T. HALL, late a merchant of Plymouth. (See No. 2173, page 279.)

A short distance north of the HALL lot is a large slate stone, 5x2½ feet, to the memory of CAPT. JOSEPH CHURCH-ILL, who was lost at sea in 1836. This is a finely executed representation of a brig at sea in a storm in bass-relief.

Erected | in memory of | JOSEPH CHURCHILL | who sailed from Boston | Nov. 1836 | in the Brig Plymouth Rock | of Plymouth | Bound to Rochelle in France, | and supposed Foundered | at Sea, aged 54 years. | Also to his Children | JOSEPH LEWIS, died at | sea on Board the Brig | Androscoggin of Portland | Aug. 1842, aged 37 years. | MARCIA GOODWIN | died May 2, 1839 | aged 22 years. (See No. 1434, page 188.)

CHURCHILL GRAVESTONE.

To the west a few feet is a granite block, on which rests a thick marble tablet 4½ feet high, on the top of which is "WHIT-TEN."

On the north summit of the hill east of the main path is a fine specimen of slate-stone cutting on the tablet, 30x48, of RICHARD FISHER, consisting of three willows, the centre spreading two others, representing three arms. (See No. 1227, page 154.)

On the left hand of the path leading from the Dr. Bartlett monument to the Russell street entrance, are the following graves in their order, viz: LUCAS, GOODMAN, BOUTELLE, DEA-CON, HOLMES, DIMON, GAMMON, FINNEY, JOHNSON, HOLMES and FARMER.

In the northeast section of the hill, on the easterly slope, is a group of names of the COLLINGWOOD family, a name well known for their faithful service in the cause of their country in the re-bellion of 1861. There are three polished granite blocks in the lot. (See No. 219, page 283, also memorial list, page 290.)

Near to this last lot is the BARNES enclosure, with a wood fence. In it is a granite block with "WILL" upon the same.

The PERRY lot, with iron rail and granite posts, is near to the Barnes lot above named.

The grave of CAPT. JOSEPH BARTLETT is also enclosed like the last.

The BROWN family has some fine slate stones at the north end of the main path, with engravings of a sarcophagus on the same.

The RIPLEY family grave is at the junction of the main path with the path leading to the west.   Here are some interesting carvings on large slate stones.

Adjoining the last named are the graves of ICHABOD SHAW'S family.

GOODWIN TOMB.

Near the above mentioned lot on the east, and near the path leading to School street, is the GOODWIN TOMB, a large thick marble slab supported by six square freestone columns.   See No. 1041, page 126, No. 2168, page 279, and No. 2222, page 286.)

The lot of FRANKLIN B. HOLMES, south of the GOODWIN tomb, is enclosed by a wooden fence.

To the east of the main path is the white granite monument of the ROBBINS family, 12 feet high, enclosed by a rustic iron fence, on the gateway of which is "L. T. ROBBINS, 1859."

Southeast of the last lot, on the easterly brow of the hill, is an enclosure with granite curbings and corners, belonging to one of the BARTLETT family.

To the southeast of the Robbins monument is a lot enclosed by a rustic iron fence, represented by another of the BARTLETT family.

On the east of the main path is the marble tablet of REV. AURIN BUGBEE.   (See No. 1831, page 240.)

On the left hand side of the path leading from the main path to Russell street is one of the oldest stones on the hill. A wooden sign has been erected beside the same, as the old slate is much defaced, and almost illegible.

Nearly opposite the head of the path leading from the First

JUDSON TOMB.

Church, in the rear of the site of the "watch house," is the JUD-SON TOMB, enclosed by a wooden fence, and containing several inscriptions on the marble top.   (See No. 1240, page 156.)

KENDALL GRAVES.

South of the site of the watch house, and under the limbs of a larch tree, is the white marble tablet to the memory of REV. JAMES KENDALL, D. D., on which is a fine sculptural design of a Reaper with a sickle in hand cutting corn. (See No. 1828, page 240.)

Also, near by is the memorial to SARAH, wife of REV. DR. KEN-DALL. (See No. 951, page 114.)

Passing along the path in a southerly direction leading towards the CUSHMAN monument on either side, we notice the names of BARTLETT, BARNES, DAVIS and PIERCE, the last lot being enclosed by an iron fence.

Directly in the rear of the latter, to the east, is the "Warren" Lot, with a lattice work iron fence. In this enclosure may be seen the marble tablet of GEN. JAMES WARREN and MERCY, his wife, 1808–1814. (See biographical sketches of his life on another page.)

Directly east of the Cushman slate stone, and between the monument and First Church, is the site of the ancient fort of 1620–1, which was about 20x20 feet. A thick oval marble block on a pedestal marks the location.

In this vicinity are the following familiar names: BARNES, DAVIS, HOLMES, GODDARD, SIMMONS and TALBOT. These lots are enclosed by iron fences. (See No. 1496, page 196.)

CUSHMAN MONUMENT,
IN BURYING HILL CEMETERY, PLYMOUTH, MASS.
ERECTED A.D. 1858.

On the southerly end of the main path, on the right hand, may be seen the tall and imposing monument erected to the memory of ROBERT CUSHMAN by his numerous descendants. It is enclosed by an iron fence, and is situated near by the original slate stone of ELDER THOMAS CUSHMAN, which has become much dilapidated by age. (See No 7, pages 5 and 6.)

South of the Davie lot is the granite curbed lot and enclosure of CAPT. SOLOMON DAVIE, with marble obelisk.

Near by is the BENJAMIN GODDARD and IVORY HARLOW lot

HERE LYER BURIED
OF THAT PRECIOUS SERVA
GOD Mʳ THOMAS CUSHMAN, W
AFTER HE HAD SERVED HIS
GENERATION ACCORDING TO
THE WILL OF GOD, AND
PARTICULARLY FE CHURCH OF
PLYMOUTH FOR MANY YEARS IN
FE OFFICE OF RULEING ELDER
FELL ASLEEP IN JESUS DECEM
10 1 691 8 IN
84 YEAR OF HIS AGE

This Stone placed at the grave of
Elder Cushman by the first Church in
Plymouth was removed to this situation in 1858, to make room for a more
enduring memorial which now exactly occupies its original position.

CUSHMAN SLATE STONE.

on the southerly brow of the hill, and enclosed with a granite curb and corners.

Also the STURTEVANTS' graves near the GEN. WARREN lot.

Directly west of the CUSHMAN monument is the heavy iron fence enclosure of HENRY ERLAND. (See No. 1644, page 229.)

To the right of this marble monument is the obelisk of JAMES BURNS, about 5 feet high. (See No. 2048, page 226.)

North of the CUSHMAN monument is the brick tomb of ICHABOD HARLOW, having a slate-stone top about 14x48 inches. (See No. 1258, page 159.)

Another CHURCHILL lot is on the southerly brow, and near the south path.

NATHANIEL CARVER'S lot contains a white monument in the rear of the church ground. (See No. 1031, page 125, and No. 1579, page 207.)

Near the last named is a polished granite monument to the memory of CAPT. HARVEY WESTON, 1876, and others.

Also another polished granite monument near by, on which is CAPT. GEO. ALLEN, 1888. (See No. 2191, page 282.)

A short distance northwest of the CUSHMAN monument is an old dark slate stone, about 18 inches high, to the memory of DR. FRANCIS LE BARON, whose name has been immortalized by Mrs. Jane G. Austin, in her work entitled "A Nameless Nobleman," a volume well worth perusing, especially for any one interested in the history of Plymouth. (See No. 13, page 8.)

Opposite to the latter is a large, thick stone, 4 feet square and 3 inches thick, of gray slate, on which is inscribed DR. LAZARUS LE BARON, son of the former doctor. (See No. 419, page 44.)

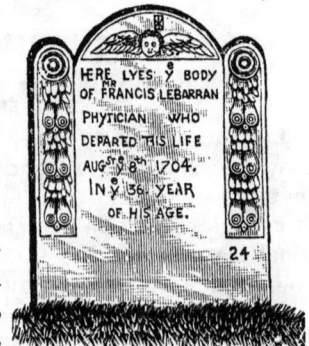

HERE LYES Y BODY
OF FRANCIS LEBARRON
PHYTICIAN WHO
DEPARTED THIS LIFE
AUG 8 1704.
IN Y 36 YEAR
OF HIS AGE.

24

LE BARON GRAVE-STONE.

LE BARON GRAVE-STONE.

LINES ON GRAVE-STONE.

My flesh shall slumber in the ground
Till the last trumpet's joyful sound;
Then burst the chains with sweet surprise,
And in my Saviour's image rise.

Dr. Lazarus LeBaron was born in Plymouth Dec. 26, 1698; studied medicine and became a physician, and enjoyed a lucrative practice in his profession, and died in 1773, aged 75 years. He had two sons, Joseph and Lazarus, who became physicians; and Lemuel, a clergyman, settled in Mattapoiset, Mass., in 1772.

WILLIAM DREW'S lot is on the top of the hill south of and near to the John Howland grave, and has two marble stones. (See No. 1283, page 164, and No. 1510, page 198.)

In the background of the annexed engraving, to the south of the main path leading to Russell street, may be seen a large granite tablet about 4½ feet by 2½ feet and 6 inches thick, which marks the resting place of REV. JAMES H. BUGBEE, the first settled pastor of the Universalist Church in Plymouth. He was ordained Dec. 22, 1826, and remained until his death, which took place May 10, 1834. (See No. 1379, page 181.)

The following lines are inserted as being exceedingly appropriate to a work of this kind: —

One of the oldest graves in the old Pilgrim burying ground at Plymouth is that of John Howland. The first stone erected to the memory of this old settler has crumbled, and another erected on the spot is in an advanced stage of decay.

HOWLAND GRAVE-STONE.

From this latter stone, the following taken from the Plymouth records is quoted: "He was the last that was left of those that came over in the Mayflower that lived in Plymouth."

The slab erected long ago
    Has yielded to destroying rust;
And with the lord who sleeps below,
    Has joined old Plymouth's silent dust.
Yet still another marks the place
    To keep remembrance fresh and green,
And link the pride of former days
    With freedom's creatures yet unseen.

John Howland!   Let that name survive
    When millions sleep in nameless graves;
Aye, honest fame shall keep alive
    This strongest of the Pilgrim braves.
Though mighty statesmen sigh for fame,
    Though soldiers fight and poets muse,
This simple-minded father's name
    Shall all their highest hopes confuse.

He sought for neither wealth nor ease —
    He only sought for freedom's air;
For this he braved the wintry seas
    And Western forests, bleak and bare.
He suffered hunger's gnawing breath,
    He dared the Red Man's wily laws,
He faced a most inglorious death,
    And all to die in freedom's cause.

Inglorious?   So thought the slave
    Who toiled in Europe's sunny clime,
While every church did wildly rave
    And stamp this hardy man with crime.
But who were they?   Where do they sleep?
    Where are their monuments? their names?
Do grateful States their memory keep
    And shield it from oblivion's flames?

No!   Death has levelled them so low
    Remembrance never can awake;
Their names shall not with lustre glow,
    They sleep unknown for freedom's sake.
But untold millions pass along
    Who stop to read John Howland's name.
And in our history and song
    A grateful people guard his fame.

—H. M. in New Bedford Standard.

LITTLE GRAVE-STONE.

To the left of the grave of Rev. Mr. Bugbee is the head-stone of the first minister who died in Plymouth, REV. EPHRAIM LITTLE. He was a native of Marshfield, Mass., and was pastor of the First Plymouth Church for twenty-four years. (See No. 59, page 12.)

Adjoining the grave of the last-mentioned is a low head-stone containing a simple inscription of the death and age of one who was a prominent figure in Plymouth in its early history, and was Secretary of the Colony after the death of Nathaniel Morton, and also a counsellor-at-law. Besides the duties of preserving the doings of the Colony, he was Clerk of Courts, Register of Deeds, as well as of Probate.

He was for a short time owner of what is known as "Clark's Island," under a grant from the King during the obnoxious reign of Sir E. Andros. It passed out of his hands to the town, and was afterwards sold to private parties, and has been held in the Watson family to this day.

CLARK GRAVE-STONE.

NATHANIEL CLARK, the engraving of whose head-stone accompanies this article, was the son of Thomas and Susanna (Ring) Clark, and is buried near his father's monument mentioned below. He married Dorothy, widow of Edward Gray, and left no children. (See No. 37, page 10.)

CLARK MONUMENT.

Alongside the last mentioned is the old slate-stone at the grave of THOMAS CLARK, which has been so often pointed out to the stranger as the grave of the mate of the Mayflower. This is not true to history, as may be seen on page 113 of the History of Plymouth County, published in 1884; also in Davis' Ancient Landmarks, page 145; and we also have the statement on a bronze tablet attached to a huge boulder brought from "Manomet Hills," which has recently been erected adjoining to the ancient stone, by Miss Kate Lincoln Clark, of Chicago, Ill., by which it appears that Thomas Clark came over in the Ann, three years later than the Mayflower. (See No. 6, p. 4.)

HERE LIES BURIED YE BODY OF

MR. THOMAS CLARKE.

Aged 98.

DEPARTED THIS LIFE MARCH 24, 1697.

Thomas Clarke came to Plymouth from
England in the ship Anne, 1623. He married
Susan Ring of Plymouth, 1634. Their Children
were Andrew, James, William, Susanna,
Nathaniel, and John, from whom descended
a numerous posterity. He married his second
wife Mrs Alice Hallett Nichols of Boston
and also in Harwich of which town he was
one of the original proprietors. He died in
Plymouth, having lived in the reigns of Six
British Sovereigns and the Commonwealth.

THIS STONE IS ERECTED TO HIS MEMORY
BY HIS DESCENDANTS
A. D. 1891.

In the rear of the Bugbee lot, to the west, is a low wooden
fence, enclosing some pink marble tablets of the NICHOLAS and
ABBOT DREW families. (See No. 152, page 20, and 2140, page
276.)

West of the Drew ground is a JACKSON lot enclosed with an
iron fence, pointed palings.

The lot of SOLOMON RICHMOND joins the Drew lot, in the
western part of the hill, and has a wooden rail fence. (See No.
1530, page 201.)

Another lot in the west part of the hill is the lot of JOHN T.
and WOODWORTH JACKSON, enclosed with an iron fence. (See
No. 1138, page 140, and No. 1180, page 146.)

Near the latter, to the east, is a lot enclosed by a wood fence,
the family lot of JACOB JACKSON. In this lot is a large marble
slab supported on columns, and several names on the same.
(See No. 1807, page 237, and No. 1574, page 207.)

In the westerly portion of the hill and directly south of the
last named Jackson lot is the monument erected to mark the
spot where sixty of the crew of Brig GENERAL ARNOLD were
buried, known as the "MAGEE MONUMENT," after the name of
the captain of the lost brig. It is a marble shaft on a granite
base enclosed within a rail, and granite posts. (See No. 472,
page 50.)

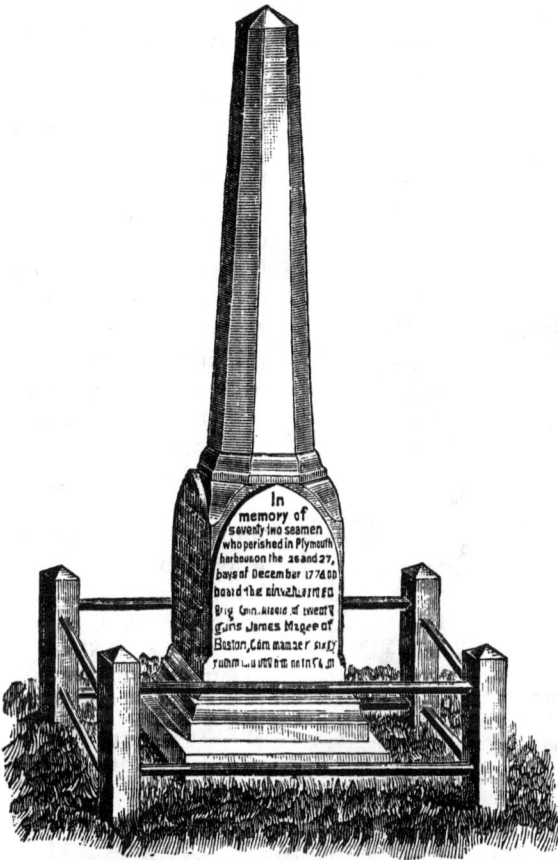

In
memory of
seventy two seamen
who perished in Plymouth
harbour on the 26 and 27,
Days of December 17800
board the private armed
Brig Gen. Arnold of twenty
guns James Magee of
Boston, Com mander sixty
[illegible]

MAGEE MONUMENT.

Here follow the inscriptions that are on the four sides of the monument, viz. :—

NORTH, OR FRONT, SIDE.—In memory of seventy-two seamen, who perished in Plymouth harbor on the 26 and 27 days of December, 1778, on board the private armed brig GEN. ARNOLD, of twenty guns, numbering in officers and crew one hundred and six persons in all, JAMES MAGEE, of Boston, Commander, sixty of whom were buried on this spot, and twelve in other parts of the hill.

EAST SIDE.—This monument marks the resting place of sixty of the seventy two mariners who perished in their strife with the storm, and is erected by STEPHEN GALE, of Portland, Maine, a stranger to them, as a just memorial of their suffering and death.

SOUTH SIDE.—
"Oh! falsely flattering were yon billows smooth,
  When forth, elated, sailed in evil hour
  That vessel, whose disastrous fate, when told,
  Filled every breast with sorrow and each eye with piteous tears."

WEST SIDE.—CAPT. JAMES MAGEE, died in Roxbury, February 4th, 1801, aged 51 years.

In the south-west portion of the hill, and south of the Magee lot, is a tall gothic marble tablet of ALLEN C. SPOONER. (See No. 1739, page 228.)

Next to the last named, south-west, is the DAVID WARREN lot, with iron posts at the corners connected by chains. (See No. 804, page 92.)

ANDREW FARRELL
of respectable connections
IN IRELAND
Aged 38 years.
Owner & Commander
of the Ship Hibernia
Sailed from Boston Jan? 26
And was wrecked on Plymouth Beach
Jan? 28.1805.
His remains
With five of seven seamen
Who perished with him
Are here interred
O pireous lot of man's uncertain state
What woes on lifes Eventful journey
By sea what treacherous calms: what sudden storms
And death attendant in a thousand Forms.

In the central portion of the west end of the hill is a peculiar shaped slate-stone erected to mark the spot where AN-DREW FARRELL, captain and owner of the ship "Hibernia," with five other seamen, were buried. They were wrecked on Plymouth Beach, Jan. 28, 1805. (See No. 884, page 104.)

In the west section of the hill are the family lots and graves of many of the well-known citizens of the town, among whom are the BRAD-FORD, CORNISH, COTTON, DAVIS, DREW, HARLOW, JACK-SON, PATY, WASHBURN and WESTON names. (For the inscriptions on the stones and monuments see the index of names.)

Among the earliest gravestones on the hill is that of EDWARD GRAY, 1681, which has been supposed to be the oldest; but the late Dr. Nathaniel Lothrop is said to have information from an aged relative by which it appears that the stone of JOSEPH BARTLETT, who died in 1703, was the earliest placed there, and that Mr. Gray's was erected at a later date. The accompanying engraving is a correct copy of the grave-stone of Mr. Bartlett, situated on the top of the hill, a short distance west of the head of the main path as one ascends from the church, and near to the grave of Rev. Dr. Kendall. (See No. 10, page 7.)

HERE LYETH
BURIED ye BODY
OF JOSEPH
BARTLETT WHO
DEPARTED THIS
LIFE APRILL ye 9th
1703
IN ye 38th YEAR
OF HIS AGE.

BARTLETT GRAVE-STONE.

THIS MONUMENT MARKS THE SPOT WHERE THE WATCH HOUSE WAS ERECTED IN 1643.

The visitor to the hill, on arriving at the summit, near the head of the path, and on the main avenue, will notice an oval marble block on a pedestal, marking the site of the old WATCH HOUSE. At the corners of the lot are short granite posts indicating the bounds of the same. (See ante pages XI and XII.)

The two following engravings represent two of the DAVIS gravestones, and are situated at the west end of the hill. This family have long been among the prominent names in the town of Plymouth:—

In memory of
HON. WILLIAM DAVIS
Born July 15, 1758
Died January 5, 1826

DAVIS GRAVE-STONE.
(See No. 1210, page 150.)

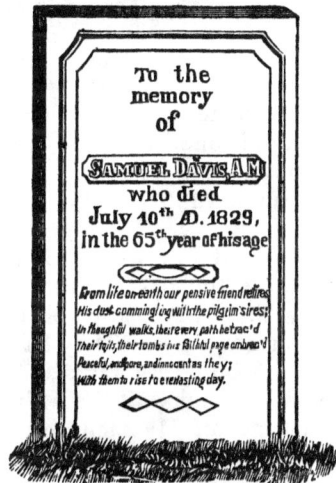

To the
memory
of
SAMUEL DAVIS, A.M.
who died
July 10th A.D. 1829,
in the 65th year of his age

From life on earth our pensive friend retires,
His dust comming ling with the pilgrim sires;
In thoughtful walks, here very path betrac'd
Their tojit, their tombs his faithful page embrac'd
Peaceful, and pure, and innocent as they;
With them to rise to everlasting day.

DAVIS GRAVE-STONE.
(See No. 1273, page 162.)

THE OLD POWDER HOUSE.

The accompanying engraving of the OLD POWDER HOUSE will be recognized by many of the older residents and others. It was erected in 1770, of brick, and stood on the north-east part of the hill. A little mound is said to have been built by the scholars of Mrs. Cotton at the time of Queen Anne's war, a short distance from the same in a south-east direction.

We present to our readers on the two following pages some of the grave-stones of the Bradford family. The oldest is that of JOSEPH BRADFORD, the youngest son of Governor William and Alice (South-worth) Bradford, born in 1630, and was a resident of what was well known as "Flat House Dock," about one-half a mile from the mouth of Jones River, and known as Kingston. He lies buried quite near his father, on the top of the hill, in immediate proximity to others of the same name.

JOSEPH BRADFORD GRAVE-STONE.

The name of Bradford has always been an honored one, and the various branches are widely scattered throughout this country. The principal seat of the family was in Plymouth in colonial days, and also at Plympton, Kingston and Duxbury. In later days they are found in Maine, Rhode Island and all other sections of the United Sates.

While the descendants of Gov. Bradford have been numerous, they have also occupied prominent public positions of honor and trust. They have been among our Governors, Members of Congress, Officers in the Revolutionary Army, as well as in the ranks of the Militia. Hon. Alden Bradford, the late Secretary of Massachusetts, and author, was a descendant from Duxbury, and Governor William Bradford, of Bristol, R. I., was a descendant from Plympton, formerly the west precinct of Plymouth. He married, April, 1751, Mary LeBaron, daughter of Dr. Lazarus and Lydia (Bartlett) LeBaron, of Plymouth.

The LeBaron Bradfords mentioned on the grave-stone accompanying this article were respectively son and grandson of Gov. William Bradford, of Bristol, and lie buried at the west section of the hill, near to the Davis graves.

NATHANIEL BRADFORD GRAVE-STONE.

The writer of these articles has always taken a great interest in the earliest families of the Colony of Plymouth, and for the purposes of information paid a visit to the English home of the Pilgrim Fathers in June, 1888, visiting the little church in Austerfield in which was the oaken chest containing the Baptismal register of WILLIAM BRADFORD, afterwards the Governor of Plymouth, and the ancestor of the Bradford family of Massachusetts. The little graveyard adjoining the stone church was also visited, to learn how many burials of the name might be found. Austerfield, on the Great Northern road, is a village in Yorkshire about two and one-half miles north of Scrooby, following the course of the River Idle, and from the old Manor House, where Brewster and other of the Pilgrims held their meetings. The manor house of their day has long since disappeared. There is but little now remaining except traces of the old moat which once surrounded the same.

Here are interred in adjoining graves, the remains of SARAH BRADFORD relict of Le Baron Bradford of Bristol Rhode Island Born June 29 1754 Died Nov. 10, 1821. and of their son LE BARON BRADFORD Born 1780, Died Nov. 1846.

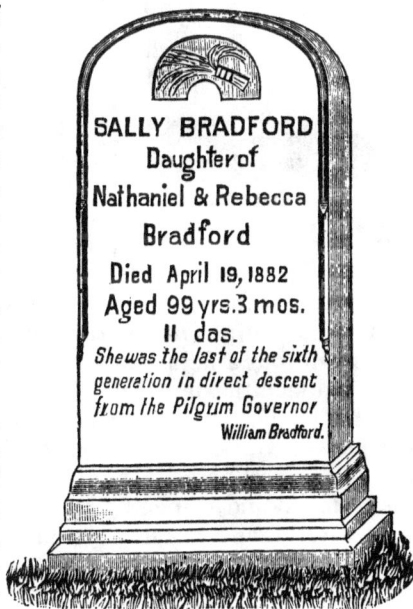

BRADFORD GRAVE STONE.

Carved oaken timbers are now doing duty in one of the farm barns of the occupant of the grounds. The The writer has some pieces of the same, presented to him as a reminder of his visit to Scrooby. There is an old Mulberry tree on the premises, however, said to have been planted during the occupancy of William Brewster, afterwards known as "Elder" Brewster in the new colony of Plymouth, America. It has been well settled that this place was where the early meetings of the Pilgrims were held, and it is appropriate that mention should be made of the English homes, as well as their last resting place here.

SALLY BRADFORD Daughter of Nathaniel & Rebecca Bradford Died April 19, 1882 Aged 99 yrs. 3 mos. 11 das. She was the last of the sixth generation in direct descent from the Pilgrim Governor William Bradford.

BRADFORD GRAVE-STONE.

BIOGRAPHICAL.

THE OLD SEXTON.

CLEMENT BATES.

Those who have made an annual pilgrimage to Plymouth of late years have missed the genial and kind-hearted "OLD SEXTON." He no longer can be seen at the entrance of the church door, tolling the bell, nor travelling among the graves of those he long since laid away. His name was Clement Bates, a native of Hanover, Mass., born Oct. 4, 1792. He was the son of Clement and Rebecca (Stetson) Bates, and died July 13, 1885, at the age of nearly 93 years. Mr. Bates came to Plymouth in 1809, and previous to 1831 worked at the trade of caulker and graver. In that year he was chosen sexton of the First Parish and of the town, to which which position he was annually chosen to the year 1883, when he resigned. His duties have been to ring the church bells daily, and to bury the dead. And it is said he has buried 3250 persons, equal to about one-half the present population of the town. He rang the bell four times a day, besides those for church services on the Sabbath, for funerals and for fire alarms for fifty-two years, without a failure and only two mistakes. His mental and physical faculties he retained to an unusual degree till his death, and his memory of occurrences was clear and reliable. In early life he was quite an athlete, of jovial disposition and fond of jokes, besides being a good story teller, of cheerful temperament, loved and respected by all. We can almost see him, with bowed form and leaning on his cane, making his way around the town at a rapid pace.

GEN. JAMES WARREN was the son of James and Penelope (Winslow) Warren, born in Plymouth, Mass., 1726. He descended from Richard Warren, one of the earliest settlers of

Plymouth; graduated at Harvard College in 1745, and became a merchant. In 1757 he succeeded his father as high sheriff, which office he retained till the Revolution. In 1766 he was a member of the General Court from Plymouth. He is said to have been the originator of the plan for establishing "committees of correspondence" in the various towns and cities. In 1775 he became a member of the Provincial Congress, and upon the death of Gen. Joseph Warren he was appointed President of that body. While the army was at Cambridge he was chosen Paymaster General. In 1776 he was appointed Major General of the Massachusetts Militia. In 1780 he was elected Lieutenant-Governor under Hancock, but declined to serve. He was for several years Speaker of the House of Representatives. He was appointed to the office of Judge of the Supreme Court, which he declined. He served as Commissioner of the Navy Board for some time. At the close of the war he retired from public life, in order that he might enjoy the ease of domestic life, and became interested in agricultural pursuits. He was soon called from private life to serve in the councils of the government. For some years he resided at the Gov. Hutchinson seat at Milton, but returned to his native town, where he resided till his decease, Nov. 28, 1808. His residence was at the corner of Main and North streets, in the house now standing. He married Mercy, the daughter of Hon. James and Mary (Allyne) Otis, of Barnstable, Mass. She was a sister of the patriot and orator. Mrs. Warren was the author of a "History of the War." She died Oct. 19, 1814, at the age of 86 years. James, son of the above, was for several years postmaster of Plymouth, and was with Paul Jones in the "Bon Homme-Richard," and lost a limb in one of the battles. He was buried in the grave with his father; and Henry was collector of the port of Plymouth, and died July 6, 1828, aged sixty-four years.

GEN. JAMES WARREN, | died November 28, 1808; | aged 82, | MERCY WARREN | his wife | daughter of James Otis | of Barnstable | died October 19, 1814; | aged 86.

REV. DR. JAMES KENDALL was the youngest son of Major James and Elizabeth (Mason) Kendall; born in Sterling, Mass., Nov. 3, 1769. After the usual preparation for college, he entered Harvard College in 1792, and graduated with high honor in 1796. On leaving college he passed two years at Phillips Academy, Andover, Mass., as assistant teacher, at the same time pursuing his theological studies under the direction of Rev. Dr. Tappan, then Professor of Divinity at Harvard College, and with Rev. Jonathan French. He received approbation to preach from the Andover Association in 1795. In that year he was chosen tutor of Greek in the college, and removed to Cam-

bridge, continuing his theological studies at the same time. He
first preached at Plymouth as a candidate in October, 1799, and
was ordained as pastor of the First Church of Plymouth January 1, 1800, Rev. Jonathan French of Andover preaching the
installation sermon. Here he continued his labors of love for
thirty-eight years alone, till 1838, when Rev. George W. Briggs,
a graduate of Brown University, was settled as colleague pastor, and remained as such till 1852, he continuing to preach in
his own pulpit and others in the neighboring towns. He died
March 17, 1859, in the ninetieth year of his age. His funeral
sermon was preached by his former colleague, Rev. Dr. Briggs,
then of Salem, Mass. Dr. Kendall married Sarah, daughter of
Dea Daniel Poor, of Andover, Mass., by whom he had six
children. (See No. 1828, page 240.)

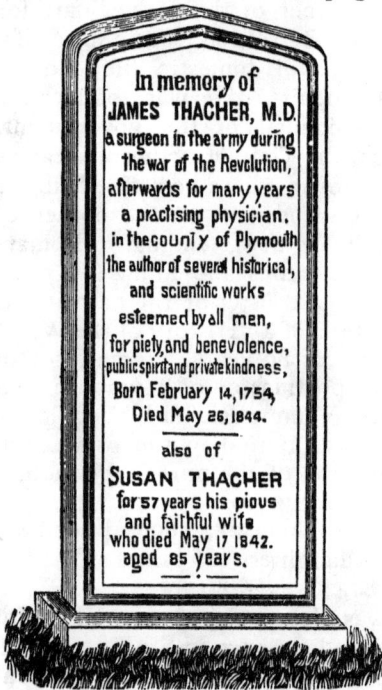

In memory of
JAMES THACHER, M.D.
a surgeon in the army during
the war of the Revolution,
afterwards for many years
a practising physician.
in the county of Plymouth
the author of several historical,
and scientific works
esteemed by all men,
for piety and benevolence,
public spirit and private kindness,
Born February 14, 1754,
Died May 26, 1844.

also of

SUSAN THACHER
for 57 years his pious
and faithful wife
who died May 17 1842.
aged 85 years.

DR. JAMES THACHER, the
late eminent surgeon and physician of Plymouth, was the son
of John and Content (Norton)
Thacher, and was born in Barnstable, Mass., in 1754. At an
early date he began to devote
his attention to medicine, and
studied the profession with Dr.
Abner Hersey, a very cele-
brated physician of Barnstable.
Upon arriving at the age of 21
years Dr. Thacher was appointed by the Provincial Congress
a surgeon in the Revolutionary
army, and in July, 1775, commenced the active duties inci-
dent to hospital life, at Cambridge. He was afterwards at
Albany and West Point, N. Y.,
and was present at the execu-
tion of Benedict Arnold for
treason. He was also present
at the surrender of Lord Corn-
wallis, Oct. 19, 1780. In 1824 he published a journal of events
occurring while he was in the army. At the termination of the
war he settled in Plymouth as surgeon and physician, where he
enjoyed the entire confidence of his fellow-citizens, and was
eminently successful in his practice. He devoted a great deal
of time to antiquarian researches, and was a member of several
literary societies. He was an active member of the Pilgrim

Society, of Plymouth, the American Academy of Arts and Sciences, the Massachusetts Medical Society, and others. He received the degree of M. D. from Harvard College in 1810. He was one of the most voluminous and elaborate writers in the medical ranks of New England. In 1828 he published two volumes of Medical Biography, and in 1832 a History of Plymouth, a highly interesting and reliable volume. A fellow-townsman, in writing of Dr. Thacher's private character, says: "As a citizen he was public spirited, a lover of order and a warm supporter of the civil and religious institutions under which he lived, and in all the relations of life he was guided by a spirit of benevolence, kindness, and disinterestedness, which gained him the attachment and regard of many friends."

Dr. Thacher married Susanna, daughter of Nathan and Susanna (Latham) Hayward of Bridgewater, Mass., 1785, and had six children.

WILLIAM SHAW RUSSELL was the son of James and Experience (Shaw) Russell, and direct descendant of John Russell of Glasgow. He was born in Plymouth, January 11, 1792, where he spent his early days, with the exception of a short time while he resided in Bridgewater. Upon arriving to manhood he engaged in active business, and married MARY WINSLOW, 1798, daughter of Dr. Nathan and Joanna (Winslow) Hayward. In 1826 he became a resident of Boston and engaged in business with Andrew L. Russell, where he remained till 1835. Returning to his native town, he was elected to the office of Register of Deeds in 1846, which office he held till his decease.

He was a genial, affable, and patient public officer and indefatigable explorer among the ancient and interesting records and annals of Colonial history. He was also the author of an invaluable compilation of the same. He was a conscientious and painstaking student of antiquarian lore, and one of the best authorities in anything pertaining to the history of the Pilgrims, and was ever ready to communicate the results of his knowledge to all enquirers. He was a member of the First Church, and a

deacon for many years. In 1846 he published a volume entitled, " Guide to Plymouth and Recollections of the Pilgrims,"
a work of about 400 pages, containing local history, statistical
and personal reminiscences of our pilgrim ancestors and their
early homes, with an appendix of hymns and poems on sub-
jects pertaining to the early history of the colony.

In the publication of the " Plymouth Colony Records," by
the Commonwealth some years since, Mr. Russell rendered valuable aid in the preparation of the same, together with David
Pulsifer, Esq., of Boston, to both of whom the public are indebted for the accuracy with which the work was completed.

When William H. Bartlett visited this country in search of information for his valuable work entitled " Pilgrim Fathers, or
the Founders of New England," Mr. Russell furnished
much of the information relating to Plymouth, Mass., and
which was in his own language. Mr. Russell had a
great fondness for Burial Hill, one of the prominent
historical features of the town, and much frequented by visitors, and in 1858 caused to be prepared a complete list of inscriptions on the stones and monuments having reference to the
publication of the same, but for some reason was never printed
but the careful and accurate labors of which are now included
within this volume.

We cannot better conclude this notice of Mr. Russell than by
inserting the following well deserved notice found in the " Old
Colony Memorial" at the time of his decease.

" By his death our town has lost one whose place as a student
of our early history and a repository of knowledge of our places
of local interest we know not how to fill. We shall miss his
ever pleasant face, his never failing courtesy, his kindly manners,
and his truly christian example. We shall miss him sadly as one
to whom all questions of history or genealogy were referred,
and no one ever applied to him without receiving a pleasant answer and a kindly interest in the object of their enquiries.

"The places that have known him will know him no more, but
the memory of Mr. Russell will never be lost while ' Plymouth
Rock and Burial Hill ' are cherished and venerated."

On the easterly brow of Burial Hill, in a central location is a marble tablet which is represented by the accompanying engraving.

EDWARD WINSLOW WATSON.

We cannot close these sketches without giving a notice of
one well remembered by a large number of our readers. But
a few moments' sail in the harbor of Plymouth, in full view from
Burial Hill, is situated the well-known spot called "Clark's

Island," the place where the first Sabbath was observed by the Pilgrim fathers. Several years since, the writer had the pleasure of spending two days with the owner, one of the most enjoyable occasions he ever passed ; and the following article by a Boston correspondent of the Springfield Republican has so well described the proprietor of the soil that we take great pleasure in placing it before our readers :

EDWARD W. WATSON
Born on
Clark's Island,
·Dec. 17, 1797,
Died Aug. 8, 1876.

"If a statue were to be made of an ideal American —neither the dollar-worshipping Yankee, nor the over-cultivated æsthetic scholar, but the plain man of the people, rejoicing in his strength and in the boundless opportunities of his country, such as Walt Whitman would describe—the late Edward W. Watson of Clark's Island might have been the model. In him nature was everything, art and literature but accidents; and it made little difference that he had been all his days occupied with the simple pursuits and the narrow vicissitudes of a sea-side farmer and countryman, living within sight of Plymouth Rock. He was at home there, but so he would have been anywhere in the world, if sea room, open air, the key of the fields and the companionship of his fellowmen were allowed him. He was a Homeric person without the Homeric proclivity to fight and steal; and I have seen him slay and apportion a lamb as deftly and gravely as Agamemnon or any of his confederate chieftains. It was good, also, to see him walk barefoot, like an old Greek, along the ooze and into the foam of the sea, tending his boat or bringing his freight or passengers on shore when the tide was low. Such common acts he did with an apostolic and joyous unconcern, quite ignoring the modern refinements of costume and attitude —stepping from boat to boat as his friend Thoreau says of a very different person, ' with a divine ease and sureness.' Yet no fine gentleman was less embarassed in good society than he —having been so long accustomed to the best society—that of his own family traditions, clear thoughts and generous purposes. The respect he won was like that the Highlander expressed when he said of his chief, ' Wherever the MacDonald sits is the head of the table.' If, now-and-then, a city lady eyed him askance, and questioned in her conventional mind the apparent propriety of his coat and shoes, it was soon revealed to her that this was a gentleman of such great courtesy that he might wear what he pleased without criticism. The homeliest surroundings were idolized by his romantic presence, and his island became a place where life, amid many inconveniences, took on an enchanted, charming aspect, for old and young.

> " There blows the clover summer-long,
>   There figs grow ripe and full,
> In orchards ring the robin's song,
>   The grapes climb up the wall;
> The lily springs to deck the bride,
>   The melon creeps to see;
> The slumbrous poppy nods beside
>   The whispering poplar tree.
>
> The gleaming water, day and night,
>   Flashes along the shore,
> And out beyond the double-light
>   Swells ocean's heavy roar.
> The breezy hill is white with sheep,
>   The fields are green with corn—
> But never deem the enchantment deep
>   Was of these beauties born.
>
> Nor yet, though more endeared than these,
>   Was all the charm from thee,
> Old friend, that walked amidst thy trees
>   As stately and as free.
> For thee that sweet enchantment found,
>   Though lord of isle and stream;
> Thee, too, did magic walls surround,
>   Thy life a gentle dream.
>
> With joy, with thee, we hailed the spot
>   Where sorrow never dwelt,
> Where all things ill were soon forgot,
>   And only bliss was felt.
> We heard thy wise and laughing words,
>   Thou lord of isle and stream,
> Mixt with the music of the birds,
>   Fresh breeze and sunny beam.
>
> Now sadly parting from the strand
>   In thy delaying boat,
> We bid farewell with voice and hand
>   To thee returning not.
> No more on this brief voyage bound,
>   Thou sail'st a brighter wave
> Than thine, which, sighing, circles round
>   The stillness of thy grave.

"Such a life as Edward W. Watson's, without being unfaithful to any duty, and with no conspicuous greatness or success, was like a long poem of fourscore stanzas—each quatrain a revolving year, in which winter rhymed with summer and spring with autumn in a pleasing melody, now lyric, now idyllic, now pastoral, and sometimes grave and diadatic, but always with a genial moral. Wordsworth, in his 'Mathew' and in other sketches, has tried to describe such men. But they do not come to full maturity in England, I suppose, lacking the perfect freedom and unconstraint of our American country life.

> 'Much doth nature's love excel
> To the souls that never fell,
> To swains that live in happiness,
> And do well because they please,
> Who walk in ways that are unfamed,
> And feats achieve before they're named.'

"Living thus embosomed in poetry and on the most friendly terms with nature in all her aspects, it was natural that he should write verses—but they had less merit than his most casual remark, which was sure to be worth remembering. It was true of him as of that friend of his who said—

> 'My life has been the poem I would have writ,
> But I could not both live and utter it.'

"What he wrote was sometimes printed, and if collected in a volume would pleasantly remind us of the writer, especially if along with them should be presented his handsome portrait, adorned with thick white hair. He was not so remarkable in appearance as his neighbor on the mainland, Daniel Webster, who used to come sailing down to Marshfield into the waters where Mr. Watson bore sway; but he was a more wholesome, buoyant and attractive person, and one who lived on better terms with himself; renouncing wealth and ambition, and contenting himself with the sovereignty of his own island and its waters, and the companionship of his friends. But better than anything that he wrote would be his daily conversation, if that could be preserved as the table-talk of more famous men have been. He talked as the birds sing and the breezes blow—without forethought or restraint, and with all the freshness of boyhood, while he uttered the mellow wisdom of age. But why strive longer to describe the indescribable? for such was he.

> ' Thou soul of God's best earthly mould,
> Thou happy soul! and can it be
> That these three words of glittering gold
> Are all that must remain of thee?' "

INDEX.

www.ingramcontent.com/pod-product-compliance
Lightning Source LLC
Chambersburg PA
CBHW071833270326
41929CB00013B/1981